AF519353

Building & Running a

Successful Research Business

Building & Running a

Successful Research Business

A Guide for the Independent Information Professional

Mary Ellen Bates

Edited by
Reva Basch

Ess Ess Publications

New Delhi-110002

In Association with

Medford, New Jersey

Building and Running a Successful Research Business: A Guide for Independent Information Professional

ISBN 978-81-7000-524-7 (13 digit)
ISBN 81-7000-524-8 (10 digit)

Rs.1095/-

First Indian Imprint 2008

Published by:
Ess Ess Publications
4837/24, Ansari Road,
Darya Ganj,
New Delhi-110 002.
INDIA

in arrangement with

Information Today, Inc.
143, Old Marlton Pike
Medford, New Jersey 08055
United States of America

Printed and bound in India at Salasar Imaging Systems.

Dedication

To my parents, Flo and Pete Bates, who taught me to believe in myself and to take risks, and to the memory of Sue Rugge, a pioneer independent info pro, who so generously shared her wisdom with anyone who asked.

Contents

Section Two: Running the Business

Appendices

Foreword

More years ago than I care to specify, I heard of a business out in California called Information on Demand (IOD). The name said it all: You ask, we answer. Working as an engineering librarian in a small Pennsylvania town, IOD gleamed in my professional subconscious like the Emerald City. What a dream job, I thought, tackling research questions about anything imaginable and earning money doing it. Through an utterly unforeseeable sequence of events, I eventually found myself in Berkeley and employed at IOD. My years there, starting as a temporary research associate and ending up as Director of Research, proved to be the best of several worlds: all the fun of doing research, plus a regular paycheck, while someone else worried about marketing and promotion—which I hated—not to mention the mundanity of office administration and the messy financial aspects of making a business succeed. IOD's culture felt fresh and entrepreneurial, but the owner, not I, bore all the risks.

My years at Information on Demand were, in retrospect, an ideal transition into the independent info pro business. I had the opportunity to absorb by osmosis the basic principles of operating a small business, including dealing diplomatically and creatively with a wide variety of clients on an astonishing array of projects; to learn more about print, phone, and online sources and techniques from my incredibly resourceful colleagues in the research department; and to observe a master marketer in operation. What luck. Before I left IOD to go out on my own in the mid-1980s, I made most of the mistakes a startup info pro could make, buffered from the harsh reality of having to pay for them myself. Again, what extraordinary luck. Not many companies like IOD exist these days (including IOD), and of those that do, very few offer opportunities to learn on the job as I was able to do.

Sue Rugge, owner of Information on Demand, is widely regarded as the "godmother" of the independent information business. I'm proud and privileged to have had her as my professional mentor. Unfortunately, *The Information Broker's Handbook*, which she co-wrote with Alfred Glossbrenner, is now out of date and out of print, and Sue herself is no longer around to provide updates or advice. But she, and the book that embodied her hard-earned expertise and insights, have found a worthy successor in Mary Ellen Bates and the volume you're holding in your hands.

Mary Ellen is the best possible person I can imagine to have written *Building and Running a Successful Research Business*. She built Bates Information Services from the ground up, learning the hard way what works and what doesn't, discovering for herself how to function more efficiently and effectively in everything from daily office operations to promoting her business, conducting research, managing her clients, staying current, and developing, enriching, and expanding her own career. She is an active independent information professional specializing in business research, as well as a columnist and writer of books and articles, a consultant, a trainer, and a familiar and much-lauded presence on the conference circuit. She has reached the epitome of what one can accomplish as an independent info pro; she does practice, on a daily basis, what she preaches in the pages of this book.

Let me caution you about one thing: This is not a book about "how to make money on the Internet." Every established independent info pro hears regularly from people (we call them wannabes) who know how to use a Web search engine, think that working from home sounds just dandy, and want to know how to "break into" this business. Breaking in is not what it's about. As Mary Ellen explains, it's about doing your homework, laying the groundwork, planning carefully, and, perhaps most important of all, conducting a candid assessment of your own personality and preferences to determine whether the life of an independent info pro is for you. If it's not, I'd advise you to keep your day job. But if you can honestly say that you're drawn to the independent information profession, that you can imagine yourself thriving, despite the discipline, hard work, isolation, risks, and uncertainties involved, driven and sustained by your enthusiasm for *information*— whether it's the power of delivering the right information to your clients at the right time, or the potential to improve their lives and the decisions they make by facilitating and improving the information environment in which they operate—then read on.

As I wrote in the foreword to Sue Rugge's book, "One thing that has characterized this profession from its inception is a spirit of cooperation, rather than competition, among its members. This has its roots, I think, in the library world, where the thrill of the hunt, and of *finding* what you're looking for, is something to be shared with your colleagues. If this excitement—this love of research for its own sake—resonates with you, you're already ahead of the game." A lot has changed in the information profession since I wrote those words—the growth and development of the Web, among other things—but a passion for this profession is still the number one requirement for success. Everything else can be learned. And Mary Ellen will show you how.

Reva Basch
The Sea Ranch, California

Acknowledgments

Sue Rugge, a pioneer independent information professional, is the person who inspired me to even consider writing this book. Sue started her first research business, Information Unlimited, back in 1971, and went on to found two more successful information businesses. She wrote *The Information Broker's Handbook* (now out of print), and many of us independent info pros depended on it when we started our businesses. Sue gave seminars on starting and running an information business and provided advice, encouragement, and friendship to thousands of people. She passed away in 1999, at the age of 58. I feel enriched to have known her, and I still catch myself wanting to pick up the phone or e-mail her to ask her advice. The Association of Independent Information Professionals established the Sue Rugge Memorial Award to recognize an AIIP member who, through mentoring, has significantly helped others establish their businesses. I was honored beyond words to be the first recipient of that award, in 2000.

As always, my editor Reva Basch has been a joy to work with. I've lost track of the number of books we've worked on together, but I've enjoyed each one. I value Reva's input in the content of this book, as well as her gentle but firm editorial pen. Reva was also my informal mentor as I began and built my independent info pro business. She gave generously of her time, managed to keep a straight face when I asked really stupid questions, and was always supporting and encouraging. Thanks, Reva.

Beyond Reva, I owe a great debt of gratitude to the other members of AIIP. They offered encouragement and advice when I launched my business, and many have become good friends. I especially want to thank a small group of friends and colleagues who let me pick their brains as I wrote this book: Linda Cooper, Marjorie Desgrosseilliers, Jan Goudreau, Amelia Kassel, Alex Kramer, John Levis, Lynn Peterson, Suzanne Sabroski, Risa Sacks, and Jan Tudor. Their insights have enriched this book, and I have credited them whenever I could. But beyond that, they have generously shared their thoughts, encouragement, and friendship over the years. Thank you all.

I must separately acknowledge the contributions of Alex Kramer, a wise colleague and a good friend. She and I have talked shop for years, and I'd write notes every time we'd get talking about business strategy, market trends, managing clients ... you name it. As I started work on each chapter of this book, I dug up those notes written on paper napkins, scrawled on the back of envelopes, or jotted down when we got back from running. Much of her wisdom, perspective, sense of humor, and—yes, Alex—incurable optimism are incorporated within these pages. I have credited Alex when I could quote her directly, but her influence on my thinking permeates this book.

I owe many thanks to John Bryans, my publisher at Information Today. He has been supportive of and enthusiastic about this book throughout the process of seeing it into print, as he has been with the three other books of mine that he's published.

Amy Pass has once again come to my rescue and helped out with all the last-minute details of pulling a manuscript together. She is always a joy to work with—professional, friendly, efficient, and smart.

While writing this book, I've become more aware of the life experiences that have brought me where I am today. Successfully running an independent information business is not an easy thing, and I doubt that I would have been able to imagine myself in this adventure without the encouragement of my partner, Dave Wild, and the unconditional love and support of my family. And I owe a special debt, which I'll never be able to repay, to Scott Smith, a dear friend and extraordinary person who, in the year I knew him before his death, taught me so much about living mindfully and listening carefully.

From the land of the midnight sun
Where the ice blue roses grow
Along those roads of gold and silver snow
Howling wide or moaning low
So many roads I know
So many roads to ease my soul
[Robert Hunter, So Many Roads]

Mary Ellen Bates
Washington, DC

Introduction

I'll never forget when I met my first independent information professional. It was 1979 and I was taking the Friday afternoon ferry from San Francisco back home to Berkeley. This was the party ferry—everyone brought wine or snacks—and we'd hold a floating happy hour as we watched the sun set over the Golden Gate Bridge and marveled at our good fortune of living in the most beautiful place in the world. I was chatting with my boss, a law firm librarian, and she introduced me to Georgia Finnigan, who had recently dissolved a partnership with Sue Rugge and launched her own information business, The Information Store. I'm not sure what amazed me more—that Georgia had just up and started a new company or that she read the *Wall Street Journal* because she found it thought-provoking. (This was back when we counter-culturalists simply didn't read the publications of "capitalist pigs.") I remember thinking that Georgia had the most exciting job I'd ever heard of, but also that I couldn't imagine how there could be more than two people in the world who could run this sort of business, and that she and Sue must have the market locked up.

Years went by, and I continued working in specialized libraries of one sort or another. I'm not quite sure how it happened; it may have been on the exhibit floor at a librarians' conference, when I stumbled onto the booth of the Association of Independent Information Professionals. There they were, in the flesh—normal-looking people who had walked away from a regular job in an office with a steady paycheck and were now running their own information businesses. I couldn't believe that there was an entire association of people like Sue Rugge and Georgia Finnigan, and that they actually got together, talked with each other, referred work to each other, and were friends.

Intrigued, I sidled up to the booth and struck up a conversation with the AIIP member who was staffing the booth at the time—Reva Basch. She encouraged me to join AIIP, even if I wasn't ready to start my own business yet. I nodded doubtfully, took the membership application, and scurried off to the more "normal" booths of information vendors and bookshelf manufacturers. "Whew," I thought, "close call!"

Well, I kept thinking about this independent info pro thing, and somewhere along the line, I decided that if all these other people could do it, I could too. As Reva suggested, I joined AIIP, I listened in on the private AIIP electronic discussion board, and I got to know a number of established info pros. I realized that it wasn't all sitting around in your bunny slippers waiting for clients to call, but I also figured out that it was the type of work that I enjoyed doing and that I would find challenging, not just at first but over the course of years. After a year or two of thinking about it, saving up enough money to pay for my first six months' of expenses, and screwing up the courage to abandon the safety net of steady employment, I finally did it—I started Bates Information Services.

I loved being an information entrepreneur from day one. I was able to try anything I wanted—no committees to run proposals by, no boss to sign off on a new strategy—and, as my business grew, I had the satisfaction of knowing that it was because my clients wanted *me* to do work for them. Yes, I've had my share of days when I longed for the relative simplicity of a regular job, where I didn't have to juggle the responsibilities of CEO, financial planner, sales staff, marketing director, file clerk, and researcher. But I've also never had as much fun in any other job. In fact, when I entered the second decade of my business, I realized that I'd been an independent info pro longer than I'd held any other job in my life, and I never cease to marvel that I managed to stumble into what is, for me, the perfect career.

And as I watch the economy go through its inevitable growth and contraction cycles, I am reminded that running my own business actually gives me more job stability than if I were working for someone else. How's that? If you're an employee, you get all your income from one source—your employer. If you lose your job, your income immediately drops to $0/year, and you can spend the next few months at that same salary until you find another job. On the other hand, if I lose a client, I see a temporary drop in my revenue, but that's only one client among many. I always have other sources of income, so the loss of any one client is never devastating. Now that no employer offers lifetime employment, the steadiest job is often one you make yourself.

Where Independent Info Pros Come From

When I first learned about independent info professionals, most of the existing businesses were run by librarians and researchers—people who had already spent years finding information in libraries, in online databases, through telephone interviews, and by going to courthouses and government agencies to dig around in files. These days, though, AIIP is full of people who come to this profession from other fields, having worked as marketing specialists, engineers, or lawyers. Lynn Peterson, owner of PFC Information Services, previously owned a business that offered recruitment and placement services for nannies and housekeepers. Tom Culbert, president of Aviation Information Research, served 21 years in the U.S. Air Force, as a pilot and then a staff officer. Chris Sherman, president of Searchwise, worked for a company developing interactive video training programs. Not a librarian among them.

Successful independent info pros may not enter the profession with all the business, entrepreneurial, research, and people skills they need, but they've figured out how to acquire the expertise they don't have or outsource the aspects of the business that they can't do themselves and that aren't mission critical. This book will show you what you need to know, give you the tools to help you succeed, and teach you where to go to fill in the gaps in your knowledge.

Getting Started as an Independent Info Pro

The comment I hear the most from aspiring independent info pros is, "I've always been an info junkie, but I never realized that I could make money from it." Well, maybe you can, but it's not as simple as that. Running a successful business means not only having the research skills but also being able to think and act like an entrepreneur—to know how to price your services, anticipate changes in the economy and the information environment, market yourself and your business constantly, and develop new skills as your clients' needs change.

Running an information business also requires courage and determination. You're it; there's no one else to help you make the tough decisions, to handle the difficult client, or to tell you that you need to work on your financial planning skills, for example. Your income fluctuates from month to month, and at times it seems like all your marketing efforts are failing and no client will ever call you again. That's when you pick up the phone or go online to get a reality check with your colleagues. We've all gone through similar difficulties; we've all weathered the same kinds of crises.

The first section of this book introduces you to what's involved in the independent information profession—what kinds of work you can do, what kinds of clients you can market to, and what kinds of resources you'll need. I talk about how to plan your business launch, how to mentally prepare yourself for your new life as a business owner, what you need to set up your office, and how to make time for life outside of work.

Now That I've Started, Where Do I Go?

Once you've hung out your shingle, virtually if not physically, what do you do next? Section Two, Running the Business, gets into the nitty-gritty of being a business owner. You'll learn about writing proposals and presenting project estimates, about finding the money to start your business and keep it going, about running a business ethically, managing and firing clients, and about functioning as your own private brain trust to provide yourself with a strategic vision. You'll also learn how to establish rates and fees that will sustain your business, send the right message to your clients (that you're an expert and worth the cost), and enable you to pay yourself the salary you want. I also cover the topic of subcontracting—taking advantage of the web of relationships we independent info pros build among ourselves to ensure that we can all provide high-quality research services to our clients.

While you may read the first section of this book just once, when you're planning and starting your business, you'll be consulting Section Three, Marketing, for as long as you're in operation. Marketing is a constant in most businesses, and independent info pros are no exception. This section will tell you about establishing your business image, about low-cost and low-effort marketing efforts that you can start now and sustain over the years, and about high-impact marketing techniques that will get your clients to pay attention to you and what you offer to them.

When I started my business, I didn't realize how much I'd need to market myself, not just at first, but even after my business had been growing for a few years. Fortunately, I started out, like the early space program, with the attitude that failure was not an option. So, when I decided that I needed to do some public speaking to get my face and name in front of potential clients, I didn't immediately reject the idea, even though my first reaction was to recoil in horror. Yes, the first four or five speeches I gave turned my knees to jelly and tied my stomach into knots, but I did them anyway, because my business was *not* going to fail. After a while, public speaking got easier, and I learned how to harness the nervous energy I'd get before my talk and direct it into the focus and enthusiasm I needed to get my points across.

There are probably some aspects of marketing that you will tell yourself you simply cannot do. At that point, remind yourself that the worst that can happen is that it won't work and you'll have to try something else. If that's all that's at stake, why not try it? Perhaps, like me, you'll learn that you have skills you didn't suspect you had, and you'll discover that you actually enjoy doing something that at first seemed impossible.

Getting Down to Research

Section Four, Researching, comes *after* the discussions about running and marketing your business for a reason. I assume you're already interested in research; that's why you're reading this book. What many new independent info pros forget, though, is that your research skills alone won't bring in the clients and revenue. You must first think through the practicalities of how you'll actually make money at it.

The section on researching covers the client information needs assessment, known in librarian circles as the reference interview. It also includes a template for developing your mental road map for research, and discusses which information resources are best for different types of research. Then, you'll get an overview of the various kinds of research that independent info pros provide: research on the Web and the fee-based online services, research in libraries and other physical information repositories, telephone research and in-depth interviewing, public records research using government agencies and courthouses, and other types of services independent info pros can offer. I also describe tools and techniques for highlighting the value of the information you provide to clients, presenting your research results in ways that your clients will find most useful.

I have included a number of Web site addresses in this book. They are current as of early 2003, but we all know that URLs change and can disappear altogether. The sites I have referenced are generally well-established, and I've included enough description that you should be able to use your research skills to track down the page if the URL has changed. Think of this as good independent info pro practice.

One final caveat: I have quoted a number of experienced info pros throughout this book and, whenever possible, have included the perspective of as many information entrepreneurs as possible. But I accept responsibility for any opinions, conclusions, or recommendations that I don't attribute to others, as well as any errors.

For new ideas on searching and on marketing your business, you might be interested in subscribing to my free electronic newsletter. You can sign up on my Web site at www.BatesInfo.com. Good luck with your new business. I trust that you will find this profession as challenging, satisfying, and fun as I have over the years.

Section One

Getting Started

Chapter 1

What's an Independent Info Pro?

What's This Business All About?

I assume that you have some notion of what the independent information profession covers—finding, organizing, and managing information—or you wouldn't have picked up this book. But different people define this profession differently, and it's a common misconception that most research can be done on the Web. While the Internet *has* radically changed how independent info pros operate, much of our work involves research outside the portion of the Web that most people are familiar with—that is, beyond what you can find by typing a few words into your favorite search engine.

In the most general terms, independent information professionals work for themselves or as partners in a two- or three-person business; they provide information services, such as research, analysis, information management, or consulting services; and they charge their clients for their services, either per project or on an hourly or daily basis. Many independent info pros worked as librarians or researchers before launching their own businesses; they may have spent years honing their research skills within large corporations or research centers. Others started out as professionals in other fields—lawyers, engineers, or marketing consultants, for example—then shifted their focus to providing research support to others within their profession. What all successful independent info pros have in common are strong entrepreneurial skills. They enjoy the challenge of building a business, they're good at managing their clients, and they're self-motivated.

The independent information profession is a wide-open field; there are far more potential clients out there than people providing information services to them. No one has accurate numbers on the total number of independent info pros in the marketplace. The Association of Independent Information Professionals, the trade association of the profession (www.aiip.org), has about 700 members. But this total does not accurately reflect the total number of independent info pros in business at any point in time; probably 10 times as many exist who aren't AIIP members. A fairly high turnover rate prevails among independent info businesses, reflecting the entrepreneurial world as a whole, in which, according to anecdotal evidence, more than half of all small businesses close within five years.

People leave the independent info pro field for a number of reasons:

- They miss the daily stimulation of a more traditional office environment.
- They have difficulty dealing with the dramatically fluctuating cash flow.
- They don't enjoy the amount of administrative and marketing work required.
- A client offers them a full-time job that they can't resist.

I have been an independent info pro for more than 10 years, and have watched several colleagues' businesses start up and then shut down. Often the closing of the business results in unexpected successes—formerly independent info pros re-enter the more traditional work force with newly acquired business skills, and often find that they are much more valuable to employers because of their experience running a small business.

So What Do You Do, Anyway?

The independent information profession encompasses a wide variety of services. This section includes brief descriptions of many of the most common types. Most independent info pros specialize in a particular kind of research and focus on a specific industry or vertical market. Many of us have a wide range of clients—mine include self-employed speechwriters, engineers, ad agencies, executives from *Fortune* 100 firms, lawyers, and doctoral students, among others—but most of us focus on a specific market. What all my clients have in common is that they call me for business research. Other independent info pros may target the healthcare industry, architectural firms, the aviation market, or the chemical industry. While many of us also have clients outside our primary market, we tend to target our marketing efforts on a specific subject area or industry. Note that some of the information services described below, particularly document delivery, are more likely than others to serve clients across vertical markets.

Online Research

With the prevalence of databases on the Web, most independent info pros who provide research services of any sort include at least some online research in their portfolios. That may include locating government statistics on international trade, analyzing company filings with the U.S. Securities and Exchange Commission, or searching online catalogs of libraries around the world. However, the professional online services described in Chapter 29 are even richer sources of information than the free or public Web. These databases include material that never appears on the Web, and they provide sophisticated search tools and value-added features that enable users to conduct in-depth research in ways not possible on the Web.

Using the professional online services can be an expensive proposition. These services charge by the search, by the document, by the amount of time you spend connected to them, or by various other pricing algorithms. As an independent info pro, you pass along the online expenses to your clients, and these costs can add up to a third or even half of the total project cost. Note that there is very little demand in the marketplace for independent info pros who only provide Web research. The public perception, whether or not it's correct, is that it takes no great skill to search the Web. We set ourselves apart by offering access to online research sources not generally available to our clients and by using uncommon and lesser-known Web-based sources.

Library Research

When the independent information profession began, much of our research involved going to libraries on behalf of clients. Some instances still call for library research or, similarly, contacting information centers or other brick-and-mortar collections of material. An info pro might travel to a government agency's information center to search a database not available on the Web, e-mail a university library in Sweden to find a copy of a doctoral thesis, arrange to visit a trade association's library to use its specialized collection, or review records in the U.S. National

Archives to determine how a particular site was used by the U.S. Army 50 years ago, in order to determine what hazardous materials may still be lurking in the soil and groundwater.

As more government agencies, embassies, associations, and other resources make their information available on the Web, demand for hands-on library research has diminished. On the other hand, library research can sometimes unearth information not available anywhere in electronic format. See Chapter 33, Library and Other Manual Research, for more discussion of this type of research.

Public Records Research

Although much consternation has arisen recently about supposedly easy access to personal information on the Web, a great deal of information about individuals has always been available in court clerks' and county recorders' offices and other government agencies. Some of these records are now available on the Web, but the majority still reside only in print files. Public records research includes:

- Reviewing bankruptcy filings to determine what assets are held by a corporation
- Conducting a pre-employment check of a school bus driver to make sure he has no criminal record or driving offenses
- Looking through articles of incorporation to identify the executives of a privately held company
- Finding prior court testimony given by an expert witness, to determine how she is likely testify for an upcoming case

Public records research is not for the faint of heart. It often requires a private investigator's license, it requires a good understanding of the ins and outs of various government agencies, and it takes a gut sense to know when you have found all the pieces of the puzzle. See Chapter 32, Public Records Research, for more information.

Telephone Research

Despite the much-talked-about "information explosion," a lot of information never appears in print or in any electronic format. Sometimes, the fastest way to obtain it is simply to call an expert in the field and ask. Telephone research is an art form, and many independent info pros—myself included—don't have the special combination of charm, patience, persistence, chutzpah, and the ability to talk to anyone about anything that a good telephone researcher needs. This type of work tends to involve more hours per project and a longer turnaround time than other types of research because of its very nature. Merely identifying the person who can answer your question might involve 10 or 15 calls. When you factor in the inevitable delays brought on by voice-mail tag and varying business schedules and time zones, it means that very few telephone research projects can be completed in less than a week, even if the total amount of time spent on the phone is only a fraction of that time.

The kind of telephone research I'm talking about here requires more sophisticated research techniques than just running through a list of survey questions with a preselected list of contacts. Usually, you'll get an assignment to find out about a specific topic and you will have to develop your own leads. That means some preliminary online or library research to identify likely sources for the information, as well as deciding on the best way to approach the project and exactly what questions to ask.

Telephone researchers get much of their work in the form of referrals from other independent info pros and from researchers within organizations. From a marketing point of view, networking is particularly important in order to develop a large client base of subcontracting sources. Chapter 31 goes into more detail about what is involved in telephone research.

Document Delivery

Tracking down obscure citations and obtaining photocopies or originals of articles, reports, and books is the job of document delivery firms. Unlike most other types of independent information businesses, doc del firms may employ a number of people, due to the amount of clerical and paraprofessional work involved. A doc del company acts, in a sense, as a librarian's—or researcher's—librarian. Once an info pro has identified the white paper, academic treatise, industrial standard, conference paper, 20-year-old annual report, or obscure article from a Polish medical journal that the client needs, the doc del firm's job is to get a copy of the item. Sometimes that means searching online library catalogs to find an institution that subscribes to the journal or maintains an archive of old corporate annual reports, and arranging to send someone to that library to photocopy the material. Sometimes it involves contacting the publisher and negotiating an appropriate royalty payment for a copy. Sometimes it means tracking down the original author or conference speaker to see if he is willing to supply a copy of his paper or presentation.

Many doc del clients are librarians looking for material they don't have in their own collections and may not have been able to find through their own network of sources. That means that doc del firms often get difficult, incomplete, or incorrect citations. So part of the job of a good doc del researcher is to think like a detective. To an extent, doc del firms are threatened by the perception that "it's all available on the Web." People are sometimes not willing to wait a week for an article when they are accustomed to getting material at the click of a mouse. And customers often balk at the price for document delivery; an article can easily cost $25 or $50, once the publisher's royalty fee is included in the invoice. Document delivery is a specialized niche for people who are detail-oriented, able to generate and manage large volumes of orders, and can identify clients willing to pay the not-unsubstantial fees. See Chapter 33 for more about this aspect of the independent info pro business.

Competitive Intelligence

Despite rumors to the contrary, competitive intelligence (CI) doesn't require diving into dumpsters and digging up a company's strategic plans from the trash. What CI *does* involve is using a variety of research and analytical skills to gather information on a company or industry and to figure out what it means. CI research may tackle questions such as "why are my competitors pulling back from Asia," "what is my competitor's product development strategy," and "what do purchasers think of our products and those of our competitors." Some of this information is available via in-depth online research—in market research reports, industry newsletters, published interviews with executives, and so on. But much of this type of intelligence resides in more obscure sources, so CI research may involve, for example, researching public records to find factory blueprints filed with construction permits monitoring company Web sites to see what jobs are being advertised or what new offices or divisions have been opened; or conducting telephone interviews with a target company's vendors, customers, and competitors.

CI often includes analyzing research findings and developing conclusions regarding a company's strategies. CI researchers find it challenging to dig up hidden information without compromising the confidentiality of their clients and without misrepresenting themselves. In fact, this is one reason why CI research may be outsourced to independent information professionals; the CI department within a company doesn't want its employees associated with the research and prefers to have an independent researcher making those probing phone calls.

The principal professional association for this type of research is the Society of Competitive Intelligence Professionals (www.scip.org). SCIP members include CI researchers and analysts within organizations, CI consulting firms, and academicians in business and related disciplines.

Information Management

While most independent info pros specialize in particular types of research, some provide more general consulting services related to the acquisition, organization, management, and distribution of information within organizations. These consultants may provide "information audits"—in-depth surveys of an organization's information needs and resources—and offer recommendations on what information sources should be acquired, how these sources should be distributed within the organization through intranets or other technologies, and how to teach employees how best to use the information. Information consultants also help set up information resource centers and libraries, develop Web sites and databases to organize and disseminate internal and external information, and offer workshops and training sessions on information-related topics. Most information consultants come from a library background or have formal training in library and information services.

Library Staffing

Libraries within organizations, sometimes called "special libraries," may need help in recruiting new staff or finding temporary help during a busy period or while a staff member is on leave. In fact, some organizations want the entire library function handled by a third party, preferring to pay a set fee to have all the staffing responsibilities managed by someone who understands the information profession, rather than trying to build and staff the library internally.

Library staffing companies usually focus on a single geographic region or a vertical market—law firm libraries or engineering firm libraries, for example—because it is difficult to maintain staffing quality when the client libraries are all over the country. With the exception of firms that only do library personnel recruitment, most staffing companies consist of the principal(s) and a number of information professionals. Thus, one of the skills that these types of independent info pros need is the ability to manage and motivate employees. This is one skill that those of us who are one-person businesses do not have to develop. Note that many of the issues related to outsourced personnel management services go beyond the scope of this book. If you are considering this type of business, be sure to expand your reading to include material on these other concerns as well.

Training and Seminars

Finally, a number of independent info pros offer training, workshops, or seminars on research-related topics, in addition to other information services. They often find that these are good vehicles for marketing their expertise, expanding their client base, and keeping their information skills sharp. (There's nothing like knowing you'll be speaking in front of a room full of people to encourage you to stay up-to-date on whatever topic you're speaking on.) Some independent info pros work their seminar schedule around trips they already have planned—to professional conferences, meetings with clients, and the like—and they handle all the marketing, registration, and administrative tasks involved in organizing and promoting their sessions. Others work with the organizers of existing professional conferences to present their workshop as pre- or post-conference sessions. They piggyback on the attendance and marketing effort of a larger conference, but give up a portion of their income in exchange for having someone else handle all the marketing. In fact, info pros who give pre- and post-conference workshops are usually just paid a flat fee, regardless of the number of people attending the session. The independent route works best if you already have some name recognition and/or a large base of contacts you can market to; generating interest in your workshops from scratch is difficult, time-consuming, and expensive. A third option, which works well for some independent info pros, is to market your workshops to professional organizations, who then handle the promotion and administrative responsibilities.

However you decide to approach it, workshops and seminars can be a nice source of supplemental income if you're a lively speaker and can develop presentations that pique people's interest. And don't worry that you're giving away the store by teaching others your research techniques. The skills that got you to this point will keep you ahead of the pack. More importantly, most of your clients will be calling you for work because they know you have years of expertise that can't be acquired overnight. Teaching others about research helps to build their appreciation of what is involved in your work and enables them to do simple research themselves.

Focus, Focus, Focus

It can be rather daunting to think about all the different kinds of information services that independent info pros can provide. However, most don't offer *all* the services I just described. The late Sue Rugge, one of the founders of the independent information profession, was well-known for her advice to "do what you do best, and hire the rest." Many independent info pros put this in practice every day as we subcontract work to fellow info pros. For example, I focus primarily on online research, and I use a small network of colleagues for all of my telephone research and document delivery work. Several public records researchers call me when they need online searches to supplement what they can do themselves. When I get calls for information audits or knowledge management consulting, I refer them to a couple of people I know who are expert in that area. This informal network ensures that all of us are able to offer a wide range of high-quality research to our clients by tapping into the skills of other info pros who can provide what we do not. This is, I believe, the best reason to join AIIP; the contacts I have made there have enabled me to provide a much deeper, richer range of services to my clients than I could on my own. See Chapter 14, Subcontracting, or I'll Scratch Your Back if You Scratch Mine, for more discussion of how these relationships work, how subcontractors get paid, and who gets to keep the client.

Where Will I Find My Clients?

I'm over-simplifying a bit, but your clients will probably be some combination of:

- Information-hungry professionals, such as speech writers, competitive intelligence researchers, and product managers
- Intermediaries such as other consultants who will pass your work along to their clients
- Organizations that do not have an in-house library but that need professional research support
- Librarians who need to outsource some of their research
- Individuals with more money than time and a specific research need

You might find these people in advertising and public relations agencies; research, strategic planning, and marketing departments of large corporations; nonprofit organizations, private investigation firms, engineering companies, hospitals and medical research facilities; and among upper-level executives who need outside research on their competitors and the industry.

Real-Life Examples

So, what does an actual research project look like? I asked several colleagues to describe a project they'd done recently, and the following are their examples. These are quite extensive in their scope; any part of one of these projects might constitute a separate research job. And each example shows a different type of research—online, public records research, or a combination of information sources. Some of the details have been changed to protect the confidentiality of the clients.

Color Printer Market

Objective: A client needed to learn what consumers thought about the quality of color inkjet printers. Did they expect the same quality as traditional photographic film processing? Did they generally just use color printers to add pizzazz to a marketing brochure or sales chart? What did they like and dislike in color inkjet printers?

Research: I searched a number of online databases, to see what was written in the trade press about inkjet printers and about consumer purchases and use of digital cameras. I also searched market research report databases to find consulting reports on the color printer market. I searched the Web for product specifications for various color printers and for discussions of these printers in various Web-based forums and online bulletin boards. After I had pulled all the material together—more than 300 pages of information—I wrote an analysis of the major concerns of consumers and an executive summary for my client to provide to her vice president.

Total time: 40 hours

Finding Funding

Objective: My client, a public/private consortium, needed to identify potential sources of grants and funding in order to expand its efforts in recruiting information technology companies as tenants for a new "technology village" office complex as well as to train IT workers directly.

Research: I started with a general Web search and identified a model program in another state. On their Web site, I found program descriptions and contact information so my client could talk with them directly. I searched the U.S. Department of Education's Web site and found two federal funding initiatives. I also found information on a new bill in Congress that would have a direct impact on my client's program and looked up information on the chief sponsor of the bill. It turned out that one of my client's senators is very interested in this issue, so I called his office and obtained further details. I also searched the Foundation Center's database and identified a number of relevant grant programs. I ended with an in-depth search in one of the professional online services for success stories of companies announcing funding they had received for on-the-job training of IT workers.

Total time: 25 hours

Automobile Aftermarket

Objective: A client that manufactures automobile accessories—hubcaps, chrome wheels, fog lights, and so on—is considering acquiring a privately held competitor. They need as much information as possible on the competitor.

Research: I went to the state Department of Corporations and looked up the company records to get information on the officers and directors. Then I went to the courthouses in three local jurisdictions and looked up court documents to see if I could find any litigation involving the company or its officers. I found a suit filed by a former employee regarding an alleged breach of an employment contract, and contacted the ex-employee to find out what she had to say about the company. I also found a divorce suit involving an officer of the company; the settlement agreement listed company assets and gave me additional details on the spouse's involvement in the company. Finally, since this industry uses a lot of plastics and paints, I contacted the state environmental protection agency and got the permits the company had filed for its manufacturing plants. This gave me information on the number of employees at the plants and the type of equipment used. I wrote all this up and gave the client the information I'd gleaned, along with suggestions on other sources of information we might be able to pursue.

Total time: 16 hours

Frequently Asked Questions

I speak and write frequently about the independent info pro business, and some questions seem to come up all the time, either from people who are considering this line of work or those who are thinking about hiring an independent info pro.

"How can you sell me someone else's information?"

Most independent info pros don't do much original research—that is, they don't spend all their time conducting surveys, studying trends, and writing their own market research reports. Instead, they gather information from a number of sources, including the Web, trade and professional journals, newspapers, magazines, government agencies, associations, and consulting reports. What they are charging for is not the information per se but their time and skill in *finding* the information, and in knowing where to go to find it.

That's why an independent info pro still charges even if he didn't find the information that exactly answered the client's question—the client is paying for the info pro's time, not just for the information retrieved. Compare it to going to a doctor for an illness; you pay the doctor for her time regardless of whether you were eventually cured. Unlike real estate agents and personal injury lawyers, few independent info pros work on a contingency basis, hoping to cash in big if their client finds the information particularly useful.

"Why do you charge me when it's all free on the Web?"

Three words: Time Is Money. Well, that's the smart-aleck answer, anyway. And, indeed, an independent info pro should be able to find useful, accurate, and relevant information in less time than her client can. But more to the point, most information is *not* available on the free Web. It's hidden in databases that don't show up in search engines. It appears in articles and white papers that never make their way to the Web. It's found in government and association reports that are hidden deep within Web sites. It's buried in a book chapter or periodical article housed only in a library somewhere, or in a document filed in a county courthouse. Or it's unearthed by doing telephone research, interviewing experts to get their take on a given situation.

In addition to finding information that simply never shows up in a Web search engine, independent info pros also add value by analyzing and synthesizing the results—by providing not just information but answers.

"What if you don't find any information?"

There are really very few research projects for which no information exists. You might not be able to find the exact answer. My guess, for example, is that no one knows the exact value of all the personal property of U.S. residents—and yes, this was a real research question. However, a good researcher can often find enough information to deduce or extrapolate an answer. To use the example just mentioned, useful statistics from insurance industry associations and from the U.S. Census Bureau enabled the client to make an educated guess.

And sometimes finding no information is just what the client wants to hear. If a client has invented a new infrared, hands-free potato peeler, he would be delighted to hear that I can find no existing patents for similar inventions. If a company is considering marketing its new children's pager to parents in western Canada, it will be pleased to learn that no Canadian newspapers or parents' magazines have mentioned a similar product in the past five years.

As I mentioned in the answer to "How can you sell me someone else's information?," independent info pros charge for their time and research skills rather than for the quantity of information retrieved. Of course, if you find, partway into a project, that you aren't uncovering anything useful, it makes sense to stop and consult with the client about expanding or changing the focus of the research.

"What training or education is required?"

Many longtime independent info pros have master's degrees in library or information science and years of experience as professional librarians. A number of graduate library schools are developing new programs that cater to the entrepreneurial interests of their students, some of whom have no intention of working within a traditional library after graduation. However, a library background isn't required, provided you have other experience as a researcher or you are willing to outsource the actual research to others. Sue Rugge, the owner of three successful independent information companies, focused all her energy on marketing and relied on a group of employees and subcontractors to do the research for her clients.

In addition to research skills, you have to be able to run a business. That means marketing yourself; developing and implementing a strategic business plan; handling the day-to-day operations of a small business including invoicing, collections, accounts payable, and cash flow; continually upgrading your information skills through professional development; and managing your clients. You need good communication skills, because you will be talking with clients face to face, over the telephone, or in e-mail, and you will be writing analyses, summaries, and reports.

You can subcontract some of these duties, but one thing you can't easily subcontract is marketing. No one knows your skills, abilities, and talents as well as you do, and no one can establish clients' confidence in your abilities better than you. If marketing isn't your strong suit, consider finding a business coach who can work with you to develop a marketing strategy that is comfortable for you.

"Will you hire me? Can I intern for you?"

Many aspiring independent info pros hope to hone their skills by working for established information businesses. Unfortunately, very few independents can absorb the overhead required to train a new info pro and, more importantly, the inevitable cost of their "learning experiences"—known to clients as mistakes. Most of us work from our homes or in one-room offices outside the home, and don't have the room and equipment to accommodate a new employee or intern. Most importantly, we are already busy providing information services to clients, as well as marketing and handling the administrative end of the business, and we just don't have the time to guide and train someone who isn't already an experienced information professional.

The two exceptions to this rule are public records and telephone research. Both are labor-intensive, and experienced independent info pros sometimes take on new employees or interns to provide an additional set of eyes and ears. Note, though, that this usually requires that you are located near the info pro you want to work with; this is hands-on research and it's hard to train someone remotely.

In general, if you want to get into the independent info profession, your best bet is to read the rest of this book, evaluate your own strengths and weaknesses, take the necessary steps to enhance your skill sets, then—as that sporting goods company admonishes—just do it, and start your own business.

"Can I do this part-time?"

Yes and no. Most if not all of the work you get will come from word of mouth, and it takes time to generate that buzz. The more hours you can devote to marketing at the beginning, the faster your network of contacts will grow. The strongest argument for holding down a paid part-time job is that it provides a source of steady income while you are building your business. However, trying to start an independent info pro business while working full time is almost always doomed to failure. This is not the kind of business that can be done evenings and weekends.

The disadvantages of working part time while running your business are that you are unavailable to talk to your clients during part of the day, you have less time to generate business, and your focus is split between your two jobs. If you do decide to work part-time, make a firm commitment to yourself that you will only do so for a specific amount of time—say, six months or a year—during which you will focus on making your business self-sustaining. Note that some kinds of research really can't be done part time or during off-hours, particularly phone research (you have to be in your office during business hours to make and receive calls), public records research (you have to be available to travel to another county at the drop of a hat, and you're limited to the hours that the public records offices are open), and library staffing (you have to be there when your clients want you in the library). Some beginning independent info pros handle such conflicts by finding part-time jobs that involve evening hours only, such as bartending, waiting tables, or working the evening shift at a library.

"How much will I earn?"

This depends on several factors—how much time you can devote to marketing your business, who your clients are, how established your business is, and whether this is a full-time or part-time business for you. During your first year, assuming you're working at it full time, you can expect to make anywhere from $15,000 to $50,000. Once you have been marketing for a year or two, and your clients have begun recommending you to colleagues, the sky's the limit. Net income (after expenses but before income taxes) can range from $40,000 to $100,000 or more. How much *you* make depends on your ability to find clients that you can charge $50 to $100 an hour and your willingness and availability to work at least 40 hours a week. See Chapter 13 for more discussion on setting your rates.

Independent Info Pro Reality Checklist

Independent info pros usually:

- Specialize in a particular type of research and client base
- Need some familiarity with online research
- Use a variety of resources in order to complete projects
- Possess entrepreneurial skills as well as research expertise

Chapter 2

A Day in the Life of an Independent Info Pro

Before I started my business, I didn't really know what to expect on a day-to-day basis. What would I spend my day *doing*? Since my prior work experience was as a corporate librarian, I knew what a day of research felt like, but I also suspected that working as an independent info pro had its own unique pace and feel.

Although I had heard this before, I did not really believe that a third to half of my day would be spent doing nonbillable work. But then I thought about it—almost every company has a sales department, a marketing staff, strategic planners, some administrative support people, an accounting department, *and* the employees who actually produce the goods or provide the services that the company's customers buy. In a one-person business, all those jobs have to be done by—you guessed it—you. Certainly, some efficiencies are achieved when you work solo, but you still have to bring in customers, keep them happy, and bill them—as well as provide the information services that those customers are paying for.

My Typical Day

So, what does a typical working day look like? There is probably no such thing as an average day; in fact, I would be happy if any given day were 100 percent predictable. But here is a composite diary of one of my days:

After an early morning walk with the dogs, a quick breakfast, and a scan of the newspaper, I braced myself for the 25-foot commute to my home office in the carriage house above my garage. After putting on a pot of coffee to brew, I spent the first half hour going through e-mail and reading postings from the seven or eight e-mail discussion lists I subscribe to. I replied to a query from a program planner who wanted to know my availability and rate to speak at a conference in six months, giving her a list of possible topics. I sent a pre-written reply to someone who asked about starting an information business from home, and deleted the inevitable spam messages offering me free satellite TV service, porn, and 24.5 million e-mail addresses that I can use to spam others for only $99.

Then I settled down to the work of the day. I was in the middle of a project to identify the major buyers, manufacturers, and uses of optical amplifiers, a job commissioned by a corporate librarian who didn't have the time to do it himself. I had already looked through Web sites of the major manufacturers, so now I headed to the professional online services to see what I could find in the industry press, technical journals, and market research reports. I often start with Factiva.com (global.factiva.com) because of its favorable pricing, but this project struck me as one that required the wide variety and power search tools offered by Dialog (www.dialogweb.com). (If you aren't familiar with these resources, take a look at Chapter 29, Professional Online Services.) I found more information than I had expected, so I refined the search to get just what I thought the client would want, and had the results sent to my e-mail account.

While waiting for the e-mail to arrive, I ran a quick search on the U.S. Patent & Trademark Office's Web site for recent patents on optical amplifiers, and wrote up an analysis for my client, listing the number of recent patents granted to the major industry players. Then I headed for some sources that specialize in in-depth market research (MindBranch, ECNext, and MarketResearch.com) and downloaded tables of contents of the reports I thought my client might want.

By now, the results of my Dialog search had arrived in my e-mail inbox, so I downloaded the files, ran them through a word-processing macro to reformat the articles and strip out the carriage returns within each paragraph, and started going through the material. I deleted a few articles that weren't as useful as they first appeared, organized the rest, and did some simple formatting to generate a table of contents and make the material easier for my client to read. I noticed that two interesting articles were not available online in full text, so I sent a fax with the bibliographic citations to a document delivery company, which could arrange to have the articles photocopied, the royalties paid, and the material faxed to me by the end of the day. (Note that I did not do this portion of the research myself; it is more cost-effective for me to outsource this kind of work to a company that specializes in it, and has someone stationed on site at a library that has the journals I need, than it would be for me to drop what I was doing and visit a local library in the hope that it would have what I'm looking for. The doc del company also handles copyright fees so that I don't have to try to figure out who gets paid what.)

I made note of several Web sites mentioned in the articles, finished off the rest of the Web research for the job, and wrote a cover letter and summary for the client. Then I put the project aside until later in the day. I like to let my work percolate in my head for a few hours to make sure I haven't forgotten anything. Besides, I had to wait for the two articles I'd ordered to arrive via fax from the doc del company.

Since it was the end of the month, I sat down to do my monthly invoices and pay my bills. I sent out reminder notices to two clients who were late in paying, and sent a thank-you note to a new client. Just as I was backing up my accounting file, I got a call from a colleague, a public records researcher out in California. "Wow," I thought, glancing at the clock. "Only 10:45. She's up early." She told me that she was digging up information on a scoundrel who, it seemed, was bent on defrauding half the state of Florida. She wanted me to run an online search to see if he or his wife were mentioned in any Florida newspapers in the past five years. We agreed on a not-to-exceed budget and deadline, and I thought to myself that my clients often send me interesting work, but rarely do they ask me to track down real estate crooks.

By now, the dogs had gotten restless, so I took them on a quick walk around the block. I saw the economist who lives across the street and also works from home, walking his dogs. There must be some mysterious canine schedule that requires walking at 11 A.M.

The dogs quieted, I settled down for some serious Web surfing. A public relations firm had hired me to develop the content for a business process reengineering (BPR) portal they were building for a client. I started out by looking through a few general business portals for leads: Business.com, the Librarians' Index to the Internet (www.lii.org), and Yahoo! (www.yahoo.com). All had valuable leads to BPR sources. I started collecting sites, annotating each as I went along. Before I got too far, though, the phone rang—a friend and private investigator who lives nearby asked if I wanted to go on a run. Why not? It was a beautiful day, and Rock Creek Park beckoned. We met in 10 minutes and spent the next hour running through the park and talking about work. A quick shower and I was back in the office, the dogs moping because I hadn't taken them along this time.

I called a telephone researcher in Boston who was working on a phone project I'd subcontracted—obtaining standards for electrical power systems on ships—to see how the work was going and to find out if she needed any additional information from the client. As I expected, she had the project completely under control. She told me that she would have a report written, using my electronic memo format, and ready for me to send to the client by the end of the next day.

I put in another hour on the business process reengineering project, made some notes on what sites to check next, and then put the project aside. The client didn't need the material for another week, and other deadlines were looming.

I would be traveling to California in a couple of weeks to give a talk on trends in the information industry. Public speaking is one of the ways I market my business; not only does it establish my expertise, I use these talks as a way to collect names and business cards of prospective clients. I had already sketched out my presentation and set up a file folder where I tossed any interesting articles that I thought might be useful. Now I pulled out the folder, opened up a fresh PowerPoint file, and outlined the talk. When I was finished, I loaded the presentation onto my Web site, where I maintain a list of recent speaking engagements, and updated the page to include the latest talk. And, while it was fresh in my mind, I called the editor of one of the information industry magazines and asked if she would be interested in having me rework the presentation into an article, since writing for publication is another form of marketing that works well for me. We agreed on a deadline, word count, and fee, and I noted the assignment on my "writing deadlines" list that hangs on the wall next to the computer. I wouldn't start the article until after I gave the talk; I expected to get some useful feedback and ideas from the conference, and knew that I would want to incorporate those into the article.

Beep! The fax machine came to life, and spit out the two articles on optical amplifiers that I had ordered earlier from the document delivery company. I looked them over, added a comment to the executive summary, and sent the report to the client.

It was getting close to the end of the day, so I picked up the phone and called a new independent info pro I'm informally mentoring. We spent half an hour talking about her marketing strategy, how she was going to handle a difficult client situation, and a seminar she was planning to teach in a few months.

By now, the dogs had started nudging my elbow; it was time for their evening walk and they were getting impatient. I breathed a sigh of relief that they had refrained from howling during any of my phone calls during the day; they aren't always this well-mannered.

I started my backup program, which saves all new files onto a Zip disk, packed up some professional reading that I might or might not get to that evening, and steeled myself for the 25-foot commute back to the house.

Your Typical Day

Everyone's day is going to have its own rhythm. Info pros with children at home will have to factor in the interruptions of child care; with young children, that can have a serious impact on the amount of time you're able to put into your business. Info pros who provide public records or other hands-on research will probably spend much of their time out of their offices—in government agencies, libraries, archives, or other repositories of hard-copy information. Telephone researchers generally have much less freedom to leave the office in order to walk the dog or meet a friend for a long lunch or a run in the park, because they're often waiting for contacts to return phone calls.

Issues We All Face

Regardless of the type of information service you provide, some basic issues will remain the same. You'll have to figure out how to make the best use of every hour of the day. You'll spend a significant portion of your day doing work that can't be billed out to a client, such as marketing, staying in touch with colleagues, and handling administrative chores. That's all work that's essential, but that doesn't contribute to your bottom line, at least not directly. You'll be juggling a lot of different responsibilities, some of which you will probably enjoy and some of which you won't. The chances are slim that you will have an entire day uninterrupted by phone calls, the noisy neighbor who thinks that, because you're working at home, you aren't really busy, or other unexpected disruptions.

Even if you don't do online research, you will be using various software applications during the course of the day. You'll be writing up summaries of your research in a word-processing program; you'll probably be using a financial management software package such as QuickBooks for basic accounting; you'll be checking and managing your e-mail with software such as Eudora Pro, Outlook, or Outlook Express, and I hope that you'll be using a file backup system—such as a Zip drive or CD—at least once a week, in order to save copies of all your business-critical files. Chapter 9, Software for Your Business, goes into more detail about what you'll need.

The consequence of relying on software, as most businesses do today, is that you are responsible for providing at least the first line of defense when your PC goes down. As an independent info pro, you have no in-house help desk, no friendly computer geek down the hall who can wander by and figure out what's wrong. If your printer experiences a meltdown, your phone line suddenly goes dead, or your PC displays the Blue Screen of Death—every Windows user knows about this, the "Fatal Error" message that means whatever you were working on has just been eaten by your computer and you will now have to reboot—you're on your own. Most of us develop a good relationship with a local computer pro who is reliable, willing to make home-office calls, and who understands that if our PC is down, our business is down, too.

Eternal Verities in the Life of an Independent Info Pro

- Time management is essential. If you're not reporting to a boss or working on a regular 9–to–5 (or whatever) schedule, it's easy to let time get away from you.
- You switch hats constantly. You need to be able to mentally put one job on hold while you deal with other projects or concerns, then pick up the first job where you left off.
- It's critical to set aside time to get some exercise or otherwise refresh yourself. Work can easily take over your life, and that's no way to live.
- There's a lot of overhead and administrative time in running your own business.
- No matter how busy you are, you never stop marketing. The format may change—you may rely more on marketing efforts that reinforce word of mouth after your business is well-established—but you will continue to do some form of marketing as long as you are in business.

Chapter 3

The Joys and Frustrations of Being an Independent Info Pro

Way back when I was considering whether being an independent info pro would be right for me, I talked to a number of people who had been in business for a while, and I lurked on the electronic bulletin board of the Association of Independent Information Professionals (www.aiip.org). What I really wanted was to get a sense of the highs and lows of this business—what made this such a rewarding profession and what caused people the most aggravation.

As you are reading this chapter, think about how important each of these aspects of the business is to you. Some of the negatives almost everyone experiences, such as isolation, the lack of a steady paycheck, and the constant need to market yourself and your business. Likewise, some features of the entrepreneurial life almost all independent info pros find rewarding—the ability to work from home, the relationships we establish with clients, and the personal satisfaction of knowing that we have built a business ourselves. If, as you read this chapter, you discover that what we find rewarding doesn't resonate with you, then this may not be the best choice of profession for you.

The Thrills of Being an Independent Info Pro

For many of us independent info pros, one of the biggest thrills is knowing that, single-handedly, we have built solid, successful businesses. Except for the lucky few who were already luminaries in their field when they started out, most of us didn't have clients flocking to our door on our first day of business. But gradually, we learned the best ways to attract customers, keep them happy, and build our revenue year after year. We know that we always have competitors, but our clients want to call *us*, and that can be very satisfying.

One of the often-mentioned benefits of being an independent info pro is the ability to manage your workload and have a more family-friendly schedule. I'm not persuaded that this is always a realistic expectation, but it is possible to build more flexibility into your schedule than can be done in a traditional work setting. As you can see from reading Chapter 2, A Day in the Life of an Independent Info Pro, I value the ability to take breaks during the day for non-work activities like running with a friend or walking the dogs. Although it's not always feasible and it takes a lot of cooperation on the part of one's family, some independent info pros are able to build their schedules around their children's school schedules—by starting their workday before the kids get up, enforcing the "no talking to me while I'm on the phone" rule, tackling administrative work in the evening, and building a client base that doesn't expect them to be available in the afternoon when school gets out.

It A ll Depends ...

A friend and colleague of mine, Alex Kramer, is a public records researcher. Until recently, almost all of her work involved going to courts and other government offices and conducting research in document files. I, on the other hand, almost never need to leave my home office, and do most of my research online. Alex would often tell me that she thought she had the better deal, since she has to stop work at the end of the day when the government offices close. She never got stuck working far into the night; knowing that she could only work during normal business hours meant that she stayed particularly focused during the day.

I would respond to her by saying that I had the better deal, because I could take time off in the middle of the day and make up the time in the evening or during the weekend. "Think of how much more flexibility I have," I would tell her. "Look at how many nights and weekends you work," she would respond.

Which type of work schedule works best for you?

Many independent info pros value the freedom to travel and to work from any location. If they have a phone line, they're in business. In fact, on my last vacation to a mountain cabin with my family, I speculated on whether I could run my office from the ranger's look-out station at the top of a nearby mountain peak. A wireless modem and a cell phone would keep me connected to the world. My only problem was that the nearest post office and FedEx drop-off location were several hours away; as wired as I am, I still need to send and receive hard-copy material every few days.

Of course, the advent of global wireless access has its disadvantages for the mobile info pro. We now feel obligated to travel with cell phone and laptop, because our clients expect us to remain in touch even when we're out of the office. On the other hand, we are the ultimate telecommuter. We can work from home. We can use voice mail, e-mail, and pagers to stay in touch while we're traveling. As long as we're willing to stay tied to our electronic leashes, we can look like we are hard at work in the office while we are working on our tans on Maui, or taking the grandchildren to the zoo.

Although I will mention this later as a drawback of being independent, I also consider the opportunity to work from home one of the joys of the business. My clothing budget has dropped to a fraction of what I spent as an employee. My commute is 15 seconds on a bad day. I can throw a load of laundry in the washer while waiting for a document to print. I can take a coffee break and water the yard. In good weather, I can open the door and windows of my office above the garage and hear the birds singing and the gurgle of the waterfall in the fish pond.

One of the most frustrating aspects of working in a traditional job, at least for me, was the bureaucracy that inevitably slowed down innovation and change. If I wanted to introduce a new service, it required meetings, proposals, focus groups, and approvals. A certain amount of structural inertia is built into almost any organization. While that provides stability, it also means that change takes time. As a one- or two-person business, you can turn on a dime. Want to offer a new service to your clients? Institute an e-mail newsletter? Refocus your marketing to a different client base? No problem! You can be fearless in your approach, because you know that you can regroup if you see that something doesn't work. Such flexibility is particularly valuable during economic downturns. If you find that one group of clients has been hit hard by a slowdown in that industry or niche, you can reevaluate your strategy and target another market. If you notice a sudden interest in a particular type of research—pre-employment screening of job applicants, for example, or the ability to analyze and read between the lines of company Web pages—you can retool and refocus your marketing efforts much more quickly than a larger competitor could.

Another joy of being an independent info pro is the opportunity to meet so many interesting people. My clients come from a wide variety of industries, backgrounds, and countries. Some are fellow entrepreneurs; some are CEOs of large companies; some are well-known in their fields. I would not have met any of them if I weren't running my own business. We independent info pros are often brought in (virtually, if not physically) as part of a team for a specific project. The client benefits from an outside perspective, and we benefit from learning how that organization perceives a problem or an industry issue. Seeing the world from the point of view of a number of clients gives us a depth of perspective that most employees don't have an opportunity to develop.

Related to this is the opportunity to see more of the world as an independent info pro. I was never attracted to jobs that required frequent travel; I'm a homebody at heart. But I love the chance to see the world, at least in short visits. I decided to look for speaking opportunities outside the U.S., in order to meet info pros in other countries and find out how the information industry in other places differed from the U.S. I began sending proposals to conference program committees in countries that I wanted to visit, and I have been fortunate enough to have made it to a number of them. Even if you don't like travel and would prefer to stay put, marketing your services internationally—and, yes, that takes some creativity—allows you to meet and interact with clients throughout the world without leaving your neighborhood.

An entrepreneur doesn't get an annual review (or pay raise) from the boss, and the lack of formal feedback and reinforcement can be difficult for some people. On the other hand, you get a lot of satisfaction from knowing that your clients keep coming back to you because they really like what you do and they're willing to pay you to do it. A related benefit is the supportive note that comes when you least expect it. I send out a free e-mail newsletter and, as I was writing this chapter, I received a message from someone on my distribution list telling me how much she appreciates the newsletter and how grateful she is that I take the time to write it. That kind of response makes my day.

Independent info pros also tend to develop strong bonds with other independents. Although we always maintain client confidentiality, we often bounce ideas and questions off each other and get advice and support from colleagues who have addressed similar problems. As a community, independent info pros are remarkably supportive; we understand the challenges of running a business, and we know how important encouragement is. We also recognize the need for plenty of other independent info pros in the marketplace—for subcontracting and as referral sources—so we are all invested in the success of each other's businesses.

One of the less-tangible benefits of running your own business is the ability to turn down projects or clients that you just don't want to work with … within reason, of course. Sooner or later, everyone runs into the Client From Hell—someone who makes unreasonable demands, is consistently rude or abrasive, or represents an organization or cause that, for whatever reason, you would rather not work with. Since you're running the show, you can decide that you simply won't do business with that person. (See Chapter 11, Managing Your Clients, for more discussion on this topic.) By the same token, you can decide to discount your rate or donate your services to a nonprofit or charitable organization that you do support. Being able to incorporate your personal values into your business can be a gratifying aspect of entrepreneurship.

The Chills of Being an Independent Info Pro

The thrills of running your own business sound great, don't they? Generally, it is—otherwise, we wouldn't keep doing it. But there are some less appealing aspects of this profession. A lot depends on your own tolerance for risk and uncertainty, whether or not you need external structure to work most efficiently, and whether you can ride out the highs and lows of running a business. But talk to any independent info pro long enough, and you'll probably hear most of what I'm about to say.

Perhaps the hardest part of being independent is that fact that you're *it*. You *are* the company. You have to do the strategic planning, the marketing, the client management, and the administrative work, as well as providing the actual information services. You have to take responsibility for all the difficult decisions and for the occasional really bad error in judgment (yes, it happens to all of us sooner or later). There will be times when no work has come in for a week or two, and you start wondering if this whole information-business thing was just a horrible mistake. There will be times when you wish you had someone else to share the responsibilities and decisions. And there will be times when you suffer burnout, when you are sick of what you do, tired of always having to hustle for new clients, and longing for the security of a steady paycheck. It happens to all of us—usually not for long periods, but it can feel crippling when it hits. As I mentioned earlier, your info pro colleagues will offer sympathy and encouragement; that is what has always kept me going. But you do have to be willing to reach out for help, which is hard for some people to do.

Related to the need to ask for support from fellow info entrepreneurs when things get rough, some people need the structure of the workplace. They are energized by the bustle and noise of a busy office, they like being able to wander down the hall to bounce an idea off a co-worker, and they're accustomed to going out to lunch with friends or business associates. When you're an independent info pro, you can e-mail a colleague or pick up the phone and talk to a friend, but you don't have regular face-to-face contact with co-workers. Some independents address this issue by developing a business that lets them work on-site with clients—perhaps the best of both worlds. They are in the workplace but not of it, as it were.

Although I consider the ability to work from home an advantage of the profession, it does have its drawbacks. It took a while to teach the neighbors that I really was working even though I was home and dressed casually, and that I wasn't necessarily free to stop and chat. Some colleagues tell me that they find it difficult to focus on work when they know that there's laundry or housework to do. Personally, I'd much rather do research than housework, but I'll take their word that this can be a distraction.

Independent info pros who must take care of children or elderly parents struggle with the need to separate work from home. In most cases, this means hiring someone to come in and handle the caregiving during work hours; trying to juggle work with family-member responsibilities means that neither your clients nor your loved ones get the attention they need.

Running your own business means conducting a fearless self-evaluation at least once a year, to assess your strengths and weaknesses and to figure out how to take advantage of the former and either address or accommodate the latter. You're not expected to be perfect, but you must know yourself well enough to recognize what you don't do well, and then either improve or outsource those jobs. In general, hire outside help for those tasks that are generic and outside the primary focus of your business, such as invoicing, paying bills, designing a brochure or logo, or upgrading your hardware or software. These are all jobs that require specific skills but don't directly involve the operation or direction of your business—as long as you keep an eye on what the person you've hired is doing. On the other hand, high-contact, high-visibility responsibilities such as talking with clients, estimating and selling projects, and marketing yourself and your services usually cannot be handed off to a third party. These activities go to the very heart of what you do; if you feel that you're weak in one of these areas, focus on developing your skills by taking a professional development course, reading up on the subject, or working with a job coach. See the checklist "With a Little Help from My Friends" for a list of what can and can't easily be delegated to someone outside your business.

With a Little Help from My Friends

Nobody's perfect at all aspects of running an info pro business. Some tasks can be contracted out fairly easily; others are more difficult to delegate.

What's easy to contract out:

- Accounting
- Collections
- Design and writing of marketing material
- Web page design
- Computer maintenance and purchasing
- Specific types of research at which you're not expert

What's difficult to contract out:

- Strategic planning
- Marketing
- Client contact
- Estimating cost and time for projects

One of the challenges that almost every independent info pro faces is pricing and cash flow. (I address this in detail in Chapter 12, Money, Money, Money and Chapter 13, Setting Rates and Fees.) Even after many years in business, you will probably find that some months you're flush with cash and some months (usually, it seems, just before you have to pay your income taxes) you're running low. Besides the obvious need to bank surplus income in anticipation of the lean times, it takes a strong stomach to ride out those periods when you've sent invoices out but none of the checks have come in.

Pricing your services is the other financial-related aspect of the business that many info pros find difficult. Quoting a four- or five-figure estimate for a job can be hard, particularly when you don't know what your competitors are charging or offering. In general, we info pros tend to undercharge, relative to what clients pay for other high-value professional services such as attorneys or strategic planning consultants. Knowing how much to charge, accurately estimating what the market will bear, and setting a price that appropriately reflects the expertise and value we offer is a challenge for many of us.

Related to pricing and cash flow is the issue of marketing. Independent info pros always have to market. When you start out, you will probably spend 90 percent of your time marketing yourself and your business. For some people, this is the most difficult part of running a business: "How can I tell people how great I am without sounding conceited or pompous?" Section Three goes into marketing issues in depth; the short answer here is that running an independent info pro business means being able to look at yourself as a brand, a product, a business. This never stops. Even after you have been in business for five or ten years, you still need to market yourself—although the amount of time you spend on marketing will drop to 20 or 30 percent.

Vacation and business-related travel pose problems for independent info pros. For starters, there is no such thing as a paid vacation for the self-employed. (That's not quite true; I have sometimes arranged to subcontract jobs when I go on vacation, so I do earn the difference between what the subcontractor charges me and what I bill the client. But most vacations mean zero income.) A bigger challenge is what you do with your clients while you're away. Yes, you can try to stay in touch while you are on the road. With call forwarding, cell phones, pagers, and e-mail, you can respond fairly quickly if a client wants to get in touch with you. But is that any way to enjoy your vacation? One reason I look forward to my annual backpacking trip to the Rocky Mountains is that I am unreachable there. If they ever put cell phone towers in Wyoming's Wind River backcountry, I'll have to plan my vacation for some even more remote wilderness.

For those times when you are out of your office and not able to respond quickly to clients' information needs, what do you do? There is no perfect solution, and it is inevitable that some clients will be dissatisfied, particularly those who are accustomed to having researchers available on-call, 24 hours a day. Some independent info pros develop relationships with colleagues, then forward their phones or leave outgoing voice-mail messages directing callers to call "my associate" or "my colleague." Others use their travel plans as an opportunity to contact all their regular clients, tell them that the office will be closed, and suggest that they take care of their anticipated information requests right away. And some hardy souls do attempt to give the impression that they are in the office, even when they aren't. But, as hard as you try, you can't offer the same degree of service that a large company can; sometimes you just can't get back to the client immediately. And that means you will lose clients who expect their info pros to be available 24/7/365.

The Best and Worst of Being an Independent Info Pro

Before you launch your own business, think about whether, for you, the "bests" outweigh the "worsts":

BEST:

- Pride of ownership; being responsible for the success of your business
- Flexibility about where, when, and how you work
- Meeting and developing relationships with a wide variety of clients and colleagues
- Freedom from bureaucracy

WORST:

- Stress of ownership; being responsible for the success of your business
- Needing to be available whenever your clients need you
- Cash flow fluctuations
- Constant need to market yourself and your business

Chapter 4

Are You a Potential Independent Info Pro?

I'm often asked why there aren't more of us independent info pros out there in the marketplace. It seems like the perfect job—sit at home all day in your pajamas, find information for people on all kinds of fascinating subjects, and send out invoices for thousands of dollars. What's not to like about that?

The curious thing about this profession is that, in fact, it requires an unusual set of skills that aren't innate in most people. Fortunately, you can fill in the gaps in your skill set by reading this book, hiring experts, and focusing your business in areas that take advantage of your strengths. But before you get too far into the planning process, let's look at exactly what it takes to be a successful independent info pro.

The People Skills

Running an information business requires great people skills—getting along with a wide variety of personality types; being able to talk with an irate client without becoming defensive, belligerent, or tongue-tied; and being able to talk enthusiastically about your business to prospective clients. Most independent info pros have clients all over the country, not to mention the world. So you have to come across well on the telephone and via e-mail, because it may be the only contact most clients will have with you. (I have clients I've worked with for many years whom I've never met face to face. Sometimes they ask me to send them a picture just so they have an image of the person they've been talking to all these years.) Conveying your winning personality and professional competence via e-mail can be challenging; depending on the client, you need to develop some combination of professionalism and informality that comes across in a plain-text e-mail message. Note that discussions with clients about specific projects are more effective when conducted via phone conversations rather than e-mail. See Chapter 25, The Reference Interview, for more discussion of the value of interactive conversations with clients.

Beyond client management, being an independent info pro means having client *attraction* skills as well. You need to be the kind of person that people enjoy working with. Information services are an expense that clients choose to incur. And your clients will call you rather than calling someone else or choosing to do the work themselves because they know you'll deliver cost-effectively, on time, and with a minimum of aggravation and effort. If you're someone they enjoy working with, someone who is personable and friendly, your clients will be more likely to want to get in touch when they need your services.

You also need the ability to evaluate people and to trust your instincts. Is this caller a legitimate potential client or just a tire-kicker, someone who loves to talk but isn't ever going to send you a real job? Does this person have budget authority to approve the purchase, or is he just shopping around for his boss and not actually interested in contracting for your services? You don't want to waste your valuable time with someone who will never become a client, but you don't want to alienate a good prospect who is simply shy or vague about what she needs, or who spends some time asking intelligent questions before deciding to engage your services.

The Entrepreneurial Skills

New independent info pros often underestimate the need for entrepreneurial skills. You may be great at finding information for your friends or family, but can you develop a business in which people will pay you $75, $100, or more per hour for your research?

What's your tolerance for risk? It's a scary thing to move from knowing that you'll be getting a paycheck every two weeks to realizing that you're going to have to hustle for every dollar you earn. You'll be making decisions about the direction of your business, how you'll market your services to clients, and when to invest in new technology. How well do you make decisions? How comfortable are you in unfamiliar situations? You don't need to be the kind of person who rappels off cliffs without a second thought, but you should be able to tolerate ambiguity and to assess new situations quickly and pick a course of action.

As any entrepreneur knows, running your own business means that you have to market—and that means marketing yourself as well as your company. You must be able to evaluate your marketing efforts as your business grows, decide what works and what doesn't, and modify your strategies to reflect a changing client base and economic environment. Marketing never, ever goes away, even after you've been in business for years.

I am often asked whether it's possible to subcontract the marketing to someone who specializes in promoting businesses. Although I suppose it can be done, it doesn't seem to be a workable option for too many of my colleagues; what your client is paying for is *you*—your skills, experience, and ability. It's hard for someone else to project the air of authority and expertise that comes naturally to you—or will. On the other hand, a number of independent info pros have worked successfully with job coaches or marketing consultants to build up their marketing skills. Because promoting your business is a never-ending task, it's wise to invest in learning how to do this as painlessly as possible.

Entrepreneurs tend to have a drive to succeed and the self-discipline to keep going when business slumps. Sometimes you're going to be discouraged. The phone doesn't ring, a client yells at you, even your dog won't wag her tail when you walk by. At such times, you'll want to take advantage of one of the biggest benefits of membership in the Association of Independent Information Professionals (www.aiip.org)—a ready network of fellow independent info pros who can give you suggestions on new approaches to your business or simply offer a sympathetic ear.

I have found that most successful independent info pros tend to be detail oriented. They can see the big picture, but they also focus on the little things that make that big picture happen. Being a one-person operation means that there's no one else to catch your mistakes, cover for you, or take the blame if you miss something. If you're the type of person who is careful about details, thinks through all the aspects of a project, and follows through on everything that has to be done, you'll have a much better chance of succeeding in this business.

Time management is a critical entrepreneurial skill. How well do you function in a work setting with very little structure? Will you be tempted to spend the day gardening, watching TV, or doing housework instead of working? Alternatively, will you be able to close the door (figuratively if not literally) on your business at the end of the day, or will it wind up taking over every waking hour of your life?

How much do you enjoy working alone? Do you need the excitement of an office to get fired up, or do you find the hustle and bustle of an office exhausting? Do you need input and recognition from others in order to feel that your work is meaningful and valuable? If so, can you get that from your clients or do you need the more immediate feedback of co-workers and a boss?

Finally, a successful entrepreneur is one who not only has a vision but is able to implement it. Can you think through what is involved in bringing an idea to fruition and take all the steps required to do it? Do you think creatively? Do you have the ability to think of new ways of doing things and new ways to build a business?

The Business Skills

In addition to entrepreneurial skills, independent info pros need to master the basics of business management. You'll be the CEO, CFO, Marketing Director, Sales Manager, and Strategic Planning VP, all in one, and although you don't have to have advanced degrees in all these areas, you will need to develop some skills in management, finance, sales and marketing, and so on.

You have to be able to set up a business infrastructure and operate as a professional entity, even if you're doing it from your kitchen table. You must keep accounting records, manage your cash flow, and comply with tax rules regarding periodic reports and payments. If you're not a detail-oriented person, hire an accountant to take care of this part of your business. You can be fairly casual about some things, but you don't want to tell the IRS "Oops! I forgot to pay my taxes. Sorry about that."

You should feel comfortable projecting a professional image to everyone you deal with. This may take some practice. Some independent info pros find it hard to sound professional when they're sitting at the phone in their bathrobe and bunny slippers, or when they're doing business with a friend. You have to be able to see yourself as a business owner, regardless of whom you're talking to or what setting you're in. Even if your office consists of a corner of your living room, you must be able to view it as the corner office of an executive.

You have to be able to close a sale. When someone asks you for an estimate on a project, you have to feel comfortable talking about budgets, what you charge per hour, and your payment terms. And if someone sounds like he's a "tire-kicker," can you send him on his way without being rude?

One of the most difficult parts of running a business is collections. Yes, we'd like to think that all our clients will pay us promptly, but that doesn't always happen. See Chapter 12, Money, Money, Money, for a discussion of how to accept credit cards and other finance-related topics. The bottom line is whether you are able to pick up the phone and say, "Hello, Ms. Smith. I notice that my invoice dated January 15 is past due. What can we do to get this invoice processed by Friday?"

I sometimes think of independent info pros as information pit-bulls. We're the people who won't take "no" for an answer, who keep on digging for what our client has asked us to find, hour after hour. Persistence is an admirable trait in a researcher, but it can get in your way if you're running your own business. You only earn money for the time that you can bill to a client. If your client is not willing to pay you for more than two hours of research, you have to stop at that point, even though you may have identified lots of other avenues to explore. If you don't stop working, you'll be giving away your time and will be training your client to expect bonus time from you on every project. It's hard to walk away when you're involved in research, but if a client isn't willing to pay for an extensive effort, you're a fool to give it away for nothing. And you're a bigger fool if you try to bill a client for more than the authorized budget. Your client may pay that invoice, but you can bet she won't call you again.

Part of running a business is the ability to watch your competition and predict what's going to happen in your market. Can you make the time to think strategically about where your business is going and what your clients will want a year from now? You're not expected to have psychic powers, but you do have to be able to hazard a guess on the future direction of your business and your clients' needs, and then take appropriate action. No one else can tell you where your market is going to be a year from now; you have to decide for yourself where you want your business to go.

Every business owner knows about money management and cash flow. If you live in the U.S., you'll have to write a check to the IRS every three months for a portion of your income for the past quarter. If you've already spent it, too bad. How do you handle cash? Do you have the discipline to set a substantial percentage of your revenue aside to pay for things like taxes or that big invoice from an online service provider or a subcontractor?

Finally, everyone who owns a business needs the ability to recognize hype and oversell. I'm amazed at the number of people who've approached me over the years, offering the chance to partner with them for an "amazing opportunity" or who—especially during the hot dot.com days—wanted to pay me in stock instead of cash. Although your experience may be different, I've found that people who really do have sustainable business opportunities are willing to pay their vendors (that's you and me) in cash. Independent info pros are usually independent for a reason—we like having control over our own destiny. And that serves us well when we're approached by people who would love to let us in on the next big thing in exchange for a substantial discount on our rates or part-ownership of their business. Until you figure out a way to pay your electric bill with a start-up company's stock options, stick to payment in cash.

The Information Skills

You may have started reading this book because you just love finding things out, or you're the one everyone comes to for help in gathering information. That passion for finding information is essential, but turning your avocation into a business means developing a whole new level of research expertise. Independent info pros don't just surf the Web for information, nor do they typically just head down to the library and bury their heads in books all day. They usually use a variety of resources, including the Web; fee-based online services such as LexisNexis, Factiva.com, or Dialog; government databases; telephone interviews; and court records. If the only information source you know is the Web, it'll be very difficult to differentiate yourself from anyone else with an Internet connection, not to mention that some of the most useful information can't be found through a Web search engine. (See Chapter 28, Web Research 101, for more discussion of the "invisible Web.")

In order to succeed in this business, you need to have experience as a researcher or be willing to subcontract out any project involving types of research in which you aren't already an expert. (See Chapter 14, Subcontracting, or I'll Scratch Your Back if You Scratch Mine, for a discussion of how you can build a business around subcontracting.) The bottom line is that you generally can't get your clients to pay for your learning curve. And it's a steep curve if you don't already have a foundation in research to build on. It takes a surprising amount of time and money to learn how to search the professional online services, how to find court documents, how to conduct effective telephone research, and so on.

You can, of course, pick up those skills by taking the long view—a year or two—and considering what kind of job you can find now that will help you build the research skills you need. It might feel frustrating to delay the launch of your business, but it's an investment in time and patience that will pay off for years to come. Does the company you work for have a research department? Does someone within your own area provide a research function? Do you have a corporate library or information center? If so, take the librarians or researchers to lunch, find out how they acquired their skills, and ask for some guidance in doing research and pointers to where you can learn more. Nothing warms a librarian's heart more than someone who says, "I want to know how you do what you do." And look outside your own organization. If you're considering public records research, see if any local private investigation firms hire entry-level investigators. If you want to specialize in telephone research, go through the AIIP membership directory and see if any of the members who provide primary research would be willing to train a smart, talented newcomer. This approach works best for telephone and public records research, both of which require creativity and persistence but not necessarily expertise in using fee-based information services. Also, neither requires that you work in someone else's office, which is often not a possibility for home-based businesses. If you're interested in developing your skills in searching the professional online services, the most feasible option is to learn through formal training rather than making expensive mistakes on the job or for another independent info pro.

Many independent info pros come from a library background, complete with masters' degrees in library science and years behind the reference desk. Librarians have the advantage of knowing where to look for information, how to find it quickly, how to organize it, how to interview clients to make sure they're looking for the *right* information in the first place, and countless other research-related skills. You don't need to get a graduate degree in library science, but consider taking some continuing education courses in reference skills and online research.

Many successful independent info pros almost stumbled into the profession, after deciding that what they really enjoy is finding information and then figuring out how to build that passion into a business. For example, Risa Sacks, owner of Risa Sacks Information Services and a top-notch telephone researcher, started out as a speech therapist. "My work involved identifying what a client's speech problem was and how to get that client to where he needed to be," Risa told me. "It was all about figuring out what people need and then finding a solution. From there, I moved into training development and technical writing, which also involve identifying problems and developing solutions. Both training development and technical writing required that I interview experts in order to learn about whatever I had to write about. About 30 percent of my time was spent interviewing, and 70 percent was writing, and I realized that I really wanted to find a profession in which I could spend 70 percent of my time interviewing people and 30 percent of the time writing. And that's how I fell into telephone research!"

Where Can You Get Help?

You've read about the skill sets involved in successfully running an information business. Unless you're a perfect specimen of humanity or are unable to conduct a critical self-evaluation, you've probably identified some areas in which you could use a little help. Congratulations! I haven't yet met anyone who came to this business with all the necessary people skills, entrepreneurial skills, business skills and research skills—myself included. If you're strong in at least two of these areas and willing to develop your skills in the others, you can join the ranks of successful independent info pros.

One of the best ways to enhance your CEO-ability is, yes, school. Your local college may offer adult education or continuing ed courses on entrepreneurship or specific business-related subjects like cash management and financial planning, marketing on the Web, and government contracting. In fact, some schools even have courses specifically titled "Home-Based Business."

The Small Business Administration offers a number of resources through its Web site (www.sba.gov), including brief tutorials—called Online Courses—on writing a business plan, conducting a self-assessment, building your business, and so on. The SBA also sponsors the SCORE program, the Service Corps of Retired Executives. SCORE volunteers provide free counseling and workshops for people considering starting a business. Go to www.score.org to learn more about SCORE's e-mail and in-person counseling, and check the SBA Web site to find locations of local SBA offices.

You might also want to check the Web site of your state or regional government. You're likely to find information not only on business licenses or permits you may need, but also on financial assistance programs, help with business planning, and workshops and other continuing education programs.

And what about the necessary information skills? A number of graduate-level library schools offer specific programs on what's often called information brokering. Check with your local university to see if it has a School of Library Studies (some library science programs are eschewing the "L-word" and are calling themselves Information Management Studies or something similar). For a list of the American Library Association-accredited library schools in the U.S. and Canada, see www.ala.org/alaorg/oa/lisdir.html. This site also indicates which accredited schools offer distance education opportunities—a great way to build your research skills if you don't live near a school that offers a library science degree.

Checklist of Key Independent Info Pro Skills

- Ability to deal with a wide range of personalities.
- Self-motivation. The flip side of never having to endure a job performance evaluation is that no one tells you that you're doing a great job.
- Knowing when to say when. You only make money on the time you can bill a client.
- Ability to market yourself and your business. This is one setting in which it doesn't pay to be shy or self-effacing.
- The skills to develop a strategic plan and direction, and then take the steps necessary to implement that plan.
- Basic money-management skills and a strong stomach for fluctuating cash flow.
- A drive to succeed and to make your business grow.
- Excellent information skills, or the willingness to subcontract to other experts.

Chapter 5

Understanding Your Competition

One of the strange aspects of being an independent info pro is that our competition is generally invisible. We don't have a storefront, so we don't see the Discount Info Supermarket down the street with "50% off all information this week only" signs in the window. In fact, you will probably find that you spend far more time thinking about how to attract new clients than you do worrying about what your competitors are up to. It's a big market out there, and it's far from saturated. However, you may find it useful to stroll down the virtual sidewalk every so often to see where else your clients could be shopping.

Who Am I Up Against?

As you begin marketing your services, one of the first questions to ask yourself is, "Where are my clients going *now* for the services I want to provide them?" The most likely answer will be the Web; although it's not always the most efficient or cost-effective way to find in-depth information, it sure is fast, easy, and cheap. When you present yourself to prospective clients, you'll have to address the perception that it's all on the Web, for free, and anyone can find it. See the sidebar, "Can You Find That on the Web?" for some thoughts on talking with your clients about what *can't* be found by searching the Web. You'll also want to evaluate specific aspects of the services you offer and the value you add that differentiate your deliverable from what your clients can find on the Web. This shouldn't be hard, but sometimes you do have to spell it out.

Special Libraries

Your clients may have the option of using an in-house library or information center. Most large companies, government agencies, nonprofits and associations have specialized in-house libraries that serve that organization's employees. Why should your clients pay you when they can get the information for free? Good question, and it has to be answered carefully. I have always viewed in-house librarians (also known as special librarians) as colleagues and partners, not competitors, and I'll usually ask my clients if they've checked with their internal library before I start working on a project. Am I crazy? No, I want to make sure that I stay in the librarian's good graces. Special librarians are great referral sources; when they get a request that goes beyond the scope of what they can handle, they *want* to refer their patron to someone who can do the work, and you'll be on their short list if you play your cards right.

Likewise, I refer clients to their own library for simple projects that aren't profitable for me to work on but that their librarian can answer quickly. And special librarians may have access to high-priced information sources that you can't afford. So, working with your client's librarian on a complex research project usually benefits everyone—your client gets your expertise as well as the specialized information that only the librarian can find, the librarian sees you as a partner rather than a competitor, and you keep your client happy.

Public and Academic Libraries

Public and university libraries sometimes compete with independent info pros, particularly if the library operates a fee-based service of its own. The hourly rates for these services are usually comparable to what independent info pros charge. They're attractive to clients because they usually have several people on staff, so someone is always available to handle calls, and they have direct access to a wide variety of information sources. They often have substantial marketing budgets, too, so they can reach most of the large prospects in their area.

As an independent info pro, you can compete successfully if you focus on what sets you apart from fee-based library services:

- You offer consistency—the client always works with the same info pro.
- You provide services that the library can't, such as telephone or public records research.

- Because you own your own business, you might be more responsive to your client's needs.

You can also market your services outside your geographic region, whereas most libraries limit themselves to their local area. In fact, some fee-based services are funded or sponsored by a university or local government and, as a result—fortunately for us independent info pros—are limited in the amount of outreach they can do, as well as in the level and variety of services they provide. By marketing to a broader base of clients, you can move well beyond the reach of fee-based library services.

Information on the Desktop

Large organizations often provide external information through an intranet, distributing news stories, market research, and articles from trade publications directly to employees' PCs. Such arrangements can be difficult to compete against—you don't know exactly what your client has access to internally, but he probably thinks that everything he'd ever need is right there on his desktop. You can respond that you have access to a broader range of publications, you can conduct primary research (telephone interviews, surveys, and so on), you provide customized answers rather than just collections of news and general industry information, and you can dig deeper than the preselected material that pops up on the client's desktop. Keep in mind that the client probably does have access to some material that you won't be able to get, particularly high-priced industry analysis and consulting reports. Work with the client to ensure that he taps into his internal information sources and that you focus on resources that his intranet can't deliver.

Joe Down the Hall

Some of your "competitors" are harder to pin down. Some clients rely on interns to do in-depth research; some ask the colleague down the hall who always seems to have the information they need; and some people just do without. Such prospects are hard to attract—they don't know what they're missing, so they're not inclined to seek out an info pro to help them find it. On the other hand, they're relatively easy to impress because they're accustomed to minimal added value. When you're talking to someone who relies on "Joe down the hall," be sure to describe the services you provide that go beyond what Joe could find on the Web, such as research in sources that don't exist online, confidential calls to industry sources, analysis of results, and so on.

"Can You Find That on the Web?"

We've all been encouraged to believe that all you have to do to find information on the Web is type a few words into a search engine. In fact, most of the useful information on the Web can't be found through search engines—at least not through the search engines you've come to know and love. This "invisible Web" includes material that search engines can't get to, such as articles within databases or Web sites that require registration; material that most search engines can't read, such as spreadsheets, images, audio clips, and, to a degree, PDF files; material that search engines don't even try to capture, such as real-time wire stories; and material that search engines simply miss, such as pages buried deep within a Web site or information on a new Web site they haven't gotten around to indexing. See www.invisible-web.net for lots of information on the invisible Web.

When you're talking with a prospect who thinks she can find everything she needs from a Web search engine, you might want to tell her:

- The information on the invisible Web is often more useful than what a search engine could find.
- Many publishers never put any of their content on their Web site; you have to use one of the professional online services to retrieve it.
- Web sites that look authoritative may be misleading or just plain wrong.
- Some information never shows up online at all. Sometimes a book or a phone conversation is your best bet.
- You can search the Web more efficiently, and your client can spend her valuable time doing something else.

You'll want to state your case gracefully so you don't inadvertently insult your client; many people believe that they're expert Web researchers. Develop a couple of examples showing how you found something important in the invisible Web, or that wasn't on the Web at all. And bite your tongue when a client says "Hey, I just found out about this great search engine. Have you ever tried it?"

Working with Your Competition

You might have noticed that I haven't yet mentioned other independent info pros as competitors. That's because they virtually never compete with you. In the 10-plus years I've been in business, I can think of only two situations in which I found myself directly competing with another info pro for a client's business. Instead, we see each other as colleagues and partners. Other independent info pros will be your subcontractors when you get a job you can't or don't have time to do; they'll hire you as a subcontractor when they need your expertise; and you will find yourself referring clients to a colleague who is the best in his subject area.

One of the biggest reasons why I renew my membership in the Association of Independent Information Professionals every year is because I value the network of fellow info entrepreneurs that I can tap into. Members use AIIP's private e-mail discussion list to ask for help with a tricky research project, the name of a good online searcher in Hong Kong, suggestions on how to use a Web site for marketing, or advice on how to keep clients happy while on vacation or traveling on business. These people aren't my competitors—they're my secret weapon! They're what enable me, a one-person business, to provide a wide variety of services to a broad spectrum of clients.

Every once in a while, I get a call from a prospective client who explains in painful detail just why he is so very unhappy with his current independent info pro. While it's gratifying that he's calling me—and I hope I'll be able to keep him happy—I also make sure that I never criticize a colleague. It's a small world, and if you bad-mouth a fellow info pro, you can bet that word will get out. In this situation, my response to the unhappy prospect is something like, "I'm so sorry that you're not happy with so-and-so. Sometimes it just doesn't work out." See Chapter 11, Managing Your Clients, for a sobering discussion of the fact that each of us will eventually experience a project that blows up in our face. Sooner or later, you will probably learn first-hand that, indeed, sometimes it just doesn't work out between an independent info pro and a client.

An Example of "Coopetition"

It would appear that Susan Detwiler, president of The Detwiler Group, and John Levis, owner of John E. Levis and Associates, are direct competitors; they both specialize in the medical and healthcare industries. However, they focus on different markets and use very different means to solve their clients' problems.

John works with small- to medium-sized consultants who need his special skills to deal with their clients' needs. Most of the time, John's deliverables are combined with the consultant's own work to become part of the finished project. Susan, on the other hand, is often the consultant to whom John is accountable. She takes on large projects and usually employs the services of several info pros such as John to do the work while she coordinates the project and writes the final report.

John and Susan described one project they worked on together. The client needed worldwide market research concerning a particular medical condition. Susan put together a team of four info pros, from North America (that was John), Europe, South America, and Asia. Susan coordinated the effort and prepared the final report based on the work of her team. This was a large project that she would not have been able to do by herself. Susan and John describe this as their coopetition—they're cooperative competitors.

John and Susan often recommend each other to potential clients. To the best of their knowledge, they have never competed head to head for the same project. And they use each other as sounding boards and reality checks when they need to brainstorm with someone else who knows the healthcare industry.

Looking for Competition

When you are considering your market and deciding whom to target, look at how many other independent info pros are in that market, and how long they've been in business. Check the membership directory of AIIP to get a general sense of who's out there doing what you want to do. Then mull over the following questions in your mind:

- Is your potential market niche full of people who've been in business for less than a couple of years? Is that because it's a really new market or because it isn't a sustainable market?

- Is the niche full of established businesses who've been around a long time? If so, can you break into it? Do you have a proven track record in that industry? Do you have contacts in the industry who could serve as referrals for new clients?

- If nobody seems to be doing the kind of work you have in mind, is it because there's no market for it, or because you're the first to think of it? Can you conduct some brief market research interviews with prospective clients to get an idea of whether you're leading edge or totally off the page?

- Do clients in this market have ready access to in-house research centers, libraries, or other in-depth internal information resources? Do they need and value the information services you can provide? Are they willing to pay what you plan to charge for your services?

Making Yourself Competition Proof

The best way to deal with competition is to eliminate it. Easier said than done? The secret is to develop a business that provides a unique set of services, and that features the irreplaceable *you.* Sell a service that doesn't lend itself to price comparisons—that way, your clients aren't going to leave you for someone who charges 10 percent less.

How do you develop this kind of competition-proof business?

- Provide "frictionless service." Make sure that getting you started on a project is as easy as using a search engine. Think about what you can do to make it easier for your clients to work with you. Get a toll-free phone number. Have an easy-to-remember e-mail address. Return phone calls as quickly as you can.

- Invest in your clients. Keep an eye out for articles they might be interested in. Subscribe to their leading industry publication. Attend the major trade conference that your clients attend and make sure they know you're there. (Offer to send them a report of the conference when you return home, for example.)

- Provide analysis as well as research services; move your services up the value chain. Find out what your client intends to do with the information you provide, and see what you can do to make the information easier to use, more valuable, more irreplaceable. If your client is pulling together material for a PowerPoint presentation, for example, deliver your research results in simple bullet-point form.

- Notify your most valuable clients before you leave town on a business trip or vacation; let them know who will be covering your phone. Make sure that your clients have someone they can call while you're gone—and that whoever's taking those calls knows that these clients are to be given the red-carpet treatment.

- Take your best clients to lunch once in a while. If they're not local, let them know if you're going to be visiting their city. Even if a client doesn't have time for lunch, you can stop by, say hello, and drop off a small gift—a fruit basket or other specialty food item, a book, or a similar token to indicate that you appreciate working with them.

Lessons Learned About Competition

✦ Most independent info pros have very little direct competition. Fellow info pros are more often referral sources and subcontractors than competitors.

✦ Competition can take the form of prospective clients' attitudes that they can find everything they need themselves.

✦ Check how many other info pros are already in the sector you plan to enter. Does their presence, or absence, indicate a strong potential market or a weak, unprofitable niche?

✦ Look for ways to make yourself competition-proof. Establish long-term relationships with clients.

Chapter 6

Structuring Your Business

Most independent info pros start out as one-person operations, and many find that this works just fine, thank you. Others begin their entrepreneurial life with a business partner, on the assumption that two heads are better than one. Some people build their businesses by hiring employees or using subcontractors extensively; others prefer to limit their growth to what they can handle themselves. You will have to make some decisions about how to structure your business before you open up shop, but you can also restructure later, as your needs and goals change.

Incorporating or Keeping It Simple

Independent info pros in the U.S. have four choices of business structure:

- Sole proprietorship
- Partnership
- Limited liability company
- Corporation

Each of these forms of business has its advantages and drawbacks, some of which will vary depending on where you live. The following sections give you a brief rundown on each type of business. You may want to talk with a business advisor, such as an accountant or lawyer, before you make a decision about which form your business will take and how to go about setting it up. Note that the following comments apply specifically to U.S. businesses, but many countries have similar provisions for structuring a business. For more information on the legal formats for businesses in the U.K., see Start in Business (www.startinbusiness.co.uk; click the "Business Formats" link) and Inland Revenue's guide to starting a business (www.inlandrevenue.gov.uk/startingup). For information on Canadian business forms, see Revenue Canada's *Guide for Canadian Small Businesses,* which walks you through setting up a business and explains the taxes for which you are liable. This publication is available on Revenue Canada's Web site; start at www.ccra-adrc.gc.ca and use the "Search" feature to find the Guide.

Sole Proprietorship

This is the simplest way to start your business and the one that most independent info pros opt for, at least at the beginning. In essence, you and your business are the same entity—you can operate under a trade name but your clients and vendors are dealing with you as an individual. The biggest advantage of a sole proprietorship is simplicity. You report your income to the IRS on the familiar personal income tax Form 1040, using Schedule C to itemize your business expenses. Bookkeeping is relatively simple, and the only mid-year filings required are the quarterly payments of your estimated income tax.

One of the main reasons why some info pros eventually change their business structure is that sole proprietors are legally liable for all the debts of the company. Companies to which you owe money can go after your personal assets (yes, that's your house we're talking about) if you don't pay your bills. In addition, some business expenses cannot be fully deducted from your income, such as health insurance payments. You may also find it more difficult to obtain a business loan or line of credit from a bank as a sole proprietor. You can't sell a sole proprietorship business because you and the business are one, so if you plan on eventually selling your business, you will need to incorporate. And finally, once your business is successful and you're earning a substantial income, you run a higher risk of being audited by the IRS as a sole proprietor than you would as a corporation or LLC.

The equivalent of a sole proprietorship in the U.K. is a "sole trader," and the concerns are much the same as in the U.S. You are personally liable for any debts incurred by your company, and you report your income directly to the Inland Revenue. Canadian sole proprietors operate similarly; note that you will have to register for the goods and services tax if your annual revenue is more than C$30,000.

Protecting Your Social Security Number

As a sole proprietor in the U.S., you will give out your Social Security number to just about every client. They need your "Taxpayer Identification Number," which in your case is your SSN, in order to file an IRS Form 1099 on which they report how much they paid you during the year. (1099s must be filed by anyone who pays a contractor at least $600 annually, supposedly to ensure that you don't cheat in reporting your income as a sole proprietor.) Since a loose SSN can be used by criminals to commit all kinds of fraud, some independent info pros are reluctant to give out that number left and right.

You can get around this remote but real possibility by requesting an Employer Identification Number from the IRS. You don't have to be an employer; you don't even have to be incorporated. You just have to fill out IRS Form SS-4, which you can download from www.irs.gov, and your EIN will be mailed to you. Then you can provide your EIN to clients instead of your Social Security number. Your clients will still have to fill out a Form 1099, but at least your SSN will remain secure.

Partnership

You can form a partnership with someone who will take an active role in the business, or with someone who provides some or all of the funding but will not participate in day-to-day operations. See the following section, "Going Solo or Playing a Duet" for some partnership issues you'll want to consider, beyond the purely legal aspects.

Partnerships are easy to set up, although you should expect to spend a good deal of time working through the partnership agreement. As with a sole proprietorship, the income of the business is reported on the partners' individual tax returns, simplifying the accounting and bookkeeping burden. A couple of the downsides of partnerships are that you and your partner are personally liable for the debts of the company, and you are each liable for the actions of the other. And if one of you wants to leave the partnership, the business itself has to be re-formed.

In the U.K. and Canada, partnerships are structured similarly; you are jointly liable for all debts of the company and you report your income individually.

Limited Liability Company

LLCs are fairly new entities, designed to provide both the tax benefits of incorporation and the flexibility of a sole proprietorship or partnership. A limited liability company exists for a specified amount of time, although the partners can extend the time limit as desired. LLCs offer limited protection from personal liability, which makes it an attractive alternative to a partnership. However, like corporations, LLCs have some additional filing requirements and less operational flexibility than sole proprietorships or partnerships.

Beginning in 2001, the U.K. introduced the option of limited liability partnerships, similar to LLCs. The LLP is a separate legal entity and the members of the partnership are somewhat protected from individual liability. As an LLP, you have more flexibility in terms of how you structure and run your business than you would as a private limited company.

Corporation

Several types of corporations can be formed, but the one most relevant to independent info pros is the "Subchapter S" corporation. Corporations have the advantage of existing separate from their owner or partners. This means that the assets of the owner—that's you—are at least somewhat protected from the debts of the corporation. That doesn't mean you can spend like there's no tomorrow and escape the consequences, but it does help shield you if, heaven forbid, your company goes into bankruptcy. If you plan on doing the kind of research that involves higher risk—trademark searching or litigation support, for example—you may want to incorporate for an extra layer of liability protection, in addition to carrying errors-and-omissions (E&O) insurance. E&O policies cover claims by clients who might sue you because you either failed to find crucial information or you provided incorrect information. See Chapter 15, Ethics and Legalities, for a discussion of how to avoid such lawsuits.

Unlike a sole proprietorship or partnership, a corporation can be transferred to a partner or sold outright, which can be an important consideration if you think you might some day sell your business. There are also some tax benefits to incorporating, and if your revenue is high enough, you reduce the risk of an audit if you are

My Newly Incorporated Life

I was a sole proprietor for the first 10 years of my business, on the advice of my accountant and my lawyer. It kept my life simple. I could manage both my personal and business finances through QuickBooks. Preparing my own tax returns was relatively simple, but then, I do have a mathematical mind.

However, after 10 years, I decided to revisit the question of the form my business should take. I consulted with a CPA and, on his advice, finally incorporated at the end of 2001. The process itself was pretty straightforward, and doing it at the end of the year made the transition fairly simple. Once a month, I e-mail him my QuickBooks file, from which he generates income and expense statements and tells me how much salary to pay myself and how much to pay the government. At the end of the year, he handles my income tax filing.

The advantages for me at this point include:

- I can put more money into a tax-free retirement fund.
- I have reduced my personal liability.
- I have reduced my chances of being audited by the IRS (knock wood).
- I can write off some expenses that I couldn't as a sole proprietor.

The downsides of incorporating include:

- I can't do all of my tax filings myself (I know ... most people wouldn't see this as a disadvantage).
- I have to be extra careful about not mingling my business and personal accounts.
- I have to pay an accountant, whereas as a sole proprietor I could do most of the accounting myself.

The bottom line is that I am glad I incorporated when I did. I recommend that you have a heart-to-heart talk with your accountant before you start your business and then every few years thereafter. Your financial situation will change, your life situation may change and, heaven knows, the tax laws will change, so it makes sense to get a reality check periodically.

operating as a corporation rather than a sole proprietorship. If you plan on hiring employees, you may want to be incorporated for liability and tax reasons.

The disadvantages of incorporating include the following:

- You are required to file certain forms and to comply with laws that don't apply to sole proprietorships and partnerships.
- You will probably have more paperwork to fill out, since you are more highly regulated by federal, state, and local governments.
- You have less flexibility in terms of how you account for your money; you can't simply run your business and your personal life through QuickBooks software.

In the U.K., your option is to form a private limited company, which gives you some protection, as an individual, from the liabilities of the company. You file your annual financial return with Companies House. Unlike the U.S., your company must have at least two shareholders, and both a director and a company secretary. Companies House (www.companieshouse.co.uk) has detailed information on the procedures for setting up a company; click the "Guidance Booklets and FAQs" at the Web site.

Canadian corporations operate similarly to U.S. corporations; income is reported separately from that of the shareholders, and owners of corporations are, to an extent, protected from the liabilities of the company.

Going Solo or Playing a Duet

For most aspiring independent info pros, "independent" implies a one-person business. But there's something to be said for finding a partner to share the risks and the rewards. Say you do find someone with whom you would like to commit partnership, if not marriage. Let's think through the ramifications. On the positive side, you have someone with whom you can talk and brainstorm, someone who will share the risks of starting a new business. Perhaps you have complementary skills—you're great with marketing and your partner is an expert researcher. Or maybe you think that, if each of you puts in three days of work a week, you'll wind up with one strong full-time business.

Forming a business with a partner really is like a marriage—in fact, it's like the most difficult parts of a marriage without the romance. You don't get the candlelight dinners, roses, and chocolates, but you do get to fight over money and how to raise the child—that is, the business. A partnership can be a beautiful relationship or a real challenge to maintain. Much depends on how well you and your partner structure the prenuptials.

How will you allocate responsibilities? Will one of you do the marketing and the other one handle most of the actual information service? Do you expect to split the responsibilities down the middle? If so, who does the bookkeeping and accounting? Who does the collections calls to the deadbeat clients? What if you both hate public speaking but you know you have to do it occasionally to generate business?

Odds are good that you'll start by dividing up the paying work. One of you will be better at telephone research. One will be better at writing reports and executive summaries. And eventually you'll figure out who is better at the administrative work—the invoicing, the filing, making the calls to the accountant, and so on. At some point, you'll probably realize that you don't contribute equal amounts of effort, expertise, time, and energy to every aspect of the business. Add to that the near certainty that eventually you will disagree about something important—a large purchase, the strategic direction of the company, or whether to introduce new products or services—and you can see how partnerships run into trouble.

This isn't intended to scare you away from a partnership—in fact, one of the wonderful things about having a business partner is that he or she is there when you're dealing with the invoicing, the collections, the strategic decisions, and the troublesome client. But you do need to think through the possibility that the two of you will have to resolve issues in which you hold opposing opinions. One important issue that you'll have to resolve at the outset—and revisit periodically as your business develops—is how you will split the income. Evenly? What if one of you does far more client development? What if one does far more of the actual research? If either or both of you intend to work part time, how will this affect the distribution of labor, responsibilities, and income? Sit down with a lawyer before you finalize the partnership, and spell out each partner's responsibilities, how the income will be shared, and how you would split up the business if you eventually chose to do so.

A partnership agreement is simpler than incorporation, but it means that if one of you chooses to leave the partnership or dies or is incapacitated, the partnership automatically dissolves. A corporation is a bit more formal and involves more paperwork, but will survive if one partner leaves. Your choice of business structure will depend on your personal style, your strategic plan for your business, your need to protect yourself from liability, and so on. Keep in mind, too, that you can always restructure your business later, as it grows and its direction or focus changes.

Hired Help or Ad Hoc Subcontracting

Very few independent info pros hire employees. On the other hand, a great many do use subcontractors, on either an occasional or regular basis, to handle overflow work or projects that go beyond the info pro's area of expertise, or simply to free up some time to focus on building the business.

I suspect that most independent info pros, if asked, would say that they have intentionally chosen not to have employees, even though that decision usually restricts their income potential somewhat. Both practical and less tangible reasons are cited for choosing not to build a business with employees.

- Employee salaries are fixed expenses, whereas an independent info pro's revenue and work flow can fluctuate wildly from month to month.
- Hiring and training employees can be difficult and time-consuming, particularly for a small business.
- Paying for an employee's learning curve (and inevitable mistakes) can be expensive.
- Many independent info pros enjoy the hands-on aspects of the business—doing the research, visiting a client's site, and so on. With employees, the info pro usually gives up some of the day-to-day work, which can often be done less expensively by a research assistant or paraprofessional employee.
- An independent info pro may not be a good manager of people; in fact, he may have left traditional employment in order to get away from the aggravation or stress of supervising others.

Some info pro businesses are better suited for hiring employees than others. Document delivery companies, which tend to be labor-intensive (see Chapter 33, Library and Other Manual Research), often have employees. Companies that provide on-site workers, such as library staffing firms, have a number of employees (see Chapter 35, Other Services You Can Offer).

Another situation in which you might consider hiring employees is if you don't have a research background and are willing to focus all your energy on marketing. In that case, you can hire or subcontract expert researchers and spend your time bringing in business. The late Sue Rugge, one of the first independent info pros, successfully built two businesses using this model. Doing so requires that you find and manage excellent researchers who enjoy working in a small business, that you dedicate yourself to generating enough work to keep your researchers busy, and that you find clients who are willing to pay the relatively high hourly rates you must charge to cover the costs of your employees plus your profit.

If you decide that hiring employees isn't for you, you can do what most independent info pros do and subcontract with colleagues as the work demands. See Chapter 14, Subcontracting, or I'll Scratch Your Back if You Scratch Mine, for a discussion of how subcontracting works and how to be a successful contractor and subcontractor.

Deciding on the Structure of Your Business

- Want to keep the accounting and paperwork simple?—sole proprietorship
- Expect to have a business partner who either contributes financially or works with you day to day?—partnership or limited liability company (LLC)
- Think you'll ever want to sell your business?—corporation
- Plan to hire employees?—corporation
- Concerned about personal liability?—LLC or corporation

Chapter 7

Before You Launch

In the first six chapters of this section, we've looked at what it's like to be an independent info pro, the upsides and the downsides, the skills you need to succeed, and how you might structure your business. This chapter helps you think through what you want for your business and how you can get there. It looks at the essence of what your business is all about.

If you don't have a background in business, you might want to take a course on how to start a small or home-based business through your local community college or university extension program. Many schools offer continuing education courses just a few weeks in duration that cover the basics of local zoning and licensing regulations, writing a business plan, finding sources for loans, and so on.

Business Plans and Other Pipe Dreams

Anyone starting a business is told that it's critical to write a detailed business plan. If you don't have a business plan, how will you know which way you're going and when you've gotten there? How can you ask a potential lender for heaps of cash if you haven't spelled out what you want to do with the money when you get it? Even if you don't plan on borrowing funds to launch your business, a business plan can be a valuable exercise.

I generally don't recommend taking out a loan to finance your start-up expenses, much less your day-to-day operations; however, this may the only option you have. If you do decide to borrow money, include in your business plan how you plan to pay back the loan and what you will use the money for. Needless to say, borrow only as much as you need and can pay back within a reasonable amount of time. You will certainly need a business plan—complete with financial projections—to apply for money from a bank or credit union, or even from family or friends. (For more information on financing your business, see Chapter 12, Money, Money, Money.)

Even if you aren't planning to borrow money, writing a business plan can be a useful reality check. If you're going to leave that $60,000/year job, with its insurance benefits, retirement fund, and paid vacation, what will it take to generate $60,000 in *profit* (not just revenue) from your new business? You'll use your business plan to set goals for how much income you intend to bring in, how much you expect to pay yourself as a salary, how much overhead you'll have, where and how you'll find clients, and so on. You'll want to write a business plan that is aggressive but realistic—there's no sense aiming low just to make your goal, nor is it wise to plan on earning $100,000 the first year.

Another reason for writing a business plan is that the process of putting your ideas into writing helps you make that vision a reality. It's a tangible commitment—to yourself if no one else—that you take this new business seriously, that you intend to make this enterprise thrive. It also enables you to think through what you need to do and how you intend to accomplish your goals. One of the characteristics of most successful independent info pros is the ability to see not only the big picture but also the details, and to pay attention to all the little things that have to happen in order for the business to succeed.

Of course, at some point down the road as your business grows and matures, you will probably notice that real life has overtaken your well-designed plan and your business has moved into areas that you hadn't foreseen. That's okay—it's an indication that you are able to recognize changes in the marketplace and your client base and adapt to new situations. That original business plan helped you organize your thoughts, plan your actions, anticipate challenges and opportunities, and get started.

There's no single way to go about writing a business plan. In fact, unless you intend to use it to apply for a loan, the only people who will see it are you and your business advisor, typically an accountant and/or a lawyer. Don't sweat the format; focus on thinking through what is involved in getting your business going.

Plenty of Web sites give pointers about writing business plans. The Small Business Administration has a useful tutorial; see the Starting Your Business area of the site, or go directly to www.sba.gov/starting/indexbusplans.html. A number of companies sell software to help write business plans, which you may find useful if you prefer to work from a template. But be careful of invalid assumptions built into the software; an independent information business isn't a typical small business like a coffee shop or hardware store. If you're concerned about presentation—how your business plan looks and how it's worded—check out the American Express corporate site, which offers a nice tutorial. From the main page at www.americanexpress.com, drill down to the Small Business section, or jump straight to home3.americanexpress.com/smallbusiness/tool/biz_plan/index.asp.

Your local library or bookstore will have plenty of books specifically on writing business plans that you can choose from.

Business Plan Checklist

Your business plan may be polished and formal, or a simple write-up of how you envision your company and its first year. In either case, you should answer—or at least think carefully about—each of the following questions:

- Why am I starting this business?
- What service am I providing to clients?
- Who are my potential clients?
- How will I attract clients?
- How many repeat clients do I expect by the end of my first year?
- Who are my competitors?
- How will I price my services?
- What are my start-up capital purchases?
- What will my overhead be for the first year?
- What is my expected revenue the first year? And after that?
- What are my personal strengths and weaknesses as a business owner?
- What are my strengths and weaknesses in this market?

Your Marketing Plan—Getting Clients to Beat a Path to Your Door

It may be true that, if you build a better mousetrap, customers will beat that path to your door. With an information business, though, it usually takes a little more work to get the attention of prospective clients. Section Three goes into detail about how to market through a variety of media. Use the ideas in that section when you write a marketing plan to attract those clients.

Like a business plan, a marketing plan doesn't have to be a formal document with headings, subheadings, footnotes, and appendices. However, it does have to provide you with a framework within which to think about how you'll find your clients. Here are some tips on what to include or consider as you write your own marketing plan:

- Describe your information service. What will you provide and why would clients pay you for it? How will it be priced? Will it be seen as a low-end service, or high-end/high-value? Which of those do you want to provide, and why? Which will be more competition-proof?

- Identify your client base. Know whom you'll be addressing. If you don't already understand their information needs, include in your marketing plan a strategy for finding out—through informational interviews or other research.

- Spell out how you will get repeat business and referral business from your clients. Are they— and possibly their colleagues—likely to need your services on a regular basis? Do your services lend themselves to return business and add-on work?

- Make your marketing plan measurable. Set quantifiable goals for the number of clients you want to have by the end of a year, how many prospects you expect to have, how much you plan to spend on marketing, and so on. Make your goals aggressively realistic—aim for as high as you think is feasible.

- Include some marketing efforts that offer short-term results and some that have a longer-term payback. You want some revenue right away, but you also want to start working on those marketing strategies that will take months to come to fruition.

- Commit to setting specific goals for every week and completing those goals before the weekend rolls around. If you have a mentor or business coach, tell her each Monday what your marketing goals are for the week. If you don't have a mentor, start a business journal and write down your goals every week. (Note that the Association of Independent Information Professionals [www.aiip.org] has a free volunteer mentoring program for new members.)

Although a marketing plan may be less structured than a business plan, it is, if anything, *more* important to the success of your business. Many people find it difficult to sit down and think through their marketing strategy, but there is no better time to plan how you'll get clients than before you've started your business.

Although lots of books and Web sites focus on writing a business plan, fewer relevant sources exist to help you develop a marketing plan for an independent info pro business. You probably won't be relying on your storefront displays, advertising, or a trained sales force to generate business, so most of the generic resources aren't particularly helpful. Instead, write a marketing plan that feels right for you, and consider it a work in progress. You will modify it as you learn what works and what doesn't work for your particular business and client base.

Who Are Your Clients?

Both your business plan and your marketing plan presuppose that you have some idea of whom your clients will be. As I discuss in Chapter 11, Managing Your Clients, assume that you will be marketing far beyond your local area, unless you expect to offer a specialized on-site service that cannot be provided remotely. If you're like most independent info pros, you will probably start out with a prospective client base of former employers and colleagues who know your work, other contacts in the industry you've come from, and people in industries or professions that are information-hungry and not overly price-sensitive.

Of course, the industry or niche you're most familiar with may not be adequate to support your business long-term. Suzanne Sabroski, owner of Sabroski & Associates, used to work as a corporate librarian for a company in the synthetic lubricants market. She knew that this was too limited a niche, so when she started her business she focused on the much broader base of clients who needed business research in general.

When I started my business, I thought I'd get lots of business from local firms, from writers who needed background research, and from law firms that didn't have a library staff of their own. I found that I was wrong on all counts. As it turns out, all of these groups are very price-sensitive—they consider $200 a large expenditure for something as intangible as information, and they generally want to do their own research rather than pay someone else to do it for them. The lesson I learned was to look for clients with an established research budget or that can pass my charges on directly to *their* clients. So I refocused my marketing toward companies with revenue of at least $50 million that needed business research, and to consulting firms and advertising agencies that would bill their clients for the cost of my research.

What if you don't know a lot of prospective clients? Perhaps your last job didn't give you much contact with colleagues. Maybe you worked in an industry that does not do much research or rely on outside expertise. In that case, follow the money and follow your heart. No, those two aren't mutually exclusive. Think about what kind of work you enjoy doing and at which you're fairly proficient. I'm not talking about the Web surfing you do for friends or neighbors—unless they're willing to pay you your regular rate for research, that experience counts as fun, not an indicator of the market. Instead, think about who would want to pay you for your expertise or familiarity with an area and what you would really enjoy doing all day long.

Are you proficient in Spanish? Perhaps you could focus on working with Latin American companies that are exploring international business opportunities. If you live in Los Angeles and find the entertainment industry fascinating, look into providing background research services to film writers and television companies. If you worked for the marketing department of an oil company, maybe you can use the contacts you have and focus on providing services to the petroleum or energy industry. If you know the pharmaceutical industry, figure out what companies and organizations need your services and which people within those organizations need information and don't have the time to get it themselves. If your background is in political science, identify think tanks and consulting companies that need your expertise on an ad hoc basis. That's your client base. As Amelia Kassel of MarketingBase says, "Find an information need and think of how you can fill it."

Before I started my business, I worked for a number of years as the librarian at a telecommunications company. Once I got Bates Information Services going, I focused on people in the communications industry—large corporate marketing and strategic planning departments, industry consultants, and fellow telecom librarians. I emphasized my expertise in the telecommunications industry, and that gave me instant credibility. As it turned out, the focus of my business broadened within a year or two to other forms of business research. What's important is that my clients drove that shift. People who had come to me originally for telecom research started asking for more general research, and then referred me to colleagues and friends who needed non-telecom research, too. But the reason my clients called me in the first place was that I'd made myself known for a specialty. If I had started by telling prospects that I could find any information they needed on any topic at all, they would have been less likely to remember to call me. There's no "hook" there—why should potential clients think of *me* whenever they're looking for information? But once they've associated me with industry-specific research, they think of me for other and more general information needs as well.

I was fortunate, in that I had already developed a network of contacts within my chosen field. All I had to do was start sending out brochures, newsletters, and postcards to my colleagues and former co-workers; they knew who I was and I knew the kind of information they needed. If you don't already have a pile of business cards from people you can market to, it's time to do some research. Select a few likely companies within your target industry, and check their Web sites for an organization chart, annual report, or a page that profiles their executives. Look for information-hungry people, such as the directors of marketing, strategic planning, corporate development, competitive intelligence, and product development. Once you've identified a few key executives in each company, call the main number and confirm the names, titles, phone numbers, and address of your contacts. No, you're not going to send them marketing material—you're going to conduct "informational interviews" to find out how people find information, what frustrates them about doing their own research, what they'd pay for, and what their biggest challenge is, informationally speaking. Write a letter (yes, hard copy, not e-mail) and ask for a 15-minute interview at their convenience. Reiterate that this is not a sales call, but that you are contacting them to learn how [marketing ... competitive intelligence ... you fill in the blank] professionals find and use information. What you learn from these interviews will help you identify the most likely prospects and understand what kinds of research services you can provide to them. Remember Amelia Kassel's advice about finding an information need and then figuring out how to fill it? These information interviews should help you do just that.

What About My Steady Paycheck?

One of the first considerations when starting an independent info pro business is whether to quit your regular job. There are two schools of thought about this—some independent info pros say that the only way you can survive financially the first year is to run your new business on the side, and others say that the only way to get traction is to focus totally on your business. Eventually, most successful independent info pros wind up working full time (and then some!). The question is whether you start out full time or not. Here are some of the advantages and disadvantages of each choice.

Moonlighting Employee

This approach, working full time and running your business only on weekends and evenings, has very little chance of success. Almost by definition, most of your energy and time will be focused on your regular job, even if it's a job you don't enjoy. In fact, it probably takes even more of your energy if it's a job you're not happy in. You cannot ethically take business calls during the workday, so your clients will find it difficult to talk with you directly. Your employer deserves your full attention while you're on the clock, and returning client calls during your lunch break is simply not feasible.

So this leaves you trying to stay in touch with clients via e-mail, and with the limitation that you cannot reply promptly to any e-mail or voice-mail queries. (And see Chapter 25, The Reference Interview, on the inadvisability of accepting projects based on e-mail or voice mail alone, without a live, back-and-forth conversation.) Most clients will be put off by your lack of availability; they are accustomed to dealing with vendors who are accessible during normal business hours and who can respond to their information needs promptly. Working full time pretty much precludes all this.

Full-Time Entrepreneur

This is certainly the scariest option. You go from a steady income and employee benefits like health insurance and paid vacations to zero—or rather, to put it in a more positive light, a full focus on your new business. This option works best if:

- Someone else in your household is bringing in a steady income.
- You have set aside enough money to live on for six to nine months.
- You already have at least one regular client, such as your last employer.

On the positive side, going full time means that word-of-mouth referrals get started that much faster. Also, you can devote more time to marketing, which takes time to show results. The more time you can spend on marketing at the beginning of your business, the sooner those clients will start calling you.

Speaking of calling, one of the under-appreciated competitive advantages of devoting full time to your business is that clients can reach you during normal business hours. Think of how much more likely you are to do business with someone you can speak with when you call, rather than having to resort to voice-mail messages and telephone tag.

As a full-time entrepreneur, you have the ability to take on short turnaround projects and large projects that need to be done quickly. Unlike someone who must somehow squeeze in the time during nonwork hours, you have eight (or more) hours a day that you can throw at a project. Also, some kinds of information work, such as telephone research and going to government offices to research public records, have to be done during normal working hours. You limit your service options if you can't work full time during regular business hours. You also have the flexibility to attend conferences and speak at meetings your prospective clients are likely to attend.

One advantage of taking the plunge and working full time for yourself is less tangible but just as important as the others I've mentioned. By devoting yourself full time to your business, you demonstrate both to yourself and to your clients that you really take it seriously. You're committed to making it work and to providing high-quality professional information services to your clients. Granted, part-timers can be just as committed, but it's substantially harder to maintain that level of enthusiasm, creativity, and persistence if you're juggling your new business and an existing job.

As for the downsides of going full time, the most obvious one is financial. Unless you already have clients lined up, don't expect to be able to pay yourself any salary for at least a few months. The first year will be lean; there's no getting around that. Before I quit my job and started my (full-time) information business, I spent a year focused on lowering my living expenses. I got into the habit of not eating out as frequently, not practicing "shopping therapy," and generally learning that a lot of discretionary spending really is unnecessary. This made my first year in business easier to handle, as I could get by with substantially less income than I'd been earning in my last job. I also figured out ahead of time how much money I needed per month just to pay the bills, and banked six months' worth of living expenses, which I drew upon when I didn't have many clients yet still had to pay my overhead expenses.

Part-Time Entrepreneur

Actually, there are two kinds of part-time business owners—people who have another part-time job and people who choose to work only part time. Some people have childcare or eldercare obligations or health limitations that prevent them from working full time. It's possible to start and run an information business part time, but it takes discipline and flexibility. If you're juggling care for others with running your business, consider hiring someone to help with your home responsibilities during the day. You'll still be available for emergencies, but you'll be freed up to make phone calls, focus on research, and plan your marketing strategies. Taking a client's call while the kids are trying to put doll clothes on the cat is doomed to failure. Although clients are much more understanding about people who work part time and from home than they were five or ten years ago, they still want to deal with someone who is professional and focused.

I've talked about the downside of continuing to work full time while starting your business. As you can tell, I don't recommend it. But what about working at a salaried job part time and running your business part time? It's do-able but difficult. The steady income and benefits are a nice safety net while you're growing your business. However, it's easy to fall into the trap of seeing your part-time job as your *real* job. Will you think of your employment as supplementing your independent info pro business, or vice versa? The first few years of a new business require a lot of attention and energy without a lot of pay-back. Being able to devote only part of your working day to your baby means drawing out its Terrible Twos that much longer. It may be necessary, but it can be tiring and difficult.

One option is to find a part-time job with evening and weekend hours. That leaves you free during the day to speak with clients, conduct telephone research, and get out to meet clients and colleagues. Of course, this choice takes a toll, since most of us are accustomed to viewing our evenings and weekends as the time to relax, run errands, and get on with the rest of our lives. On the other hand, it does offer the advantage of freeing you up all day for your clients. In essence, you offer them full-time availability while providing yourself with a part-time salary on the side.

Alex Kramer, owner of Kramer Research, started her business while working an off-hours job. I asked her how she managed to stay focused while working part time, and she said: "If people think of their start-up company as a serious business and not just something they can do on the side, then I can see how they might make it work. That is to say, they will need regular office hours, work space dedicated for this business, and perhaps a telephone message or Web site that states their office hours. I don't think it can really happen if someone tries to do this on the sly while working full time, or if they think that business will come to them as if by magic. Constant marketing is essential, especially when you're just starting your business."

Just Do It!

While it's important to think through the ramifications of your choices regarding employment and income, eventually you will probably have to take the leap and become a full-time independent info pro. It involves planning, and it's a risk—but starting any business is a risk. In fact, when you think about it, you have more job stability as an independent than you do as an employee. Your employer is your sole source of income; if you lose your job, your income goes from substantial to zero. If, on the other hand, you're in business for yourself and have a number of clients, the loss of any one client only reduces your income slightly. As long as you continue to market yourself, you will always have other sources of revenue.

It's easy to let all the preliminary tasks—writing a business plan, setting up your office, talking with a lawyer or accountant, identifying your client base, determining your niche—impede you from actually starting your business. I like to compare all this preliminary work to taking up a new sport. For the first few weeks, you're going to be stiff and sore; it seems like all pain and no gain. But once you get your muscles toned up, you start seeing dramatic results. Likewise, all these administrative and strategic planning tasks are hard at first—they're new jobs, they're unfamiliar, and they require you to sit down and really think about what you want. But once you've gone through the process, it's a lot easier to continue. You'll always have administrative and high-level management responsibilities; now is the time to learn how to handle them and to start feeling comfortable in your new roles.

A wise friend once told me that starting a business feels like standing on the edge of a cliff. Then you suddenly realize that what appeared to be empty space is actually a path up, or that you have the equipment to rappel your way down, or that you can fly.

Checklist for Launching Your Business

- ✦ Write a business plan, even if you don't intend to use it to raise capital.
- ✦ Write a marketing plan and promise yourself that you will set and meet weekly marketing goals.
- ✦ Identify your market niche and your client base.
- ✦ Plan ahead of time for a drop in income the first year.
- ✦ Decide whether you can run your business full time or not.
- ✦ Take that leap of faith and launch!

Chapter 8

Setting Up Your Business

I remember when I moved away from home and into my first apartment. What stunned me (besides the price of rent) was how many little things I needed, and how much the cost added up. Bookcases, a desk, stocking the kitchen cabinet, silverware, cleaning supplies, a vacuum cleaner ... I felt like I needed another student loan just to cover the expense of moving into my own apartment!

When you get ready to set up your office, you may suffer similar sticker shock. In addition to the usual office accoutrements such as pens, paper, desk, chair, phone, and so on, you'll need to get a business checking account, stationery, business cards, possibly a business license, and so on. This chapter will cover all the practicalities you have to deal with *before* you open your door for business. What about paying for all this? See Chapter 12, Money, Money, Money, for some ideas. And, if you're serious about starting your own business, set up a separate savings account *now* and start putting money aside. Think of it as an investment in your future success.

Who Am I?

For starters, you'll need to figure out how to answer the phone when it rings (and yes, it *will* start ringing). What will you call your business? You have several basic options: You can use your own name (Jane Smith and Associates); you can incorporate your name into your business name (Smith Information Services); you can have a name that describes what you do (Healthcare Research, Inc.); or you can make up a name (InfoSource Solutions). Although it is important to feel comfortable with whatever name you give your company, most info pros find that their clients know them by their personal name rather than their business name. Don't count on the company name itself to generate much business just because it's memorable or clever; as I've said before, most of your business will come from referrals, and a happy client will make just as strong an endorsement whether your company name is Smith Information Services or InfoSource Solutions. Each type of company name has its benefits and drawbacks.

Jane Smith and Associates

Advantages: You are your own brand; you can be reasonably sure that your business name will be unique.

Disadvantages: It is difficult to sell your business when it is so closely identified with you. Clients may not know how to "file" you—under J for Jane, under S for Smith? An "and Associates" name often signifies a one-person business—Reva Basch once commented, "when I see 'and Associates', I think 'and cat'"—which may make you less attractive to some clients.

Smith Information Services

Advantages: You can be reasonably sure that your business name will be unique. It may sound somewhat more established than Smith & Associates. Your clients can find your listing in a directory if they remember your last name.

Disadvantages: It is difficult to sell your business because your name is part of the business name.

Healthcare Research Inc.

Advantages: Your name makes clear what you do. Prospective clients know when it's appropriate to call you. You can sell your business without having to change the name.

Disadvantages: You limit your ability to provide a wide range of services because your specialization is part of your business name.

InfoSource Solutions

Advantages: You can design a unique business name. It can be generic enough to allow you to expand the business. You can sell your business without having to change the name.

Disadvantages: Clients may not easily remember your business name. The name may sound dated after a few years.

Note that even if you are a sole proprietor (see the section later in this chapter on the form of your business, and the more extensive discussion in Chapter 6), you should not simply operate under your own name. Some accounts payable departments are reluctant to pay an invoice for Jane Doe, preferring to issue payment to a business entity.

Regardless of which type of business name you choose, make sure it's not already being used by someone else. Here are some simple steps to check for any established businesses with the same name you've selected.

- Search for the name using several Web search engines. Try variations of the name; if you've selected the name InfoSource Solutions, try "Info Source Solutions" and "InfoSourceSolutions" as well.

- Look the name up in an Internet domain registry, such as www.netsol.com.

- Look up the name in the membership directory of the Association of Independent Information Professionals (www.aiip.org) and of any associations your clients belong to.

- Look up the name in the trademark section of the U.S. Patent and Trademark Office (www.uspto.gov), or the equivalent agency in your country. Note that an identical name in an entirely different line of business may not necessarily be a conflict, at least in the U.S., as long as there is no possibility of confusing your business with the existing one.

- Check the telephone directory and Yellow Pages for your local area. You can also use one of the many Web-based "yellow pages" services that let you search for business listings by city and state. See, for example, www.yellowpages.com, which includes both U.S. listings and links to Yellow Pages sites around the world.

- Search the published literature—general and business news plus trade journals and magazines—for mentions of the company name, using one of the professional online services described in Chapter 29, Professional Online Services.

You may also want to consult a lawyer to determine whether you should take additional steps to ensure that you are not infringing on any trademarked names, and to establish your right to the name you choose.

Are You My Employer?

U.S. info pros, particularly those who work extensively for one client, have to be careful of running afoul of Internal Revenue Service rules. In response to the practice of hiring "perma-temps"—contract workers who are, for all intents and purposes, employees, but who are classified as temporary workers or contractors by their employer—the IRS has established a set of criteria for determining whether you are truly an independent business or essentially an employee. Of course, the best way to avoid any appearance of being an employee is to ensure that you have a number of clients and that no one client accounts for more than, say, a quarter of your income. The distinction between employee and independent contractor is important for both you and your client. The IRS has a publication available on its Web site (www.irs.gov) that spells out the criteria for being considered an employee. It's Publication 15-A, Employer's Supplemental Tax Guide. Look through it and make sure that you don't meet the criteria for employee status.

What Am I?

When you set up your business, you will need to decide what *form* of business you will be. For those of us in the U.S., the main choices include sole proprietorship, partnership, limited liability company, and Subchapter S corporation. Each form has its benefits and drawbacks. (See Chapter 6, Structuring Your Business, for more discussion of various business forms.) Many independent info pros begin as sole proprietors, which is the simplest form of business.

Forming a limited liability company or Subchapter S corporation makes sense if you plan to hire employees, bring your spouse into the business, or eventually sell the business. I was a sole proprietor for 10 years, as I explain in Chapter 6, and finally decided, for a couple of reasons, to incorporate in 2001. First, as my income rose, I became a more attractive audit target for the IRS as a sole proprietor. Related to my income status, it's more important for me to take advantage of deductions now, and I have more options as a corporation than I did as a sole proprietor. And, as I get closer to retirement age, I want to be able to put as much money into tax-sheltered retirement plans as I can, and corporations have more options than individuals. Given the important legal ramifications of this decision, you should consult with an accountant or lawyer to decide which business form is best for your current situation. Switching from one form to another is usually not very burdensome.

Where Am I?

Most independent info pros work from their home, or at least start their businesses at home before moving to an outside office. The decision on where to set up shop will depend on a number of factors:

- Whether you have space at home in which to set up a permanent office
- Whether you are willing to commit to the monthly overhead expense of office rental
- Whether you find working in your home too distracting
- Whether other personal considerations dictate your immediate availability

For most people starting a new business, just the thought of having to pay rent every month, regardless of how much money is (or isn't) coming in, is daunting. On the other hand, someone who lives in an efficiency apartment may cringe at the thought of turning essentially her entire home into an office. Who wants to live at work? Look at your own housing situation and think about how realistically you can carve out office space separate from your living space.

You'll need room for a good-sized desk on which to put not only your PC, keyboard, and mouse pad but all the other items you reach for during the day. For me, that includes a phone, a coffee cup, pens, a note pad, the notes for whatever projects I'm currently working on, my pending project files, my Rolodex, and my Franklin Planner. As you can tell, regardless of the high-tech hype, I'm not even close to achieving a paperless office. And you'll need at least one desk drawer—where else will you put your stamps, paper clips, scissors, rubber bands, and so on?

In addition to a generously proportioned desk, you'll need space for your printer; fax machine; a filing cabinet; a bookshelf for reference books, manuals and documentation, phone directories and the like; and a place to store office supplies (your brochures and marketing materials, printer paper, file folders, stationery and envelopes, note pads, sticky notes, and on and on). A comfortable reading chair is also nice, for those times when you want to catch up with professional reading or just take a break. While some people assume that it's not an office without a copier, I've never seen the need for an in-house photocopy machine. If I have to copy a few pages for my files, I just run them through my fax machine, which has a copy feature. If I'm copying more than four or five pages, I take them to the local copy shop. Given the high cost and maintenance expenses of a copier, I would only recommend that you purchase (or lease) one if you plan to do high volume copying.

Another factor in deciding whether to start out with a home or outside office is how often you expect to meet clients face to face. See Chapter 11, Managing Your Clients, for some thoughts on this issue. You can usually meet at your client's office or at a restaurant over lunch or coffee. You can even sign up with one of the "office space" businesses that exist in many cities. They provide you with a mail drop, a receptionist, and the ability to book a meeting room or office as needed. On the other hand, if you expect to have people working for you, an outside office may be preferable—for both you and your family—to sharing your house with nonfamily members.

Some independent info pros who work from home are reluctant to use their street address on their business card. One option is to use a post office box as the business address. Although this solution does protect your privacy, it has a few disadvantages. The most obvious is that carriers such as UPS and FedEx can't deliver to post office boxes, so you'll still have to give your home address to vendors and clients who need a street address. Another downside of P.O. boxes is that, at least in some clients' eyes, one- or two-person businesses look suspect if they don't have a street address. If you live near a Mail Boxes Etc. or other storefront business center, you can rent a mailbox and get some of the benefits of a regular office. You'll have a street address, they'll accept packages for you, and you can call to find out if there is any mail in your box before making the trip to the office.

If you do decide to set up your office at home, think hard about where you want to spend the majority of your day. The guest bedroom is a good option, although if you have frequent houseguests, it can get tense when you need to evict them at the start of your business day. Your own bedroom can work, as long as you don't mind sleeping in your office. Some people do elect to establish their office in a corner of the living room, dining room, or kitchen but this can be very difficult. You force your family to co-exist with your office, and you are never able to shut the door on your work—either to leave it at the end of the day or to close yourself *in* to get work done. The basement can be a good solution, as long as you're comfortable with all-artificial lighting and working next to the washing machine. I know of one independent info pro who took her two-car garage and split it in half, turning one car's worth into a nice office. Think creatively about whatever extra space you might have, and how you might turn that area into an office. If you were considering remodeling or making substantial improvements to your house anyway, consider the feasibility of adding a simple office to your plans.

Wherever you decide to put your office, take note of the natural lighting, ambient noise, ability to moderate the heating and cooling, the number of electrical outlets, and whether you'll need to upgrade your wiring to handle all the appliances you'll be running. Think, too, about how easy it will be to run phone lines and a cable modem or DSL line to the office. You'll live with these features (or lack of same) every day, and most of them are difficult, disruptive, and expensive to change once you've settled in.

Office Equipment Checklist

Here's your shopping list for setting up your office. Make sure your checkbook has a healthy balance; this is one area where you don't want to scrimp. You are investing in *you* here. You'll be spending a lot of time living with your choices.

- Desk—make sure it's at a comfortable height, has plenty of space for all the equipment and supplies you'll store on and in it, and convenient drawers for the items you'll need to get at all day long.

- Chair—shop carefully for this, because you'll be spending a lot of time in it. Make sure that, when it's at a comfortable working level relative to your desk, your feet rest on the floor, your armrests are at the right height and angle, your back is supported, and you can shift positions. Consider a "kneeling" chair; some people find them uncomfortable or awkward, but I've had mine for years and love it.

- PC—if you're shopping for a new system, get as much disk space, RAM, speed, and processing power as you can afford; make sure it includes a

3.5" disk drive (yes, the medium is becoming obsolescent, but you'll probably need to deal with it for a while longer), a CD-ROM drive, and either a Zip drive or read-writeable CD capability, for mass storage and backup. You'll probably also want a high-speed modem. (See the section "Staying in Touch" later in this chapter for more discussion of modems and connectivity.) Invest in the latest version of your choice of word processing, presentation, and spreadsheet software, assuming it's not preinstalled on your computer when you buy it. If you already have a PC that you can devote full time to the business, make sure it meets the performance and functionality requirements I've outlined here, and that its speed, memory, storage, and other limitations won't handicap your productivity.

- Printer—unless you already own one, think twice about buying a color printer for your business, as the maintenance and ink costs are higher than black and white, and you can always print the occasional color piece at a local copy shop. Look for speed, reliability, and reasonably priced toner cartridges. I recommend a laser printer over an inkjet printer, because of the higher quality output. And see the "Shopping Perils, Pitfalls, and Precautions" sidebar for a discussion of multifunction machines that combine the features of a printer, fax, and scanner.

- Telephone—I prefer corded to wireless for security reasons; get one with a mute button and at least two lines (more about your phone lines later in this chapter). Consider buying a hands-free headset as well, if you expect to be on the phone for long periods of time.

- Fax machine—a separate fax machine is simpler than using fax software on your PC, and enables you to send outgoing faxes from hard copy. Be sure to look at the cost for the ink or toner as well as the purchase price. A separate machine also means you don't have to leave the PC on to receive faxes, and you can tell at a glance when one has come in.

- File cabinet—for tax and security reasons, you will need to keep paper copies of your invoices, receipts, project notes, correspondence, and other business documents. Buy a sturdy cabinet with at least two drawers. Lateral file cabinets take up less space than the traditional pull-out kind. I have found that hanging file folders (see, for example, the Pendaflex folders at www.pendaflex.com) last longer and are easier to use than cramming manila folders into a drawer.

- Lights—depending on your set-up, you may need a good desk lamp as well as a floor lamp and ceiling lighting. I find compact fluorescent lights easy on my eyes; try several kinds of bulbs until you find what works for you. Some people swear by "daylight" or "full spectrum" bulbs.

- Bookshelves—at least two 4-foot shelves, sturdy enough to hold telephone books and directories.

- Shelving (or a closet or drawers) for supplies—your extra boxes of stationery, envelopes, invoice forms, brochures, printer paper, diskettes, light bulbs, file folders, paper clips, and so on.

- Fire extinguisher—if you're lucky, you'll never need it. Don't tempt fate; keep one in your office and know how to use it.

If your budget is tight, visit second-hand stores for a large desk, bookshelf, lamps, and filing cabinets. You might also check your local "penny saver" newspaper or community bulletin board to see if anyone is selling grandpa's desk at a bargain. But be sure to buy the sturdiest and best quality you can. You don't want to have to lug that flimsy file cabinet out the back door and down the stairs when it breaks.

How will you pay for all this equipment? The simplest solution is to start setting money aside now, so that you can purchase what you need without going into debt. Some entrepreneurs lend their business the money, and pay back the loan—with interest—gradually. Look into the possibility of grants for new businesses, particularly those owned by women or minorities, if you fall into one of those categories. If you feel that you have to borrow money for start-up costs, look into low-interest loans through the U.S. Small Business Administration (see the Financing Your Business section at www.sba.gov/financing) or an equivalent government organization. The one option to *avoid* is putting all these expenses on a credit card and then paying off the balance gradually. Your first year will be tight enough without having to pay 18 percent interest every month on a substantial balance.

Shopping Perils, Pitfalls, and Precautions

Even though I live within a mile of several office supply stores, I order all my supplies on the Web. Why? Because once I step inside an Office Depot or Staples, my willpower disappears. Oh, look! Sticky notes in bright new colors! A nifty new filing system! Software guaranteed to make me more organized! You get the idea. If you do enjoy doing your shopping offline and in person, bring a shopping list and stick to it—yes, just like grocery shopping.

Likewise, when you are shopping for office equipment, think hard about what you truly need. Do you really need a scanner, or does it just seem like a cool piece of equipment? Can you justify the ongoing expense of a color printer (those cartridges add up)? Would you really use that photocopier enough to justify the cost? Consider doing without and using a nearby copy shop or office supply store for the occasional scanning or color print job. If eventually you do find that you honestly do need the equipment and that it is more cost-effective to buy, then you'll be in a better position to purchase something that fits your needs.

Think twice about buying multifunction devices. A printer/fax/scanner saves space on your desk, but when it needs to be repaired, you're suddenly without your printer, your fax machine, and your scanner. On the other hand, a high-quality unit from a reliable vendor can be a good choice. The cost of a good printer-scanner-fax machine is less than what you'd pay for three separate machines.

Think about the total lifespan cost of any piece of equipment. Look at the cost of ink cartridges and see how many pages the manufacturer claims each cartridge will print.

Alex Kramer, owner of Kramer Research Services, recommends using a computer consultant when purchasing any computer-related hardware. "I find that having someone shop for me who knows my needs and knows the places to get a good price costs the same as me buying the equipment myself. But this way, I get a setup that's just right for me, and I don't have to spend any of my time running around looking for the best deal."

Other Office Expenditures

Before you set up your office, call a couple of the office supply super-stores and ask them to send you their catalogs. Then start paging through them and make a list of all the little things you need to set up your office. You'll be amazed at how fast it adds up:

- Extra toner cartridges for your printer and fax machine
- Box of plain bond printer paper
- Box of pens
- 10" x 12" mailing envelopes and padded envelopes
- Presentation folders for your marketing material
- Stapler
- Trash can
- Stacking trays for documents
- Sticky notes
- Postal meter or scale
- Stamps
- Paper clips, staples, binder clips, tape

If you're working in an office now, take a look around and make a list of *everything* that you use within a month. You'll either need to buy everything on that list, make separate trips whenever you realize you're without some critical item, or learn to do without.

Your Public Face

Early in your business, if not at the moment you open your door, you will need stationery and business cards. See Chapter 19, Your Business Image, for a discussion of designing your company letterhead and logo. This may be one of the biggest investments you make in your business, and one that sends a powerful message to your clients and prospects. Unless you have a strong artistic bent, this should not be a do-it-yourself project.

There is an alternative, though I think it's a second-best option, if you can't wait for the graphic designer to finish your logo. Paper Direct, for example, sells predesigned color letterhead paper and envelopes, business card stock, and brochures (www.paperdirect.com). You feed this preformatted stationery into your printer and add your company name and contact information to give it a customized feel. You can also purchase designer paper from some office supply chains such as Office Depot and Viking Office Products.

The advantages of this approach are a low initial investment, no more than the cost of a box or two of predesigned paper stock; your order can be delivered within a day or two, so you can start sending out marketing material with minimal delay; and the coordinated designs available give a consistent "look" to your stationery, business cards, envelopes, mailing labels, brochures, and postcards.

The disadvantages of using predesigned paper include selecting the same design as someone else in your industry, thus diluting the distinctiveness and impact of your material; the relatively high cost compared to ordering your own stationery from a printer; and the chance that your supplier will decide to discontinue your design in the future. Although most of the paper is relatively heavyweight, the business card stock is light when compared to regular business cards, and the microperforations along the edges are a give-away—the sign of a do-it-yourself print job. That can give a prospective client the impression that you are just starting out and are unwilling to invest in professionally printed cards.

If you decide on a very simple one-color letterhead with no graphics, a local print shop can help you design a professional-looking suite of stationery, envelopes, and business cards. The only option I would recommend you avoid is the complete do-it-yourself approach of using your word processor, an assortment of clip-art, and a color printer to design your own corporate logo. You might be able to get away with a self-designed logo if you have a graphics art background or an exceptionally good eye. To me, though, do-it-yourself marketing materials scream "I'm new, I'm cheap,

I may not be in business tomorrow!" Clients may wonder whether it's worth investing in you if you aren't willing to invest in your own business.

Just one more item: Depending on your accounting software, you'll either need to order preprinted invoices or use the software to design an invoice form that you can print on your letterhead.

Tackling That To-Do List

It's tempting to put off some of the to-do items in this chapter until you've quit your day job and launched your business. Don't do it. You want your first day of business to be focused on marketing—on getting paying clients—rather than on administrative details. Because nature abhors a vacuum, it's easy to let this to-do list of, let's face it, mostly relatively trivial items, take all your time during your first few weeks of business. Instead, plan on getting everything in this chapter completed before you open your doors for business. That way, you get into the habit of focusing on productive activities from Day One.

Staying in Touch

Your customers can't call you if they can't find your phone number. You'll need to figure out how to arrange your phone lines before you order your stationery and business cards, so you can list your numbers appropriately. Some independent info pros who already have an extra residential phone line simply appropriate that line for their business. Others order an additional residential line. And others order—and pay substantially more for—a separate business line. Think carefully about which option you choose, because you don't want to have to change your business telephone number once you've printed it and promoted it to clients and prospects.

The advantage of having a business line is that your business name will be listed with directory assistance. A prospective client who remembers that Smith Information Services is located somewhere in Illinois can call directory assistance, or locate the business name in one of the Web-based phone book services such as www.whitepages.com. If you are using a residential line for your business, you won't be able to list Smith Information Services. A separate business line also ensures that you have a line totally dedicated to your business. You haven't "stolen" the phone line your children use for their own Web surfing or chatting with friends. The line will only ring in your office, so you can safely ignore it if a call comes in after business hours. This avoids the awkwardness of having a family member answer your business line and project a less-than-business-like image, or feeling that you have to lunge for the phone whenever it rings, on the chance that it's a client calling.

The next best alternative to an official business line is a new residential line dedicated to your business. You do give up the ability to list your business name in the phone directory, a consequence I consider a disadvantage, but many independent info pros don't mind it, focusing instead on making sure their phone number appears in professional association directories, on their Web site, and on other marketing material. The cost of an additional residential line is substantially less than that of a new business line. If you take this approach, see if your local phone company can set up the new line with what is sometimes called "distinctive ring." This lets you determine immediately whether the call is personal or business, even without checking to see which line is blinking on your telephone.

You'll want a multiline phone (or phones), and a multiline answering machine or voice mail that lets you record different outgoing messages for your home and business lines. You'll also have to train your family not to answer the business line or use it during business hours. And, of course, you'll have to train yourself not to answer after business hours, lest your business takes over your life!

The final options are to simply take over an extra residential line or—hardly an option at all—use your residential line as a combination home/business line. If you do use a residential line, be sure that other family members understand that the phone is off-limits during work hours. And you'll have to figure out a way to handle after-hours calls. As with adding a new residential line, consider using a multiline answering machine or voice mail; you don't want a client to get a constant busy signal while your spouse is on the Web searching for cheap air fares for your next vacation. And think twice about simply using a single line for home and office. It's certainly the cheapest option, but it means that you'll wind up taking client calls at 6 in the morning and 10 at night—and compromising their chances of getting through to you during normal business hours if your family is on the line.

If you do use residential phone lines for your business—either for incoming calls or for your modem or fax lines—be sure to keep track of which expenses are business and which are not. Your company can pay for the long-distance calls that you made for work, but you can't write off the calls to Grandma (unless she's a client, of course).

What about a toll-free number? Surprisingly, this can cost very little, and giving out a toll-free number to important clients is a great way to show them how much you value their business. Call several long-distance carriers and see how much they will charge you to add a toll-free number onto your existing phone line. Often, the monthly fee is minimal (or waived altogether) and the per-minute charges are usually competitive with what you pay for your regular outgoing calls.

While you're at it, look into any voice mail capability that your local phone company, or an independent answering service, may offer. Yes, it's an ongoing expense, as opposed to the one-time cost of an answering machine. On the other hand, voice mail means that your callers never get a busy signal; if you're on the phone when they call, the call rolls straight to voice mail. Note that some answering machines, too, will pick up the call if they detect the "call waiting" tone.

If you expect to be on the Internet for much of your day (no, I mean *working*, not downloading music files), high-speed access is a good idea. The three primary choices are:

- Digital subscriber line (DSL), provided by a telecommunications company, and supplied through a regular phone line

- Cable modem, provided by a cable communications company, and supplied through a specialized modem that connects to your cable feed

- Satellite, provided by satellite services such as DirecPC or Dish Network, requires a satellite receiver installation that connects with your computer. Currently comes in one-way and two-way systems; one-way requires a dialup modem in addition to the satellite connection. (Note that satellite may be your only high-speed option if you live in a rural area.)

DSL, cable modem, and two-way satellite all offer always-on, fast connection to the Net. If you aren't sure which is best for you, read the tutorials and comparison guides available on Zdnet.com or cnet.com.

Your subscription to any of these options will probably include an account with an Internet service provider (ISP). However, be sure to sign up with a second ISP as well. I don't know anyone whose primary ISP has not gone down at some point for a day or more. If you count on communicating with your clients via e-mail and your ISP is down, you're toast. When it comes to Internet connectivity, redundancy is a good idea; although I use a DSL line, I also have a regular dial-up modem for those times when my DSL service is acting up. It doesn't happen often, but when it does, my clients can't wait 24 or 48 hours for me to deliver that electronic file they're waiting for. If you don't expect to do a tremendous amount of online research, a standard dial-up account with an ISP may be right for you, and about half the cost of high-speed access.

What about a Web site for your business? See Chapter 20, Marketing on the Web, for details; at this point, you will want to consider reserving a domain name, even if you aren't ready to put up a Web page. Many ISPs will hold or "park" your domain name for you for a small fee. Expect to pay from $15 to $35 or so to register your domain name. Even if you don't have a Web site yet, you can use your domain name as an e-mail address—that would be you@yourdomain.com—and have it forwarded to your regular e-mail account. That way, you can give out an e-mail address that won't change, even if you change ISPs; e-mail to your personalized address can always be forwarded to your current ISP. You may have to pay a small monthly fee to have e-mail forwarded to your regular ISP. Register.com and NameZero.com are two Web sites that offer free e-mail forwarding, once you have registered your domain name through them.

Setting Up Office Procedures

It's hard to imagine that you actually need a written list of office procedures if the only person in the office is you. On the other hand, most of us work best with at least a bit of structure, and when you're building your own business, you have to set up that structure yourself.

For starters, figure out how you are going to keep track of your appointments, deadlines, and to-do lists. I became a convert to one of those daily planning binders (see FranklinCovey.com and DayMinder.com for two examples) and now can't imagine living without one. Most of these "organizers" are now available in both binder form and as software, and of course you may opt for one of the ever-popular PDAs such as Palm Pilot and Handspring. Whatever organizing tool you choose, get in the habit of using it. As a one- or two-person business, it's critical that you develop good time management and project planning skills. And, to start you out on the right foot, your first job once you have selected your organizer is to write yourself a weekly reminder to back up all your business-critical files.

Decide how you will keep track of your clients and prospects. You will be contacting them regularly (see Section Three: Marketing for more on keeping in touch with your clients), and you need some system for storing, sorting, and retrieving their mailing addresses, phone numbers, and e-mail addresses. You may also want to keep a record of other information about each client or prospect—when you first contacted them, how they heard about you, any preferences about deliverables, and their charming quirks ("high-maintenance" or "likes to see list of search strategies used"). Contact management software, such as Act! or Goldmine, lets you maintain a database of your clients and prospects, keep track of when you last spoke with each person, set up reminders of when to call someone next, and so on. If this seems like overkill for your needs, consider just creating a table in your word processor, or a spreadsheet, either of which allows you to generate mailing labels and sort your list by name or any other field you want with a minimum of grief. For example, my client "database" is a table in Word that looks like this:

Brown, Jane	Jane Brown Public Relations Acme Tire Co. 123 Elm St. Chicago, IL 60606	312.123.1234; fax: 312.123.2345; e-mail: jbrown@acmetire.com	May 2001: met through AIIP referral program
Smith, Patrick	Patrick Smith Smith Consulting 123 Spruce St. Berkeley, CA 94709	510.111.2222; fax: 510.111.2345; cell: 510.111.2468; e-mail: pat@smithconsulting. com	Oct. 1999: met at Internet Librarian conference. Likes to see all search strategies.

The first column is last name first, so I can sort my list alphabetically. The second column is in mailing label format. The third column holds any other contact information. The fourth column is for notes for when the clients started, how they heard about me, and anything else I want to remember about them.

Paying Your Dues

If you haven't already joined the Association of Independent Information Professionals, now's the time to do so. AIIP, described in more detail in the Appendix, is the primary association for us independent info pros, and can be an invaluable resource for beginning entrepreneurs. Members have access to a lively private e-mail discussion group, a volunteer mentoring program, sample forms for subcontracting and confidentiality agreements, a quarterly newsletter, a referral program, and the opportunity to tap into the expertise of hundreds of people who have been doing this kind of work for years.

In addition to AIIP, join the major trade or professional association that your clients are likely to belong to. Do you plan to do research for HR departments? Then join the Society for Human Resource Professionals. Are you focusing on product marketing professionals? Join the American Marketing Association, or its equivalent. Not only will you hear industry-related news when your clients do, but you'll have the opportunity to take on volunteer responsibilities for the organization, which get your name out there to prospective clients.

Now is also the time to look into health insurance, office (or home office) insurance, and professional liability insurance. In addition to general liability coverage, which is available through your homeowner's policy to cover incidents like someone falling down your stairs, you might want to consider errors-and-omissions (E&O) insurance. E&O insurance is particularly important if you provide research in situations in which a great deal rides on the results of your work. For example, suppose a patent searcher tells a client that no patents currently exist for the client's new invention. If the client proceeds to market his invention and is later sued for millions of dollars by someone who does, indeed, hold an applicable patent, the client may sue the patent searcher. If you're doing research in areas of intellectual property, law, or medicine, you may want to investigate the cost and coverage options of E&O insurance. Also, see Chapter 15, Ethics and Legalities, for a discussion of avoiding liability issues.

Finding affordable health insurance, at least for those of us in the U.S., can be a challenge. Call several of the major insurance companies in your area and find out what options they have for individual coverage. If you're leaving full-time employment, check with your existing health insurance provider to see if the rate and coverage for individuals is comparable to what you're getting now. Also, check with any associations you belong to; some larger associations offer at least basic health insurance at a group rate.

And finally, you will need to open accounts with any online information services you expect to use for research. (See Chapter 29, Professional Online Services, for information on these resources.) My approach has always been to subscribe to as many sources as I can, as long as they don't charge a subscription or minimum usage fee; it's frustrating when I need immediate access to a publication that's only available on an online service I don't subscribe to, and find that I have to wait two days to get all the paperwork done. Keep in mind that AIIP members are eligible for discounts and special deals with a number of online services, including the waiving of monthly or annual subscription fees.

Final Thouthts on Setting Up Your Business

- Expect to spend $8,000 to $10,000 setting up your office and your business. Buy the best you can afford, and you'll only have to buy it once (with the exception of computers, of course, which you'll probably replace every few years)
- Do as much of the setup as you can ahead of time. Go office furniture shopping on the weekend. Get your letterhead designed before you launch. Be prepared to start marketing on your first day in business.
- Think five years out. Does your business name give you the flexibility you need?
- Be honest with yourself about your ability to work well in whatever setting you've chosen. Moving an office is not something you want to do more than once.

Chapter 9

Software for Your Business

I'll start by confessing that I'm not one of those early adopters who loads every new piece of software that comes down the pike. I run as few programs as possible, on the assumption that no one pays me for my learning curve, so I might as well minimize the time I spend getting familiar with new software. I upgrade when I have to—primarily when the version of my operating system is a couple of versions behind the leading edge. I make sure that my software is compatible with what my clients and contacts use. That means, for example, that I switched from WordPerfect to Word years ago, once Word became the dominant word-processing program.

The software packages that I'll cover in this chapter are what most independent info pros would consider the bare necessities, along with a few utilities that are helpful in specific situations. All of these programs run on Windows PCs and most also come in Mac versions.

Entrepreneur magazine has a Web-based guide to software. Some of it is overkill for a one- or two-person business, but it's useful nonetheless. Go to www.entrepreneur.com/features/softguide for the latest version of the guide.

The Basics

Let's start with the can't-live-without software, much of which probably came preinstalled on your PC. In some cases, I recommend that you stick with whatever is commonly used. It's easier to find colleagues or friends who can help you troubleshoot any problems you run into, and it's much more likely that your clients will be running the same program.

Word Processing

Microsoft Word; need I say more? But I will. When you start your business, make sure you have the latest, or next-to-latest, version of Word, then plan on upgrading every couple of years. You probably won't need any of the bells, whistles, and bugs added with each new iteration, but your clients are likely to be using a current version and you want to make sure that you can exchange documents with a minimum of trouble.

These are the Word functions I've found most useful in my business over the years:

- Create a table of contents
- Create a template for reports
- Add and edit headers and footers
- Build simple macros for repetitive tasks
- Build simple tables
- Insert images and files

Microsoft Word (www.microsoft.com); Windows and Mac versions available.

E-Mail

Most people use Microsoft's Outlook or Outlook Express, but this is one case where I've chosen to go against the tide and use something other than a Microsoft application: Eudora Pro. The advantage of using less-standard e-mail software is that viruses written to exploit the vulnerabilities of Outlook usually aren't as virulent on other e-mail programs. It's one way to ensure safe computing—along with obeying the rule about never, ever opening an attached file you're not expecting, even from someone you know, without first running it through a virus-checker (see the discussion later about virus-checking software). The only disadvantage I have encountered with using Eudora instead of Outlook is that I get less support from my Internet service provider when I run into problems with my account. A small price to pay, in my opinion, for a setup that is more resistant to e-mail-borne viruses.

These are the e-mail functions I use the most:

- Attach files
- Create address lists and nicknames for frequently e-mailed addresses
- Filter your incoming e-mail into folders (one folder for e-mail discussion lists, one for 'stuff to be read later,' and so on)
- Run your outgoing e-mail through a spell-checker, and format your messages in plain text (some e-mail software doesn't handle formatted text well, but any e-mail software can read plain text)
- Create 'signature' files

Microsoft Outlook Express and Outlook (www.microsoft.com); Windows and Mac versions available.

Eudora Pro (www.eudora.com); Windows and Mac versions available.

Web Browser

The browser battles appear to be over, and Microsoft's Internet Explorer seems to have conquered the field, at least in terms of the size of its user base. Netscape Navigator is always an option, and it doesn't really matter which browser you use. You may even want to try one of the second-tier browsers such as Opera, a nifty piece of software that loads fast and takes up a lot less disk space. Make sure you have the free versions of the usual plug-ins such as Adobe Acrobat Reader, an audio player, and a video player. Normally, you'll be directed to a download site by a Web page that requires any of these plug-ins.

These are the browser features I use the most:

- Create and edit a bookmarks/favorites file
- Create and edit the toolbar of frequently visited sites
- Set a default home page
- Modify the security settings to your tolerance of risk

Microsoft Internet Explorer (www.microsoft.com); Windows and Mac versions available.

Netscape Navigator (www.netscape.com); Windows and Mac versions available.

Opera (www.opera.com); Windows and Mac versions available.

Accounting

Intuit's QuickBooks products are by far the most popular accounting packages for independent info pros. In addition to the fact that they're powerful and easy to use, you're much more likely to find an accountant who uses QuickBooks than one who uses Microsoft Money or some other financial management program. Intuit sells several versions of QuickBooks; even the most basic versions have all the features you'll probably need. (Note that Quicken, the personal finance software, probably isn't adequate for a small business, unless you buy the version specifically designed for home businesses. The personal finance versions don't include invoicing and accounts receivable features, which are an important part of running your business.)

Work with your accountant to set up QuickBooks initially. As streamlined as the software is, an information business is not a typical business and you may need to modify some expense and income categories. It's a lot easier to pay an accountant to get you set up properly than it is to re-do a year's worth of transactions at tax time when you realize that the categories you've set up aren't what the IRS uses (and yes, I'm speaking from first-hand experience).

You'll need to be able to do the following functions in QuickBooks:

- Create invoices
- Write checks
- Receive and deposit payments
- Generate profit & loss reports
- Generate past-due collections reports
- Balance your checkbook

Intuit QuickBooks (quickbooks.intuit.com); Windows and Mac versions available.

Backups

I feel fortunate that I learned early in my career to back up my PC regularly. My first computer, bought in 1984, crashed fatally within two weeks of purchase—everything I had stored was gone forever. No great loss of data at the time, but I've been scrupulous about backing up all essential files once a week ever since. (In fact, I back up data files daily for projects I'm actively working on.) The appropriate software is usually included with whatever system you use for backup—a high-capacity disk drive or a writeable CD drive.

Symantec offers a Norton product, Ghost, for PC backup to CD; Iomega (maker of Zip drives and disks) provides backup software with its high-capacity disk drives; and your computer may come equipped with a backup utility program. What you use doesn't matter half as much as that you use it regularly. Note that you don't usually have to back up application software, particularly if you have the original installation disks. However, if you purchase software from a Web site and download it to your computer, make a backup copy on disk or CD before you've even installed it.

Focus on backing up files that you have created or modified—word-processing documents, online search results you intend to send to your clients, your accounting software data, and so on. Keep your backup in a safe place, preferably someplace away from your office. The point of making backups is to protect yourself from loss; if your office is flooded, suffers smoke or fire damage, or is ransacked by a thief, you don't want to lose both your PC and your backup files. Have your spouse take your backups in to work, keep a copy in your garage, or stash them in your car.

The following are the basic functions your backup software should handle:

- Back up all essential files
- Schedule unattended backups
- Restore files from the backup

Iomega Zip Drives (www.iomega.com); Windows and Mac versions available.
Norton Ghost (www.symantec.com); Windows version only.

Virus Protection

Like backup programs, antivirus software is something you only truly appreciate after you've been caught without it. The leading virus protection programs are McAfee VirusScan and Norton AntiVirus. Either one is a good choice, and both offer automatic Web updates to keep your software alert to the latest viruses in the wild. Of course, you also have to practice safe computing; never open an unexpected e-mail attachment without scanning it first, regardless of who it's from, and always virus-check any files you download from the Web, even those you purchase from a reputable vendor.

Mac users are safer from viruses simply because they constitute such a small proportion of total computer users, and therefore present a less attractive target to the low-lifes who create viruses. However, Mac users, too, should stay vigilant, as Mac viruses do occasionally appear.

Make sure you know how to do the following in your virus protection software:

- Schedule automatic scans of your hard disk
- Automatically scan all incoming e-mail and downloaded files
- Get updates from the vendor's Web site

McAfee VirusScan (www.mcafee.com); Windows version only.
Norton AntiVirus (www.symantec.com); Windows and Mac versions available.

The Nice-to-Haves

This section covers software that you'll probably want eventually but may not use every day. If you've got the cash to spare and you like knowing that you've got a fully equipped tool bench, add these to your shopping list. Like a number of the basic applications I described in the earlier sections, some of these categories are dominated by a single vendor. Go with the name brand, particularly in something like presentation software where it's important that you use what your clients and colleagues are using.

Adobe Acrobat

I'm not going to bother using a generic name to describe Acrobat—this is one software application that not only owns the market but has, in fact, defined the market for PDF, or Portable Document Format, files. Acrobat allows the user to create text and image files that can be read across platforms, regardless of whether the recipient has the software that created the original file. You can download the free version of Adobe Acrobat Reader, which enables you to read PDF files, from www.adobe.com. But the full-featured Acrobat suite is nice to have, as it enables you to convert word-processing documents, PowerPoint presentations, and so on into PDF files. I often find this the best way to supply information to a client; PDF is universally readable and ensures that the material remains intact, as PDF files are 'sealed' and cannot be modified by the reader. (See Chapter 34, Deliverables, for more discussion about sealing material for clients.)

Adobe Acrobat (www.adobe.com); Windows and Mac versions available.

PowerPoint

Like Acrobat in the electronic publishing arena, Microsoft's PowerPoint pretty much owns the market for presentation software. It's easy to use, a great tool for public speaking, and comes in handy when providing an executive summary of a report to a client who is accustomed to PowerPoint files. If you want to stand out from the rest of the presenters at your next conference, you can purchase CDs of additional PowerPoint design templates and background images from third-party vendors. Some Web sites such as Corbis' BizPresenter.com also sell templates on an a la carte basis, although that can get expensive.

Microsoft PowerPoint (www.microsoft.com); Windows and Mac versions available.

Corbis BizPresenter (bizpresenter.corbis.com); Windows and Mac versions available.

Screen Capture

You'll occasionally have the need to take a snapshot of what's displayed on your monitor. You may want to include the information in a report, you may want an example of a certain Web site to show as part of a presentation, or you may want to document what a Web page looked like at a given moment. The Windows default Print Screen function doesn't give you much flexibility; sometimes you want to capture just a portion of a screen, or snap a picture of a page that requires that you scroll down through several screens' worth of material. Popular Windows screen capture programs include Snag-It, FullShot, and Paint Shop Pro. Snag-It and FullShot are particularly useful for their scroll-down feature; Paint Shop Pro is a full-featured graphics program that comes preloaded on many PCs, and offers a wide range of image manipulation features as well as screen shots. Mac users can opt for Snapz Pro.

Snapz Pro (www.ambrosiasw.com); Mac version only.

FullShot (www.inbit.com); Windows version only.

Paint Shop Pro (www.jasc.com); Windows version only.

Snag-It (www.techsmith.com); Windows version only.

FTP

I didn't realize how much I needed an FTP utility until I started using one. If you maintain your Web site yourself—and of course you made sure that whoever designed your site kept it simple enough for you to maintain without tears—you have to be able to upload fresh versions of your Web pages as you update them. This involves using FTP, the Internet file transfer protocol. Most Web browsers have an FTP facility built in, but these tend to be clumsy at best. A utility like WS_FTP (for Windows) or Interarchy (for Mac) handles FTP much more smoothly.

Interarchy (www.stairways.com); Mac version only.

WS_FTP (www.ipswitch.com); Windows version only.

Dedicated Search Software

Back in the days before the Web (yes, online research existed way back then), some professional online services developed specialized software to streamline the search and retrieval process on their systems. (See Chapter 29, Professional Online Services, for more information on these value-added information resources.) Some of these software packages are still supported by the vendors, and they sometimes offer features not available through the service's Web interface. Dialog's DialogLink, for example, lets you type in several search queries at a time, even while the system is still working on the first one, which saves a bit of time; capture an entire search session to disk as you go so you have a record of your search strategy as well as the results; and display graphic images. It also helps manage multiple passwords. Dedicated software also has the benefit of being generally more stable than a Web browser. If you plan to use any of the professional online services regularly, you may want to try out the vendor's specialized search software, if available.

DialogLink for Dialog (support.dialog.com/products); Windows version only.

Research Software for LexisNexis (support.lexisnexis.com/lndownload); Windows and Mac versions available.

Imagination 2 for Questel*Orbit (www.questel.orbit.com); Windows version only.

File Compression

Very large files are often compressed by the sender in order to reduce the time it takes the recipient to download them. While most files are self-extracting—you click on the file and it automatically restores the files to their original format even if you don't have a copy of the software used to compress it—you'll need to invest in appropriate compression/decompression software if you want to compress files prior to sending them. Big players in this field are WinZip (for Windows), ZipIt (for Mac), StuffIt, and StuffIt Expander (for Windows and Mac).

WinZip (www.winzip.com); Windows version only.

ZipIt (www.maczipit.com); Mac version only.

StuffIt and StuffIt Expander (www.stuffit.com); Windows and Mac versions available.

Other Cool Tools

Loads of nifty tools and utilities are available for just about all those tasks you do frequently and wish you could streamline. Here are a few with a big following in the independent info pro community.

- HTMASC—a conversion program that turns HTML text to plain text quickly, removing HTML tags and reformatting. (www.bitenbyte.com), Windows version only.

- Link-management programs that check whether links on a Web page are still valid. I use a quirky program called Xenu (home.snafu.de/tilman/xenulink.html); Windows version only. NetMechanic is another option (www.netmechanic.com); hosted remotely, so platform-independent.

- Web research software that turbo-charges your search capability, such as BullsEye (www.intelliseek.com) and Copernic (www.copernic.com); both are Windows version only.

- Time-tracking software for recording the time you spend on a project, down to tenths of an hour. This is particularly useful if you do work for law firms or other organizations that track time in small increments. Business versions of Quicken handle this to a certain extent, but Timeslips is a specialized tool for just this purpose. (www.timeslips.com), Windows and Mac versions available.

- Firewall software is essential if you have DSL, cable modem, or other 'always-on' Internet access. Products include ZoneAlarm (www.zonealarm.com), Windows version only; Norton Personal Firewall (www.symantec.com), Windows and Mac versions available; BlackICE (www.black-ice-firewall.com) Windows version only; and McAfee Personal Firewall (www.mcafee.com), Windows version only.

Software Lessons Learned

- You don't have an IT department on call to provide PC support. Keep your computer free of unnecessary tools and utilities; you're the one who has to maintain them.
- Avoid version 1.x of anything. Why be an unpaid bug tester?
- Be as frictionless as possible for your clients; find out what version of a particular application they use, or what file format works best for them.
- Back up everything you wouldn't want to lose. Keep the backup files outside your office; if you experience a fire or theft, why lose both your PC and your backup files?

Chapter 10

Work and the Rest of Your Life

So far, I've covered lots of practical issues—setting up your office, writing a business plan, even "softer" factors like making sure you have the personality to enjoy and succeed at being an independent info pro. But I haven't talked much about integrating your work into the *other* hours of your day—the time that you spend outside the office, having a life. This chapter will look at some of the issues that frequently arise when you own a one- or two-person business, especially if you work from home.

Living Abundantly

There are different ways of living life richly. You can spend money as fast as you make it and live from paycheck to paycheck (or, as an independent info pro, from client payment to client payment). Or you can focus on finding richness and wealth in whatever situation you're in, in ways that don't involve cash. The first six months or year of a new business are going to be hard; you'll be working like crazy to find new clients, and you may be spending more money than you take in at first. You can react to this by feeling desperate, making cold calls to random prospects, accepting work in which you don't have enough expertise, and generally losing your cool. Or you can focus on the ways in which you *are* wealthy, right now at the beginning of your life as an entrepreneur. Here are a few of the riches I reminded myself I had during my first, lean year:

- I can set my own schedule and take time to take the dogs on a walk.

- I can develop a network of fascinating fellow independent info pros through the Association of Independent Information Professionals (AIIP).
- I can play music as loud as I want, all day long.
- I can try out new ideas without running them by my boss for approval.
- I don't have to sit through committee meetings.

You can pull together your own list of things that gratify you as you work. The point is that, right now, you are rich in ways that you might not have realized. You are following your dream, you are creating a business from scratch, you are embarking on a new adventure, and you are challenging yourself in ways you might not have thought possible. Think about what you feel rich in right now, and focus on that when you start feeling discouraged. I found it helpful to read the daily essays in *Simple Abundance: A Daybook of Comfort and Joy*, by Sarah Ban Breathnach (Warner Books, 1995). This may be a bit New Age-y for your tastes, but try to find something that helps you focus on wealth beyond the bottom line.

Time Management, or "I think I'll take a little break now"

Unstructured time is difficult for some people. You show up at your office in the morning and find none of the usual cues to buckle down and start working—no ringing phones, no voices from the next cubicle, no boss walking by asking about that report that's due at noon. Unless you have a client's project staring you in the face, or some administrative tasks that absolutely have to be done, you'll need to create your own structure for the day. Assign yourself the task of spending a certain number of hours today working on marketing.

If you find that the days keep slipping away from you and you feel like you haven't accomplished anything by 5:30, work on being mindful of how you spend your day. If you have to, keep a diary for a week and see how you spend every hour (the business versions of QuickBooks financial management software enable you to track your activities during the day). At the end of the week, add up the time and see where it went. Some people find that working at home creates all kinds of little time sinks. "I'll just run out now and do the grocery shopping while the store isn't crowded." "I'll just take care of the dry cleaning and run a few loads of wash." "I'll just meet a friend for a quick cup of coffee." It's great to be able to get a load of wash done while you work, but if that turns into two hours of tidying up the house, then you're not working at your business. Likewise, the flexibility to meet friends, go for a walk, and take care of personal errands during the week is a real benefit of being an independent info pro, but if you find that you're spending a quarter of your week this way, it's time to rethink your schedule.

"The Info Pro Is In"

Even if you have great time management skills, it sometimes takes a while for your family, friends, and neighbors to realize that, just because you're home all day, you're can't necessarily drop everything and chat. When I started my business, I stopped answering my home telephone during the day. (Yes, you *do* need a separate business line. See Chapter 8, Setting Up Your Business.) I found that I was getting too many calls from friends who thought that I had turned into a lady of leisure who had nothing to do all day long but chat on the phone.

Take a Day Off

Laurie Kauffman, owner of Net Worth Consulting Inc., a wise friend of mine and a longtime consultant who also works from home, schedules one weekday off every month. She says that she works hard enough all week, and often works on the weekends, and this is one way of paying herself back—comp time, if you will. She takes her kids to the zoo, goes to an afternoon matinee, meets a friend for coffee, or does something that's fun and feels special, especially if done while most people are working diligently in their offices. I'm not as good as Laurie about scheduling my monthly play-hooky day, but when I do, I really look forward to that day—and I do enjoy the time off.

Set firm office hours. It seems that there are two kinds of independent info pros; some have trouble sitting at their desk from 9:00 to 5:00, working all alone; others have trouble leaving the office at the end of the day and tend to let their work take over their lives. Figure out which type you are and develop a strategy for sticking to the office hours that you've set for yourself.

If you can hear your office phone from the rest of the house, you might want to get in the habit of turning off the ringer when you leave for the day (but remember to turn it on again in the morning!), so that you're not tempted to take after-hours calls. If your clients discover that you'll pick up the phone at all hours of the day and night, they'll call at all hours, and that way lies madness. Instead, really *leave* the office at the end of the day.

Creating a Good Office Environment

I talk about the nuts and bolts of setting up your office in Chapter 8, Setting Up Your Business. Now let's think of the ambiance of your office beyond the desk and PC. Look around the room and think about what you need to make it feel *right*. Pictures of your family? A beautiful bowl you picked up on vacation? A comfy chair to sit in while catching up on your professional reading? Some hardy houseplants? You're going to be spending at least a third of your day in the office, so you might as well make it as inviting, pleasant, and soothing as possible.

My first office was in the basement of my house, with one small window that looked out onto a busy alley with trash trucks rumbling by all day. Because I didn't get much natural light, I installed full spectrum light bulbs that replicated natural light. I hung a calendar with pictures of the Rocky Mountains, where I go backpacking every year, to serve as a reminder that I *do* have a life. I brought in a funky old couch so that my dogs and I could curl up on it when I had reading to do. And I invested in a small boom-box so that I could play music during the day. I even hang my marathon medals in the office rather than in the house; it's another daily reminder of my accomplishments outside the work environment.

Going on Vacation

Yes, you will go on vacation—or you'll go crazy. Some independent info pros like to tack on a few vacation days at the end of a business trip or attendance at a professional conference. I find that difficult, on several levels. On a practical level, it means I have to pack two wardrobes—one for business and one for play—which doubles the luggage. I also tend to go into marketing overdrive while I'm at a conference, and it's hard for me to switch from business professional to tourist overnight. Finally, by the end of a business trip, I'm ready to get back in the office and get caught up with e-mail and backlogged work.

On the other hand, these mini-vacations can be a nice way to get a few days of relaxation without the hassle of planning a separate trip. You've already written off the travel costs as a business expense, so your only nondeductible expenses are the extra days of hotel and food. And, let's face it, professional conferences are often held at nice destinations.

In any event, you'll need to plan what to do with your office while you're away. During business trips, you might conceivably check voice mail and e-mail throughout the day, and subcontract out any work that comes in. However, trying to do this during a vacation is insane. (That's why I go backpacking every summer; because I am completely unwilling to tote a laptop and satellite phone in my pack, I'm blissfully and completely offline.)

You have several options for taking care of clients while you're on vacation. Whichever you choose, be sure that you manage your callers' expectations. One is simply to record a voice-mail greeting that tells them when you will be back in the office and when they can expect a return call. You don't want clients to hear the standard "I'm not in right now, but leave a message" and then not get a call back for a week. If you are concerned about alerting burglars that your home is unoccupied, leave a message like "I'm attending a local conference this week but won't be able to handle any calls until Friday" or even "The office is closed this week" without any indication that you will be away from town.

"Call My Associate"

The option I usually choose when I'm traveling is to have a trusted colleague handle any calls that come in. We agree ahead of time on what hourly rate to charge, how to handle calls from new clients, any special needs that existing clients may have, and so on. I then leave a message on my voice mail saying "My office is closed this week. If you have any urgent research needs, please call my associate ..." and I give her name and number. The advantage of referring callers to someone else is that they can talk with a live person rather than just leaving a message and waiting a week for a reply. The disadvantage is that I am sending callers to someone else, with the inevitable risk that they may decide that they'd rather do business with my colleague than with me. That's a risk I'm willing to take, especially since the independent info pros to whom I refer callers when I travel are scrupulous about sending subsequent calls back to me.

"Here's My Password"

Linda Cooper, an information consultant in Pennsylvania, takes a different approach. When she was running an independent info pro business and had to leave the office, she would give her voice-mail password to a colleague, who would check it several times a day and return any important calls. If you can arrange this, it may be the best solution, because it appears more seamless to your clients. They don't have to call anyone else; someone returns their calls and can handle their information needs, and you don't have a voice-mail box overflowing with messages when you return.

"Good Morning, Research"

If it's very important that your clients reach a live person when they call you, another option is to arrange to have your calls automatically forwarded to a colleague. There was a period of a few years when I had a lot of clients who needed work done within 24 hours, and they didn't want to wait until I got back in the office, nor did they want to have to call someone else for the work. Several colleagues had similar fast-turnaround clients, and we set up an arrangement to handle each others' calls when one of us was out. We all got in the habit of answering our phones "Research" instead of with our name; this more generic greeting meant that, when Kim's calls were forwarded to me, her caller wasn't disconcerted by having someone answer the phone with an unfamiliar name. Of course, once the clients started talking, I could figure out that this was one of Kim's clients, and I would handle the job as she had instructed me, and would let Kim bill the client when she returned. This arrangement can work well if you have a colleague who is in the office most of the day and who can handle the type of research your clients usually ask for, and if you can arrange some way of answering the phones so that clients who've had their calls forwarded don't immediately assume they have the wrong number.

"I'm Outta Here"

Alex Kramer of Kramer Research is of the opinion that sometimes it's best to just shut down the office. When she is out of town, either on business or vacation, she usually leaves a voice-mail message telling callers that the office is closed and the date that she will return. She found that her client base tended to assume that the person to whom she referred callers when she was away was, in fact, someone who worked for her. They would call the colleague directly the next time they needed research, and Alex would lose the client's business. Now, she may have an intern answer phone calls or faxes that arrive while she is gone, and provide guidelines on how to handle any assignments. Otherwise, her clients just wait until she returns.

Use whichever approach works best for your clients. If your clients typically contact you via e-mail, you might want to set up an autoreply that tells them you are away. See the sidebar "E-Mail Vacation Message" for some thoughts on this approach. If you're not sure how your clients will respond to your planned method for handling their business while you're out of town, ask two or three of your best clients for their reaction and suggestions.

E-Mail Vacation Message

E-mail vacation messages, or autoresponders, are settings on your e-mail software or on your Internet service provider's mail server that generate an automatic response to every incoming e-mail message. You can usually supply the text of the response, so you can tell senders when you'll be back and, if you'd like, whom to call in your absence. Most Internet service providers—at least most of the nonfreebie services—let you set up an autoreply on the server end; the advantage is that you don't have to keep your PC turned on while you are out of the office. For example, my current ISP has a user-support Web page where I can provide the text for my "vacation message" and specify whether the message should be sent every time I receive an e-mail or only once to each sender. If you opt to use your own e-mail software for autoresponses, you will also need always-on Net access (through DSL or cable modem), or else set up your software to automatically dial up and check your e-mail at least once a day. I live in Washington, DC, where we get frequent thunderstorms during the summer, so I'm always reluctant to leave my PC on when I go on vacation and run the risk that a nearby lightning strike will fry my plugged-in PC. I'll opt for the server-side autoresponder, so that I can unplug my PC and keep it safe from electrical storms while I'm on the road.

Be aware, however, that deployed inappropriately, an autoresponder can earn you infamy. Anyone who's been on an e-mail discussion list has seen messages like this: "I'm out of the office until February 15th. If you need immediate help, contact Susan Smith at x1254 or Jim Brown at x4327, or go to the intranet site at private.acme.com for more information." The message might as well say "Hi, I'm clueless about the impact of my vacation e-mail message on others."

If you subscribe to any e-mail discussion lists, keep the instructions on how to suspend your subscription while you're gone, and make sure you put your lists on hold before you set up an autoreply. Otherwise, every time anyone posts a message to a list you subscribe to, they may get a copy of your out-of-office reply—and that may result in your banishment from the list, or at least a scolding from the administrator. Check the autorespond instructions on your e-mail software or ISP's site; some allow you to specify that your autorespond message be sent just once to any given sender, or no more frequently than once a week. That way, you don't bombard a discussion list or colleague with "gone fishing" messages. I manage a couple of professional discussion lists, and during holiday seasons I handle six or eight out-of-control autoresponders a day.

Business Coaches: Help, I Need Somebody

If you have issues to work out in your personal life, you might see a therapist or counselor. If you need help working out business issues, a business coach could be a godsend. Jan Tudor of JT Research has worked with a business coach and described her experience this way: "Business coaches get into the psychology of running a business—the personal baggage we may bring to the business as well as the issues of running our business in synch with our personal goals and values. They hold us accountable for the priorities we set, such as taking time off, raising rates, and saying 'no.' I found the experience of having a weekly phone conversation with a business coach very worthwhile. Like therapy, there were things I learned about myself that I didn't necessarily like but that I needed to change in order to run a business harmoniously. Having a business coach really is like having a business therapist."

Note that business coaches aren't mentors in the sense of unpaid guides or advisors. Rather, they are professionals with training and expertise in helping people identify and think through the things that are keeping them from achieving their full professional potential. Finding a business coach is often a matter of word of mouth, asking colleagues whom they would recommend. A number of business coaches have been trained by Coach U (www.coachu.com), a training program for business and personal coaches. They offer a free referral service at www.coachreferral.com.

Life Lessons Learned

- Focus on the things that enrich your life. What are the less tangible benefits you receive every day from being an independent info pro?
- Bring to your office reminders of the rest of your life—things that relax and inspire you.
- Create enough structure in your schedule that you can leave the office behind at the end of the day knowing that you spent your time well.
- Teach your family and friends that, even though you're at home, you're at work.
- Find the right setup that lets you truly leave the office behind when you go on vacation.

Section Two

Running the Business

Chapter 11

Managing Your Clients

Clients are strange creatures whom you love but who sometimes drive you crazy. If you didn't have clients, you'd be out of business; but how do you know what kinds of clients to cultivate, how to manage their expectations and keep them happy, and how to handle those occasional situations in which everything seems to blow up?

Monogamy vs. Playing the Field

No, I'm not offering couples counseling or marriage advice—just a recommendation that, when it comes to clients, the more the merrier. It's great to have some big clients who consistently call you for large projects, who refer others to you, and who pay you promptly. Would that we were all blessed with many such clients. But relying on one or two big clients for all or most of your revenue can be a risky business. Here's why:

- Without diversity in your client base, you are much more vulnerable to an economic downturn, because a dip that hits one will probably affect everyone in the same industry. Downturn or not, your clients will have similar seasonal fluctuations in their business, which means that certain times of year will be particularly lean for you in terms of cash flow. If you have clients in a number of industries, or at least a variety of types of clients (large corporations, small consulting firms, and so on), it's much more likely that at least some portion of your customer base will need your services all year round.

- If most of your work is for a single client, you may even be discounting your hourly rates in exchange for the steady income. But your client isn't really doing you a favor by giving you all that work. It means that you are, in essence, providing the client with an employee who doesn't need benefits, paid vacations, a retirement fund, or a steady paycheck. And if you're in the U.S., it means that you are running the risk of having the IRS classify you as a de facto employee. That's not a good thing—you will lose the ability to write off your office expenses, and your "employer" is hit with a tax bill for its portion of employee taxes.

- If one or two big clients take up most of your time, you're less inclined to think about marketing and building up your base of other clients and prospects. "Who cares?" you ask, "since I've got a steady gig." Unfortunately, all good gigs end eventually, and usually with little or no warning. Your contact person will change jobs or get laid off. The client will have a budget freeze and eliminate contractors, despite contractual obligations or assurances to the contrary. The department you work for will be reorganized out of existence or into another group that doesn't need your services. Stuff happens, and unless you've been busily building new client relationships during the good times, you'll find yourself with no work and no prospects when times turn lean.

- Limiting yourself to one or two large clients means limiting your vision of what you're capable of doing. All you see are the skills and abilities that your one or two clients draw on. Most of the growth in my business, in terms of services I offer and types of work I do, has sprung from a client saying, "Hey, I don't know if you can do this, but I really need someone to do such and such." You are far less likely to hear that from a client who has you pigeonholed as "the person we pay to do 25 hours of X a week."

The bottom line is that, while monogamy may be the way to a happy marriage, don't plan to marry any one client. Instead, think of yourself as a charming, attractive singleton, interested in going out for dinner and a movie but not in a full-time commitment any time soon. Don't let one or two clients monopolize your time; there's too much at risk.

Is Any Client Too Small?

You've probably seen those ads for general contractors and repair people—"no project too large or too small." It's true that I've never had a job too big for one of them to handle, but I have a heck of a time finding someone to come and do all the little jobs around my house—repair a faucet, rewire a light fixture, or paint a closet. Whenever I hear a contractor complain about a slowdown in work, I wonder why he's not willing to pick up a day's revenue, at least, doing all the handyman jobs I've accumulated.

Independent info pros aren't looking to fix leaky toilets or patch the hole in the roof, but we do have to figure out whether small clients are worth the trouble. My policy is that small jobs are worth it if I think I can cultivate the clients into becoming more valuable over time, or if I have the free time and this small job won't displace a larger project. (By "small" I mean a job that doesn't take more than an hour or so and that isn't likely to provide any follow-up work; examples include looking up which Congressional committees have oversight over the Federal Aviation Administration, or a quick search to see what newspapers reviewed a particular book.) Perhaps they'll be a source of repeat business, or good referral sources; maybe I can turn the small job into a stepping stone for bigger projects. It sounds cold-hearted to assess potential clients this way, but you have to work one of these angles; it doesn't make much sense to attract clients who offer nothing but low-end one-time jobs. The cost of attracting a client is significant; if you can't recoup that expense with repeat business or steady referrals, you're losing money.

How small is too small? In part, the answer comes down to the type of work you do. Manual research such as public records research or document delivery services are sometimes simpler to juggle, so you can take on a lot of little jobs and turn them into a steady source of income. Online research and telephone projects, on the other hand, require a certain amount of overhead and uninterrupted time, and most require more than an hour or two to complete. Of course, if you charge a one-hour minimum for online or telephone research, then even those small jobs can add up.

Sometimes, doing work for a small client or one that you can't charge your regular rate is better than doing nothing. Small jobs give you valuable practice in estimating projects, negotiating with clients, and writing executive summaries of your research results. You can always ask smaller clients if they can recommend any colleagues for you to contact, and you can include their positive feedback (with permission, of course) on your Web site or in your marketing package. Alex Kramer, the owner of Kramer Research, puts it this way, "The bottom line is that the value in business is always more than just numbers. Looking at any one client solely on how much you can bill him often underestimates his value."

Working for the Cause

I know of a number of independent info pros who will work for nonprofit organizations they support, or for a local startup business, or who will work on a project that's interesting but doesn't pay well, with the understanding that, when the info pro's time gets tight, that small client will have to wait. One reason to take on this kind of work is to keep you from going crazy when the phone does not ring; another is that it's satisfying to be able to provide your services to a nonprofit cause that you care about. When you don't have a lot of spare cash to give, offering your research expertise is a great way to support an organization in a tangible way. (And remember that even nonprofits often have board members and trustees who are executives in their "real" jobs, and you'll get to know them and show them the services you provide.)

Tire-Kickers, Lookie-Loos, and Low-Ballers

I think we all know what tire-kickers are—they're the people who wander through the used car lot, kicking tires and tying up a salesperson's time without intending to actually buy a car. "Lookie-loo" is the name given by real estate agents to the folks who love to wander through open houses and look around, but who have no interest in purchasing real estate. And low-ballers are the clients who always work on getting a "better deal"—who try to negotiate down any project and get the most they can from you for less than you want to charge.

I can almost guarantee that, within a month after you've opened for business, you'll get a phone call from one of these characters. They'll talk and talk and talk, they'll ask you all about your services and imply that they're just about to buy ... but they have to shop around a bit first. Your challenge is figuring out how to get off the phone gracefully without offending the caller or wasting your time with someone who's not going to turn into a good client.

My solution is to watch the clock. I've gotten into the habit of always noting the time at the beginning of a phone call. If we haven't gotten down to talking about the specifics of the job and the budget within five or ten minutes, I assume that I'm dealing with a tire-kicker. At that point, I'll tell her that it sounds like a fascinating project, but it would be best if she could outline her needs and either e-mail or fax me a description of the job so that I can review it and submit a proposal. The message that comes across, without my having to put it in so many words, is that this is going to cost money and we need to get down to business. In the vast majority of cases, the tire-kicker will simply go away rather than go to the effort of writing up a description for a project that may be no more than a gleam in her eye.

How do you deal with someone who's shopping around for the lowest bidder? Easy—bid high. Who needs a client who only hires you because you're cheap? This is a client who will be gone as soon as he finds someone cheaper, and clients like this can turn into clients who don't pay their bills. If the caller tells you, or implies, that he's contacted other info pros, you may wish to end the conversation right there—"Well, it sounds like you have already identified several excellent companies. Rather than tie up your time talking about this project, I'd recommend you just go with one of the people you've already called." If that doesn't work and he insists on getting an estimate from you, give him a budget that's as high as you can name with a straight face, and tell him that you require prepayment of at least 75 percent of the not-to-exceed budget. If he really does want you and comes up with the deposit, then you've got yourself a new client. If not, he'll go away and you won't be bothered by him again. Either way, you were polite, gracious, and professional.

Free Samples, Anyone?

Prospective clients sometimes ask independent info pros (IIPs) for samples of their work. Occasionally this makes sense; usually, though, you are better off responding to the request by addressing the underlying hesitancy your prospect is probably feeling. Is she worried that you won't be able to meet her needs? Did she have a bad experience with another researcher? Does she think that all you'll do is surf the Web and send her some URLs? Since most IIPs offer customized information services, a sample project won't reflect the added value we can provide to each client. Focus your conversation on the kinds of services you provide and on how you can tailor the deliverable to just what your prospect needs.

Amelia Kassel, owner of MarketingBase, commented, "The point of providing a sample of work is supposed to be to make a sale. But my experience has been that it never works in this profession. The client will make a purchasing decision based on other aspects of how you present yourself. These factors include personal chemistry (a very important aspect of business), your background, your reputation (including whether you've been referred by someone the client respects), and so on. In my experience, anyone requesting a sample is usually wasting your time and is probably not a serious or qualified buyer."

Providing a sample project does make sense in one particular situation—when you offer, as part of your product mix, standardized, relatively low-cost, high-volume information services. If you provide fixed-price company profiles, for example, or news updates on a specific industry, you might want to show clients what they would receive for their money. The danger, however, is that by showing prospective clients one cookie-cutter product or service, you limit their expectations of what you're capable of doing; be sure to emphasize, if you do furnish a sample of such a work product, that you also provide higher-end, customized, value-added services.

Sample projects should carry no indication of the client for whom you did the work. Going still further, you might have to change the description of the project or other particulars to ensure that competitors can't identify the client by the nature of the request itself. Pick a project that sounds intriguing but that could have been done for just about anybody. Avoid technologies, marketing ideas, and issues that are closely identified with a particular client. Depending on the agreement you have with your client, you may have to get permission before sending out even a sanitized version of the work you did for them.

Let's *Not* Do Lunch

One of the advantages of marketing to clients outside your local area is that they seldom expect you to get together for meetings or for lunch. Even though face-to-face contact is sometimes nice, it's also a significant investment of your time, when you count the hours it takes to get dressed in your meet-the-client clothes, travel to the meeting, travel home, and change back into your home-office clothes.

If a prospective client asks you to meet her in her office to talk about a possible project, think twice before accepting. For one thing, you almost certainly won't be able to charge for this time, since you haven't started working for the prospect. And look at how much time you are investing in marketing to one person. Unless you are almost positive that you will walk out of the meeting with a *signed contract*, you are gambling with one important asset—your valuable time. Agreeing to what is, in essence, a sales call sends a message that you have time on your hands and that you can be summoned into the office as needed. Keep control of your time. You would probably prefer to send a message like, "Although I'd love the chance to meet face to face, I'm really quite tied up with other projects at the moment. Is it possible that we could schedule a telephone interview at a time that works best for both of us?" And finally, the time you would invest in this one sales call could be spent doing other, more efficient marketing efforts that put you in front of a large number of people at once. See Section Three, Marketing, for more thoughts on cost-effective marketing techniques.

Of course, if the request for an in-person meeting comes from an existing client, your approach may change. Does the client expect to pay for your time, portal to portal (that is, from the moment you leave your office to the moment you return)? I try to pitch every face-to-face meeting with a client as consulting time, and bill accordingly. If I can't charge for the time, I do make sure my client introduces me to as many other people within the office as possible. The more people who know me, who have my business card (and, more importantly, whose business cards I have), the more I can count on keeping this client, even if my original contact moves on to another job.

The bottom line, then, is to think about whether the meeting will pay off, either immediately or soon. One-on-one meetings are not an efficient marketing tool, but they can be a good way to cement a relationship with an existing client.

Handling RFPs

It's great when a client calls and says, "I want you to do this project for me. Just tell me how much it'll cost." For most independent info pros, negotiating with a client regarding the scope or budget of a project doesn't involve bidding against other info pros—your clients call you because they're already sold on your ability to do the work.

However, there will come a time in your business that you encounter a Request for Proposal, or RFP. Government agencies are often required to competitively bid all contracts with outside vendors. Some corporations also have formal bidding procedures in which at least three or four contractors must be solicited for any project over a certain size. Responding to RFPs, by definition, puts you in a situation where you're bidding against other providers, and your odds of winning that contract are, all other things being equal, at best one in three. And you have no assurance that the organization issuing the RFP will award the contract to *any* of the bidders. If all the bids come in higher than expected, the organization may simply decide to cancel the project. Given the amount of work involved in responding to an RFP—they usually require extensive descriptions of what you intend to do, how, and when—you are investing a significant chunk of time with no assurance that it will result in a paying job. But, to be fair, let's walk through the advantages and disadvantages of responding to RFPs.

Advantages of RFPs

- Contracts that are awarded through RFPs are usually substantial.
- You have spelled out all the particulars of the project ahead of time, so any add-ons can be billed separately.
- Even if the person you originally deal with leaves the organization, your contract remains intact.
- If you always have a number of RFPs in the pipeline, you have the chance of at least one contract coming through at any given time.

Disadvantages of RFPs

- RFPs often require extensive descriptions of your services and can take hours to prepare.
- The odds of being awarded a contract through a competitive RFP are low; you will lose more RFPs than you win.
- There is no guarantee that anyone will be awarded a contract through an RFP; the agency may decide that no proposals were acceptable.
- RFPs are sometimes poorly written, but bidders have very little leeway in modifying the proposal.

Government Contracts the Easy Way

Bidding for government contracts can be a time-consuming process, but there are other ways to land contracts with the government. Instead of looking for solicitations for bids, focus on finding contacts within government agencies that need your services. In a sense, you can treat the government like any other prospective client. Identify an agency's information needs. Figure out how you can solve those needs. Write a one-page description of what you offer and what problems you can solve. Look through the agency's Web site to identify who is most likely to need your services, recognize your value, and authorize a contract. Get on the phone and confirm the name, title, and address of each of your prospects. Then send each a personalized letter spelling all this out.

After all this, you still may have to respond to RFPs, but if you stay in contact with your prospects and talk with them about what they need and how you can meet those needs, it's much more likely that the RFP will be written with you in mind.

If you do decide to respond to RFPs, you may find it useful to consult the Small Business Administration's site (www.sba.gov). Its Government Contracting section (www.sba.gov/GC) includes a collection of resources to help companies contract with the federal government. And if you decide that you are not interested in responding to RFPs, consider using the response that Amelia Kassel, owner of MarketingBase, gives when asked: "MarketingBase does not bid but instead looks for a fit between ourselves and potential clients. We are not in the business of 'competing'; rather, we base our success on working with clients who understand our particular methodology and reputation, and who consider us an excellent choice for their situation."

The Art of Proposal Writing

Although responding to RFPs may not be an efficient use of your time, writing a proposal for a client is different matter. In this case, you've already been talking about a project, you agree on the scope of what's involved, and you prepare a formal proposal explaining what you'll do and what it'll cost. Such proposals are generally completed in a noncompetitive environment—that is, you aren't bidding against anyone else for this job. Instead, you are formalizing the relationship, defining all aspects of the job, and getting a written commitment from your client.

I am mindful, though, of the late Sue Rugge's advice. She cautioned independent info pros against calling the proposal a "contract" or writing it in legalese with lots of whereases and party-of-the-first-parts, since that might trigger an automatic review by the organization's lawyers—and we know how long that process can take. It might also scare the client, who suddenly thinks, "Gee, what am I getting into here? Perhaps I should just reconsider the whole thing." A signed proposal or letter of agreement, while it doesn't contain all the dotted I's and crossed T's of a formal contract, indicates the understanding between you and your client—you'll do the work and your client will pay you for it. Call it a statement of work, or a project description ... just don't call it a contract.

A proposal serves several purposes. It defines the scope of the project, which ensures not only that you and your client are in accord, but also that you can charge separately for any work the client requests that falls outside the original scope. The proposal also serves as a marketing tool; if you write it well, your description of the project will help answer the question, "Why should I pay you that much for your work? What am I getting for it?" And it articulates your payment requirements, which is particularly important if you require prepayment or payments at certain stages of the work.

It's a wise investment to have your attorney draft a generic proposal that you can modify for each situation. Just make sure she writes it in nonlegalese—to avoid intimidating the client and to enable you to tweak it as necessary. The proposal can be as short or as long as you want, but must include the following:

- Outline of all aspects of the project—the questions you're addressing or the problems you're there to fix, described in as much detail as you and the client think necessary

- Description of deliverables—a written report, a spreadsheet, a PowerPoint presentation, an in-person consultation, and so on

- Time frame and due date—if this is contingent on receipt of prepayment, you can indicate the total length of the project instead of an actual deadline

- Budget—either a not-to-exceed figure or a description of what you estimate the project will cost

- Whether the work will be done at your client's site or at your office (you may not need to spell this out, unless you want to ensure space at the client's office)

- The resources you'll need from the client—if your client expects you to use online information services for which he has an enterprise-wide subscription, you need to spell out how you will get access to those services

- Terms of payment—how much you require before work can begin and how soon after completion of the project you require the final payment

- Liability statement or disclaimer—ask your lawyer to write this in clear terms that a non-lawyer can understand

- Copyright limitations—spell out that you are providing information for one-time use by the client, and that posting the material on an intranet or redistributing multiple copies must be negotiated separately

- "Sell-by" date for the proposal—specify how long the quote is valid, lest someone come back next year asking you to perform the work at this year's fee structure

A Sample Proposal

123 Main St.
Buena Vista, CO 81211
719.123.4567

To: Pat Adams
From: Robin Sullivan
Subject: Proposal for Research Services
Date: December 1, 2003

Based on our telephone conversation, the following is a proposal for the market research we discussed.

Scope of Work

A World of Information Inc. will provide the following research services to The Denton Corp.:

- Identify companies that provide products in direct competition to Denton's Widgelator
- Provide company information, description of products, and samples of products, if possible, of Widgelator competitors
- Determine trends in the Widgelator market

Research Methodology

We expect to conduct research using several professional online services and the Web. We will also contact companies directly, without disclosing information about the client for whom we are working and while abiding by the Code of Professional Business Practices of the Association of Independent Information Professionals. The attached sheet describes the professional backgrounds of the principals of A World of Information, who collectively have over 30 years of research experience.

Deliverables

Industry analysis, company profiles, and a discussion of trends in the market will be prepared in Microsoft Word. The report will be delivered electronically; the product samples will be sent via overnight courier at the end of the project.

Budget and Time Frame

The total budget for this project will not exceed $10,000. This includes researchers' time billed at $150/hour; the cost of online research, telephone calls, delivery charges, and other miscellaneous expenses, billed at cost. Prepayment of $5,000 is required before work can begin. The work will be completed within four weeks of receipt of the deposit payment. The remainder of the cost will be billed at the conclusion of the project. Payment terms are net 30 days.

Liability and Copyright Statement

A World of Information, Inc. shall make a good faith effort to provide services and work product that are of a high quality and that meet The Denton Corp.'s needs and expectations. Every attempt is made to ensure accuracy; however, A World of Information has no control over the quality of the information retrieved from the various sources used. We cannot guarantee the accuracy or completeness of the material provided. Due to the highly subjective nature of research, we cannot guarantee results. If you plan to distribute copies or make the material provided on an intranet or Internet Web site, you must negotiate payment with the copyright owners.

This quote is valid for 45 days.

Get It in Writing?

Some independent info pros write up a proposal or statement of work for each job they do. Others—and I'm in this latter group—only use written proposals for first-time clients and for projects that exceed a certain threshold in terms of either budget or complexity. One consideration is whether the client needs something signed before the work begins in order to get your invoice processed. Another factor is your gut instinct; if your client sounds like he may not feel confident about the scope of the project, or if you have any concerns about whether the client will pay your invoice, a written contract is essential. And if you require prepayment of all or a portion of the not-to-exceed budget before you'll begin work, you will need a written proposal.

If the project isn't big enough to justify a formal proposal and you work with the client regularly, it's a good idea to at least confirm the request via e-mail or fax. Your confirmation might be no more than the following:

> Susan:
>
> It was nice talking with you today. Glad to hear that the speech you gave was so well-received. This is to confirm that you want me to see what I can find on the current state of K-12 math and science education. I'll e-mail this information to you by close of business on Friday, and the total cost won't exceed $500.
>
> As always, thanks for calling me. It's always a pleasure working with you.
>
> Best regards,
>
> Robin

It's not fancy, but it reiterates the key elements of the project—subject, budget, and deadline—so that you know that you and the client are in agreement. Some info pros ask their clients to either initial a fax copy or reply to your e-mail indicating that they agree with the description of and budget for the project. It depends on your comfort level and your clients' schedules. I find this additional step a burden, and I want to offer my clients as frictionless an interaction as possible. On the other hand, if you have no prior experience with a particular client, it makes sense to be a bit more formal. It sends the message that you take this business relationship seriously and expect your client to do the same, particularly when it comes to processing your invoice.

When to Say "No"

I know—it sounds crazy to turn down work. However, sometimes it just doesn't pay to accept a job, and it's better to recognize this ahead of time than to try to extricate yourself from a mess later. Here are some situations that have "Just Say No" written all over them. If you find yourself in one of these scenarios, read Chapter 14, Subcontracting, or I'll Scratch Your Back if You Scratch Mine, to find out how to pass the work along to someone better suited for the project.

- Subject specialization. No one can do all kinds of research well, and we all have limited expertise outside our primary subject area. If you're a legal researcher, for example, you probably aren't proficient in chemical research as well. If your expertise is in radiology, you probably shouldn't take on research that requires in-depth analysis of financial statements. The time it takes you to get up to speed in an entirely new area will far exceed the hours you can justifiably bill your client and, frankly, you just may not have the background knowledge to do a competent job in an entirely unfamiliar area.

- Time crunch. There are only 24 hours in a day, and you don't want to spend every one of them working. Sometimes a client will call with a project that you simply don't have time for, unless you do work around the clock. Take it from someone who has tried the work-all-night trick—you can't do a decent job at 2:00 a.m., regardless of how many cups of coffee you drink. Suppose a client calls at 4:00 on a Friday afternoon and asks if you can get the results to him by Monday morning? Sure, you could work all weekend, but the message you're sending is, "I'm available whenever you need me. No need to plan ahead; I'm always ready to drop what I'm doing for you." That sounds very customer-friendly, but it also means that you are willing to give up any free time you have—and that's a first-class ticket to a big case of burn-out. Instead, train your clients to plan ahead rather than assume that you will routinely give up your weekend for their last-minute requests. Believe it or not, they will find a way to call you earlier in the process once they learn that that's what it takes.

- Client conflict. This is a tough call; if you work for one company, can you also work for its competitor? It depends on what the project entails, how much access you have to proprietary information, and whether you have signed a contract with a client that forbids working for its competitors. Use the "headlines test": How would you feel if tomorrow's lead story in the *New York Times* was that you were providing research services to both Ford and General Motors? If you're simply gathering public information, my gut tells me you don't have a conflict. On the other hand, if the work you're doing for Ford involves an intimate knowledge of its proprietary designs for new vehicles, you shouldn't be doing similar work for GM. (See Chapter 15, Ethics and Legalities, for more discussion of conflicts of interest and client confidentiality.)

- Personal conflict. If you're a strict vegetarian and get a call from the American Veal Association, you might want to turn down the work. If you believe that abortion is wrong, you probably don't want to take on a project from Planned Parenthood. But handle your refusal professionally; there's no need to go into the details of why you want to have nothing to do with a prospective client. All you have to say is, "I'm sorry, but I have a conflict of interest and can't do any work for your organization." Period. Let the prospective client think that the conflict is with an existing client rather than with your conscience. It's not worth getting into an argument about why you find their stand morally repugnant; remember, the person you're talking with may eventually change jobs and call you from an organization that you'd be glad to work for—or at least wouldn't have qualms about considering a client.

The Project from Hell

What happens when you *don't* say no when you should? You can wind up embroiled in the project from Hell. Established info pros have all, at one point or another, accepted a job that their gut told them to turn down. The result? The client is angry because he didn't get what he expected, or he thinks the bill is excessive, or he wants you to do far more than what you thought you had agreed to.

The one thing not to do in a situation like this is argue. Your client is already unhappy/anxious/impatient/frustrated/you-fill-in-the-blank. If you get an irate-sounding phone call or e-mail, try to put yourself in the client's shoes before getting defensive. At the moment, it doesn't really matter what happened; what your client wants to hear is that you care and that you'll make it better.

What *not* to say in this situation:

- "This has never happened before."
- "But this is what you told me you wanted! I did just what you asked for. What's your problem?"
- "Well, as soon as you pay my invoice, I'll see what else I can do for you."

What you can say to defuse the situation:

- "I feel terrible that this happened."
- "I am so sorry that this wasn't what you expected; let's talk about what I can do to fix it."
- "Thanks so much for explaining what you had expected. Let me get back to work and see what I can find."

Note that you don't necessarily have to admit fault—although, of course, if the problem was your fault, or due to a misunderstanding or faulty assumption that might well have been yours, you should say so. The object is to demonstrate to your client that you "share her pain." Once you both calm down, you can figure out where and why the miscommunication happened. When you get down to it, projects from Hell are usually caused by a failure to communicate. You didn't explain to the client that you might not find exactly what she wanted, or the two of you didn't come to an understanding on the parameters of the project, or you didn't alert her early in the process that her initial expectations were not reasonable, or you took on a project that you didn't fully understand, or you didn't listen to your gut when it said, "Walk away from this one … it's a loser."

You might notice a pattern here; just about all the reasons that this project went bad include you. That doesn't mean that the customer is always right; in fact, the client may be a raving idiot. But it's your responsibility to recognize and watch for those pitfalls and address problems before they become unsolvable—by taking more time to discuss and manage the client's expectations, by articulating the limits on what you can and will do within the client's budget, and by walking away from a job that you don't think you could do splendidly. Of course, this assumes that you keep your part of the bargain—you do deliver what you promised, on time and within budget. And what if you can't? You pick up the phone as soon as you realize that there's going to be a problem, and you negotiate, with the understanding that this is *your* problem and the client is under no obligation to let you off the hook. Your job is to take responsibility—although not necessarily blame—for any project that went bad.

What do you do if, despite your best efforts, your client is not happy with the results of your work? Up to a certain point, it makes sense to absorb the cost, at least for the portion of your invoice that covers your time as distinguished from your direct expenses. Call it a learning experience. Remember that a client whom you treat respectfully will probably call you again. See what additional work you can do to make the client happy, and don't bill the additional time. Consider charging the client for your out-of-pocket expenses (such as online research) only, or invoicing for expenses and just a portion of your time.

I have several long-time clients with whom I have occasionally experienced miscommunications. I have always apologized, expressed my mortification that this misunderstanding happened, and either not billed them for the job or charged them only for my out-of-pocket costs. They have always returned with more work; I have demonstrated that I want their business and am willing to give them the benefit of the doubt. Up to a certain point, it's a good investment to let one invoice go, if it's likely that the client will call you again.

Of course, you must see how the client behaves in the future. If you sense as you start to negotiate the next project that you are going to have problems, you might want to politely turn down the work and refer the client to someone else.

How to Fire a Client

Wait—you're supposed to *find* clients, not fire them, right? In general, that's true, but one of the perks of running your own business is that you can gracefully get rid of clients whom you just don't want to work with any more. It's always a hard decision; you hate to lose the income from any client. On the other hand, being an independent info pro means having to manage yourself, your time, and your energy. If a client becomes a burden, it might be time to let him go.

When should you think about firing a client, or, to put it more gently, helping a client find another independent info pro who can better handle his unique needs?

- When you feel angry or anxious whenever the client calls
- If working for the client is significantly more time-consuming and less profitable than doing similar jobs for other clients
- If the client is consistently verbally abusive, offensive, rude, or demanding
- If the client often complains about your rates
- If the client is habitually very slow to pay your invoices
- If the client pressures you to do something that you believe is unethical or illegal

Even though it's tempting to simply call the client and yell, "I'm never going to work for you again! Ever!", this is probably not the wisest approach. Life's too short and the market is too small for you to create a scene. The person you slam the telephone down on today may be working for your best client next month. And, in most situations, the softer path is just as effective and far easier. The secret is not to let the client know he's being fired, or at least not *why*.

Think back to high school. When you were dating and wanted to break up, the standard line was, "It's not you, it's me. I'm just not right for you." Take that sentiment, tune it to the business world, and it really can work. When I started my business, one of my first clients had me coming on-site for 20 hours a week at a greatly reduced hourly rate. For the first six or nine months, that was great; it was welcome revenue at a point when I didn't have much other work. But I finally realized that it was taking the time I needed to devote to growing the business, and the money did not justify it. After a year, I sat down with my client and said, "Ken, I have really enjoyed working with you folks. Unfortunately, I'm going to have to raise my rates next month to double what I've been charging you. I know that's probably more than you can pay, and I'll work with you to find someone else who can take my place." A month later, we parted ways amicably, Ken never realizing that I'd fired him. And, scary as it was to give up a client who took up half my time, within a week I had found two new clients who paid my full hourly rate and who more than made up for the lost income.

Another approach, if you can't just double your rates, is to tell the client that her projects are falling outside your area of expertise, or that you are becoming so busy with other work that you can no longer fulfill her requests within their deadlines. And if the client doesn't believe you, turn down her next requests, using whatever reason you gave her—you simply can't meet the deadline, or you can't take on the request because it goes outside your realm of expertise. Yes, it takes nerves of steel to turn down work this way, but you can do it. If possible, refer the client to a colleague, or to the referral program of the Association of Independent Information Professionals (www.aiip.org/AboutAIIP/referral.html). Just because the client didn't work well with you doesn't mean that someone else can't handle her. Dog trainers say that there are no bad dogs, only untrained ones. Similarly, perhaps there are no bad clients, just ones who haven't yet found the independent info pro with whom they can work happily and productively.

Top Tips for Managing Clients

- A variety of clients makes for a stronger business than a client base of one or two.
- Value your time; try to turn down requests for face-to-face meetings with prospects.
- Learn to gracefully extricate yourself from conversations with prospects who will not turn into clients.
- Think twice about responding to competitive bidding requests.
- Use proposals to sell yourself and manage your clients' expectations.
- Turn down projects and fire clients if the chemistry isn't there.
- Accept responsibility (if not blame) when a project goes bad.
- Don't let a client know he's being fired; let him down gently.

Chapter 12

Money, Money, Money

I suppose that all of us start our own businesses because we love the work, love the independence, and love the challenge, but we also do it for the money. This chapter looks at the financial issues that are central to starting and running an independent info pro business.

Financing Your Business

Section One of this book talks about the things you need to do and the equipment you need to buy before you launch your business. It might feel rather daunting, particularly after you've read through Chapter 8, Setting Up Your Business, and you total up all those startup expenses. For many people, this can amount to $8,000 or $10,000—probably more than you have sitting around in your checking account.

You have several options for funding your business. The simplest and most typical is to pay for it out of your savings. If you're thinking about starting a business, set up a separate savings account now and plan to put several hundred dollars in it every month. Yes, that may mean eliminating some discretionary spending, but it also means that you'll start your business without the burden of debt.

Another option is to write a thorough business plan (see Chapter 7, Before You Launch) and present it to selected family members and friends. Ask them to lend you a portion of what you need, at an interest rate equivalent to what they would earn from the bank on a certificate of deposit, and for a period of, say, five years. Of course, you will treat this loan as one that absolutely must be paid off as promised—the last thing you want to do is lose a friend over a business debt.

The U.S. Small Business Administration provides information on low-interest loans. The SBA doesn't provide loans directly, but works with a number of lending organizations to enable start-up and growing businesses to obtain financing. In order to qualify for an SBA-guaranteed loan, you must meet certain criteria, including having already tapped into your personal assets to fund the business and being able to repay the loan from your business's cash flow. See the Financing Your Business section of the SBA's Web site at www.sba.gov/financing.

Local banks and credit unions may also be willing to lend you money, provided you can demonstrate that you have a sound business proposal. Some independent info pros tap into the value of their house by taking out a home equity loan. Note that most lending organizations—whether an SBA-guaranteed source or a local financial institution—expect you to invest your savings or personal equity in the business as well. A lender generally won't finance more than 50 percent of your business, which means that you will have to invest your own money even if you do take out a loan.

The last, and least attractive, option is to put your expenses on a credit card and pay off the debt as you can. Given that the interest rate on credit cards is usually at least 18 percent, this can be a quick path to failure. The total cost of an item purchased on a credit card and paid off gradually can easily double, once you factor in what you're paying in interest. If the only way you can finance your business is through credit card debt, my suggestion would be to hold off on starting your business until you are in a stronger financial situation.

The Small Business Administration has a discussion of finding startup money at its "Small Business Startup Kit" Web page (www.sba.gov/starting/finding.html). The section on how to write a loan proposal is particularly useful.

Accounting 101

Fortunately, you don't need to know much about accounting to run your business, particularly if you work with an accountant to set up your books. Unless you have a background in finance or accounting, you're probably better off with simple money management software such as QuickBooks (www.intuit.com), rather than trying to maintain your accounts manually. If you choose Quicken instead of QuickBooks, be sure to purchase the "Home & Business" version, which includes essential business functions such as invoicing, rather than the Home version, which focuses on cash management for personal use.

If you choose not to have an accountant set up the initial accounts for you, and you live in the U.S., go through the most current IRS Form 1040 and Schedule C and note how the IRS categorizes expenses and income. For Canadian companies, you'll be filing a T2 tax return and Schedule 1 if you're incorporated, or Form T2124, Statement of Business Activities, or Form T2032, Statement of Professional Activities, if you are a sole proprietor. Note how the CCRA (Canada Customs & Revenue Agency) categorizes income and expenses, and set up your accounting software with those same categories. I'm afraid I can't claim any expertise in the tax laws of other countries. My best advice is to talk to an accounting professional who works with small businesses, especially service businesses, and one- or two-person consultancies.

In addition, think through how *you* want to track your income and expenses. For example, I have separate income categories for regular research and for research that I provide at a discounted rate, for online charges that I bill to clients, for speaking fees, for consulting services, and so on. To the IRS, it's all just gross receipts, but I can generate reports in QuickBooks that show me how much of my revenue comes from each type of work, how much of my research time I discount, and so on. For expenses, I track the IRS forms as closely as possible, with a few subcategories that help me monitor my cash flow. For example, I have categories for advertising, referral fees, business travel, health insurance, and utilities, all of which are line items on Form 1040. But I also break out my office expenses into specific subcategories that I find useful for various purposes. The "online costs" category, for example, enables me to compare my online costs to the online charges I bill back to clients (they should be roughly equal).

You will need to set up a business checking account and savings account in addition to whatever personal bank accounts you already have. The IRS looks more favorably on sole proprietors who keep their personal and business money separate, and it's just simpler this way. Note that some banks require proof that you are already in business before they will open business accounts. Make sure you have your business license or whatever other forms your local jurisdiction requires before you head to the bank.

Why should you have a business savings account? You'll need to put money aside regularly for quarterly tax payments (see the section below on paying the tax man), and you'll want to set aside funds for new equipment and unplanned expenditures. And, as you learn about the inevitable ebb and flow of income, you will have to have saved enough money to cover your overhead expenses during those months when your income is exceeded by your outgo.

The accounting issue that puzzled me most when I started my business was how I actually paid myself and reimbursed myself for petty cash expenditures. I finally realized that, as long as everything is eventually processed through my business checking account, it would all get accounted for. So, for example, I save my receipts for business expenses that I paid for out of my own pocket, such as cab fare and postage, until it amounted to $100 or so. Then I write myself a check from my business account just as I would pay any other bill, and categorize the expenses appropriately. Likewise, I pay myself a salary by writing myself a check and categorizing the expense as either draw (when I was a sole proprietor) or salary (now that I am incorporated). If this sounds complicated, pay an accountant to walk you through the steps the first time. It's pretty simple once you get used to thinking of your checking account in business terms.

Billing and Collections

Unlike employees, who receive a steady paycheck, independent info pros only get paid after they've billed their clients and collected the money. In order to maintain at least some semblance of a steady cash flow, it's important to invoice quickly and follow up promptly on any invoices that are past due.

The Check's in the Mail

Some info pros require prepayment in full for every job. This works well if you price your projects on a flat fee basis rather than on time plus expenses. (See Chapter 13, Setting Rates and Fees, for a discussion of the pros and cons of each approach.) However, you often won't know the exact cost of the project ahead of time. It's still wise to require prepayment of at least a portion of the not-to-exceed budget, particularly if it's a large project. The advantages of requiring prepayment are:

- You ensure that the client is willing and able to pay you.
- You are protected from a total loss if the client contests the invoice.

- You help your cash flow by receiving money up front for expenses that will come due before your client pays your invoice.

The disadvantages of requiring prepayment include:

- Some organizations cannot generate a check quickly enough to let you get started in time to meet the deadline.
- Your client may be reluctant to pay you before seeing the results of the work

An alternative to requiring a prepayment is to set up what is called a merchant account with a bank so that you can accept credit card payments. Then you have the choice of either charging the client immediately for a portion of the project or holding his credit card number so you can charge him at the end of the job. Of course, worst-case scenario, the client might dispute a charge, but I have found that any client who trusts me enough to give me her credit card number is going to be a good client. See the sidebar "Will That Be Visa or MasterCard?" for a discussion of how to accept credit cards.

My informal guideline is to require either a credit card number or partial prepayment on the first job I do for any client, and whenever a project's not-to-exceed budget exceeds $1,000. Use your own judgment, balancing the need to manage your cash flow with the flexibility and trustworthiness of your clients.

And what happens if your client tells you that the check is in the mail? Should you start work immediately? Only if you have money to burn. If I've decided to require prepayment from a client, I always wait until I have the check in hand. Even then, I sometimes call the bank and ask for confirmation that the account has enough money in it to cover the check. Banks will not disclose an account balance, but they will tell you whether, at the time you call, it contains sufficient funds to honor the check. In these days of electronic funds transfer and overnight courier, if a client really wants you to get started immediately, she can figure out a way to get the prepayment to you quickly.

Be Explicit

When you are discussing a project with a client, take time to explicitly discuss payment terms, and listen to the client's response. If your client is a consultant and will be billing a third party for your work, you must spell out that you expect your

"Will That Be Visa or MasterCard?"

Back in the old days when I started my business, it was very difficult to convince a bank to grant me merchant status so that I could accept credit cards. Fortunately, banks' attitudes toward small and home-based businesses have changed a lot over the years, and now the hardest part is figuring out which bank offers you the best deal.

The easiest approach is to go to the Web sites for Visa and MasterCard and look through their lists of "acquirers" or "merchant service providers"—banks and other financial institutions through whom you can process credit card charges. Visa's list is at usa.visa.com/business/merchants/get_account_list.html (or go to www.visa.com, then the Business area, and select the Merchants area). MasterCard asks you to fill out a profile of your business at www.mastercardintl.com/merchant/acqdir/; when you've filled out the form, you get a list of merchant service providers that match your needs (or go to www.mastercard.com and click the link to Accepting MasterCard to get to the form).

Shop around and compare costs before you sign up. As with any other banking service, charges vary considerably. Expect to pay either a one-time charge or a monthly service fee for a terminal or the software to process charges. The bank charges a certain percentage of each transaction (usually 2 to 4 percent, depending on how fast you want to get paid), and most also impose a monthly minimum fee of $20 or $30. While the monthly minimum may cause you alarm, think of it as payment insurance and just build the cost into your overhead.

American Express has a different setup than MasterCard and Visa; instead of going through a bank, you establish a merchant account directly with Am Ex. Go to www.americanexpress.com and click the Merchants link to apply for a merchant account.

invoice to be paid within the agreed-upon time. My usual speech goes something like this: "Although I know that you're working for your own client on this job, *you* are *my* client so I'll need to be paid within 30 days of the invoice, regardless of when or whether you're paid by your client. Will there be any problem with that?" If the client sounds hesitant or ambiguous, I ask for prepayment or a credit card number. It is always foolhardy to agree to wait for payment until your client gets paid; you'll have no idea when that happens and, in any event, his cash flow (or lack of it) is not your problem. You have to manage your cash flow, and your client must manage his.

Listen to your gut. There are times when, as soon as you bring up the matter of payment, you get a sense that this client just isn't going to pay the bill. If that happens, it is perfectly reasonable for you to require prepayment or to decline the work.

Ask if They're Happy

Always ask your client at the end of the job whether she's satisfied with the results, even—especially!—when you think she may not be entirely happy. Does she have any questions? Would she like any additional work done? Unresolved client dissatisfaction is what leads to slow- or no-pay clients. I know, it's hard to ask clients if they're happy, because then they might complain. But my experience is that an unhappy client whom you talk with right away can be turned into a satisfied client by doing a little extra work on the project. But an unhappy client whose problem you don't attempt to resolve can turn into a *very* unhappy client.

Presenting the Invoice

When you invoice a client, you are sending a message about the value you attach to your services. Whether you use preprinted invoices from QuickBooks or other stationery forms, or simply your letterhead, you want an invoice that looks official and is clear and concise. Be sure that, whatever format you use, you include:

- The date
- The word "INVOICE" (some accounts payable departments will not pay from a "statement of accounts," for example)
- Your company name, address, and telephone number
- The name and address of your client
- The invoice number
- The payment terms (e.g., net 30 days)
- A description of the services provided and the cost for each item

- The total charges for the work
- Your Taxpayer Identification Number (See Chapter 6, Structuring Your Business, for more about your TIN)

With a new client's first invoice, I include IRS Form W-9, which provides my Taxpayer ID number in a format that accounts payable departments expect. If you don't include it, your invoice may be delayed while the accounting folks mail you a copy of the W-9 to fill out and return. Save them the trouble and time by sending it with the invoice. You can download a PDF version of the W-9 from the IRS's Web site (www.irs.gov).

Make your description of the services you're billing as professional-sounding as you can. Rather than charge for "library research," say "provided analysis of the Chinese tungsten industry." Make sure that the invoice reflects value provided, not just work done. Some independent info pros like to list all aspects of the project individually: "Conducted six telephone interviews, obtained three market research reports, conducted extensive online research," and so on. Others prefer to simply describe the focus of the project without going into detail. I think the latter looks more professional, but some clients like to have all the charges spelled out.

Some independent info pros send out all their invoices at the end of the month. There is a certain efficiency in this, but it also delays payment, in some cases by several weeks. Instead, consider sending out the invoice as soon as the project is completed and you have confirmed with the client that he is satisfied and no additional work is needed at this time. One exception is if you are doing several small jobs for a single client. As a courtesy, ask the client if she would prefer to receive one combined invoice at the end of the month or individual invoices as you go along. Some of my small-but-steady clients like separate invoices, because they pass along the costs for each project to their clients; others prefer one invoice, because it means less paperwork to process on their end. If a project extends over several months, establish at the beginning that you will invoice at the end of each month for the work conducted during that month.

Net 30 Means Net 30

Most companies send out bills with an indication of the date by which you are expected to pay. In the business world, this is often written as "net 30" or "net 15." Net 30 means that you are expected to pay the net total (that is, the total after taking into account any credits or refunds) within 30 days of the date of the invoice. Net 30 is typical, but other payment terms exist. You can set any terms you like, but regardless of what you tell your clients, most of them will cut you a check 30 days after the date of the invoice. I always chuckle when I receive invoices marked "payment due upon receipt." Unless the vendor and I negotiated that beforehand, I pay the next time I'm writing checks; I'm not going to stop what I'm doing and pay it immediately, or even the next day.

It's important to stay on top of your receivables. Your accounting software can generate past-due reports that show you which invoices haven't been paid on time. I usually give my client a few days after the due date, because I've found that some companies have a policy of mailing the check the day it's due. But once an invoice is more than two or three days beyond the due date, call the client to confirm that the invoice was received and to check whether the accounting department needs any additional information. (Did you include a W-9 with your invoice?) If everything is in order and the accounting folks say the check is coming, give it a couple of weeks and then call again to check the status. Be courteous but firm. See Chapter 15, Ethics and Legalities, for a discussion of collections issues, and keep in mind that it is sometimes better to walk away from a deadbeat client than to take him to court. If you have a client who is habitually slow to pay, you may want to require prepayment of some or all of the budget before you begin work. There is no reason for you to act as a short-term lender for clients who have trouble managing their cash flow.

You might also offer to let the client establish a deposit account; they pay you a certain amount up front and you provide service until the account is depleted. It's a great idea but very few independent info pros ever find clients willing to do this. It does work well in doc del businesses that bill multiple small amounts to the same client over a period of weeks or months. If you do set up a deposit account for a client, make sure that:

- The client understands that any money not used by the end of the year or another agreed-upon deadline belongs to you (after all, your client is paying for your promised availability).
- You provide a monthly statement of the account.
- You establish how low the account balance can go before it must be replenished.

Cash Flow

Do you remember the character named Wimpy in the Popeye cartoon? He struggled with cash flow and his refrain was "I will gladly pay you Tuesday for a hamburger today."

During your first couple of years in business, you may feel a bit like Wimpy. The telephone bill comes in and has to be paid, regardless of whether you've been paid by your last client. Get in the habit of banking any extra money. You don't know yet where your business's peaks and valleys are going to be, and you need enough money in the bank to pay the bills. This is particularly true if you do a lot of research using the professional online services; you will inevitably receive the invoice from your online vendor before you get payment from your client.

Watch your overhead expenses—the costs you incur independent of how much work you're doing and how much income you expect. (See the sidebar, "Overhead vs. Cost of Goods Sold" for a discussion of what overhead is.) It's nice to take potential clients out to lunch, and Caller ID seems so handy, and, gosh, you're going through those expensive color inkjet cartridges awfully fast, and, and, and ... suddenly you wonder where all the money has gone. Think long and hard about any potential expense that isn't directly related to gaining new clients or providing billable information services to existing clients. After you've been in business a year or two, you can think about buying that high-end color printer; until then, keep your overhead to a minimum.

Some professional online services impose monthly service charges or minimum usage fees. If you are a member of the Association of Independent Information Professionals (www.aiip.org), you can take advantage of vendor discount programs that eliminate the monthly fees for a number of online information sources. In general, avoid buying anything in bulk that you can pay for à la carte. For example, instead of signing up for unlimited online searching at $1,500 a month, stick with the pay-as-you-go option, even though you'll be paying a nondiscount rate per search. Why risk not being able to bill out the entire $1,500 every month, when you can buy (and charge the client for) only what you use?

Keep track of when bills are due and make sure that you pay your vendors on time. Your credit rating is a valuable asset and, once lost, is difficult to restore. If you think you're going to be late in making a payment, call the vendor, explain the situation and see if you can negotiate a better payment option. You don't want your phone line to go dead or your e-mail address to disappear because you didn't pay your bills promptly. Your clients will be inclined to shop elsewhere if they have trouble getting in touch with you.

Even if an accountant or assistant routinely manages your invoices and payments, you should monitor your cash flow weekly. Know how much money you have available, what bills are coming due, and when you can expect to receive payment from clients. Legally, *you* are the one responsible for your finances, so get used to monitoring them regularly.

Overhead vs. Cost of Goods Sold

There are two broad types of expenses in business—overhead and the cost of goods (or services) sold. Overhead is what you spend to establish your company and stay in business, including items like your Internet connection, business cards, health insurance, and office supplies. These are expenses you have to pay, whether you have any money coming in or not. You can't charge any of them directly back to a client, although your hourly fee is calculated to cover overhead costs. (See Chapter 13, Setting Rates and Fees, for more on setting your hourly fee.) It's important to keep an eye on your overhead expenses, because they can eat up a good deal of your profit.

The cost of services or of goods sold is what you spend in the process of providing your research or other services. It includes expenses such as searching professional online services, photocopying journal articles for a client, books or reports you purchase on behalf of a client, long-distance charges incurred during telephone research, and fees you pay subcontractors for research. These costs are directly tied to how much and what kind of work you do. Generally, you pass along all these charges to your clients. Make sure that your cost of services per project isn't so high that there's nothing left in the budget to bill for your time; if you have a not-to-exceed budget of $800 and you spend $700 in direct costs to obtain the information, your profit on that project is awfully low.

Paying Yourself

Believe it or not, paying yourself is sometimes one of the hardest aspects of managing your money. How do you determine how much to take out of the business checking account as salary or draw? What if you need the money later to pay bills?

I have found it helpful to work backward. At the end of each month, look at how much money came in. Subtract any income you collected for expenses you must pay, such as online research; you'll just be sending that money right back out when the vendor's bill arrives. Assume that 25 percent of what's left will go to the IRS soon, as an estimated tax payment. Then take out whatever is required to pay your overhead bills, including regular payments to a retirement fund, and set aside an amount for the business savings account—for new equipment, unexpected repairs, and to pay other bills when you don't have enough income to cover them. What's left after that is your salary.

Some info pros find it difficult to be this disciplined about money; they tend to spend it on whatever seems most pressing at the moment, as soon as it comes in. If that sounds like you, just remember that you don't have a choice about paying bills and the IRS. If what's left over only pays for peanut butter sandwiches and spaghetti, well, next month you'll redouble your marketing efforts.

Paying the Tax Man

If you live in the U.S., about one-fourth of every check you receive will go right back out again to the IRS. You're no longer a payroll employee; no one is withholding the IRS's take on your behalf. Four times a year, even before they ask for it (yes, I know it's painful), you'll have to pay the IRS—or, outside the U.S., the equivalent government tax collection agency—25 percent of your estimated total income tax for the year. This process is commonly known as paying your estimated quarterlies.

But how do you know what your total income tax liability will be? After you've been in business a year, it's pretty easy. The IRS lets you base your quarterly payments on the prior year's total tax liability. Even if this year's revenue is much higher than last year's, you probably won't be penalized for underpaying your taxes during the year, as long as you base the payment on the prior year's tax bill. (Of course, you'll have to pay the difference when you file your formal tax return in April, but at least you've been able to delay the day of reckoning.) Note, however, that tax laws change all the time, and if you expect your revenue this year to be significantly larger than last year's, consult a tax advisor.

All well and good, but what about the first year you're in business? Ask colleagues who went through a similar start-up what you might expect to spend, talk with an accountant, and then make a reasonable guess. Revisit your business plan as the year progresses, and make any necessary adjustments in your cash flow projections. But remember to make those quarterly payments. Go to the IRS Web site (www.irs.gov) to read about estimated tax payments and to download Form 1040-ES. And note that if your state has an income tax, you will have to send quarterly estimated tax payments to the state revenue office as well.

Be sure you keep careful receipts for and records of all your business expenses. And keep in mind that your definition of a "business expense" has to match that of the IRS. Sole proprietors and small businesses are disproportionately targeted for audits, and you want to be sure that you have documentation for anything you claim as a business expense. The IRS has a fairly clear description of what constitutes a business expense for a small business or self-employed individual. From the main Web site, www.irs.gov, drill down to Businesses, then Small Business/Self-Employed. The common-sense answer to "what is a business expense?" is that it has to pass the straight-face test. You can often tack a vacation onto the end of a business trip, for example, but you can't write off the entire expense of your housecleaning service if your office occupies only one-tenth of the total floor space of your house. And, though your health club membership keeps you fit and alert, it's not a legitimate business write-off.

Living Large, or Managing Your Money

- Be prepared to invest your own money in your business before you start looking for loans.
- Watch out for unnecessary overhead expenses and recurring costs.
- Keep your business finances separate from your personal accounts.
- Consider requiring prepayment from clients, particularly for large projects.
- Learn to be comfortable talking about payment terms with clients.
- Stay on top of your receivables.
- Monitor your cash flow.
- Plan ahead for your quarterly tax payments.

Chapter 13

Setting Rates and Fees

As any marketing manager knows, setting prices is an art as well as a science. It's a combination of covering your costs, ensuring a fair profit, and determining what the market will bear. For most retail products, a business owner can easily compare his prices against his competitors'—he can just walk down the street and see what Joe is charging for *his* widgets. But info pros generally don't run storefront shops with prices in the window. And, because the cost of our work varies with the requirements of each project, we don't usually have rate cards, either.

Your fees will be based on a combination of factors, including the type of work you do, your client base, the going rate both for the industry you're marketing to and for the independent info profession itself, and the salary you want to pay yourself. This chapter will help you think about how you want to charge for your services, what your hourly rate should be, and how to talk to clients about your fees.

Setting an Hourly Rate

There are two ways to determine your hourly rate. The first is to just do a gut-check, decide that you're worth, oh, $150 an hour, and go with it. (And I hope that, if you do set your rate this way, you have a healthy amount of self-confidence. If your gut tells you you're worth $25 an hour, keep reading.)

If, on the other hand, you prefer to take the analytical approach—or at least be able to justify your fee in your own mind—here's a formula to help you. It takes a little while to work through this process, but you'll end up setting an hourly rate that will sustain you.

- First, decide what annual salary you want to pay yourself. Be honest; don't estimate too low and don't expect to pay yourself $200,000 the first year. Self-employment has some intangible benefits, such as flexibility, independence, and the satisfaction of running your own business. However, you also have to factor in the downsides—erratic cash flow, no employer-sponsored retirement pension or paid vacations, the constant need to market. Be sure that the salary you set for yourself reflects the added stress of running your business. Remember that this won't be your take-home pay; you will still pay taxes on your income, just like a regular salary.

- Next, figure out your nonreimbursable and overhead expenses for a year. This includes everything except expenses you can bill back directly to clients, such as the cost of online searches or overnight package delivery. It does not include your one-time office setup costs (described in Chapter 8, Setting Up Your Business), but does include just about everything else you'll be writing checks for, such as:

  - Office rent for 12 months

  - Utilities (electricity, telephone, Internet service) for 12 months

  - Insurance payments (health, property, liability) for 12 months

  - Online information service fees for 12 months (subscription or minimum usage charges; not actual search costs, which you will bill back to the client)

  - Office supplies (paper, toner, business cards, stamps, brochures, envelopes, etc.) The amount of office supplies you will consume in a year may surprise you; estimate $2,000 or so annually.

  - Annual membership dues for professional associations, both info pro-related and those of your client base

  - Travel and registration costs for a minimum of two professional conferences a year (yes, you need to attend at least two—to market yourself, refresh your research skills, and stay on top of the issues in your clients' industry)

- Retirement fund contributions (since you don't get a pension from an employer, you need to fund your own retirement)
- Office equipment (assume that you'll have to replace your PC every three to five years and that you'll eventually need to purchase or upgrade other equipment, such as a laptop, cell phone, and so on)
- Accountants' fees, magazine subscriptions, and other miscellaneous costs

Yes, it's hard to estimate all of this ahead of time. For most people, these overhead costs add up to between $20,000 and $40,000 a year.

Now let's figure out how many hours you can bill in a year. It's probably not as many as you think. Start with 52 weeks. Subtract one or two weeks for vacation. Subtract one week for doctors' appointments and sick days. Subtract another two to three weeks for nonbillable holidays (all the holidays that regular employees get; they won't be calling you on those days—and, let's face it, do you really want to be in your office working on New Year's Day?). Then subtract one to two weeks for attendance at professional conferences (as I said, this is essential for your business). That probably leaves you with about 45 weeks. It's amazing how fast the time flies.

How many hours will you bill each week? For most independent info pros, the answer is no more than 20 or 25—and that assumes a 45- to 50-hour work week. If you plan to do primarily manual research in libraries, court houses, and government agencies, your billable time may be more like 30 to 35 hours. You will be billing your clients for your travel time, and you can bill *each* client for a share of the travel time even when you combine several projects into a single trip. You'll spend the rest of your time marketing, answering e-mail, marketing, preparing for presentations, marketing, sending out invoices, marketing, paying bills, marketing, and so on. Trust me on this, you *will* spend a lot of your time marketing. Even if one major client takes up most of your time, you still need to invest in marketing. As I explained in Chapter 11, Managing Your Clients, relying on one client for more than 30 or 40 percent of your revenue is dangerous; if you lose that client your income will plummet. Bottom line, you'll be able to bill roughly 1,000 hours a year, assuming you can generate that much work.

So what do we have? In simple math, it's:

Your annual salary plus your overhead
divided by
The number of hours you expect to bill in a year

What's the result? Probably somewhere between $85 and $150 an hour (or $50 to $70 an hour for manual research, since you can bill more hours in a week than you can for online research). That's how much you have to bill per hour in order to pay your salary and cover your overhead expenses.

For many beginning independent info pros, this rate may sound absurdly high; others may look at the number and imagine six-figure salaries their first month in business. Reality lies somewhere in between. Your clients probably won't focus on your hourly rate—particularly if, when you quote on a project, you emphasize the total, not-to-exceed budget. Most clients—the kind you want to attract, anyway—are accustomed to paying hefty rates for consultants. If your intended client base is likely to balk at your rate, think long and hard about whether you are willing to take a substantial pay cut to work for people who can't afford your fees. If, on the other hand, you look at an hourly rate of $100 and imagine that you really will be able to bill 40 hours a week, 52 weeks a year, think again. Finding clients means marketing, and marketing takes time, particularly the first year.

Hourly Rates or Flat Fee?

There are two approaches to pricing a project: You can bill at an hourly rate, plus expenses, or you can set an all-inclusive flat fee. Of course, both are based on your hourly rate; the difference lies in the amount of risk you want to build into the estimate.

If you are billing a project by the hour, you and your client have probably established a not-to-exceed budget—you agree that the *total* cost will not exceed a set amount. If you finish the work in less time than you expected, the cost will be lower than the estimate. You have a strong incentive to watch your time and your expenses, because you have agreed to a cap on the total amount. Once you begin work, if you realize that the project will take significantly more time or money to complete, you can go back to the client as early in the process as possible and try to negotiate a larger budget.

If, on the other hand, you set a flat fee for a project, you are in a sense gambling that you know how much time the job will take. The advantage of flat-fee pricing for the independent info pro is that, if you finish the job in less time than expected, you can still bill the full amount—in essence, earning a higher per-hour rate. If you offer a prepackaged product or service, such as a standardized profile of a publicly held company or a two-hour workshop on Internet research, flat fee pricing makes sense. The disadvantage of set prices for individual, custom projects is that you are gambling that you *will* be able to finish the job in the time you expect. If you guessed wrong and it turns out to take twice as long, your hourly pay suddenly drops in half. For the first year or so, you are probably better off using hourly pricing; once you have developed a sense of what kinds of projects are predictable enough to price on a flat fee basis, you can institute per-project pricing.

Estimating a Project

So you get a call from a client who wants you to identify the latest trends in intermodal transport in Australia. You discuss the parameters of the project, figure out how much information your client is expecting, and agree on a deadline. Now, she wants to know how much it'll cost. Gulp. What do you say?

There's no easy answer for "how do I estimate the cost of a project?" After a while, it becomes second nature—"Hmm, this sounds like a five-hour project, plus about $300 in online costs," for example. But even if you've been doing research for years, it still takes a while to develop that gut feeling for how long a job will take. There's no firm guideline for estimating projects, but here's my first piece of advice: Resist the urge to blurt out a price. Say, instead, "Let me think about this for just a bit, and I'll call/e-mail/fax you with an estimate."

What's Involved?

Now, take a deep breath and think through all the aspects of the project carefully. Do you understand the subject matter? Will you need to allow extra time to familiarize yourself with industry terms? How much information do you think is out there? You might want to run a very quick search in one of the professional online services to get a sense of the scope of the material available. Note that this is *not* the time to start spending money; instead, check a Web search engine and see what comes up in five minutes of quick research, use Dialog's free Dialindex service, or run a search in the Publications Library of Factiva.com, none of which will incur charges.

What about telephone research? Will you need to contact experts for information that doesn't exist in print or online sources? If so, will you be doing extensive interviews? Allow at least an hour or two per interview. The interview itself won't take that long, but when you factor in the time to get the contact's name and phone number, exchange voice-mail messages a few times, conduct the interview, and write up your notes, it may take several hours. Estimate $1 per minute for long-distance charges for each interview you conduct. Your actual per-minute cost will be lower, but this rate also covers all the short phone calls that you probably won't track—leaving messages, talking with assistants, and so on.

Next, think about whether you need to factor in time for manual research in a library or government agency. Will you do this yourself or subcontract it out? If you're doing it yourself, be sure to include your transportation time. You're charging your clients for your dedicated time. When you are en route to and from a library, you are *not* available to take calls from other clients, to work on marketing, and so on. If the project requires that you leave the office, the meter starts running as soon as you walk out the door. If you're subcontracting this aspect of the project, be sure you know in advance how, and approximately how much, your subcontractor will charge you, so you can build it into your estimate. See Chapter 14, Subcontracting, or I'll Scratch Your Back if You Scratch Mine, for more on this topic.

I find it helpful, both for myself and for my client, to write out a detailed "scope of work" proposal for each project. I begin with a paragraph describing what I understand the project to entail. Then I spell out all the types of research I'll be doing—for example, a Web search for company product specifications, online research for relevant patents, a search of trade and industry publications, interviews with government industry analysts, and so on. As I write a paragraph on each of these approaches, I often think of additional aspects of the project that my client may not have thought of herself. In fact, I often find that the intended scope of a project increases significantly, once I've thoroughly thought through the specific approaches I might take.

What'll It Cost?

Even if you're an experienced researcher, it helps to map out how much time each part of a project will take. It's easy to minimize the labor involved in preparation and administrative tasks, but if you don't factor it in, you'll wind up seriously underestimating the total cost of the job.

Task:	Time (hours)	Cost
Reference interview	________	________
Research preparation	________	________
Online research	________	________
Telephone research	________	________
Manual/library research	________	________
Transportation	________	________
Reports or documents purchased or photocopied		________
Subcontracting costs		________
Editing and formatting online search results	________	
Review of results	________	
Analysis of results	________	
Report preparation	________	
Total time:	________	
Time x hourly rate:		(a)______
Total costs:		(b)______
Total expenses (a + b):		________

Pricing Permutations

Once you have a feel for the extent of the research involved, use the worksheet in the sidebar "What'll It Cost?" to develop a rough estimate of the budget for the project. Notice the wide range of activities involved, from the initial conversation with your client; traveling to and from libraries and other locations; doing the actual research; cosmetically enhancing search results by removing extraneous material, adding page breaks, and so on; down to the final analysis and report preparation. It's tempting to charge different rates for different kinds of labor; why should your client pay you $100 an hour while you're driving through traffic? Remember, your client is paying for the exclusive use of your time. Your time is worth whatever rate you set—remember the math you did earlier in this chapter—and discounting any of that time is cheating yourself. When you are driving to the library, cleaning up a file, or entering figures into a spreadsheet, you are not able to work for or market your services to other clients. This is sometimes referred to as the "opportunity cost," that is, what you give up by choosing to do something else. If you were not working on this job, you might be back in your office, calling a potential client or working on a new proposal. Whatever you're doing now, it's time that you cannot devote to something else.

One exception to this rule is when the job requires a large amount of nonprofessional work, such as data entry or photocopying. At that point, it might make sense to bring in an intern, a student, or someone from a temp services agency to help out, and charge their time at a discounted rate. However, any time that *you* spend on the project ought to be billed at your full hourly rate.

What if the client needs the project sooner than you'd normally be able to deliver? What if it requires that you work evenings and weekends in order to meet the deadline? Most independent info pros charge a rush fee for anything that will require putting aside other work, or working outside normal business hours. Think of it as overtime pay—or as a means of ensuring that your clients really, truly need the information right away. If they aren't willing to pay a rush fee, it probably isn't an emergency after all. If you demonstrate that you're always willing to drop everything to work on a client's "rush" jobs, never charging a fee for the added service, you have in essence trained that client to wait until the last minute to call you.

How to charge a rush fee depends on the type of project. You can simply tack on a specific amount—say, $500—on top of the normal cost of the job. Or you can place a surcharge on your hourly rate, charging 50 percent more, for example. Obviously, the first alternative is more attractive for smaller jobs, and the second is better when the project involves more hours of labor.

Another add-on to the bottom line is the mark-up you may choose to add to out-of-pocket expenses. When you use a professional online service for research, you may incur significant charges, which you'll have to pay whether or not you have collected the money from your client yet. Likewise, you may have to purchase consulting reports, books, articles, or other material on behalf of a client. Those charges often go straight to your credit card, which means, again, that you have to pay them before your client has paid you. Because carrying expenses like this can have an impact on your cash flow, you may want to mark up out-of-pocket project costs by a small percentage. Note, though, that some professional online services forbid mark-ups. Be sure to read your service contract carefully.

Working 9–5, Monday–Friday, Period.

I'll admit it ... I'm in my office way before 9 in the morning, I don't leave at 5:00 p.m., and I usually put in some time over the weekend. In fact, I sometimes take on work knowing that the only way I'll get it done is to work all weekend. But I never, ever admit that to a client. In fact, I have turned down clients who called on a Friday afternoon and asked if I could work on a project over the weekend and get it to them first thing Monday morning.

Am I crazy? No, I'm just training my clients. If they know that they can get me to work on a weekend, they'll start expecting it—or at least they'll hope I'll be willing to change my weekend plans. The more I meet their expectations, the less incentive they'll have to call me before the last minute. And the more I'll feel that I have completely lost control over my free time.

What I will tell that Friday-afternoon client, though, is that I can get started on the project the very first thing Monday morning and get it to him by the end of the day. He doesn't have to know that I might in fact tackle it over the weekend—and yes, I make sure that I don't send it to him until at least mid-afternoon on Monday. It's important to manage your clients' expectations.

What about fees for small jobs that you estimate will take less than an hour or two? I impose a one-hour minimum for projects; some independent info pros draw the line at two hours. The rationale for a minimum fee is that every project, no matter how small, requires a certain amount of overhead time for routine tasks such as logging in the job, preparing and sending out an invoice, and so on, not to mention simply the time it takes you to shift gears and think about a new project. Half-hour jobs don't pay, and if you accept them, your clients will begin to think that you're the person to call just for those little jobs. Instead, if a client calls with a project that won't take more than 45 minutes, tell her that you have an *X*-hour minimum, then offer to provide additional research or analysis to bring the project up to your minimum. Your client benefits from the extra work; you benefit because you've demonstrated that you're capable of more than quickie research.

Bid High or Don't Bid

It's tempting to bid a job at the lowest price you think you can manage, in order to get the work. Resist that urge! For starters, you're probably not competing with anyone else. Most clients aren't shopping around and comparing prices—they call someone they know will do the work well. If you *are* in a competitive bidding situation, think twice about bidding for the job. Why? Because you're dealing with someone who is basing his decision to work with you on cost more than anything else. Even if you get this job, your client is one you'll have to "win" over and over, for each new project, based on the fee you set. Yes, it's nice to get the work, but if you cut your fee in order to get the job, you have lowered that client's expectations of how much you're worth. Also, my experience has been that cost-sensitive clients tend to be the most labor-intensive. They're the ones who call during the project to add "just one more little question"—without an increase in budget, of course—and who call after the project is completed to ask for clarification of this item or that Web site you pointed them to. In a competitive bidding situation, bid what you normally would and stick to your price, and focus on finding clients who don't feel the need to get competitive bids for every project.

Be sure that your bid is high enough to reflect your value. This is hard to gauge; you often don't know what other independent info pros are charging, so it's difficult to know if you are high or low. My technique is to listen to the clients' reactions to my estimate. If they accept without hesitation, I suspect that I'm pricing too low. When I first started my business, I would work up an estimate and then gasp to myself: "Eight hundred dollars! Oh my gosh! That's a lot of money!" Well, it is a lot of money when you compare it to the cost of a meal out, but in the business world, $800 is chump change.

Price your services as high as the market will bear. That sounds awful, doesn't it? What's funny is that clients really do believe that the price you assign to your work reflects its true value. If you price yourself low, you are unintentionally telling your client that you don't think your work is worth much. Price high and you project the image that you're expensive and worth every penny.

Presenting the Estimate

Once you have written up a description of the scope of the project, thought through all aspects of the research involved, estimated the total charges using the table in the sidebar "What'll It Cost?", tacked on any additional fees, and done a final reality check, it's time to negotiate with the client.

I usually quote a total, not-to-exceed, budget rather than bringing up my hourly rate. Most clients have no idea how efficiently an info pro can work. Imagine the following conversation:

Info Pro: Yes, I'd be happy to work on that project. I charge $150/hour, plus online costs, and this job might take me about ...

Client: [interrupting] Oh, no! Forget it. [thinking "I already spent eight hours on this and found nothing. I can't afford to spend another $1,500 or $2,000!"]

Now imagine this conversation:

Info Pro: Yes, I'd be happy to work on that project. Based on my past experience, this type of research usually runs around $900. What if we set a not-to-exceed budget of $1,100, and I'll just charge you for my actual time plus expenses?

Client: That sounds okay. You promise you won't bill me for more than $1,100?

Info Pro: Absolutely. And if it looks like there just isn't anything out there, I'll stop before we spend very much time or money and we can talk about other ways to approach the research.

For larger projects, it's even more important to couch the estimate in terms of a possible range of prices, with a corresponding range of services. For $*X* amount, you'll provide the in-depth research, analyze the information, and prepare an executive summary of the results. For 75%-of-$*X*, you'll provide the research and write up a summary of what you've done and found. For 50%-of-$*X*, you'll provide preliminary research and a set of recommendations about further research options you would suggest. Note that you offer the high end first, and then work down. This conveys the message that a *complete* research package includes all of these services, but your client can choose to receive a less complete package by selecting one of the less expensive options.

What happens if your client balks at the price you quote? What if she says that she thinks the job is worth only half of what you bid? That's when you offer a slimmed-down version of the project, priced accordingly. Instead of doing in-depth telephone interviews, you'll limit the search to what you can find online. Instead of a high-level summary of the results, you'll just clean up the results of your search and let her do the analysis herself. Be sure that you draw the line before you negotiate the project down to a budget that doesn't allow you to do a creditable job. Sometimes the answer simply has to be, "I'm sorry, but even the preliminary research will cost you $X. Perhaps your best bet would be to go to your local library and see what information they can offer you at no charge."

What if your client says that other independent info pros would cost much less than you? My favorite response is one suggested by T.R. Halvorson of Synoptic Text Information Services, Inc.: "We set our prices according to the value we know we provide." If you have trouble saying that, practice it in front of a mirror until you can say it with confidence. And keep in mind that the client may be comparing you to someone who doesn't have access to the value-added online services, who can't offer telephone research or public records searching—someone, in other words, who isn't in your league at all.

Can You Get the Money Up Front?

As independent info pros, cash flow is always in the back of our minds. On a big project, I may be incurring hundreds of dollars in out-of-pocket expenses doing online searching, purchasing hard-copy reports, and so on. Perhaps I'm also subcontracting work to other info pros, who will expect to be paid promptly. I generally require the client to prepay one-third of the not-to-exceed budget for any project over $1,000 or so. This ensures that I'll have cash up front to cover online charges, subcontractors' bills, or other direct expenses. It also ensures that the client is serious about the job.

Requiring a prepayment does have downsides. Some companies seem to find it impossible to cut a check in less than 30 days, and delaying work until you receive the money may be difficult if not impossible. Ask the client if his organization has provisions for expedited payment or electronic funds transfer to your business checking account. You might also consider establishing merchant accounts so that you can accept major credit cards, assuming that your clients can pay that way. (See

Chapter 12, Money, Money, Money, for information on accepting credit cards and on cash flow generally.) My experience has been that if the client really wants the work done, he'll find a way to get payment to me within a few days.

Another option is to have your clients establish retainer or deposit accounts. In this arrangement, they prepay a set amount and then use your services until the account is depleted. In theory, this is a great deal for the independent info pro. You get the money up front and you're assured of a certain amount of work from the client. In fact, you may be able to offer priority attention to the client's requests in return for a use-it-or-lose-it monthly minimum. If they don't call on you during a particular month, you still deduct a predetermined amount from their account in exchange for your willingness to give precedence to their research needs.

In practice, very few independent info pros have clients on a retainer basis. The exception is document delivery businesses or other services that typically bill small amounts to clients with predictable research needs on an ongoing basis. Most clients are reluctant to obligate themselves to a set number of hours of research in a given period of time. Many clients simply don't know how much work they will be giving an independent info pro at all, so are not inclined to send any money up front. Also, the accounting for retainer clients is less straightforward than for your pay-as-you-go clientele. The bottom line is that deposit accounts are great if you can get them, but don't expect them to be the norm.

Recalibrating Rates

Picture yourself in business for three or four years. You're charging the same hourly rate that you started with. However, you're worth more now, quite likely, than when you started, even if you came from a library or research background and did similar work for years. You've become more efficient in your research, so you take less time to do the same amount of work. You have probably been subcontracting with other info pros, so you have a better sense than you did initially of what other people are charging, what their deliverables look like, what added value they provide, and so on. And the cost of living has certainly gone up since you started your business. It's time to think about raising your rates.

After I had been in business for a few years, I wanted to up my hourly rate but I hesitated—because I couldn't figure out how to tell my clients. Somehow, a postcard saying "Guess what? I cost more now!" just didn't seem appropriate. Then I realized that practically none of my clients knew what my hourly rate was. It doesn't appear on my invoices; I just list the total cost for my time. When I estimate the budget for a project, I give a round number without breaking it out into "this much for this many hours at $\$X$ an hour, plus this much for online, plus this much for telephone costs," and so on.

I realized that if I raised my hourly rate 15 percent, each project was simply going to start costing a little more. It would take the same amount of time, but that time would now cost X plus 15 percent. As it turns out, I have raised my rates twice since then, and no client has commented, or even, as far as I can tell, noticed the increase. I do have to renegotiate with my corporate clients with whom I have an annual contract that spells out the hourly rate but, as businesspeople, they expect that rate to rise over time.

Of course, I'm not suggesting that you initially set your rates low, with the assumption that you can raise them to an acceptable level later. Start out with a rate you are happy with, and raise it when you feel that you can justify the increase.

Top Tips for Rates and Fees

- Take the time to figure out an hourly rate you can live with.
- Be sure to include all overhead expenses when calculating your hourly rate.
- Get comfortable pricing jobs at what the market will bear.
- Prepare for clients' questions about the budget for a project.
- No hourly rate is set in stone. Reevaluate your prices every year or two.

Chapter 14

Subcontracting, or I'll Scratch Your Back if You Scratch Mine

One of the most important reasons to establish your own network of independent info pros is that you'll eventually land a project that you can't do yourself, and you'll have to bring in someone else. You may get a question in an area that you know nothing about—for me, that would include medical, legal, and chemical searching—or a request for a type of research you don't offer—patent searches, perhaps, or in-depth telephone interviews—or perhaps you're just swamped with work, don't want to turn down a client, but can't accommodate the work because of other projects you're doing. In all these situations, as long as you have a network of other experienced info pros, you can keep a client happy even though you can't do the work yourself.

How Does Subcontracting Work, and Why Should I Share?

Subcontracting turns you into a client: You have a project that needs doing and you contract with another independent info pro who will do the work for you. As a matter of professional courtesy, the subcontractor agrees to work at a discounted hourly rate. You invoice your client at your regular rate, and the difference between what your subcontractor charges you and what you charge your client is profit. If you prefer, the client needn't even know that you didn't do the work yourself.

Depending on the situation, the subcontractor may not ever talk with your client directly; you act as the intermediary between the client and the subcontractor. This arrangement works best if you thoroughly understand the client's request and are able to accurately pass questions and answers back and forth between the subcontractor and the client. Sometimes, you may not want the client to know that the work is being subcontracted, and there are some situations in which you just don't want the subcontractor and client to talk. (I have a couple of clients who are, well, challenging to work with, and my subcontractors are grateful that I buffer them from any direct interaction.) The situation in which this arrangement may not be ideal is when both your client and your subcontractor are much more familiar with the subject area than you are; in this case, it's probably better to let the two of them talk directly.

You may choose to introduce the subcontractor as your associate and indicate that, although the client may call the sub and interact with him directly, all the accounting, project management, and so on will come through you, and that all *new* projects should be directed to you, not to the sub. Quite often, over the years, I have been the subcontracted researcher, and I usually feel more confident that I have filled the client's information need if I am able to speak directly with the client. However, when I am working on just part of a larger project, it's usually simpler for me to talk only with the contractor, who is managing the process and who knows what specific part of the puzzle I am responsible for. In any event, be sure that you discuss the issue of client contact with your subcontractor up front, so that the sub understands with whom he will be dealing.

Calling in the Experts

Why would you send work to someone else instead of doing it yourself? The simplest answer is that you want your clients to come to you for all their research or information needs, regardless of the scope or topic; you're their one-stop shop. But the challenge lies in providing high-quality research involving topics or methodologies that you aren't familiar with; the last thing you want to do is take on a project in an area you know nothing about and wind up providing erroneous or incomplete information to your client. This is one major benefit of membership in the Association of Independent Information Professionals (www.aiip.org). AIIP's annual conference and private e-mail discussion list help you get acquainted with colleagues, watch how professionally they present themselves, and learn about their backgrounds and where their expertise lies. (That's why you should maintain a professional demeanor whenever you participate in work-related e-mail discussion lists. If you are argumentative, unprofessional, or rude, your colleagues will be disinclined to subcontract with you.) Working within your network, you can call on fellow info pros who have the skills you need for particular projects, thus enabling you to provide your clients with information from the best possible researchers.

On the Road Again

Bringing in subcontractors is also a way to provide services to clients while you are traveling or on vacation. When I am on the road, for example, I often ask a colleague to handle my clients for me. I leave a message on my voice mail explaining that I am out of town but that for rush research needs, clients should call "my associate" so-and-so at such-and-such phone number. My colleague then handles any calls that come in and bills me for her time (at a discounted rate) and expenses; I then bill my client for my colleague's time (at my regular hourly rate) plus expenses. I make a little money, my clients are happy, and I didn't have to leave the office unattended while I was away. See Chapter 10, Work and the Rest of Your Life, for more discussion of how to handle your clients during a vacation.

Needing Low-End Labor

You may occasionally need to hire subcontractors to help with simple research that you don't have time for, or that you don't want to bill out at your regular hourly rate. I ran into one of these situations when a client asked me to look at more than 800 Web sites. I knew that not only would I go crazy and run out of time, but my client couldn't afford to pay my hourly rate for this kind of work and didn't actually need my expertise in looking at each site. For projects like this, you might find graduate students who want to work a few hours a week, or a mom with small kids at home who isn't interested in full-time employment but wants to stay in the work force. You will have to supervise these subcontractors more closely than you would a colleague, because you must train them from scratch and they're bound to make some mistakes in judgment as they learn. On the other hand, you'll probably be paying them a fraction of your hourly rate, so you can build in some overhead time for training and review.

The Challenges of Subcontracting

Some disadvantages come along with subcontracting out work, of course. The issue foremost in most contractors' minds is that they must rely on someone else's work. It's usually not feasible (or even possible) to replicate the subcontractor's work, or check it thoroughly before it goes to the client, so you have to accept on faith the subcontractor's assurance that she did a thorough and competent job. When you send a subcontractor's work to a client, *you* have to answer for its quality even though you didn't do the research yourself. If the client isn't happy with the results, you can't simply throw up your hands and say "Well, I didn't do the work ... go talk to my subcontractor."

I routinely subcontract out a portion of my research work, and in one or two situations I was left high and dry by a new subcontractor. The person didn't do a good job, or overlooked a crucial piece of information, or completely misunderstood the scope or focus of the project, or missed my deadline. The few projects that have gone bad have been learning experiences for me. I now know how to avoid most of the problems that can arise—by staying in touch with the subcontractor, by having her send the information to me during the course of the project rather than all at the end, and by making sure that she isn't overworked or distracted.

Your subcontractor may legitimately need more hours than you expected the project to take. That of course eats into your profit, because you've probably agreed on a not-to-exceed budget with your client. The subcontractor may not use the same resources that you would have used, or may not write up the results the way you would. Given that some of us independent info pros have a stubborn streak a mile wide—"It's my way or the highway"—dealing with subcontractors who have their own way of doing things can be an exercise in frustration.

In addition to the problems inherent in having someone else do the research for you, a remote possibility does exist that your subcontractor will approach your client directly and solicit business. This is considered unethical and it shouldn't happen, but there are a few less-than-sterling people in any profession. Make it clear when negotiating with a new subcontractor that such conduct would be unacceptable.

It's important to spell out all the details of the subcontracting relationship, in writing, before you begin. It's tempting to just call a colleague, describe the project, and let it go at that, particularly if you're in a hurry. Resist the urge; in my experience, the most significant cause of subcontracting relationships going bad is treating a subcontracted job too casually. Even if I've discussed a project with a subcontractor,

I always follow up with an e-mail that spells out the details of the project (at least, the details that I can disclose to the subcontractor without violating client confidentiality), an itemized list of what I expect the subcontractor to do, a description of the deliverable (that is, the form and format in which the results will be delivered), the final deadline for the project and any interim deadlines, and the maximum number of hours, the hourly rate, and the dollar amount of expenses authorized—or just the total not-to-exceed budget the subcontractor has to work within. See the sidebar "Points to Ponder" for the items to include in your subcontracting agreement.

Points to Ponder

The Association of Independent Information Professionals offers a sample subcontractor agreement that its members can use. Whether you use the AIIP form, have a lawyer draw up a contract, or write your own, you'll need to spell out the following:

- ✦ A detailed description of the nature of the research to be done, analysis to be provided, and other aspects of the project
- ✦ Whether the subcontractor can contact the client directly
- ✦ The format of your search results—the full text of articles, an executive summary, printouts of Web pages, and so on
- ✦ How you want the material delivered to you—hard copy sent via overnight courier, or e-mail, fax, etc.
- ✦ The not-to-exceed budget or the maximum number of hours the subcontractor is authorized to work, and the hourly rate you will pay
- ✦ The deadline by which the information must be delivered to the contractor (you)
- ✦ Whose fee-based online accounts to use—the subcontractor's or yours
- ✦ The payment terms—e.g., within 30 days of the invoice date
- ✦ A statement that your subcontractor will maintain client confidentiality and not disclose the name of the client or the nature of the research without prior approval

Following the Golden Rule

If you're like most independent info pros, you will eventually find yourself on both sides of the subcontractor relationship; you'll be sending work to others and others will be asking you to work on their behalf. The Golden Rule of doing unto others certainly applies in this setting; the person to whom you subcontract a job today may hire you as a subcontractor tomorrow.

If You're the Contractor

Buddhism teaches the practice of "detachment"—the art of appreciating and enjoying life without focusing on possession or need. As a contractor, you must develop a form of detachment as well. Your subcontractor will work the way he thinks best, using the sources and techniques he believes will get the best result. You have to let go of the urge to second-guess and micromanage the process. Take a deep breath. Detach. Understand that many paths lead to the same truth, or at least to the information your client needs. No two researchers ever approach a project in quite the same way, and there is seldom only one right answer to a research question. As long as you have confidence in your subcontractor's abilities, let him follow his own path.

But how do you develop the confidence to let go? To switch metaphors from Buddhism to romance, consider going out for coffee before you start dating seriously. Try a new subcontractor on a small project with a long lead time. If it doesn't work out, you can still find someone else to finish the job. You might be less worried and prone to micromanage on something that isn't a major, rush-rush project. Starting off this way also lets you discover what communication style works best with that particular subcontractor. Does she need a lot of hand-holding? Does she like to check in every day to give you an update? Do you like it when she does? Does she ask questions if she isn't clear on the parameters of the project? Is she flexible about the format in which the results are to be delivered?

Speaking of deliverables, make sure to tell your subcontractor how you want the results delivered to you. Supply a copy of your Word template, with whatever formatting you prefer and the headers and footers that you normally insert. (Headers and footers are a nice way to polish your report; the page numbers help the reader locate specific items from a table of contents, and a footer that contains your company name and contact information ensures that every reader down the line will know who's responsible for this fabulous report. See Chapter 34, Deliverables, for more discussion of packaging your research results.) Do you want the subcontractor to highlight key portions of the documents he has found? Do you want a table of contents at the beginning of the report? Do you want a list of all the resources used during the search? Be sure your subcontractor knows your requirements so that the material he sends you is ready, or nearly ready, to forward to your client. And when you first negotiate a project with a subcontractor, be sure to factor in enough time for you to tweak the deliverable to your own specifications. If your client needs the results by Friday, ask your subcontractor to send you the material by midday on Thursday at the latest. Once you've established a working relationship with a subcontractor and have confidence in his ability to deliver results that are up to your standards, you might want to send him some of your letterhead and envelopes or mailing labels, so that he can send material directly to your client if time doesn't permit sending it to you first.

Tell your subcontractor as much about the project as you can, within the bounds of client confidentiality. The more he knows, the more focused and on-target the research results will be. Stay in touch during the course of the research. For complex projects, it's usually best to get interim results as the job goes along, to make sure that the subcontractor is on schedule and generally in the right area. Even though that principle of detachment I mentioned applies throughout the project, *you* are ultimately responsible for the results of the research, and your client will expect you to stand behind what you deliver.

Remember that the subcontractor's client is you. That means that you'll have to pay his invoice within the agreed-upon terms, whether or not you've been paid by your client. If you're working on a large project and you're concerned about cash flow, negotiate with your client for prepayment of a portion of the not-to-exceed budget. That way, you can afford to pay your subcontractor on time.

Much as you want to be able to handle anything a client asks you to do, in some situations it makes more sense to refer a project to a colleague—taking yourself completely out of the loop—rather than subcontracting and retaining ultimate control of the job. When I get requests for complex medical or legal research, for example, I know that I wouldn't be able to do a competent job of translating the client's needs for a subcontractor. I wouldn't know what questions to ask during the reference interview with the client. I wouldn't know if the information delivered by a subcontractor was reliable or not. And sometimes I step out of the middle of a transaction for reasons of liability. I don't take on intellectual property research, for instance, because there's a risk—small but real—of being held liable for enormous damages if a relevant patent or trademark was missed during the search. Rather than subcontract the work to an expert intellectual property researcher—which would mean sharing any potential liability—I simply refer the client to someone who I think would do a thorough and professional job.

John Levis, owner of John E. Levis Associates and an expert medical researcher, said it best. "It takes a healthy ego to be an information entrepreneur—you have to be confident that you've got what it takes to provide high quality information services. But successfully running an information business also takes a healthy *lack* of ego. You have to be able to recognize when you just don't have the knowledge or expertise to do the best possible job for a client. And believe me, if you take on a job that goes beyond your abilities, your client can tell, and he just won't call you again."

What About Referral Fees?

Independent info pros have various policies regarding the payment of referral fees when a colleague directs a client to them. I work on the assumption that, in the long run, referrals go both ways and it's more trouble than it's worth to pay referrals whenever a colleague sends someone to us, and vice versa. Some info pros will pay either a fixed amount or a fee equivalent to some percentage of the time they billed to the client. If you expect a fee for referring a client to a colleague, be sure to discuss this with the colleague ahead of time. And remember that there's no assurance that the colleague will actually complete the sale; even if you do agree upon a fee, it is usually contingent on the info pro getting the job. Referral fees, unlike payments to subcontractors, are usually sent after the client has paid the invoice.

If You're the Subcontractor

What I enjoy most about being a subcontractor is the variety of projects I get to work on. I can see how other independent info pros package projects for their clients. (See Chapter 34, Deliverables, for more on packaging research results.) I enjoy having colleagues as clients—someone who understands what information I need in order to do the research. And I enjoy being spared from having to interact directly with problematic clients. The downside is that I don't get to hear from the happy clients who were impressed with the research, and I generally can't call the client directly to ask questions or clarify a point.

When a colleague asks me to subcontract, it's a sign of trust. It's my responsibility to decide whether I really can do the work. Do I have the time? Am I familiar enough with the subject to do an excellent job? Am I comfortable with the budget, deadline, and description of the work? I know that my contractor is depending on me; if I botch the job, I've made her look bad to her client.

A subcontractor's responsibilities are pretty straightforward:

- Don't take on a job you can't do well.
- Never, ever exceed the agreed-upon budget without authorization by the contractor.
- Do whatever it takes to get the job done by the agreed-upon deadline.
- If you run into problems as you're working on the project, contact the contractor immediately. No surprises!
- Make sure you understand how the contractor wants the results delivered.
- Be professional. The contractor is your client. Even if you're just getting started as an independent info pro and relying on subcontracted work for most of your income, you should cultivate a number of clients, not just one contractor.
- Above all, be mindful that your contractor is counting on you. He has made a commitment to his client and is relying on you to deliver the goods.

Being a subcontractor also means that the contractor is trusting you to maintain client confidentiality. In some instances a contractor directs me to contact the client directly in order to clarify the research; I then introduce myself as my contractor's "associate." Once in a while, the client, assuming that the contractor and I are partners, later calls me directly with a request for another project. It's important to pass any such requests to the contractor; this wasn't my client to begin with, and I am ethically bound to decline any work from the client directly. When this situation comes up, I usually talk with the client just long enough to figure out generally what the project entails, then explain that my colleague so-and-so handles all new projects, that I will call her right away and relay the request, and that she will be calling the client back shortly to firm up the budget and other details.

Before you start a job for a contractor, find out how the end result should look. Does she want a Word file? If so, ask her to send you her template so you can use her standard formatting. (See the earlier section, "If You're the Contractor" to see the same questions from the point of view of the contractor.) Does she want a cover memo? Even if she plans to incorporate your work into a larger deliverable, write up a thorough description for *her*, if not for the client—of what you did, what you found, what you *didn't* find, and what additional research you would recommend (remember—one can always do more work on a job).

Finally, you have to market yourself as a subcontractor just as much as for any other type of work. The subcontracting portion of your client base will consist of your fellow independent info pros, but you still need to remind them occasionally of the services you provide. You're more vulnerable to economic downturns as a subcontractor; if the economy gets tight, independent info pros may have less business coming in, which means that they'll have less work to subcontract to you. So this kind of work should not be your only marketing focus. If you have your own base of direct clients, you have a better chance of drumming up business than if you have to wait for your contractors to do so.

Running a Subcontractor-Based Business

Up to this point in our discussion of contractors and subcontractors, I've pretty much assumed that both parties do most of their own research, farming out work to colleagues occasionally. However, in another model for independent info pro businesses, the business owner focuses almost entirely on marketing and relies on a small cadre of subcontractors for all the research. Sue Rugge, one of the pioneers in our industry, built several successful businesses this way. Others have as well. This type of business works well even if you don't have a research background, as long as you enjoy—or at least don't mind—marketing.

The idea behind a subcontractor-based business is that you, the owner, focus on building the business and managing clients, while subcontracting the work to expert researchers—all of whom are independent info pros running their own businesses; they're not your employees. You will want to develop strong relationships with five or six subcontractors, all of whom are willing to give your jobs top priority. In exchange for a steady income stream, they agree to discount their hourly rate for you. Assuming that you can mark up your subcontractors' rates by a third or half, this can be a profitable business model.

You may have to hire someone to help you manage the flow of work through your office—taking the initial calls from clients, conducting the reference interview if you aren't available to do so, tracking which subcontractor has which job, making sure the results of each job are returned to you and then sent on to the client in time, keeping track of expenses for each project, and so on. You don't have to be a researcher yourself to run a subcontractor-based business, but you do need an understanding of information resources and realities so you can discuss the project intelligently with the client. You can either estimate the budget yourself or discuss the details with the subcontractor who will be working on the job and get his or her estimate of the total hours and expenses involved.

If you are going to rely on subcontractors to do most or all of your research, you need to identify info pros who are very good, who are not so busy that they can't set aside a certain amount of time for your work, and who are willing to discount their hourly rate in exchange for steady work. This may be harder than it sounds; most independent info pros who are worth their salt are busy with their own clients, and many are not willing to substantially reduce their fees. The effort to find the best info pros you can is worth it, though; they'll enable you to offer top quality research services to your clients.

For this kind of business to succeed, you have to be a good marketer, because that's what you'll spend much of your time doing. You have to be organized and willing to set up procedures for managing the flow of work through your office; when every project goes out to a subcontractor, it's a lot easier for an occasional job to slip through the cracks. You have to focus on the bottom line, because overhead for your office administrator can't be directly billed out to a client. And you have to be comfortable relying on others to do your research for you. Unlike the ad hoc subcontracting that the typical info pro occasionally engages in, running a subcontracted research company requires that you involve your subcontractors in your business.

They will get to know your clients, they may use your account to search the professional online services, they will occasionally mess up, and you will have to cover for them with your clients.

In spite of such challenges, the subcontractor-based business model can be lucrative. You can grow your business as large as you want; your only limitation is how much marketing you want to do and how many subcontractors you want to manage.

Top Tips for Subcontracting

For contractors:

- Treat your subcontractors as partners. Give them as much information as possible about each project.
- Detach. Find the best subcontractors you can and then let them approach projects however they want.
- Pay your subcontractors promptly, regardless of when your client pays you.

For subcontractors:

- Never exceed the agreed-upon budget.
- Always deliver your results on time or, better yet, early.
- Never take on a job you can't do superbly.

Chapter 15

Ethics and Legalities

I'll begin this chapter by saying that I assume you will treat all your clients, colleagues, and vendors with courtesy and integrity. It's a small world, and your actions do have a way of coming back around to you. Your reputation is one of your most valuable assets, and it's far easier to maintain a good reputation than it is to repair a bad one.

The best way to maintain your sterling reputation and avoid the aggravation (not to mention expense) of lawsuits is to err on the side of caution, to run your business as if your spiritual advisor, your mother, the IRS, and an investigative reporter were watching every move. It's great to be a risk-taker when it comes to trying new marketing strategies or expanding your business; risk-taking in legal or ethical matters is just foolish.

IANAL

IANAL is an acronym for I Am Not A Lawyer—and I don't pretend to be one in this chapter. I'll provide commonsense guidance on how to conduct your business ethically and legally, but what I have to tell you, based on my own and my colleagues' experience, is no substitute for legal advice. You will probably need to consult a lawyer occasionally; I recommend that, as soon as you start your business, you find one you're comfortable with and who understands your concerns as an independent info pro.

For a more thorough discussion of legal issues pertaining to independent info pros, I recommend T.R. Halvorson's white paper, *How to Avoid Liability: The*

Information Professional's Guide to Negligence and Warranty Risks (available through AIIP at www.aiip.org).

Ethical Quandaries

All independent info pros place certain limits on what they consider to be ethical behavior. One, who will remain nameless, told me about a client she had when she first went into business. The client had a project funded with grant money and at the end of the info pro's work, there was still a bit of money left over. Apparently it would have been unseemly not to have spent all the funds allocated, so he asked the info pro to just bill him for some extra time without actually doing any additional work. As she told me later, "I didn't have the moxie to say no, but I regret to this day that I did as he asked. When I later came to my senses, I gave an equal amount of money to a charity, and I severed my relationship with the client. No client is worth compromising my basic ethics." Although the client may have characterized his action as a bonus for work well done, the info pro felt that it was simply a form of theft.

Of course, it is also unethical—as well as unprofessional—to accept work that goes beyond your area of expertise, or that, because of time or budget constraints, you know you won't be able to do well. It's great to challenge yourself by taking on new types of work, but be sure, in your heart of hearts, that you can confidently provide the client with high-quality, professional service. Likewise, there will be periods when you're fully booked with work and a client calls offering you a project you really don't want to turn down. If accepting it means giving short shrift to one client or another, you must turn down the job, or subcontract it to someone else. Taking on a project that you are not confident you can handle harms the entire profession; a client once burned is unlikely to use any independent info pro again.

This is where the network of colleagues that you've built up comes in handy. One of the reasons I belong to AIIP, the Association of Independent Information Professionals, is that I am able to meet experienced info pros in virtually every area of specialization—legal research, document delivery, medical information, even fields as specialized as architectural research. I have a small cadre of people to whom I routinely refer projects that I can't handle or subcontract out myself. These are people I've gotten to know over time, most of whom I've met in person at an AIIP annual meeting or at other info pro conferences. If I don't have an appropriate referral among the people I already know, I'll browse the AIIP membership directory to remind myself who does what among the info pros I already know and might have dealt with.

If no one comes to mind, then I take advantage of AIIP's free referral service (www.aiip.org/AboutAIIP/referral.html), through which potential clients in search of an info pro can get the names of up to three members who match their needs. The Web site also features a searchable version of the AIIP membership directory (www.aiip.org/AboutAIIP/directory_home.asp). You can always refer clients with whom you personally choose not to work to the AIIP site.

Handling Conflicts

Many independent info pros specialize in a particular industry—pharmaceuticals, advertising agencies, and so on. Sooner or later, they encounter the situation in which two of their clients are direct competitors. How would you handle this? If you are working closely with the marketing department of one company and you get a request from its competitor to dig up marketing strategy of your client, you may want to turn down the job. Even if you limit your research to publicly available sources, your original client might not want to learn that you're providing information to its competitor on a topic about which you've had access to proprietary information. You may also have been required to sign a contract with your first client, promising not to do any work for any of its direct competitors. I use the "clear light of day" test—what would happen if both clients found out that you were doing work for the other? If you are simply providing research services to both using publicly available resources, my gut tells me that you don't have a conflict. If, however, you know that one client or the other would find this objectionable—or if you signed a contract not to work for a direct competitor—then you'll have to turn down the work. (See the section, Reading the Fine Print, later in this chapter, which discusses how to handle contracts that unduly restrict your business activities.)

You may also run into situations where a personal conflict of interest prevents you from providing the best possible service to a client. If you lost a parent to lung cancer after a lifetime of smoking, you might not be willing to accept work from a tobacco company, for example. One of the benefits of working independently is that you *can* turn down jobs if—for whatever reason—you just don't feel comfortable accepting them. Keep in mind, though, that one person's evil empire is another person's shining example of corporate excellence. You need not explain to a prospective client why you are declining the work. Just tell him that you have a client conflict and, regretfully, cannot accept the assignment. You don't need to go into details, and of course it would be unprofessional to tell them you think they are a wicked company and the scourge of the earth. Remember, even a prospect for whom you won't work might be a good referral source. And, for all you know, they might change jobs next month and call you with a project that you would be happy to accept.

Client Confidentiality

It should go without saying that independent info pros must maintain strict confidentiality with regard to every project and every client. That means you never disclose the nature of a project to a third party. (You can usually describe projects in very general terms in your marketing material or when discussing the kind of work you do, such as "provided in-depth information on the ice cream market" or "developed a profile of the information technology needs of a government agency.") Likewise, you don't mention or list the names of your clients on your promotional material or Web site without specific, written permission from the client. Some info pros get around this by coyly describing a client as, say, "a major software company based in Redmond, Washington." Yes, they don't, strictly speaking, mention Microsoft by name, but most people will be able to figure it out. It's better to stick with a more vague and generic description ("a *Fortune* 100 information technology company") or get permission to list the company by name.

Similarly, don't use clients as references without asking. They may have a corporate policy prohibiting employees from endorsing a third party, they may not want outside entities—possibly their competitors—to know whom they use for information services, or they may simply not want to be bothered with calls from your prospective customers.

Reading the Fine Print

Reading the small print in contracts, licenses, and agreements gets harder every year, at least for those of us who have graduated to bifocals. But you ignore the fine print at your peril. Signing a contract without reading it, or hoping that no one will actually enforce all of its provisions, is asking for trouble. I will never forget the difficulties I went through the time that I unthinkingly signed a client's contract requiring that I carry $1 million (!) in automobile insurance—this for a job that did not require me to leave my office chair. When I submitted my not-insignificant invoice, the client's billing department asked for proof of that million dollar coverage before they would cut a check. Eventually I was able to get a short-term retroactive policy from my insurance carrier, but I learned then to always read the fine print and cross out any provision that I could not or would not fulfill.

As it turns out, it is sometimes easy to eliminate onerous and unreasonable requirements like that $1 million in auto insurance coverage for an in-office project. Just cross out the offending paragraph, initial it, and note the change when you send the signed copy back to the client. Ask that they return a signed copy to you, and you're done. And if the client refuses to modify the contract? Well, you can take a chance like I did back then, or you can walk away from the job as I would do now.

Some clients will ask that you sign a confidentiality or nondisclosure agreement (commonly known as an NDA) before you begin work. This is standard operating procedure for larger companies, and these agreements are usually not objectionable. However, look for a clause that also prohibits you from doing similar work for their competitors, often for a period of years. Unless you truly intend to comply with such a requirement—and how do you know ahead of time whom they might consider competitors?—be sure to negotiate. My experience has been that clauses like this one can sometimes be eliminated. Often it's just a matter of pointing out that (a) you're a small business serving their industry, and the restriction is unduly onerous, and (b) their basic concern is confidentiality, isn't it, and the rest of the contract—which you have *no* trouble signing—assures that you'll comply with that. Sometimes, however, they just won't budge and you'll have to consider declining the work, as I do.

You'll also have to scrutinize the fine print in contracts you sign with online information providers. By now, most of them have learned what independent info pros are and what we do. One of their concerns was that we would act as "resellers"—that is, we would turn around and remarket access to their information to third parties. Of course, that's not what independent info pros do; we just pass along selected information for one-time client use. However, some contracts do prohibit users from passing the information along to *anyone* else. AIIP members get the benefit of special contracts that the association has negotiated with a number of information vendors. These contracts specifically grant us the right to pass along the results of any search to a single client. If you're not an AIIP member, be sure to read carefully any information vendor's contract to ensure that it doesn't prohibit you from passing work along to your clients.

Playing by the Rules

Many independent info pros start their business while still working in a corporate environment. It's tempting to sneak in some of your own work during the day—accepting clients' calls on your cell phone, using the information resources available to employees for your outside research projects, and so on. It's especially tempting to take advantage of your organization's flat-fee contracts with the professional online services such as Factiva.com or LexisNexis. "Hey, we're paying for all-we-can-eat as it is; what's a little additional research?"

Just Say No. It's wrong, it's unprofessional, and it's cheating. It's as tacky as stealing office supplies to furnish your home office. On top of all that, you'll never learn how to determine the true cost of online research if you piggyback onto services that you don't have to pay for yourself; when you finally do quit your day job to run your independent business full time, you will have no idea how to accurately estimate costs. And finally, you will never forget or forgive yourself for these ethical lapses.

The same principle applies when using public library resources. It's tempting to call your local library and ask the reference librarian to conduct a search for you. "I mean, they'd do it if my client called directly, wouldn't they? I'm just the client's agent, right?" In this case, no. You're passing off the results of someone else's work as your own; you are using the scarce resources of a local library on behalf of someone who probably does not live in the community that the library is intended to support and that, in turn, supports the library through its taxes. Last but not least, you are using the necessarily limited resources of a public library when you should be providing your client with the full breadth and depth of resources available to you as an independent info pro.

Contracts and Agreements

As I discussed in Chapter 11, Managing Your Clients, you'll need a standard form for contracts or letters of agreement, as well as a basic disclaimer statement that spells out what your client can and cannot expect from you. While it's not cost-effective to have a lawyer draft each contract or proposal for you, it's wise to have a generic one that you can modify as necessary. As long as you're at it, you might also ask your lawyer for a standard nondisclosure agreement that *you* can offer to clients—thus avoiding the problem I described earlier with noncompete clauses hiding in clients' NDAs—and for a subcontracting agreement for when (not "if") you subcontract work to another independent info pro. If you're a member of AIIP, you have access to sample nondisclosure and subcontracting agreements, which you can take to your lawyer and ask for any recommended modifications based on your specific situation and business model.

Remember that a contract by itself doesn't necessarily protect you from being sued by a client. Good communication and listening to your instinct are just as important. Make sure that you have managed your client's expectations. Is he asking for a promise up front that you will find specific information? Does he sound like he expects more than you think you'll be able to deliver? Is this the kind of project that may require a lot of research with very little in the way of results? If so, make sure you've confronted, discussed, and dealt with any unfounded assumptions or unrealistic expectations. And by "dealt with" I don't mean just spelling out your caveats and cautions in a liability statement. Rather, you must say directly to the client, "I can't promise ahead of time what I'll find. In fact, I may find very little information on this subject. I will use the sources that I think are most likely to produce the information you want, but remember that you are paying me for my time and expertise, not for the information per se. Even if I don't find what you're looking for, you will still have to pay me for my labor and my expenses." If this sounds harsh, consider how much more harsh a collections call will sound three months from now when the client refuses to pay your invoice because you never dispelled his mistaken assumptions about the services he engaged you to provide.

Although it's tempting to turn every conversation about a potential project into a sales call, with the objective being to close the sale, this is the time to be modest and actually *under* promise. If a client can't deal with the possibility that you might not find what he wants, you don't want this client.

Dangerous Words

Every research project is restricted by budget and time constraints. Information resources are inevitably incomplete. All published sources contain inaccuracies. Given the limitations that we info pros have to live with, make sure that your marketing material, Web site, and client contracts don't include any of the following words. All of them promise what—by definition—you can't deliver.

- Complete
- All-inclusive
- Exhaustive
- Comprehensive
- Thorough
- All sources
- Best

Keeping Your Word

"I meant what I said and I said what I meant. An elephant's faithful, 100 percent." Dr. Seuss's *Horton Hatches an Egg* featured an elephant who, having promised to tend to an egg newly laid by a bird who then disappears for months, maintains his post on the nest until the egg finally hatches.

Even though your jobs probably won't entail hatching bird eggs, Horton's promise to live up to his word is instructive. Clients don't like surprises, particularly when they involve invoices that are higher than estimated or results that are not as promised. My policy is to provide every research client with a not-to-exceed budget estimate, even when I have no idea how long the project might ultimately take. *I* would never sign an open-ended contract with a car repair shop that couldn't give me an upper limit on how much a job would cost, and I don't expect my clients to do that either.

It's often difficult to estimate at the outset how much time and money a project will involve. Rather than guaranteeing a complete job for a set fee, you're much better off phrasing your quote in terms of what it will take to "see what's out there" or setting a cap on how much you'll spend on the "first phase" of the project. If, when you reach that point, you haven't found what the client wants, your report should spell out the approaches you took, what you *did* find, and what further research you recommend. If the client wants additional work, fine; you'll negotiate a fee for the next phase of the project. If not, at least you have kept within the originally approved budget. In either case, you never, ever exceed an agreed-upon budget cap without clearing it first with the client.

This concept is hard for some researchers to accept. "But there's so much more that I could find." "I'm not providing my client with truly professional service if I don't follow up on research leads I uncover." This train of thought can go on forever, though. You can almost always do more work on a project, but without your client's approval, you have no right to expect him to pay you for that extra work. And if you deliver a package that's disproportionately information-rich for what the client has agreed to pay you, you set up false expectations of what the client can expect in the future for a similar budget.

Copyright Perils

Copyright, in its most elemental form, is intended to protect the rights of authors, photographers, artists, musicians, and other creators of original works. The owner of the copyright has the exclusive right to reproduce the work, distribute copies or make other use of the work, and to authorize others to do so. For example, I own the copyright on this book, but I have authorized the publisher to make and sell copies of it and to pay me a portion of the revenue from the sale of the books. If you want to make a copy of a chapter of this book for a friend, you'll have to arrange for permission from the publisher or from me. Similarly, if you want to provide a copy of an article to a client, you need to arrange for permission from whoever owns the copyright—either the publisher or the author.

AIIP sells a white paper by member Stephanie Ardito, *Copyright & Information Professionals: Complying with the Law,* that will give you a thorough background on copyright issues as they pertain to info pros. See the description and catalog at AIIP's Web site: www.aiip.org/Store/aiipcatalog.html. Ardito writes frequently about copyright issues and is a long-time independent info pro, so her advice is particularly valuable.

Copyright is a tricky issue, and is still an unsettled question, at least in the U.S. It's become even more complicated since the Web, where electronic copying is easy—and rampant. Although the "fair use" provision of the copyright law permits one-time photocopying under certain specific circumstances, copies made in a business or for-profit context may be subject to a copyright fee. As I noted at the beginning of this chapter, I Am Not A Lawyer, so I am not going to opine on what exactly current copyright law does and does not cover. What I can recommend is that, if you anticipate needing to make photocopies of articles or sections from books on a regular basis, you either establish an account with a copyright licensing organization such as the Copyright Clearance Center (www.copyright.com) or subcontract to a document delivery service that will handle payment of the appropriate copyright fees for you. (See Chapter 33, Library and Other Manual Research, for a description of document delivery firms and how they operate.)

What about copyrighted Web sites and material downloaded from professional online services? The party line among independent info pros is that we are merely acting as agents for our clients, so as long as we comply with copyright restrictions on their behalf, we're in compliance with copyright law. That means, for example, that downloading or printing a page from a Web site is generally okay, because we are only doing what our client would do for his own use. A royalty payment to the copyright holder is built into the fee we're automatically billed for material we download from professional online services; again, we are simply acting on behalf of our client, who is not obligated to pay any additional fees for his own use of the information.

However, our clients do not automatically have the right to redistribute material you provide to them, whether by posting it on a Web site (either internal or public), making photocopies, or forwarding electronic copies to others. If your client wants to distribute copies of the information you send him, you can offer to help him negotiate with the appropriate Web site owners and online information providers. Dialog and DataStar offer a streamlined method for "purchasing" the rights to redistribute or archive individual articles through their Electronic Redistribution and Archiving program (support.dialog.com/searchaids/era).

To ensure that your clients understand that they don't have unlimited use of the information you provide them, you might want to include a copyright notice along with your cover memo when you send your research results. An example of such a notice is:

> The attached has been compiled [or derived] from copyrighted sources and is provided for your personal use. If you plan to archive or distribute copies of this information, you must seek permission directly from the copyright holder. [Independent info pro's company name] is not responsible for copyright violations by you or your organization.

Recycling Results

I'm often asked whether clients have requested the same search twice and whether I wind up using the information from one research project for another client—to recycle the results, as it were. In more than a decade of business, I have not once run into a situation in which two clients asked for exactly the same research. Every project has a slightly different spin or emphasis, and, of course, you're obligated to check the most up-to-date sources you can. In the extremely unlikely event that two clients asked for exactly the same information at the same time, the answer would still be that I have to redo the work on behalf of the second client. A colleague of mine once received a project from a law firm client on an aspect of engineering technology. It was very broad, and the client insisted he wanted "everything" on the subject. Ultimately, my colleague complied and handed the client reams of search results, along with a very hefty bill. Just a few days later, she got a call from another client, an engineering company, asking for a search in a particular technical area, one that happened to be a subset of the information requested by the law firm client. As she did the search, using the same databases and pulling up much of the same information that she had for the first client, it struck her that the two requests must have been connected. Indeed, they were—the two clients were on opposing sides in a patent infringement suit. Effectively, she had done the same search for two clients. But the second client, who focused his request much more tightly, paid a small fraction of the cost for essentially the same quantity of useful information.

The rule for research using any commercial, fee-based online information service is "one search, one client." That means that the results of a given search can be provided to one client only. If a second client wants the same results, you have to pay for the material again. The same is true for photocopies of copyrighted material. Note that most professional online services do allow you to keep a backup copy of information you send to clients—and, yes, there have been times when I've had to send the results again because a client lost the file. The online vendor may stipulate how long you can keep the backup copy; some limit you to several months. I generally keep backup copies no longer than six months; if the client needs the information again, he'll probably need an updated version of the research anyway.

Legal Collections

Very few independent info pros have been sued directly as a result of work they performed. What does sometimes happen, though, is that the results don't meet the client's expectations, the client decides not to pay the bill, the info pro threatens to take the client to small claims court, and then the client starts talking about the poor quality of the research. Suddenly the info pro is put on the defensive and things get ugly. (See Chapter 12, Money, Money, Money, for a general discussion of how to avoid getting stiffed by a client.)

So how do you deal with slow- or no-pay clients? To begin with, for any job that's large enough to really hurt if you don't get paid, obtain at least partial payment up front. Period. A client who doesn't have enough confidence in your work to put down a deposit may also be difficult to collect from at the end of the job. And be willing to walk away if the client disputes your invoice at the completion of the project. Suing a client for nonpayment is not worth the risk of being counter-sued for damages on the basis of having done an inadequate job. You may feel confident that you can defend the quality of your work, but do you really want to be put in the position of having to do so? And despite your best efforts, you may fail; any lawsuit is a gamble.

However, there are ways to encourage a client to pay that don't involve harassment, lawsuits, or undue anguish. First, make sure you contact the client as soon as the invoice is past due. Ask if the client needs another copy of the invoice, on the chance that the original was lost in the mail. If you forget to include your Taxpayer ID or Social Security number (or other business identification number, if you're not in the U.S.) on your invoice, your client's accounting department may delay payment. Offer to fax any necessary documentation such as the IRS form that provides your Taxpayer ID number or Social Security number.

Keep in mind that your client may not be the person actually responsible for writing and mailing out checks. More likely, she signs off on the invoice, sends it to someone else for approval, then sends it to the accounting department for processing. Many companies cut checks only once or twice a month, so if you just miss a payment cycle, you're out of luck and will simply have to wait. Once you have ascertained that your client has done her part, limit your calls to the accounts payable person responsible for your invoice, and escalate the discussion to that person's manager if necessary. Your contact with your client should be positive and focused on your services, not on getting your invoice paid. Of course, if you find that your client is sitting on the invoice, then you do need to impress upon her the necessity of doing whatever paperwork is necessary to get it off her desk and into the AP system.

You might consider having someone else make collections calls for you—subcontract them to a colleague or hire a skilled temporary worker with a business background to make the calls. You might even ask a spouse or other household member who's willing and able to make the call, or a business partner who is less inclined to get emotional than you are. It's easy to get emotional when calling about an invoice that is seriously in arrears, and if you're not careful, you'll wind up personalizing what is in fact just a business matter. Someone who is paid simply to make such calls in a professional manner may be better able to negotiate with the client. Be sure to give the person some negotiation points ahead of time; you might offer to accept payment in several monthly installments, or to put the charge on a credit card, or, if circumstances warrant it, to forgive a portion of the total amount due. In any event, having a friendly but stern and emotionally uninvolved person make your collections calls may keep an unpleasant situation from turning into a hostile one.

As I mentioned earlier, be willing to walk away from an invoice if it becomes clear that your client simply will not pay you. Interestingly, I have only had to do this a couple of times. After it became obvious that the client was not going to pay me, I wrote him a letter forgiving the debt, expressing my regret that he was not able to live up to his promise to pay, and hoping that he treated his clients better than he had treated me. In each case, I eventually *did* get paid by the client, albeit a year late. But the biggest benefit was that I didn't let the debt weigh me down in the meantime. Running an independent info pro business requires an extraordinary amount of energy, and expending that energy on a deadbeat client is simply a waste.

Top Tips for Remaining Lawsuit-Free

- Be modest in what you promise your clients, and manage their expectations.
- Establish a not-to-exceed budget for every project, and never, ever exceed it without prior approval.
- Be courteous, fair, and generous in dealing with clients.
- Subcontract or refer out any project that goes beyond your area of expertise.
- Keep clients in the loop when you're not finding what you expected. If you're not finding anything, tell them early in the process.
- Listen to your gut and gracefully turn down work that doesn't feel right to you.
- Read the fine print in any contract you sign, and be prepared to negotiate.

Chapter 16

Professional Development

Back when I worked in corporate libraries, I always made sure to include money in my budget for professional conferences and subscriptions to library-related publications. Now that I not only set but approve and fund the budget for my one-person business, I still set aside a certain amount for professional development. It's hard to make time to read up on new developments in the field, and it's tough to get away from the office to go to conferences, but I know that my clients are paying me for my expertise. I have to continually refresh my skills or I'll become stale and lose my edge.

AIIP: Your Secret Weapon

I mention the Association of Independent Information Professionals (www.aiip.org) in virtually every chapter of this book, and there's a reason for that. AIIP is an incredible resource for anyone who is running an independent info pro business or considering becoming an information entrepreneur. I joined AIIP before I went independent, and even took personal leave from my job to attend the association's annual conference. I'm so glad I did; the opportunity to meet with experienced independent info pros, to just sit and listen to them talk about their current challenges and triumphs, was invaluable. It gave me a real appreciation for what I was getting into. I'll never forget one of the sessions I attended at that meeting—a panel discussion on "My Biggest Marketing Mistakes." It was so surprising to see such a collegial group, willing to share their own follies in the hope that others wouldn't make the same mistakes.

AIIP was founded in 1987 by a couple of dozen independent info pros who barely knew each other but who shared a vision of forming an association of fellow information entrepreneurs. Since then, it has grown to more than 600 members in 20 countries. AIIP offers several types of membership, including Full membership for people who have already established an information business, Associate membership for those who are considering becoming an independent info pro or who are otherwise interested in the profession, and Student membership for individuals enrolled in a degree-granting college or university. Dues are relatively modest when you consider the benefits that come with AIIP membership.

Why do I renew my membership every year?

- I have access to the lively private e-mail discussion list, AIIP-L, in which members discuss topics ranging from strategies for dealing with difficult clients to converting PDF files to project-specific help such as tips for finding famous hot dog stands.

- My business is listed in the AIIP membership directory. My listing includes a description of my background, the type of work I specialize in and the services I provide, my Web site URL, and the specialized resources to which I have access. Other info pros who want to subcontract work can find me through the directory.

- As a Full member, I can enroll in AIIP's referral program, which links prospective clients with members who can meet their needs, and its speakers' bureau.

- I can attend the annual AIIP conference and learn first-hand how other information entrepreneurs deal with business issues similar to mine.

- I can develop business relationships with info pros from around the world.

- I am eligible for discounts on a variety of information-related services and products, many of which have been negotiated specifically for independent info pros.

- I can participate in the volunteer mentoring program, which matches experienced AIIP members with new info pros who need informal assistance in developing some aspect of their business.

And finally, through AIIP I have built friendships with some of the best and the brightest people in the information industry. Working as an independent info pro can be an isolating experience; most of your friends probably have no firsthand knowledge of what you're talking about when you complain about cash flow, collections, or the challenge of closing a sale for something as ephemeral as "research." Imagine tapping into a network of hundreds of people who experience these same challenges every day. *That* is why I belong to AIIP, and that's why you should seriously consider joining as well, even before you launch your business.

Associations Galore

In addition to AIIP, you may find a number of information industry-related associations useful to join. Librarians and other info pros are often great sources of referrals—even librarians occasionally are stumped by patrons' questions, and they sometimes outsource such requests—and being active in a librarians' association is a great way to both learn from the pros and develop informal business relationships with them. See Section Three, Marketing, for more discussion of how to promote your business within associations.

The following associations would be of most interest to independent info pros:

- Special Libraries Association (www.sla.org): "Special" in this context means specialized; SLA is an association of librarians who work in corporations, government agencies, business and industry organizations, and universities. The membership also includes independent library consultants. SLA has about 15,000 members internationally, although the group as a whole has a U.S. focus.

- Society of Competitive Intelligence Professionals (www.scip.org): Membership consists of CI practitioners within corporations, competitive intelligence consulting firms, and academicians. If you plan to provide business or competitive intelligence to clients, SCIP can be a useful association. SCIP has about 3,500 members worldwide, although most of them are in the U.S.

- Public Record Retriever Network (www.brbpub.com/prrn): Members conduct research in and obtain copies of public records from government sources. Note that this is not an association per se; it is hosted by BRB Publications, and principals of BRB serve as the directors of PRRN. It has 700 members, all in the U.S.

- The Chartered Institute of Library and Information Professionals (www.cilip.org.uk): Based in the U.K., membership ranges from corporate librarians to public librarians to library consultants. CILIP has about 23,000 members, most of whom are in the U.K.

Other country-specific librarian associations abound; some are more business-oriented than others. Associations also exist for librarians in specific industries and fields—the American Association of Law Libraries (www.aallnet.org), the Medical Library Association (www.mlahq.org), even the North American Sport Library Network (www.sportquest.com/naslin). You may want to join a subject-specific library association, depending on the focus of your business and the type of information services you provide. The San Jose State University School of Library & Information Science maintains a reasonably thorough list of library associations at slisweb.sjsu.edu/resources/orgs.htm.

If your business focuses on a specific industry or subject, don't forget to join your clients' major professional association. If they are primarily advertising and public relations professionals, you'll join the Public Relations Society of America (www.prsa.org) or equivalent. If your clients are in the chemical industry, you might join the American Chemical Society. Use your research skills to identify the leading association in your clients' industry, or ask some of your clients which association they consider most valuable. Keep in mind that you can often join as an associate member, which may not include all the privileges of full membership (e.g., voting or serving as an elected officer), but is often less expensive. In addition to the benefits of networking with potential clients and getting your name out to members, joining an association usually entitles you to a journal or newsletter that will help you keep on top of issues that matter to your clients, and to anticipate their research needs.

Hi, My Name Is ______

It's hard for a one-person business to close up shop in order to attend an information industry conference. You have the direct costs of travel, hotel, meals, and the

Getting the Most Value from a Conference

In addition to the marketing benefits of attending a conference (which I cover in Section Three), here are some tips for keeping you focused on professional development while you're there:

- Look through the program before you arrive and decide which sessions will be most useful. Plan to spend at least three-quarters of the day in sessions, not playing hooky and visiting the local tourist attractions. (This is not to suggest that I've ever been guilty of that!)
- Allocate time to visit the exhibit hall. Don't just walk down the aisles avoiding eye contact with the vendors; stop at each booth and ask the exhibitors to tell you, in 30 seconds or less, what sets them apart from their competition. If the vendor offers a product or service that's even remotely interesting, leave your business card so they'll send you marketing material.
- Talk to your clients ahead of time, if the conference is related to their business, and let them know you're attending. Offer to collect relevant exhibitor material or make contacts on their behalf and send the information to them when you return to the office.

  If the conference is organizing groups for dinner at local restaurants, sign up. It's amazing what you can learn from colleagues over the course of a meal.
- Bring plenty of business cards, and commit to handing them all out over the course of the conference.

conference registration itself, as well as the indirect costs attached to being away from the office and unavailable to clients who might have revenue-producing work for you. On the other hand, attending at least one info industry conference a year will keep you informed about new resources, research tools, vendors, and search techniques. Unlike the hours you might spend reading industry newsletters or magazines, attending a professional conference is a full-immersion experience. You are (or should be) totally focused on the information profession while you're there, and that's a useful annual exercise. Conferences also present a great opportunity to meet fellow independent info pros, build your subcontracting and referral network, and get inspired and re-energized.

When you figure out the overhead expenses for your business (I walk you through this exercise in Chapter 13, Setting Rates and Fees), include the cost of at least one information industry conference. Save up your frequent flier miles if you have to. I use a credit card that awards me a frequent flier mile for every dollar I charge—an easy way to accumulate those miles. Set aside $20 a week and within a year you'll save up enough to cover the cost of a conference. If your budget is tight and you don't mind giving up a little privacy, consider sharing a hotel room with a colleague.

Staying on Top of the Industry(s)

Part of your job as the CEO of your company is to stay on top of developments in the information industry as well as whatever field your clients are in. In addition to joining the appropriate trade or professional association and reading its publications, you'll want to subscribe to at least one other major industry-related magazine.

If you provide online research services, your subscription list should include at least a couple of the leading info industry magazines, such as:

- *Searcher* (www.infotoday.com/searcher)
- *Online* (www.infotoday.com/online)
- *The CyberSkeptic's Guide to Internet Research* (www.cyberskeptic.com)
- *The Information Advisor* (www.informationadvisor.com)

(Full disclosure: *Searcher*, *Online*, and *The CyberSkeptic's Guide* are published by Information Today, Inc., the publisher of this book, and I am either a contributor to or an editor of most of the magazines I've listed here.)

Numerous print and electronic journals and e-mail discussion groups also cover specific areas of research. Use your research skills to identify the ones in your areas of specialization. Two directories of public e-mail lists are Topica (www.topica.com) and Tile.Net (www.tile.net). Topica's directory is better designed for browsing; both include instructions for searching the archives of messages that have been posted to lists. Searching a list's archives lets you identify any prior discussions of the topic you're researching and avoid annoying the list participants by asking about matters that have been discussed recently.

You can also go to groups.yahoo.com and search or browse the directory of lists hosted by Yahoo!. And finally, there are Usenet discussion groups, sometimes called newsgroups. Usenet is an Internet old-timer that predates the Web and most e-mail discussion groups; some Usenet groups have been around for 20 years. In the early days, you could count on many of them to be valuable sources of information. In the last few years, though, many newsgroups have been overwhelmed by spam and other unrelated postings. However, moderated newsgroups (that is, those in which all postings have to be approved in advance by a moderator) and those that deal with arcane or narrowly focused topics can sometimes be useful. For example, I was working on a research project that involved finding out about radio interference with 800 mHz public safety radio systems. A search in groups.google.com, which has a full, searchable archive of Usenet newsgroups going back to 1981, turned up some useful material in the misc.emerg-services and alt.radio.scanner newsgroups.

In addition to periodicals, numerous Web sites offer industry- and market-specific news and information. For the research and information profession, you might consider these, among others:

- AIIP-L, the private e-mail discussion list for members of the Association of Independent Information Professionals (www.aiip.org)

- Marylaine Block's "Neat New Stuff I Found on the Web This Week" (marylaine.com/neatnew.html) and Ex Libris, a newsletter for librarians (marylaine.com/exlibris/index.html)

- Tara Calishain's ResearchBuzz, which covers Internet research (www.researchbuzz.com)

- Gary Price's Weblog of Web research sources (www.resourceshelf.com)

- Chris Sherman's SearchDay, a daily newsletter with Web research tips (www.searchenginewatch.com/searchday)

- Netsurfer Digest, a weekly digest of news from the world of the Web. $20/year (www.netsurf.com/nsd)
- Search Engine Report, a monthly update on search engine developments (www.searchenginewatch.com/sereport)
- Search Engine Showdown, another monthly update on search engines (www.searchengineshowdown.com)

Most of my research is business-related, so I also monitor some Web sites and discussion groups that focus on business and industry.

- Best Biz Web, a monthly description of selected business-related Web sites (www.bestbizweb.com)
- BUSLIB-L, an e-mail discussion list for business librarians (to subscribe, e-mail listserv@listserv.boisestate.edu; as the text of the message enter: subscribe buslib-l first-name last-name)
- FreePint, an extensive fortnightly e-mail newsletter and Web-based discussion forum, based in the U.K. and with a U.K. and European flavor (www.freepint.com)

The Invisible Network

In addition to published news sources, don't overlook the invisible network of experts available to you as an independent info pro—people who know something you don't know about the information industry or about research. I make a point of tapping into my network of colleagues whenever I can. I subscribe to several e-mail-based info pro discussion groups. In addition, I make a point of staying in touch with independent info pros whom I know and respect. Once a week, I'll call one of them just to say hello and see what's new. I'll ask what amazing new Web resource they've found lately, and of course I'll share with them an interesting source, product, tip, or technique that I've turned up.

When I talk to clients about their research projects, I often ask if they have done any initial research themselves, or have any sources to recommend. Often, they'll simply tell me to use my best judgment, but once in a while I'll learn about a great resource that I would never have found on my own. We independent info pros don't have a monopoly on research skills, and it's useful to remember that our clients may know about industry-specific sources that we can and should use.

I have been publishing a free monthly e-mail newsletter of research tips (www.BatesInfo.com/tip.html) as a marketing tool. (See Chapter 20, Marketing on the Web, for more discussion of this type of marketing.) An unexpected benefit has been the response I get, every month, from readers who point me to additional sources or other ways to find information. I think I gain more from my readers than I give them; my newsletter is one more way to tap into that invisible network of expertise that surrounds us as information professionals.

Top Tips for Maintaining Your Expertise

- Join and become active in the Association of Independent Information Professionals.
- Find out what associations your clients are most likely to belong to, and join those associations.
- Attend info pro conferences and focus on making the most of your time at each conference.
- Identify and participate in discussion lists that address your area of expertise.
- Plan to spend several hours a week on professional reading.
- Solicit recommendations of new information sources from clients and colleagues.

Chapter 17

Strategic Planning

"Strategic planning" sounds so formal—and formidable, too. *Fortune* 500 companies dedicate entire departments to this function. But independent info pros can, and should, do their own strategic planning as well. It needn't involve a Harvard MBA; fortunately, all that's required is the ability to look at your business from an arm's-length perspective once a year and evaluate where you are and where you'd like to be heading.

Getting a Yearly Check-Up

Think of this as your annual visit to the doctor, except without the embarrassing paper gown. Every year, schedule a day to sit down and evaluate where you are and, just as important, where you want to be a year from now. It's easy to coast along from year to year, particularly because we independent info pros don't get to participate in annual reviews with a boss or annual meetings with a board of directors. But if we don't take time to reflect on our business and our competitive environment, we might find ourselves adrift, or headed in an undesirable direction.

Go through your annual accounts (I hope you're using a financial management package such as QuickBooks; see Chapter 9, Software for Your Business) and print out a report of your sales for the year, sorted by client. Look at your records on every client for whom you did more than one or two projects. Where did the client come from—a referral from an info pro colleague or another client, a conference you attended, an article you wrote, a contact from your last job? Ask yourself if you can get more clients from the same source.

Saying "Thank You"

I do my annual review of my business in December, when the pace is a little slower. As I look at the work I've done for my steady clients, I want to express my gratitude for their business over the year. That brings up the question of whether or how to send holiday gifts to clients. Some independent info pros send boxes of candy, fruit, or snacks to their good clients. Others make a donation in their client's name to a noncontroversial charity. But some info pros worry either that clients will expect generous gifts every year, or that corporate policy prohibits them from accepting gifts from vendors.

I don't have a set policy on gift giving; it depends on my relationship with the client. For a couple of clients I know well, I donate to a charity I know they support and send them a card telling them what I've done. For a speechwriter client, I sometimes send a book I think he'd enjoy. One of my favorite clients gets flowers every so often, just because I know she likes them and I want to tell her that I'm thinking of her.

Having been on the receiving end of vendors' holiday gifts, I know that the thought really does count. I don't keep track of who sent me something last year and who didn't, but I do remember the occasional gift that shows that someone really thought of me. I forget within a month who sent me a tin of popcorn but I remember for years a gift that has personal value. One year, a publisher I worked for sent me a beautiful print of a photo he had taken in the mountains. I will always be grateful for that one gift, and I hope that some day I'll be able to give a client something with equal impact.

What More Can I Do for My Clients?

Look at the kind of work you've gotten from each client. What else could you do for him? What is driving your client? Is his business growing or shrinking? What about the industry he's in—is it healthy or struggling? What could you provide to your client to help him grow his business? John Levis, of John E. Levis Associates, once told me, "If you're going to grow your business, you need to be able to solve problems, not just find information. I wound up getting into the competitive intelligence field by listening to my clients and understanding their needs, sometimes even when they didn't know what they needed. Most clients are interested in getting answers to solve yesterday's problems; strategic planning focuses on solving tomorrow's problems. That's what keeps your clients—and you—in business."

Review your sales records to see if any one of your clients accounts for more than 20 or 25 percent of your revenue. If you find one that fits this criterion, ask yourself:

- What would happen if I lose this client? What impact would that have on my business?

- Why is this client giving me this much work? What can I do to generate similar amounts of revenue from other clients?

The practice of reviewing how much revenue each client brings in also helps you recognize how much business a "small" client may give you, cumulatively, over the course of a year. I remember my shock upon realizing the number of projects one consultant had sent me over the course of several months. It was all in one- or two-hour increments so I never thought of her as a particularly large client, but the business she sent my way certainly added up.

Spotting Troublesome Clients

As I do my annual review, I watch to see if anyone in particular has referred a disproportionate number of questionable, difficult, or potential deadbeat clients. If so, I make a mental note to impose a more stringent rule regarding prepayment for clients referred from that person.

Reviewing your accounts will also help you determine whether you have clients whom you need to drop altogether. Do any of your clients call frequently for estimates without following through with the project? Do you spend an inordinate amount of time with them during or after each project, answering follow-up questions or justifying your bill? If so, it's probably time to fire the client, because the time you spend with them could more profitably be spent doing billable work for other clients. And, yes, you *can* fire a client, provided you do it gently and professionally. See Chapter 11, Managing Your Clients, for more information on how to gracefully let go of a client.

Looking at the Revenue Mix

After I've reviewed the work I've done for my clients over the past year, I generate a report of income sources—how much I made from subcontracted research, how much from consulting work, how much from speaking fees, and so on. I try to keep my income stream diversified; that way, even if one industry or group of clients is hit hard by an economic downturn, other clients may be unaffected, which means that my revenue isn't hit as severely as it would be if all my work came from one small market niche. Having different types of clients and offering a variety of services also helps even out the work flow over the course of the year; a slow period for one group of clients may be a busy time for another.

Planning to Plan

Doing a yearly check-up is simple, provided you have set up your accounting system in a way that lets you easily extract useful information. With most financial management software, you can set up separate income subaccounts for the different types of work you do. For example, I maintain subaccounts for regular research, subcontracted research (work that I do as a subcontractor for other independent info pros), consulting, speaking fees, royalties, and other writing income. Using these separate categories takes no additional effort during the year—I just select the appropriate subaccount when I'm writing each invoice—but doing so makes it easy for me to review my income at the end of the year. I can look at the totals and see exactly how much of my revenue comes from each type of work. In addition, I can categorize my clients by industry or market. For example, you may want to track how much of your revenue comes from law firms, consumer product companies, or whatever your major client groups might be. What's important is to think about how you want to keep track of your work, and then build the tools that will enable you to do that. And remember, you can always set up new account types and update the account codes in existing invoices as your business grows and diversifies.

Not only do I review the diversity of my revenue sources, I also consider whether and how I might like to change that mix in the coming year. Do I want to travel more or less? Are my workshops profitable? If so, how can I increase the number that I do in a year? What impact will that have on my ability to maintain the other parts of my business?

I also think about maintaining a mix of clients and markets that respond quickly to marketing efforts—perhaps small clients with quick-turnaround projects who just forget to call—and big-ticket spenders who require longer-term marketing. With a blend of both types of clients, I can continually market to the latter group and can ratchet up my marketing efforts to the former group if I find that I'm not as busy as I'd like to be.

Taking Time to Think

Some businesses actually schedule formal retreats for top management to spend a weekend at some nice resort and think about the coming year and the company's strategic plans. That may be a bit much for a one-person business, but you will want to identify opportunities to sit back and reflect on where your business is going and your vision for the coming year. I travel frequently and have found that train trips to New York and cross-country airline flights are great times for contemplation. I'm away from the phone and e-mail, and the distractions are limited (believe me, airline food is *not* a distraction). I usually bring some professional reading and either a handheld PC or a set of index cards for jotting down thoughts. I intentionally let my mind wander as I read, thinking about alternative ways to run my business, new services I could provide, or new markets to break into.

As Alex Kramer, owner of Kramer Research, reminded me once, this kind of thinking can be done during a vacation or while attending meetings as well. "I use the AIIP conference as a time to do strategic thinking about my business," she said. "It's time away from the day-to-day worries of my business, but it's still a business-oriented setting. Hearing myself talk with colleagues and hearing what others say during all the conference chit-chat helps me a lot. Even the session during the conference in which everyone has two minutes to introduce themselves helps me think about how I define myself."

Building a Brain Trust

When Franklin Roosevelt was governor of New York and during his first term as president, he had an informal group of advisors whom he consulted regularly; he referred to that group as his Brain Trust. Consider taking a cue from FDR; a small cadre of advisors can be immensely helpful. As one- or two-person businesses, we sometimes lose that broader perspective; we can all benefit from ideas and feedback from people outside our business.

Some independent info pros create relatively formal advisory boards, comprising selected clients, colleagues, and others who understand the issues pertaining to small, service-oriented businesses. Other info pros simply pull together small groups of clients for dinner and brainstorming. What matters is that you identify people who understand your business, who are articulate, and whose instincts you trust.

Amelia Kassel of MarketingBase took this less formal approach, and has been happy with the results. She invited four good clients within driving distance of her home, treated them to dinner at a local restaurant, and offered a certain number of free hours of research in compensation. She asked for their thoughts on her services in general as well as for recommendations on how to expand her business by finding other, similar clients. Because her clients represented ad agencies and public relations firms, they had all kinds of ideas about approaches she could take. In fact, they contributed so many thoughts that Amelia spent much of the next five years putting their suggestions in action.

It can be scary to solicit this kind of advice and feedback from customers. "What if they tell me they don't like my work?" you might be thinking. "What if they suggest things that I can't do?" For starters, if they didn't like your work, they wouldn't be your clients. And listening to ideas generated during a brainstorming session can be enormously useful. Some may be nonstarters, but you'll probably want to try out one or two. The fact that your clients came up with the ideas is a good indicator that other clients will want similar products and services, too.

If you aren't comfortable asking clients to offer their thoughts, consider contacting SCORE, the Service Corps of Retired Executives, which is sponsored by the U.S. Small Business Administration (www.score.org). A volunteer from SCORE can help you think through where your business is going and how you want to get there. SCORE offers both face-to-face and e-mail counseling at no charge. Some independent info pros prefer to work with a business consultant or coach; if your finances are tight, see if the consultant will agree to a barter arrangement in which you supply him or her with research services in exchange for help with strategic planning.

Listening to Your Clients

Kids may say the darndest things, but clients do, too. Pay attention to offhand remarks they make; their casual suggestions can provide great marketing tips. Years ago, I was talking with a client who commented that she'd had trouble finding my phone number. "I knew I had your phone number in my contact management software somewhere, but I wish I'd put you in my plain old Rolodex." As soon as we finished the conversation, I headed out to the local print shop and ordered 500 Rolodex cards printed with all my contact information and the word "Information" on the tab. Total cost? Maybe $100, tops. I had them printed on bright yellow card stock, and included them with the next newsletter I mailed out. Sure enough, a number of clients called to thank me for the card and to say that it would make it easier to remember to call me in the future. Bingo! If I hadn't spent a moment chatting with that client, I wouldn't have imagined that a Rolodex card would make such a difference.

Expanding Your (and Your Clients') Vision

Once, in the middle of teaching a workshop, I had an epiphany. *Clients won't ask you to do anything they don't think you can do.* As simple as that sounds, it helped me recognize two things.

- Clients tend to pigeonhole you. "I call John when I need a profile on a competitor." They forget—or never realize in the first place—that you can provide other information services as well. Your job is to constantly remind your clients of all the ways in which you can make their lives easier or provide the information they need to do their jobs better. If they don't think you offer a particular service, they'll never ask you to supply it.

- You may pigeonhole yourself. "I do secondary research for public relations and advertising firms." Suppose a client asks you to provide a market analysis, or to develop a PowerPoint presentation based on the information you've located? Your client may recognize a skill or ability you don't see in yourself; listen to the requests that push at the edges of what you think your capabilities are, and be open to saying "yes, I can do that." Of course, if you just don't have the skills or background to do a competent job, either subcontract the work or refer it to a colleague. Many independent info pros have formed alliances to enable them to provide more complete information services to their clients. Sometimes these are formal partnerships; more often, they are casual arrangements to subcontract work to someone they know and can rely on. As you talk with clients, and as you do your own strategic planning, think about identifying areas in which you can better solve clients' business problems by expanding the services you provide, either directly or via subcontracting. (See Chapter 14, Subcontracting, or, I'll Scratch Your Back if You Scratch Mine, for a more thorough discussion of subcontracting.) Recognize the difference between being asked to tackle something you haven't done before but are capable of doing, and taking on a request in an area you know nothing about.

Finding a Sounding Board

I am immensely fortunate to live near several other longtime independent info pros, one of whom even shares my passion for running. She and I meet at least once a week to get some fresh air and, inevitably, the conversation drifts toward our businesses. The ability to bounce ideas off someone who is not only a sympathetic listener, but who understands the issues involved in being an independent info pro, is tremendously valuable.

You may not live close to anyone else who does what you do, and I suppose that advising you to move would be a bit drastic. However, you can still establish relationships with other info pros with whom you feel a bond. Reva Basch, editor of this book, and I first got to know each other when I rather presumptuously adopted her as my informal mentor when I started my business. Although we live on opposite coasts, we talked in e-mail frequently. Living in the same city—or even the same time zone—isn't a requirement. What is important is to find someone whom you can bounce ideas off and with whom you feel comfortable. You're not looking for a teacher or an expert to guide you through all the steps of your business (if you *are*, then consider paying a consultant). Rather, you are looking for an empathetic colleague whose instincts you trust and who can, by listening and occasionally offering the benefit of his or her own experience, help you think through thorny issues. The Association of Independent Information Professionals (www.aiip.org) offers an informal volunteer mentoring program through which new members hook up with more experienced info pros who have agreed to provide occasional advice, encouragement, and coaching.

Top Strategic Planning Tips

- Schedule time once a year to evaluate and reflect on your business.
- Track your best clients and figure out how you can find and attract similar clients.
- Identify any problematic clients and evaluate whether to retain them as clients.
- Use clients or, if you prefer, a business coach or consultant for brainstorming and guidance about the direction of your business and new ideas you can implement.
- Listen to your clients' suggestions. Let them expand your vision of
- what you can do.
- Find at least one colleague who can serve as your sounding board.

Section Three

Marketing

Chapter 18

Marketing Do's and Don'ts

Okay, you've read Section One, Getting Started, you've set up your office, and now you're sitting there, waiting for the telephone to ring. I don't know about you, but during my early days I would actually pick up the phone every few hours, just to make sure it was still working.

The rest of Section Three, Marketing, goes into detail about specific techniques and approaches for telling people about your business. This chapter will set the stage for those marketing efforts. Here, I'll talk about what to look for in your clients, finding clients beyond your local area, and feeling comfortable talking about yourself and your business.

Who Needs You?

The first question to ask yourself is, "Who are my potential clients?" Whom should you be marketing to? There are a number of factors to take into account as you decide on the clientele you'll be targeting.

What subject(s) do you know best? If you have experience in a subject area—patents, biotechnology, advertising, chemistry, architecture—professionals in that field represent a natural client base for you. You speak their language. You understand their concerns. You know the subject matter and you know the information sources. You have instant credibility. Of course, most independent info pros eventually expand from their core expertise. When I began my business, as I described in Chapter 7, I focused on research in the telecommunications field, because that was my background and I knew that there weren't many other independent telecom researchers. Pretty soon, though, my clients started asking me for research on other business-related topics, and I was happy to tackle those projects, too. Note, however, that there's a fine line between taking on projects that go beyond your core expertise and accepting jobs for which you just aren't qualified. See the section "Can You Do This for Me?" later in the chapter for more on this subject.

Who is willing to pay for information? You may be an expert in a particular field, but unless you can find clients who are willing to pay you for your expertise, all your knowledge won't pay the rent. Your neighbors may appreciate your ability to help them with their genealogy research, but they would be shocked, most likely, if you started charging them your professional rate for your time and expertise. Instead, you need to focus on a client base that is not particularly price-sensitive and that puts a high value on information—people who have more money than time, who need information in order to do their jobs, and who are willing to pay for that information. That means that your local grocer or hardware store owner is probably not a likely prospect, but a speechwriter, consultant, marketing professional, or strategic planning director would be a good target.

Who doesn't already have easy access to free research? Because I had worked in law libraries earlier in my career, when I first launched my business I considered marketing to small law firms without in-house libraries. After some conversations with colleagues and a few lawyers, though, I realized that this wasn't the best market for me. Many small law firms and sole practitioners view online research via the professional legal services such as Lexis or Westlaw as a profit center. They mark up the online costs and make money from each search, and they can't easily do that if an independent info pro does the research. (Note, however, that law firms do use independent info pros for specialized nonlegal research, particularly in connection with litigation.) Medical researchers tell me that marketing to physicians is also very difficult. Most medical professionals have access to librarians at their local hospital or through the American Medical Association, and are reluctant to use a for-profit researcher when they can get the research done for free or at cost. That's not to say that you should cross law and medicine off your list of possible market niches, especially if you have expertise in either area. Litigation support is a varied and potentially lucrative research area, and independent info pros who can market successfully to law firms, either directly or indirectly, can dip into a significant revenue stream. And doctors aren't the only people who require medical research. Although the Web has empowered consumers seeking medical information to an incredible degree, healthcare industry consultants are often in need of detailed, authoritative journal articles that only a researcher familiar with the ins and outs of the specialized medical databases can effectively provide.

Information-Hungry Professions

What kinds of people are likely to need and value information and be willing to pay for it? The following job titles and functions represent likely prospects.

- Marketing director
- Analyst
- Strategic planner
- Corporate development director
- Market researcher
- Consultant
- Speechwriter
- Research and development director
- Advertising professional
- Public relations officer
- Competitive intelligence director
- Product development manager
- Librarians (yes, librarians need expert researchers too, as I explain in Chapter 23, Starting the Word of Mouth)

Who will be a consistent source of referrals and/or repeat business? John Levis, owner of John E. Levis Associates and an expert in the healthcare and medical industries, used to specialize in providing medical information to consumers. In fact, I called John when my companion was diagnosed with a heart condition and I wanted to figure out what it meant. But John changed the direction of his business when he realized that most individuals who need medical information aren't the kind of clients that help build a business. Why? For starters, they generally used John just once—unless they had multiple diseases, which isn't something you would wish on your clients!—so he couldn't count on their repeat business. John also found that an adequate answer to even the simplest question involved fairly extensive research. Because most consumers wanted the work done for a set price rather than at an hourly rate, John would either have to charge more than the client wanted to pay or perform work for which he couldn't bill. "I don't think anyone is providing consumer medical information for a fee successfully now, given all the free medical sites on the Internet," he told me.

As John knows, it costs far more to get a new client than it does to keep an existing one. And the best—and least expensive—way to get new clients is by word of mouth from your existing clients and colleagues. That's why successful independent info pros focus their marketing time and attention on people who they think will use them repeatedly, and why they stay in touch with "influencers"—people whom others go to for advice, suggestions, and referrals. Concentrating on prospects like those can increase the scope of your marketing immensely.

Know What the Client Needs

It's easy to think about what services you can provide: You offer online research; you locate public records for law firms; you conduct primary research through telephone interviews. But that's not enough to make a prospect turn into a client. The crucial step that some independent info pros forget is to think beyond what you *do* to what your clients *need*. Your most powerful marketing approach is to offer an information service that your client didn't even realize he needed until he talked with you. Yes, being proactive in this way requires more upfront effort on your part; you have to think of yourself as a member of your client's team and focus on what information services your client needs and would be willing to pay for. Of course, this is a challenge if you don't have any clients yet. As I suggest in Chapter 17, consider joining your clients'—or potential clients'—major industry associations, and read the trade publications they read to keep up on their key issues. And see Chapter 7, Before You Launch, for a discussion of how to conduct "informational interviews" to identify their information needs.

The advantage of this approach is that it makes you virtually competition-proof. You have demonstrated to your client that you are focused on her business needs rather than on your own set of stock information services, and it's clear from the research and interviews that you've conducted that you understand her business and industry. It also enables you to charge a higher hourly rate; your client isn't going to shop around for the cheapest information service when you've already demonstrated that you want and value her business.

Think Globally, Not Locally

When you first ponder where your clients will come from, it's natural to think locally—the corporations headquartered or with large offices in your town, the local Chamber of Commerce, even your friends and neighbors. That's great; you might get some business from nearby people and organizations. But it's a very limited field. Even if you live in the middle of Chicago, there are only so many companies in the area for you to market to. You are vulnerable to any economic slump that hits your region particularly hard. And if you live in a small town, your chances of supporting yourself on local businesses alone are pretty slim. Besides, why restrict your horizons in such an artificial way? With the growth of the Internet, defining your market in geographical terms is, generally speaking, an obsolescent and career-limiting assumption. See Chapter 20, in which I talk about marketing your business via the Web.

Another factor to keep in mind is that it is usually much easier to target a *vertical* market (e.g., pharmaceutical companies, labor organizations, architects) than it is to focus on all prospects within a geographic region. Why? Vertical markets have well-established communication tools—industry publications to write for; professional associations to join (and, more importantly, volunteer with); electronic mailing lists to participate in; conferences and trade shows at which to network, speak, or exhibit; and so on. You can reach prospects around the country, or around the world, by taking advantage of the opportunities provided by such channels of communication. Oddly enough, it's much harder to market cost-effectively to a local audience. Very few independent info pros have successfully built a business using time-intensive marketing efforts such as in-person sales visits or cold calling, or broadcast efforts such as direct mail. By going deep and narrow, you get much more bang for your marketing buck.

You're Always "On"

Although it's important to look beyond your local area for clients, never miss an opportunity to market yourself—subtly—in person. Perfect your "elevator speech"—a quick two- or three-sentence description of what you do that you can deliver while riding the elevator with someone, or in the grocery store, on a plane, or at a meeting. Here's how I might perform my "elevator speech" as I chat with someone while we're waiting to board the train.

Prospect: That's an interesting assortment of reading material. What do you do for a living?

Me: (spoken with enthusiasm) I have the greatest job in the world! I run my own research company, finding decision-making information for business professionals.

Prospect: Really? I sometimes need information on competitors. Can you do that?

Me: I just finished a project analyzing the competitors for a financial services company. Say, why don't you give me your business card, and I'll mail you some information about what I do?

Notice that I didn't just hand the prospect my business card; it's much more important for me to get hers. Who knows if she'll remember to call me when she gets back to her office? More likely, she'll lose my card, forget about the conversation, and that's the last I'll hear of her. But ... she gave me her card. When I get back to my office, I send her a marketing kit (see Chapter 19, Your Business Image, for details on creating your marketing kit), along with a cover memo mentioning how much I enjoyed chatting with her at the train station on Tuesday, so that she is reminded of who the heck I am. Then, three weeks, later, I send her a copy of my newsletter. And a couple of weeks after that, I send her a second Rolodex card, along with a reminder that she can subscribe to my free e-mail newsletter simply by e-mailing me. The net result of having asked her for her business card instead of just giving her mine is that I'm able to do three nonintrusive follow-up contacts with her—instead of possibly none at all.

"Can You Do This for Me?"

As I explain in the "Calling in the Experts" section of Chapter 14, Subcontracting, or I'll Scratch Your Back if You Scratch Mine, even though your prospective clients may think of you as "the expert on the aerospace industry" or "the business valuation researcher," they may ask you to do research in other areas as well. If it's a subject on which you know you can educate yourself quickly, or that's related to a topic you're familiar with, or that requires the same information resources you use all the time, it's a safe bet that you'll do a fine job. However, if it goes way beyond the subject areas and the research tools you know, consider outsourcing the extra-challenging jobs to colleagues who *do* specialize in those areas. Chapter 14 says more about how to subcontract or refer work out and still make points with your clients.

Amelia Kassel, principal of MarketingBase, described one exception to the rule of always subcontracting or referring out what you don't know how to do. On two occasions, clients have asked her to use specialized software or a professional online service that she wasn't familiar with. She explained that she didn't routinely use the product and that the client would have to pay for her learning curve. In both situations, the client knew her, valued her expertise, and was willing to be billed for the time required for Amelia to get up to speed. This was a great solution for both parties—the clients could use an info pro in whom they already had confidence, and Amelia was able to expand her knowledge of information systems into new areas while being paid to learn. It worked because Amelia explained in advance that she would need time to teach herself how the new information service worked; also, as an alternative, she offered to outsource the work. The clients appreciated her willingness to bring in an outside expert and, fortunately, could spare the time for Amelia to get proficient.

You must be confident that you can deliver what you promise. Clients—for that matter, people in general—are attracted to people who are positive, upbeat, and self-confident without being arrogant. Presumably, you are in this business either because you are an excellent researcher or because you can subcontract the billable work to people who are the best in their field. You have a right to be confident, but that right only lasts as long as you resist the urge to tackle jobs that are way over your head in terms of subject expertise, access to resources, or availability of time.

Ten Mistakes New Independent Info Pros Make

One reason why starting an information services business is so challenging is that it is unlike most other small businesses. The corner market can put big signs up in the window advertising this week's special on strawberries or dog food. The dry cleaner can place flyers on all the neighborhood cars. Web site promoters can—and, alas, do—send out unsolicited e-mail by the thousands, offering to increase traffic to your site for a "modest fee." These techniques may work for some entrepreneurs, but they are not particularly useful for marketing an information business. Think about how you'd go about finding a lawyer, accountant, or real estate agent. You'd ask your friends, neighbors, or colleagues; you wouldn't wait for a cold call or a postcard in the mail, nor are you likely to look in the Yellow Pages. Word of mouth is how most people locate someone who provides professional services. And that's how people will find *you*, too.

Of course, I read a paragraph similar to what you just read when I started my business: "Direct mail, cold calls, and Yellow Pages ads don't work." Sure, I thought, maybe they don't work for *you*, but I've got this great idea, you see ... Suffice it to say that sometimes I need to learn things the hard way. In the interest of keeping you from wasting too much time and money on marketing efforts that don't pay off, here is my top ten list of what *not* to do. And yes, I tried most of them myself during my first year.

1. *Sending out brochures to everyone on a mailing list.* Regardless of where you found or purchased the list—a professional association, a local business directory, the phone book—a mass mailing is more than likely a waste of time and money. Unless the recipient already knows you and recognizes your name, it will be seen as junk mail and dropped in the nearest recycling bin.

2. *Focusing on marketing to your local area.* It's easy to assume that local businesses are more likely to use a local researcher. From that conclusion, you may decide that the best way to find those local customers is to attend Chamber of Commerce meetings or informal networking groups such as "leads clubs." The disadvantage is that you wind up spending your time marketing to a broad cross-section of people rather than focusing on your target audience.

3. *Telling prospects that you can find any kind of information.* "Whatever you need, I'm an expert at finding it!" Sounds like a compelling marketing line, doesn't it? However, most prospects will figure that you're promising more than you can deliver, or that you're not actually expert at finding anything at all. People will remember you if you tell them that you specialize in tracking down government files from a hundred years ago, or that you focus on research services for the non-profit sector, or that you help consumer food companies understand their competition. Concrete examples make you instantly memorable. While many people won't need your expertise themselves, they may know someone else who does. That

means that every person you tell about your business becomes, in effect, part of your marketing staff.

4. *Offering to discount your fee for new clients.* Supermarkets know all about "loss leaders," the practice of pricing an item below cost in order to bring customers into the store—where, presumably, they will buy plenty of other products at the regular price. Cutting prices makes sense in the consumer retail industry. Customers understand the practice and they know that the sale price won't last. In addition, most shoppers wind up filling their carts with enough other items that the store actually shows a profit from each one. However, loss leaders don't work in the independent info pro business. Customers expect you to maintain the same price over time, even if you've told them explicitly that the first project was discounted. Research or consulting time isn't a tangible like toothpaste; clients find it difficult to understand why you're charging them a higher rate now if you could "afford" to offer them a discount the first time. And, of course, you *can't* afford it. You're not running a supermarket or a drug store, so you can't make up the lost profit by convincing your customer that he should also purchase toothpaste, laundry detergent, and dog food at the regular price while he's at it. No matter how you present it, returning to your regular rate after an initial discount will feel like a price increase to your client. Offer new clients one price—your regular rate—and stick to it.

5. *Making cold calls.* One side of your brain may be saying, "Cold calling must work. Why else do stock brokers, insurance agents, and aluminum siding contractors insist on calling me, usually right at dinner time?" But if you're like me, the other half of your brain is screaming, "No! I'll do anything but make cold calls!" Fortunately, you can listen to that screaming half; in my experience and that of the vast majority of other independent info pros, cold calling simply doesn't work. There are several good reasons why cold calling is a bad idea. First, how many customers do you think would decide to spend hundreds or thousands of dollars, in preparation for making an important business decision, on someone they've never heard of who just happened to call them up? That's right ... mighty few. Secondly, in these days of voice mail and effective administrative gatekeepers, you'll spend an enormous amount of time just getting a live person on the phone. Third, you'll have to get 15 or 20 people to answer the phone and engage in a conversation before you find one who is vaguely interested. That means that you've spent an entire day (or two), with one prospect to show for your efforts, and that person may never actually

get around to using your services. At that rate, you'll *never* land a real, live, paying client.

The only exception to the No Cold Calls rule is what some people call "warm calling." This presumes that you have already made contact with your prospects in some way, so that they will recognize your name when you call. One way to do this is based on an approach described in the book *The Consultant's Calling: Bringing Who You Are to What You Do* by Geoffrey M. Bellman (Jossey-Bass, 2001). First you need to identify a specific, high-level position within a group of organizations for which you believe you can provide unique, high-value services. Perhaps your target position is the head of international accounts in *Fortune* 500 food companies. Then, using the companies' Web sites or annual reports, identify the person in charge of that function in eight or ten corporations. Be sure to call the company to confirm that the information is still current. Then write a letter to each executive, introducing yourself, and offering "name a topic and I'll send you an article a week for six weeks—no charge"—or a similar offer that highlights the custom research services you provide. Be sure to include your e-mail address and toll-free phone number, if you have one. Follow up a week or so later to ask what topic the executive would like monitored. If you can't get through to your contact, try his or her assistant, who may be able to help you identify a topic of interest. Then, monitor the leading business and industry publications, major newspapers, and news headline services on the Web, and send each executive one article a week, with a brief cover memo. Remember to abide by copyright restrictions in choosing your articles; download them from an online service that permits redistribution of the material, or avoid the copyright issue by sending your prospects the headline, a brief summary of the article, and perhaps a pointer to the URL where the rest of the story can be found. (See Chapter 15, Ethics and Legalities, for more information on copyright issues.) At the end of six weeks, you can place a warm call to these executives; if nothing else, they will probably remember who you are. But have you noticed how time-consuming this approach is? All that work just to make a sales pitch to a handful of people who might be prepared to accept your call. This illustrates why cold calling, without any preparatory work and demonstration of your value, is usually pointless.

6. *Marketing to the wrong people.* It's easier to market yourself to people you know and feel comfortable with than it is to market yourself to strangers. Unfortunately, unless all of your friends and family members just happen to be people who are anxious to use—and pay for—your services, you won't generate much business talking

only to the folks you know. Deciding on your client base requires a combination of cold-eyed realism—will these people be regular, repeat customers; good sources of referrals; and relatively price-insensitive?—and following your heart. If you can't stand working with your clients, you won't be in business for long. If you share a common bond with your customers, you will find communicating with them that much easier. But take a good hard look and make sure that you are not letting your comfort level override the basic business considerations of finding good, steady clients.

7. *Relying on a Web site or a listing in a business directory or the Yellow Pages to generate business.* "Build it and they will come" might have worked in the movie "The Field of Dreams," but it doesn't work for independent info pros. Although it's important to have a Web site and a listing in the business section (*not* residential listings) of your local telephone book, very few clients are going to find you through either of those means. I have had a Web site since 1996 and I can recall only two clients who located me through a Web directory or a search engine and then actually picked up the phone and called me. Instead, I get lots and lots of e-mail spam, solicitations to pay for listings in other directories, and e-mail from people interested in getting into the independent information profession. Yes, I maintain my Web site and pay for listings in a few business directories that my clients use. But I do this as a way to confirm the stability of my business, not as a marketing technique. Prospects expect me to have a Web page, and they like being able to find out about my background and see how I present myself on the Web. Likewise, if a prospect hears me speak at a conference, she can go back to her office, look me up in an association directory, and find that, sure enough, I'm listed there; that suggests that I am familiar with the issues that she deals with every day. Web sites and directory listings are great ways to reassure clients that you are in business, but you can't count on them as primary marketing tools.

8. *Sending unsolicited e-mail promoting your business.* As long as e-mail exists, so will unsolicited commercial e-mail, affectionately known as spam. However, spam is also one of the most effective ways to repel potential clients. Not only that, it's forbidden by most Internet service providers. Even if you have already had contact with a prospect, unsolicited e-mail is just that—unasked for and probably unappreciated. Do you really want to be seen in the same light as those companies that offer to sell you a college diploma, an improved sex life, or a way to erase all your credit card debt immediately? Rather than sending e-mail ads, write a short newsletter and offer a free opt-in subscription to your clients and prospects. See Chapter 20,

Marketing on the Web, and Chapter 21, Print Marketing, for more discussion of newsletters and other regular marketing contacts.

9. *Designing your marketing materials yourself.* Unless you are a professional Web site designer or you have years of experience designing marketing material, resist the urge to develop your own graphical business image. I have seen far too many brochures, logos, and Web sites designed by independent info pros themselves, and the majority of them are, well, awful. Yes, your marketing materials are an investment you have to make when you're just starting out, and graphic designers don't come cheap. But the money you invest at the beginning will be well spent; you'll have a business image that looks established, professional, and polished. The same applies to your Web site. Some software packages provide you with fill-in-the-blanks templates for building your own home page, but they often don't project much of a corporate image. See Chapter 19, Your Business Image, for more on your marketing materials.

10. *Scaling back your marketing if you have one big client.* Imagine the scenario: You just landed a big client, who's paying you for 30 hours of work a week. The client promises that you'll be kept busy for months—nay, years—at this rate. You sit back and think, "Now, this is how to run an info pro business." Unfortunately, you still have to market, because all that work from that one great client *will* eventually dry up. It always does, regardless of the client's well-meaning assurances and best intentions. Sometimes your contact leaves the company or is transferred. Sometimes the client's business slows down and the first budget item cut is outside contractors. Sometimes, the client decides to take the work in-house. And even a contract promising you a certain amount of revenue every month isn't really a guarantee, as it probably wouldn't be worth the expense of litigating if the client chose to cancel it. So, although a steady gig is nothing to complain about, it's important to realize that sooner or later it will end, and the end of a contract is not the time to start marketing efforts that often take months to produce results. Because you frequently can't anticipate when the work will end, you need to market constantly, even when you're fully booked with work.

Successful Marketing Techniques

- Identify a client base that needs information, is relatively price-insensitive, in a field that you're already familiar with.
- Listen to your clients; they'll give you ideas for new products and services.
- Market vertically rather than to a geographic region.
- Only accept projects you know you can do well.
- Use focused marketing techniques, not direct mail or cold calling.
- Think niche, not generalist. Focus on services that set you apart from your competitors.
- Show self-confidence and enthusiasm when you contact prospective clients. People are drawn to upbeat, positive people.

Chapter 19

Your Business Image

Everything you do is part of your image, down to how you answer your phone and how you package your deliverables. Every time your client sees you, hears about you, or looks at your work product, you're sending a message. Fortunately, what that message says about you is, for the most part, under your control.

Here's My Card

As much as we all seem to have gone "virtual," there's still a need for something as quaint as business cards—not to mention stationery, mailing labels, envelopes, and all the other accoutrements of the hard-copy world. We do still meet people face to face, and—old-fashioned as I am—I believe that sending a thank-you note or follow-up letter on paper makes a positive impact.

Designing a Logo

As you set up your business, it's tempting to simply browse through Microsoft Word's clip art collection to find a nice image, slap it at the top of a document, add your company name in some unusual font, and call that a letterhead. Resist the urge. Having a professional design your corporate image is an investment with both immediate and long-term payoffs. Trust me, people can tell the difference between a company logo designed on a word processor and one custom-designed for your business. Having a professionally designed logo and letterhead sends the message that you are an established and committed business person, not just a hobbyist. (And if you *are* entering the independent information profession as a hobby, I'd advise you to change your thinking immediately and turn it into a real business!) Whenever I see stationery or a business card that was obviously created from generic clip art or otherwise designed by an amateur, I wince. It's a short-term saving that costs you in the long run. If you're planning to do most of your marketing through your Web site, a professional image there makes a huge difference, too. (See Chapter 20, Marketing on the Web, for more discussion of your Web site.)

What your logo looks like will depend on who your clients are. You'll want a design that speaks to your client base. If you're marketing to law firms, think Staid and Serious. If you're targeting high-tech advertising or public relations firms, you might try a flashier logo that resonates with those creative types. If you work with unions, it's probably wise to use a union printing firm so you can display the tiny symbol at the bottom (called the union bug) indicating that it was printed at a union shop. Know your audience and make sure your image is appealing to them.

How do you find a design professional to develop your logo and letterhead? Ask around! If you know any consultants or small businesses whose logos you find appealing, ask whom they used. Many office supply stores provide customized logo design as well as printing services, often for a relatively modest cost. Make sure that what you get has been designed exclusively for you, and is not simply clip art with your name and contact information appended to it. In fact, if you want to do without a logo and just use text in your letterhead and other marketing materials, most printers can design something for you in a pleasing font, layout, and, if you choose, color at a modest cost. Be sure to get a copy of your design in digital form so you can incorporate it into your Web site, handouts, and so on. This last bit of advice comes from having had my logo designed long before the Web or electronic publishing, and then spending a considerable sum having it converted to a professional-looking electronic format.

Paper Matters

When you order your stationery, envelopes, and business cards, spend the money to buy high-quality paper stock. As one independent info pro commented to me, "Printing and the quality of the paper is important. I can always tell when someone has designed their own logo and printed it on a laser printer, and it makes me think they're really small-time." Considering how few printed letters you'll probably send out, it's worth the additional cost to invest in a heavy paper stock.

You won't have to replenish your supply very often, so the investment lasts for quite a while.

Several companies offer stationery preprinted with colorful designs, along with coordinated envelopes, mailing labels, and business cards. Paper Direct (www.paperdirect.com) is the best-known, although some of the large office supply chains such as Office Depot (www.officedepot.com) and copy stores such as Kinko's (www.kinkos.com) also carry "specialty paper." While preprinted stationery is an easy way to create a colorful and professional-looking letterhead, it looks like what it is—a fairly generic design run through a laser printer or photocopier with your name across the top. When I see a letter on preprinted paper, my first impression is of someone who is not sufficiently committed to his business to invest in custom stationery; then I wonder how long he intends to *stay* in business. Preprinted papers can be useful for brochures and other specialized printings such as promotional mailings, but you run the risk of sending the wrong message if you use them as your regular letterhead.

Don't Forget to Call

In Chapter 17, Strategic Planning, I described how listening to a client made me realize that I should send out Rolodex cards. It seems like such a low-tech marketing tool, particularly in these days of Palm Pilots and contact management software. But for every person who eschews hard copy, there's at least one other person who still has a Rolodex file on her desk. You can set yourself apart from your competition by getting your card in that file.

Just about any office supply or print shop can design a Rolodex card for you. Just make sure you include all the essentials—your company name, address, phone number, and e-mail address. And, speaking as someone who has graduated to bifocals, let me encourage you to make sure the print is large enough to be read easily. Include a tab along the top of the card that says *Information*, *Research*, or whatever word you want your clients to remember you by. If you have a slogan or tag line ("Building Information for the Architecture Industry" or "We Find the Hard-to-Find"), add it at the bottom of the card. Have it printed on colored card stock—I use bright yellow—and include that card whenever you give or send material to a client or prospect. Rolodex cards cost so little to print—no more than $200 for 1,000 or 2,000 cards—that you can enclose them with everything you mail out.

Business Cards and Logos That Work

You'll live with your logo for quite a while. You may eventually decide to update your corporate image if you change your company name or feel that your logo looks dated, but you want to start with a business identity that you're going to be happy with for a long time. What you select will depend on your client base (do they expect something flashy or conservative?), the type of work you do (do you want your logo to indicate that you specialize in aviation research?), and your personality and taste. Here are examples of a variety of business cards used by several established independent info pros. As you can see, they vary widely in design and "feel," but they all look professional and the company name is clear and easy to read.

Figure 19.1 Sample independent info pro business cards

Your Brochure

Most experienced independent info pros are of two minds about the usefulness of brochures. Our clients and prospects expect us to have a brochure; it's an indication, along with a professional-looking business card, that we're an established business. On the other hand, brochures aren't as flexible or easy to update as a Web page, and some info pros simply refer people to their Web pages instead of bothering to print brochures. Although I certainly don't hand out as many brochures now as I did five or ten years ago, I still get requests for brochures and I still include them in my marketing kit (see more on marketing kits later in the chapter).

If you provide several types of services, you may want to develop several brochures and hand out the one that addresses a prospective client's needs. For example, I wear several hats in my business. I specialize in business research, so my brochure talks about that. I also offer consulting services to the online industry, so I have a one-page fact sheet on my background relevant to these services. And finally, I have developed several workshops and seminars that I tailor to specific audiences, so another handout describes the types of training I provide. I never give all of these to any one prospect—I want each person to focus on the aspect of my business that I think is most pertinent to his or her needs.

Make sure that your brochure looks professional—that means no generic clip art. Talk about the services and the expertise you offer that set you apart from the competition. You may want to address the misperception that "it's all available on the Web, for free" and to briefly discuss what information you can provide beyond what's available on the open Web. Have a friend or colleague review your brochure before you have it printed; make sure it communicates your services clearly to the reader.

Some info pros have their brochures custom-printed professionally; others use preprinted brochure stock from Paper Direct (www.paperdirect.com) or an office supply store. The advantage of custom-printed brochures is that they do look more professional, and you're assured that no one else will have a brochure that looks quite like yours. On the other hand, they're more expensive to print and, printing economics being what they are, you usually wind up printing a large quantity. That means that you will live with that brochure for a long time. Using preprinted brochure stock, on the other hand, gives you a full-color brochure without the expense of custom printing, and allows you to print small batches at a time, making updating easier and more cost-effective. However, you run the risk of selecting the same stock as another independent info pro, and the finished product will probably look less professional than a custom-printed brochure.

Whether you go with a full-fledged brochure or a simple one-page fact sheet describing your services, be sure to include a tangible explanation of what you offer rather than a generic description such as "we find information on any topic." Provide some "anonymized" examples of research projects you've done, changing enough of the details to protect the confidentiality of your clients. If you don't have any clients yet, use descriptions of research you did in your last job, or offer to do some research for another professional—a business coach, accountant or graphic artist, for example—in exchange for their services. (Given the costs associated with using the professional online services, you'll probably want to barter your labor fee but pass along any out-of-pocket expenses.) Although barter relationships don't generate cold hard cash, they enable you to obtain services you might not be able to pay for immediately. (Note that, at least in the U.S., you are expected to report the cash equivalent of the bartered services to the IRS.)

As I suggested earlier when talking about Rolodex cards, you may want to develop a tag line or slogan that you can include in your brochure, on your Rolodex card, and so on. A tag line is a short sentence or phrase that memorably and succinctly describes your business specialization:

- "We Know the Aviation Industry"
- "Competitive Intelligence for the Biotech Industry"
- "International Trade Consultant"
- "Research Services for Nonprofits"

Make sure that your name, company name, mailing address, telephone and fax numbers, e-mail address, and Web site URL appear prominently somewhere in your brochure, in print large enough to be easily read. (If you aren't ready to set up a Web site yet, at least register a domain name and get a personalized e-mail address. See Chapter 20, Marketing on the Web, for how to do both.)

Your Telephone Image

Fortunately, video phones still haven't caught on, despite predictions that by now we would no longer be able to answer the phone without first stopping to comb our hair and tuck in our shirt. While we don't have to worry about our physical appearance on the phone, we do need to think about the messages we send even before we pick up the receiver.

For starters, it's important to have a separate telephone line for your business. Nothing says "I'm not serious about my business" like a child answering your phone when a client calls, or an answering machine telling callers that the Jones family is away right now but please leave a message. See Chapter 8, Setting Up Your Business, where I discuss telephone set-ups.

You will need some way to answer business calls when you're out of the office. The obvious solution is an answering machine, but I advise against that option unless you are seldom on the phone yourself. Why? Because it doesn't address the "busy signal" problem, unless you buy an answering machine that includes a feature that detects when you're on the phone and handles any incoming calls. Chances are that calls will come in when you are on the phone, and people are so accustomed to voice mail that a busy signal sounds unprofessional and gives the caller no alternative but to try back. And you might lose business that way. A better option is setting up voice mail through your local telephone company so callers can leave a message if your line is busy.

One possible downside of voice mail is that—unlike an answering machine with its blinking light—you sometimes have to pick up the phone and listen for a "stutter tone" that indicates you have messages. Some phones can signal a stutter tone with a flashing light, or you can buy a gizmo to accomplish the same thing if your phone doesn't have this feature built in. The Hello Direct catalog (www.hellodirect.com) offers an assortment of products. See Chapter 8 for more discussions of the cost and feature considerations of voice mail and answering machines.

Answering Your Phone

It seems unnecessary to advise you to answer your phone when you're available and to return calls promptly, but you'd be surprised. Paul and Sarah Edwards, home-office gurus, once told of calling five independent info pros, leaving five messages, and having not a single call returned. Nada. Zip.

Being in your office to answer your phone can be a competitive advantage, particularly now that so many businesses seem to rely heavily on automated responses and voice-mail menus. It demonstrates to clients that you are available when they need to reach you. If you are going to be out of your office for more than an hour or two, change your voice-mail or answering machine message to let callers know that you won't be able to call them back immediately. I can't count the number of times I've left messages after hearing "I'm in the office but can't take your call right now" or "I'm either away from my desk or on another call but I'll get back to you as soon as I can," and found out a week later that the person was actually on vacation but never bothered to change the outgoing message. By managing your callers' expectations, you can leave the office and still assure your callers that you really *are* glad they called. If you anticipate being out of your office frequently to do on-site research or consulting, don't advertise or guarantee 24-hour turnaround.

What about giving clients your cell phone number and listing it on your business and Rolodex cards? Maybe it's just me, but I'm put off when someone gives me a laundry list of numbers to call if I want to reach them. Why should I have to call your voice line, your pager, your cell phone, and your home phone, and leave messages at each number? If you plan to be away and want to take calls on your cell phone, pay for call forwarding on your business line and then forward your office phone to your cell when you leave the office. Of course, those incoming cell phone calls add up because most cell phone plans charge you for incoming calls, but this may be an acceptable price to pay in order to be easily accessible to your clients.

But think about whether you really want to take calls wherever you are. Suppose you're in the car or out with your family; you won't be able to concentrate on your client's needs when you're negotiating traffic or watching your daughter score a goal. As Alex Kramer of Kramer Research commented, "Your callers can hear what's going on around you, and if you're not doing something business-related at the time the call comes in, you may not be in the right frame of mind to take the call. That's why my voice mail refers people to my pager number and not my cell phone. I'll answer a page if I'm someplace quiet and I can focus on the call; otherwise, I wait until I'm back in the office."

Wherever you are when the phone rings, you'll want to sound polished, professional, and focused when you answer. Many independent info pros answer their phone with their name—"Robin Smith" or "Hello, this is Robin." I prefer this approach because it reminds my clients that they are dealing with me, not with a faceless company. Other info pros prefer to answer the phone with their business name. That's okay, if the name is easy to say out loud, since it reinforces the brand of the company. And some info pros simply answer the phone "Research" or "May I help you?" While it may seem off-putting to some callers, this rather generic greeting is a good choice if you're subcontracting and talking with your contractor's clients or acting as someone's "associate" while he's on vacation. However you choose to answer the phone, watch your tone of voice. You want to sound upbeat, crisp, and professional. One of the tricks recommended by a telephone researcher—and who would know more about cultivating an effective phone manner?—is to stand up when you talk on the phone. This helps you feel more focused and energetic.

Creating a Marketing Kit

What do you do if a prospective client asks you to send her some information on your company? Sure, you can refer her to your Web site or toss a brochure in the mail, but that doesn't create a particularly strong impression. If you get the sense that she is a strong potential client rather than a tire-kicker, you'll want to send her a more professional package—something that tells the story of who you are and why you're the answer to her dreams.

Your marketing kit can be as simple or as elaborate as you want; think about what your client base would expect. At the least, it should include the following:

- A good-looking two-pocket folder (sometimes called a portfolio folder) in a color that coordinates with your logo. Make sure it has slots where you can insert your business card.

- Your brochure or fact sheet describing your services.

- A reprint of a recent article you've written or that has been written about you.

- A page of client testimonials (don't be shy about soliciting testimonials from satisfied clients or even from people for whom you did research in your prior job).

- A short biographical profile—not a resumé (you're not looking for a job!), but a brief sketch that highlights your expertise as an information professional.

- Your business card and Rolodex card.

- A cover letter addressed to the prospect, thanking her by name for contacting you, and highlighting your capabilities and how you can best meet her needs.

Word processing makes it easy to tailor every package you send to the information needs of the individual prospect. You don't want a potential client to think "boiler plate" when he opens your envelope. By taking time to understand each prospect's business and what is going on in that industry, you can customize your cover letter to each person's concerns.

If you offer a free or for-fee client newsletter, either print or e-mail, you can also include a postage-paid postcard soliciting a subscription. Yes, it'll cost you a little extra for each marketing kit you send out, but a prepaid reply card makes the offer more attractive and easier to respond to; the more newsletter subscribers you have, the easier it is for you to stay in touch with your clients and potential clients on a regular basis. See Chapter 21 for more about using a newsletter for marketing.

Whether to include a rate sheet in your marketing kit depends on your business and your client base. I usually include one because I price most of my work at a single hourly rate, and the printed fee schedule alerts prospective clients to the fact that, while I'm good, I'm not cheap. Some independent info pros prefer not to quote their fees until after discussing the specific project, particularly if they expect to charge a per-project fee rather than an hourly rate. (See Chapter 13, Setting Rates and Fees, and the sidebar "Publishing Your Rate Sheet" in Chapter 20, Marketing on the Web, for more discussion about this issue.) If you do enclose a price sheet, be sure to include a date limit: "These rates are valid through December, 2004." I make a habit of re-evaluating my rates at the end of each year, so putting an expiration date on my rate sheet lets me raise my rate without prospective clients crying foul.

Checklist for Polishing Your Business Image

- ✦ Have your logo and letterhead professionally designed.
- ✦ Have your business cards and stationery professionally printed on high-quality stock.
- ✦ Send Rolodex cards to all your clients and prospects.
- ✦ Develop a brochure that highlights what sets you apart from your competitors.
- ✦ Come up with a tag line or slogan that is descriptive, memorable, and succinct.
- ✦ Invest in a separate business phone line; consider a toll-free number as well.
- ✦ Develop a marketing kit that projects an established, professional image.

Chapter 20

Marketing on the Web

Entire books have been written on how to market your business on the Web. They're useful as far as they go, but most potential clients don't surf the Web looking for an expert researcher. If they had the spare time to search the Web, they wouldn't need you. You'll probably want a Web site for credibility's sake; it seems to be a component of one's business identity these days. At minimum, it will provide a description of your company, your expertise, and the services you offer.

But don't count on your Web site as your ultimate marketing device. Even more useful than a site of your own is making sure you're listed in the appropriate professional directories on the Web. Prospective clients *will* check Web directories for research services. That's one of the reasons I value my membership in the Association of Independent Information Professionals; prospective clients and subcontractors can see a description of my business and a link to my Web site in the AIIP membership directory at www.aiip.org/AboutAIIP/directory_home.asp.

This chapter will show you how to set up a professional looking site, and will also give you some pointers for marketing yourself more actively on the Web.

Establishing Your Web Presence

Most Internet service providers (ISPs) will let you put up a Web site if you're a subscriber. The URL to your site will be something like www.ISP.com/joeblow. While you probably won't pay much, if anything, for the site beyond your monthly service fee, it's a false economy. For starters, you will eventually change ISPs. Even if you plan to stay with one company, odds are good that it will be acquired, change its name, go out of business, or suddenly raise its rates. And that means that all your printed literature is suddenly out of date. A personalized domain name, on the other hand, won't change when you switch ISPs. In addition, www.ISP.com/joeblow just doesn't look as professional. These days, the only URLs without personalized domain names seem to be on personal—not business—Web pages.

Reserving a Domain Name

Even if you're not yet ready to set up a Web page, you may want to reserve a domain name for your business as soon as you've decided on your company name. You can start using your customized domain for e-mail even without a Web page, and have the e-mail automatically forwarded to your regular e-mail account. A personalized domain name makes you look more established, and it enables you to give out a permanent e-mail address that won't change when you switch ISPs. For example, my "public" e-mail address is mbates@BatesInfo.com and the domain is hosted by Radix.net. However, my primary ISP (and hence my "real" e-mail address) varies, depending on which ISP I'm using. So Radix automatically redirects all incoming e-mail to my current ISP, and I set my e-mail software so that it looks as if I'm sending messages from "BatesInfo.com."

First, check to see if the domain name you want is available. Use one of the domain name look-up services (such as www.allwhois.com or www.amnesi.com) and type the domain name you'd like in the search box. I recommend that you stick to the .com extension, or .co and the country domain, rather than one of the new extensions such as .biz or .info. Your clients, along with the rest of the world, are probably accustomed to typing .com at the end of a URL; an address that ends in something else means that they'll have trouble finding you. Network Solutions used to have sole authority over domain names in the U.S., but now other companies are allowed to register domains as well. The registration costs as little as $15 a year. Note that this does *not* include ISP hosting services; it's just the domain registration fee. Your ISP will usually help you register your domain name if you don't want to go through the "paperwork" yourself and, for a nominal fee, will let you "park" it and use it for e-mail even if you're not yet ready to put up a Web site.

If you already have an ISP you're happy with, find out what they'd charge to host your site. Or check the sites that provide comparisons of various Web hosting companies, such as Web Hosting Ratings (www.Webhostingratings.com) or C|Net (www.cnet.com), for example. When you are considering a Web host, think about technical and customer support as well as price. A low-end domain host may not offer the support you need. And those free hosting services? Most are geared to folks who want to set up a personal Web page; they often impose severe limitations on the number of pages you can put on your site and the amount of traffic it can handle on a daily basis. Imagine your prospective clients getting a message like "Sorry, this Web site is over its limit for the day. Try later."

Creating a Web Site

Once you've reserved a domain name and "parked" it with an ISP, it's time to consider developing a Web site. First, give some thought to what you want your site to accomplish. For most independent info pros, a Web site isn't a major source of clients or leads, but it does lend credibility and the occasional client will call if you have a professionally designed site. To get an idea of how independent info pros describe themselves, and how they position and market themselves through their Web sites, go to the Association of Independent Information Professionals' Membership Directory, search for AIIP members who provide services or specialize in an industry similar to yours, and click through to their Web pages. Note what you like and don't like about each one. Then sketch out what you want your Web page to say about you.

Any professional Web site should include the following:

- Your name, e-mail address, and phone number on the main page and in plain text, not as part of a graphic. (People now use Web sites as a substitute for phone directories; instead of calling directory assistance, a potential client will likely pull up your Web page and see if your phone number is there. But remember: Text in a graphic is not searchable; someone using their favorite search engine to look for you by name may not be able to find your page. Make it easy for them to find and call you!)

- A link to your e-mail address, so a visitor can simply click once to send you e-mail.

- No animated graphics, large image files, or other multimedia bells and whistles that look unprofessional or that presume that visitors have the latest software plug-ins and add-ons on their PCs.

- A clear description of the services you provide, written in terms that your client base understands. Use industry buzz words and acronyms if appropriate.

- A brief description of who you are and your background and qualifications.

- Logical navigation, including clearly visible links from every page back to the main page. Don't let your visitors get lost in your site.

In short, make your Web site easy to use, relevant to your clients, and informative about your services. Remember, you're selling yourself as well as your company. Make sure your site focuses on what your clients need to know, not just on what you want to sell. Sell the benefits rather than simply listing the services you provide.

You're responsible for planning the content of your Web site, but resist the urge to design your site yourself. Unless you're a graphics professional or an experienced Web designer, you run the risk of winding up with a site that looks, well, like an amateur designed it. A Web site designer can develop a site that is simple enough for you to update yourself, if you don't mind learning a little HTML. How do you find a Web designer? Remember those AIIP-member Web sites you looked at? Contact members whose sites impressed you and ask them whom they used. Remember, you needn't limit yourself to someone who lives in your area; you can exchange files via e-mail just as easily from around the world as from down the street.

After your designer comes up with a preliminary design, ask a few friends and colleagues to give you their blunt and honest feedback—and listen to their comments. Is it easy to find information on the site? Can they tell what you're offering? Can they tell when or whether it's appropriate to call you? Can they find your phone number easily? Does the page load quickly over a 56K modem? Does it look professional? If not, change the wording to get your message across more clearly, or ask your designer to make the necessary adjustments. Most Web site design efforts go through at least a couple of iterations before they're exactly right. Designers are generally willing to change a few things here and there—as opposed to starting from scratch with a totally new concept—under the terms of your original contract. Discuss this up front just to be sure your designer is willing to be reasonably flexible.

Publishing Your Rate Sheet

What about listing your prices on your Web site? My advice is that you probably shouldn't, for a number of reasons.

- ✦ You may want to quote a flat fee for each project. By definition, a per-project estimate can't be done on a rate sheet.
- ✦ Prospective clients may seriously overestimate how long a project will take. If they see an hourly rate of, say, $150, they may jump to the conclusion that a project will be beyond their budget without even talking to you.
- ✦ A rate sheet doesn't convey all the value-added services you provide—analysis and synthesis of results, customized presentations, and so on.
- ✦ When you estimate a project, you will probably factor in what the job is worth to the client. If it is vital to him, you will estimate high; if it's a nice-to-know question, you will probably present a lower estimate. If you post a rate sheet, you lose some of this flexibility.
- ✦ Your hourly rate is only part of the total cost of a project. It's difficult to explain or anticipate direct expenses such as the cost of a search on a professional online service or copyright fees for academic papers, which you also bill back to the client.

I did an informal survey of a number of independent info pros' Web sites. Interestingly, the only ones who listed their rates were those who priced their services at the low end of the range for independent info pros. (See Chapter 13, Setting Rates and Fees, for more about pricing your services.) My theory is that people who post their rates on their Web sites are catering to clients who shop for price rather than value. Do you really want that kind of client?

Getting Listed in Search Engines and Directories

Search engines and directories have to be told about your site; they're not going to somehow just intuitively sense that you're out there. Some services will submit your site—often for a fee—to hundreds of search engines. My feeling is that a better approach is to manually submit your site to the major search engines, since some search engines let you add comments or a title to the entry. If those major search engines pick up your site, most Web searchers will be able to find you.

For a list of the largest search engines, go to Greg Notess's Search Engine Showdown (www.SearchEngineShowdown.com) and click [Total Size] to identify the six or eight largest search engines. Then go to each of these search engine sites and look for a link labeled "Add a URL" or "Submit Your Site." Note that it often takes several months before the search engine gets around to indexing your site and including it in search results, so be patient after you've submitted your URL.

An entire industry has developed around what's called Search Engine Optimization (SEO). The idea behind SEO is employing particular techniques to make your Web site appear near the top of a search engine's results list. See Search Engine Watch (www.SearchEngineWatch.com) for a thorough discussion of what's involved. As I said at the beginning of this chapter, however, most of your clients aren't going to spend time searching the Web for the kinds of services that independent info pros provide, so it probably doesn't make sense to go through a lot of trouble to tweak your Web site to appear at the top of a results list. As long as your site observes the basic principles of good Web design, such as using descriptive page titles with words that search engines will pick up and that people are likely to use when they search, you're probably fine.

You should also consider submitting your site to the major Web directories such as Open Directory Project (dmoz.org), LookSmart.com and Yahoo!. Do your homework before submitting your Web site. For each directory, figure out what subject category you want to be listed in. You might try searching for other independent info pros you know by name and see where they are classified; consider, too, how your prospective clients would look for you. Write a 25- to 50-word description of your business, using phrases that you think people will use when searching for services like those you offer. Avoid marketing hype. For example, here is an effective description of an independent info pro's business: *Value-added market analysis and competitive intelligence services to the biotech industry.* But this one runs the risk of instant deletion by the directory's editor: *Super-fast information research by the TOP EXPERT in the field!!!*

Some of the larger Web directories now charge a fee for inclusion of commercial sites (yes, that would be you). In fact, you pay just to have your submission considered; there is no guarantee that you'll get listed, although almost all nonpornographic sites are included once they pay the fee. Yahoo! charges $299 a year (yep, not only do you pay for submission, but you pay for continued inclusion); LookSmart.com charges $149 for a "Basic Submit" (they'll consider your submission within eight weeks) and $299 for an "Express Submit" (your submission will be evaluated within two business days).

If you're pausing to consider whether the expense is worth it, keep in mind that some of the largest search engines incorporate directory listings in their search results, often displaying the directory listings at the top of the results list. So investing in a listing in a directory means that search engine users will also see your listing, sometimes at the top of the search results page.

You should also do some Web research to identify any Web guides or portals specific to your client base, and investigate whether and how to get listed. For example, if you focus on business research, you might want to pay the $99 fee to submit your listing to Business.com; if your clients are in the healthcare industry, a listing in MedWebPlus.com might be useful.

Getting People to Visit Your Site

Although listing your site in directories and search engines is useful, it's even better to create content that makes people want to bookmark your site and visit it frequently. When I look through my Web page statistics (see the sidebar, Tracking Your Web Visitors), I find that at least 50 percent aren't coming to my site because they found me in a search engine but because they typed in the URL directly.

Make your site worth going to, and worth going back to. Think about why you visit the sites that you have bookmarked yourself—they contain valuable information, updated frequently, in a format that's easy to use. You can create a destination that your clients will find just as useful, with a bit of creativity and time. Write a client newsletter and publish it on your site (see Chapter 21, Print Marketing, for more about newsletters). Build an annotated guide to the best Web resources for your client base, and be sure to update it often. Post your press releases (see Chapter 24,

Public Relations) and announcements of upcoming speeches. And be sure to check all your Web links regularly to make sure they're still live. You can use a shareware or inexpensive software package to check all your links automatically. Two that I like are Net Mechanic (www.netmechanic.com) and Xenu's Link Sleuth (home.snafu.de/tilman/xenulink.html).

If you give a presentation, put your URL at the bottom of every PowerPoint slide. Post a copy of the talk or the slides at your site and tell the audience that they can download them. Make sure that all your printed material includes your URL—brochures, Rolodex cards, invoices, and so on. And if you post anything in an e-mail discussion group or Web forum, always include your URL at the bottom of your posting. (See the section "Participating in Electronic Discussions" for more thoughts on low-key marketing through discussion groups and forums.)

Susan Detwiler, president of The Detwiler Group, used her Web site to get some great coverage for her company. She conducted a survey of consumer-oriented health Web sites, evaluating how current and accurate the information was and describing how much misinformation she found. She then published her report on her Web site and sent out a press release announcing her findings. She got great coverage of both her report and her company, and was invited to testify before the White House Commission on Complementary and Alternative Health Policy.

Tracking Your Web Visitors

How do you know who's been to your site and how they got there? A number of inexpensive Web counters will not only count the number of visitors to your site but also provide data on what brought them there. See TheCounter (www.thecounter.com), WebSTAT (www.webstat.com) or 1.2.3. Count (www.123count.com), for example. Costs range from $16 a year to $10 a month. Note that some Web hosts offer detailed statistics at no additional charge; check with the customer service folks before you pay for a Web counter.

Once you've signed up, the service will send you a small bit of HTML code that you add to the bottom of your Web page. This generally results in a visible counter showing the number of visitors you've had to your site; most of these services also offer the option of different coding that results in an invisible counter. In addition, the service captures generic information about each visitor to your site. As a rule, they won't disclose visitors' e-mail addresses or any other explicit identifying information. However, they do provide clues about what people were looking for when they found your site by supplying data such as:

- Each visitor's top level domain (.com, .edu, .uk, and so on)
- The total number of hits, by time of day and by date
- What search engine (if any) visitors used to find your site
- What search terms visitors used to retrieve your site
- The URL of the site that referred a visitor to you, or whether they typed the URL directly

This information can be useful as you tweak your Web site. Are people searching for you by your name rather than your company name, or by a description of your services? After reviewing the search words that people use to find you, you can modify your Web site to ensure that those words appear near the top of the page. For example, I have found that most people who search for my site now look for me by name, although a few years ago they were looking for the phrase "information broker." I make sure that my name is in the top portion of my Web page, so that search engine spiders are sure to find it, as well as my company name, when they index my site.

It's also useful to learn about Web sites that link to your page; I watch for those links in the report that I get from my counter service and visit the sites to see how they describe me, my business, and my Web site and in what context the mention occurs, and to discover what brings people to my site. If you find that a good percentage of your visitors are coming directly to your site by just typing the URL in their browser's navigation box, that tells you that your efforts to draw people to your site are paying off.

Marketing with E-Mail

While it's smart to develop a Web site that provides valuable information and presents your business in a professional light, and to promote it in some of the ways

I've just described, you may also want to consider adding an e-mail element to your Web marketing efforts. If you develop a newsletter for your clients and prospects, offer to send it via e-mail to anyone who's interested. The cost to you is minimal (more about that later), and it lets you expand the reach of your newsletter to anyone who asks. It's also a regular and relatively nonintrusive reminder to your prospective clients of what you do and who you are. They may forget to visit your Web site, but *you* can remember to communicate with them on a regular basis. Even if you don't want to send out a full-fledged newsletter, you might opt to notify Web visitors whenever you've added something new and interesting to your Web site.

Rule number one of running an e-mail list is to make it 100 percent opt-in. That means adding no one to the distribution list unless they specifically request it. (In fact, if you send unsolicited e-mail, you can run afoul of your ISP's acceptable usage policy, and that can get you kicked off the service.) The second rule is to include instructions on subscribing and unsubscribing with every mailing. In my monthly newsletter, I remind readers in the first paragraph that "You are receiving this because you have subscribed to this free newsletter as {theirname@their domain.whatever}. If you would like to unsubscribe or change your e-mail subscription, just go to www.BatesInfo.com/subscribe.html." Alternatively, people can just e-mail me and I remove their e-mail addresses myself. The point is to make it as easy as possible for people to unsubscribe, if they want to.

When I first started sending out an e-mail newsletter, I maintained the list using my e-mail software, manually updating it whenever someone wanted to be added or removed, or when an e-mail address bounced. That worked fine when I had a couple hundred subscribers. But once my mailing list grew to 500 or 600, it became too time-consuming. At that point, I shopped around for a service that could host my e-mail list for a modest fee. (I didn't want to use a free service such as Yahoo! Groups, because free services usually insert ads at the bottom of each mailing, and because the return address indicated that the mailing was from a Yahoo! Group rather than my own e-mail address. I felt that both of these "features" detracted from the professional image I wanted to maintain.)

There are a number of e-mail list hosts, among them:

- FreePint (www.freepint.com/bulk)
- Elist Express (www.elistx.com)

- SparkLIST (www.sparklist.com)

These hosts handle most of the administrative details of a one-way (also known as broadcast or announcement) e-mail list. They handle any rejected e-mail addresses, they deal with subscription/removal requests, they will send out a message from you when someone subscribes or unsubscribes, and they provide the HTML code for you to add a subscription box on your Web page. The cost for any of these services is determined by the size of your mailing list and the frequency and file size of your mailings. As an example, a monthly mailing to about 2,000 people will cost between $30 and $60 a month. That sure beats the cost of snail-mailing a newsletter!

Participating in Electronic Discussions

An effective way of establishing your expertise is to participate in the e-mail discussion lists and Web-based forums where your clients and colleagues congregate. AIIP-L, the private e-mail list for members of AIIP, is a tremendously useful way to network with fellow info pros, brainstorm about difficult situations and projects (while maintaining client confidentiality, of course), and get to know fellow AIIP members with whom you might be able to set up subcontracting relationships.

In addition to AIIP-L, do some research to find electronic discussion groups that your prospective clients are likely to read, or that other researchers in your field participate in. Obviously, this approach is not as useful if your clients aren't particularly Net savvy. Ask those who you know are comfortable using e-mail whether they're aware of any discussion lists or would recommend one in particular. If they give you a blank look, assume that this may not be the best use of your marketing time and effort. If they rattle off the names of several groups they find stimulating or useful, take note.

You might also search the major Web sites that host discussion lists, such as Topica (www.topica.com) and Yahoo! Groups (groups.yahoo.com) to turn up public discussion lists in the industry or subject area you're targeting. You'll also want to identify the trade and professional associations your clients belong to; like AIIP, these associations may host useful e-mail discussion lists that make the membership dues a worthwhile investment. For more discussion of leveraging your association memberships as a marketing device, see Chapter 23, Starting the Word of Mouth.

Once you have identified a few electronic discussion groups that look promising, subscribe to them and just sit back and listen—well, read—for a week or two. Get a feel for the audience and the "culture" of each group. You don't have to scan more than a handful at first; in fact, you probably shouldn't. It makes more sense to subscribe to three or four at a time rather than spend all your spare time trying to keep up with 10 or 20. One of the unexpected benefits of reading these lists is that you may learn about additional, perhaps even more productive lists. The private discussion list for AIIP members often includes references to other lists of interest to many independent info pros—the BUSLIB-L list for business librarians, or the Competia.com discussion forum for competitive intelligence researchers, for example.

When someone posts a question or raises an issue that you can address, do so. Remember that this is a long-term marketing approach; you need to establish your expertise with the list participants over the course of months before you can expect people to contact you for work. Any posting on professional lists that smacks of blatant advertising is verboten; it can get you thrown off the list and will hurt your reputation. Be subtle. Saying "I know the answer and I'd be happy to do the research for you for a fee" will not win you clients. Rather, provide helpful pointers and advice when you can, and be sure to include your name, company name, e-mail address, and Web site URL at the bottom of every posting.

When networking, whether in person at a conference, electronically in an e-mail discussion group, or in private e-mail with a colleague, people notice the small things. If you are rude or snippy with someone, others may decide that they don't want to refer clients your way. If you're argumentative in a discussion forum, your colleagues may well conclude that they have no interest in engaging you one-on-one in the context of a subcontracting relationship either. Think of every professional encounter as a marketing opportunity. Just as you would never get into an argument with a prospective client during a sales call, so you should avoid needless or pointless arguments in an electronic discussion group. If you're unfamiliar with the concept of "netiquette" or would like a refresher on how to apply good manners to your online interactions, you can read a useful summary at list-etiquette.com.

Top Tips for Marketing on the Web

- Reserve a domain name and use it for e-mail, even if you aren't ready to develop a Web site yet.
- Make sure your Web site looks professional.
- Avoid over-engineering your site with cutting-edge technology or special effects.
- Make sure your name, address, telephone number, and e-mail address are easy to find on your site.
- Submit your Web page to the major search engines and, perhaps, to large Web directories.
- Provide valuable content on your site.
- Participate in e-mail discussion lists, and remember the rules of netiquette.

Chapter 21

Print Marketing

It sounds so old-fashioned, but people still read material that's written on paper. Chapter 19, Your Business Image, covers your hard-copy image—business cards, stationery, and brochures—but there's more to marketing than handing someone a business card. And even though much of your marketing will consist of activities that generate word-of-mouth buzz, there are some traditional print marketing techniques that work well for independent info pros.

Starting Your Mailing List

One marketing guideline states that a business has to "touch" or contact a prospect at least five times before the prospect remembers the business and responds to the marketing pitch. That sounds like a lot of touching, doesn't it? Fortunately, it doesn't mean that you have to pick up the phone and make five sales calls; you can send out a periodic newsletter or postcard to remind your prospects of your services.

How do you develop a mailing list of prospective clients? If you're reading this book *before* you've started your business, begin collecting business cards from everyone you meet. Once you do launch your business, you'll have an initial list to work from. I encourage you to send material to everyone you've encountered in a business-related setting. When I started my company and was flipping through my collection of business cards, I almost didn't send a brochure and marketing letter to a speechwriter I'd worked with briefly a couple of years before, thinking that it wasn't even worth the cost of the stamp. I'm glad I did, though; he turned into a wonderful client and a great source of referrals. You just never know.

As you build your mailing list, retain every name unless the mailing is returned as "addressee unknown." In saying that, I'm assuming that you have at least minimally prequalified all prospects before adding them to the list; you have ensured that everyone to whom you send mail has met you, heard you speak, or otherwise had some direct contact with you. You never know who among your prospect list doesn't use you directly but is passing along your mailings and your name to colleagues. I learned this lesson when I met a prospect to whom I had been mailing newsletters and postcards for four or five years, with no noticeable results. But when we got to talking, she commented that she was so glad that she was still on my mailing list, that she routed my newsletter to five other people, and that she routinely gave out my name as someone to call for research.

If you do any public speaking (see Chapter 22, Marketing by Writing and Speaking), view your audience as a source of leads. For some events, the organizer will supply you with a list of attendees. Otherwise, offer a door prize as a way to collect business cards. Buy a copy of a recent book by a respected author that relates to the subject of your talk, and bring it to the meeting along with a book stand and an attractive basket. Display the book prominently and announce that you'll have a drawing for it at the end of your talk. (Note that you can sometimes obtain free copies from the publisher if you offer to promote the book during your talk.) Hand the basket to the closest audience member and have the audience pass it around the room while you speak, putting in their business cards. When you're finished speaking, draw a name, award the book to the winner, and—more importantly—save all those business cards. When you get back to the office, go through the cards, weed out those from organizations that you don't think are likely prospects, and add the others to your mailing list. (See the discussion on promotional postcards later in this chapter for more thoughts on staying in touch with your prospects.)

Mass Mailings: Directly to the Wastebasket?

Your mailing list will probably grow rather slowly, and that's not necessarily a bad thing. Information services are not a commodity that can be mass-marketed, and a list of 200 qualified prospects who have heard of you is worth much more than a list of 2,000 random names of people who have no idea who you are. But it's frustrating to have to build a prospect list from scratch, and my hunch is that 75 percent of all independent info pros try a direct mail campaign at some point. Maybe you're tempted to harvest names of executives from a directory. Perhaps you're thinking about building a mailing list from a professional association's membership roster. Or maybe you're looking into purchasing a mailing list from a list broker.

I won't get into a lengthy discussion of the copyright issues involved in taking names from a directory or membership list. Generally, that information is covered by copyright. Most publishers specifically state that you can't compile your own mailing list from their directories without written permission and payment for the use of the information. But this approach is seldom cost-effective, anyway.

Traditionally, a direct mail campaign is considered successful if two to four percent of the recipients *respond* to the mailing. That doesn't necessarily mean that any of that small percentage of respondents ever become paying clients. Those aren't very good odds, particularly for a small business selling an intangible and relatively high-priced service. My hunch is that the response rate to direct marketing for info pro services is much lower than 4 percent. Would you choose a lawyer, doctor, accountant, or other professional based on a mass mailing? I don't think so; I wouldn't either. Likewise, the odds of a likely prospect deciding to use your services because of a mailing—no matter how polished—are very low.

That said, there are circumstances in which some form of direct marketing can be effective. If you have an identifiable product—company profiles, succinct analyses of a market, a weekly news update with summaries of key articles in a narrowly defined industry—you may be able to develop a direct mail piece that works. To be effective, though, you'll need to describe what you're offering in clear terms, demonstrate the value to the prospective client, and compel the prospect to follow up with an order. The product must be something that many people in your client base would find cost-effective and valuable, something that they cannot do themselves and that isn't available through other sources. Expect to send out hundreds, if not thousands, of marketing pieces on a regular basis; remember that it takes five exposures for the prospect to remember who you are and to decide to make a purchase. Even with an excellent direct marketing pitch, don't expect more than the usual 2 percent response rate.

The more qualified your mailing list, the better. Rather than purchasing a generic list from a list broker, consider buying the membership directory mailing list from an association that your prospects are likely to belong to—and do some judicious pruning of that list before sending your mailing out. What's important is to purchase a list of people who, because of their membership in an organization, have already indicated that they are interested in a specific professional area—film production, patent research, electrical engineering, or whatever your area of specialization is.

Amelia Kassel, the principal of MarketingBase, built her customized mailing list with an innovative technique. She worked with an author who was selling a book to a market that was likely to want her information services as well. The author sold her the names and addresses of people who bought his book, at 50 cents a name. This approach worked because she was able to target an audience that had already proven that it was interested in the market, and the names came to her at a manageable rate—usually 30 to 50 names a month—that allowed her to send out a mailing to the new contacts on a monthly basis.

Targeted Mailings

Although mass mailings are often ineffective, very focused mailings can be successful in some markets. The secret is to invest time up front in identifying the organizations and individuals to target. First, identify 25 or 30 companies, government agencies, or other organizations that you *know* could use your services. Use your research skills to identify the name of a likely prospect in each organization, and that person's direct mailing address. Don't rely on printed directories, which are often out of date before they're even published. Either confirm the contact information on the organization's Web site or pick up the telephone and call the organization directly.

Once you have your contact's name, write a one-page letter describing the information need that you are addressing and how you can meet that need. Tell the prospect that you will be following up with a telephone call to answer any questions. Some independent info pros prefer to fax the marketing letter if they can get the prospect's direct fax number. Although some people still view a fax as something that demands their immediate attention, I think you run the risk of having your marketing material dismissed along with all the unsolicited faxes for vacation travel packages and laser toner refill offers.

However you send your marketing letter, pace yourself so that you can indeed follow up each one with a phone call. By sending five letters, say, at a time, you can track the response you're getting and, if necessary, modify your approach for the next five letters. And even if a prospect doesn't immediately turn into a sale, be sure to keep him on your mailing list unless he asks to be removed from it. He may just need to hear from you a few times before he decides to give you a try. Evaluate your success rate after you've tried this technique for a while. If it doesn't seem to be paying off in terms of actual sales, consider switching to another marketing strategy.

Client Newsletters and Postcards

Client mailings can be an effective tool for showcasing your expertise and reminding your client base of your capabilities. Unlike advertising, a mailing to someone you've had at least some contact with usually gets noticed. The key is to make sure that your clients and prospects hear from you regularly, that they receive something from you every month or two.

Newsletters

Writing a client newsletter isn't as intimidating as it might sound. For starters, it doesn't have to be a 10-page affair; you can begin with a simple two-sided sheet. The main point is that it be readable and frequent. As for what to write about, think about interesting Web sites you've encountered, a particularly intriguing research project you tackled (maintaining client confidentiality, of course), or a description of new products or services you saw at a recent trade show.

While you may also wish to post your newsletter on your Web page, don't count on your clients going to your site to read it. Push technology—sending information directly *to* the reader—has a lot more impact than pull technology—placing it on a site that readers have to remember to visit. And, while turning it into an electronic newsletter is tempting, especially when you look at the cost of first-class postage, think of how it will appear to your clients. Plain text embedded in an e-mail message looks, well, plain. And sending an attached PDF or Word file guarantees that it won't even be opened by anyone wary of e-mail viruses. In addition to being more user-friendly and easier to read, printed newsletters are also much more likely to be passed along from one person to another. It's nice to offer an electronic version for clients who prefer it, but these days, anyone who actually goes to the trouble and expense of sending a newsletter in the mail projects a more established image. If you're concerned about costs and reducing the amount of paper consumed, another electronic option is to send e-mail with a live link to the newsletter on your Web site.

That way, interested readers can click through easily to the newsletter, but you're not clogging up their e-mail with a large attached file.

If you do decide to send out a single-page hard-copy newsletter, you can simply use your letterhead as the paper stock. You can also purchase special newsletter stock, complete with full-color designs, from companies such as Paper Direct (www.paperdirect.com) or from the larger office supply chains. You can just print your newsletter on colored paper if you want, but it will have a lot more impact if it's on interesting-looking stock. Unless you use at least 38-pound stock (the kind used for sturdy brochures), factor in the cost of envelopes as well; regular bond paper isn't sturdy enough to be used as a self-mailer. Use your company envelopes, complete with logo—you want this mail to look important, not like an anonymous letter in a plain envelope. Use commemorative stamps rather than metering—it's particularly neat if you can find a commemorative appropriate to your business or your clients' industry—and, of course, send them via first class rather than bulk mail.

Since you're creating your newsletter from scratch, you have a lot of leeway in deciding what it looks like. Keep in mind that you want to make it appealing, easy to read, and entertaining as well as informative.

- Leave plenty of white space. If their first impression is one of dense text, people are less likely to read it.
- Use a font size large enough to be read by less-than-youthful eyes.
- Break up the text into columns. Format small items in boxed text.
- Include a fun or odd feature—a link to How Stuff Works (www.HowStuffWorks.com), or an interesting fact culled from DidYouKnow.cd, such as the collective names for various groups of animals (a drift of hogs, a gang of elks, a float of crocodiles).
- Print your phone number and e-mail address in bold on all pages of the newsletter.
- Come up with intriguing article titles.
- Use clip art sparingly, if at all.
- Proofread your text. Twice. Better yet, have someone else proof it, too.

- Have a friend or colleague review the layout and content of your newsletter. What looks great to you may not strike other people the same way.

Promotional Postcards

You probably don't have the time or inspiration to create a newsletter every month. Postcards are a useful tool for getting your name out to your clients even when you don't have much to say. Be sure to include your company name, something to pique the client's curiosity, such as a list of interesting recent projects or a discount on industry profiles or another product you offer, and a "call to arms" suggesting that the client call or e-mail you today. Make sure your name, phone number, and e-mail address appears in a large, bold font. See Figures 21.1 and 21.2 for two sample client postcards. Keep in mind that the postcard has to stand on its own; that is, don't simply point people to your Web site or ask them to call to find out what

Q:?
A:!

Bates Information Services

Recently, I've researched:

- **remote environmental sensing**
- **David Letterman impersonators**
- **trends in community banking**
- **the patentability of business processes**

How can I help you find the answers you need?

Call Mary Ellen Bates at:
202.332.2360
mbates@BatesInfo.com

Figure 21.1 Sample promotional postcard

Help! Can't keep up with news in the automotive industry?

We can help! Auto-Info-Direct offers a weekly email newsletter with the hottest news in the automotive industry.

10% discount for new subscribers

Call us today at 313.555.1212 for a free sample issue!

Figure 21.2 Sample promotional postcard

services you provide. An effective marketing postcard has to be so compelling that your client is motivated to pick up the phone.

You can also use postcards as follow-up contacts after a presentation. How does this work? Collect business cards during your talk with the offer of a door prize drawing (see the earlier section in this chapter about building your mailing list, which discusses ways to solicit business cards). While you're speaking, notice which points generate the most interest. When you get back in the office, create a postcard that—briefly!—reminds people of your talk, highlights four or five key points, and invites them to call you for their next research project.

You can buy colorful preprinted postcard stock from Paper Direct and the major office supply chains. Normally, these come two- or four-to-a-page with microperforations, so you can run them through a printer or photocopier. My experience has been that the larger postcards, 5-1/2 inches by 8-1/2 inches, are more effective. You have more space for text, and they don't look like junk mail. They normally require standard letter postage, though, rather than the lower postcard rate.

Mailing Services

All these mailings sound like a great idea for marketing your business, but who has the time to fold newsletters, stuff envelopes, slap on mailing labels, and attach those commemorative stamps that I recommended? A lot depends on whether you intend to do a selective form of mass mailing as I described earlier, or work from a home-grown list of no more than a couple hundred names.

During the first few years of my business, my mailing list had fewer than 500 names on it, so I didn't mind doing the manual labor myself. In fact, I rather enjoyed the chance to insert personal notes in the newsletters that went out to favorite clients and prospects. I saved this chore for the evening, when I could pop an audio book in my cassette player and listen to the latest bestseller as I folded and stuffed.

Once my mailing list got beyond a certain point, though, I found that I was dreading the chore of sending out mailings. That's when I discovered the mailing services offered by a local sheltered workshop. These are workplaces that offer meaningful employment for people with disabilities. They provide intensive staff support and encouragement, and they help develop independence, job skills and self-confidence in their workers. On top of that, they are very reasonably priced and the quality of the work is first-rate. You can find sheltered workshops in the Yellow Pages, usually under a listing such as Mailing Services, or use your information skills to search for *sheltered employment*, *vocational rehabilitation*, or *sheltered workshop* on the Web.

Tickler Files

You've sent a marketing kit to a prospect. You want to follow up a couple of weeks later with a copy of your newsletter and, a few weeks after that, with a postcard or other marketing piece. How do you remember when to send out what? Contact management software packages, which are designed primarily for salespeople, can help. A couple of the well-known ones are Act! (Symantec) and SideKick (Starfish Software).

But I prefer a low-tech solution: Four manila folders, labeled "7th," "14th," "21st" and "end of month." When I get an invoice, I note its due date and put it in the appropriate folder; if the bill has to be paid by the 12th of the month, I toss it in the "7th" folder. Likewise, if I mail out a marketing kit on the 12th, I put a copy of my newsletter in an envelope, address and stamp it, and toss it in the "end of month" folder so that my prospect receives it a couple of weeks later. For client projects that need updating once a month, I keep a reminder in the appropriate week's folder. On the 7th, 14th, 21st, and last day of the month, I go through the appropriate folder and write checks, mail whatever marketing materials are in there, and deal with anything else I stuck in the folder. It's not a fancy system, but it's foolproof.

Directories

Most of your business will come from recommendations, from people who have heard you speak or read what you've written, or from existing clients. But you want to make it as easy as possible for prospective clients to find you. A Web site is one alternative, as are listings in Web-based directories such as Yahoo!. See Chapter 20, Marketing on the Web, for more discussion of these options. You can also pay for listings in print directories.

Do Clients' Fingers Do the Walking?

If you have a business phone line, you are automatically entitled to a standard listing in the local Yellow Pages directory. Before you specify the category you'd like to be listed under, browse through the other listings in that category and see if they are similar to your business. Bates Information Services was initially listed under "Information Bureaus," which seemed at first glance like the appropriate place. Had I looked at the other listings, I would have realized that my company would appear between the American Kurdish Information Network and the Chittenden Press Service. Needless to say, the few calls that I got from that listing were from people looking for news agencies, not research services. (The local Yellow Pages still doesn't have a category for Research Services, so now I appear under Market Research—not ideal, but at least callers know that I'm a fee-based business rather than a wire service or a source for free information.)

Regardless of the category in which you list your business, don't count on getting much actual work from a Yellow Pages listing. You can expect many more calls from tire-kickers and people who aren't prepared to pay for your services than from bona fide prospective clients. That's why I'm not persuaded that display ads are worth the expense. The money you spend for a larger ad in the local phone book would probably be better spent on listings in more targeted directories (see the following section). Remember, the vast majority of people who pick up the Yellow Pages are *not* going to be your clients. You'll get better results with a listing in a directory that goes directly into the hands of people who are likely to be interested in the services you provide.

A possible exception to this rule is if your business is strictly local—if you provide library staffing services, for example, or specialize in a market that has an unusually strong presence in your immediate area. But even if you are a pharmaceutical researcher in New Jersey, a hotbed for biotech companies, how likely is it that your prospects would look in the Yellow Pages for an independent info pro?

If you do decide to purchase a display ad, be sure to prequalify callers by specifying that you charge for your services. You might think that would be obvious, but anything with the word *information* in it is linked in many people's minds to the idea of public libraries, which translates into "free." Include a bulleted list of examples of the type of work you do, to make it clear that you aren't in the business of helping students with their homework, and so that people browsing the listings can tell what kind of business you are. Be careful that your ad appears in the appropriate category; try to think like your clients, and anticipate which category they would look at to find someone like you.

Specialized Directories

Clients are more likely to look up an independent info pro in a directory that is specific to their industry or market, rather than in the local phone book. That's why many info pros join associations that their clients belong to—to ensure that they're listed in the association's membership directory. Some associations have a less-expensive category for vendors or associates, as distinct from regular members. This usually entitles you to a directory listing, even though you may not want to take advantage of all the other benefits of membership.

If you market your services to librarians or other information professionals, or if librarians are a good source of referrals for you, you may want a listing in the major library directories as well. The primary association for corporate and other specialized libraries is the Special Libraries Association (www.sla.org). You don't have to be a librarian to join SLA. Once you've joined, you'll not only be listed in the SLA membership directory; you can participate in the e-mail discussion lists sponsored by SLA's subject-oriented divisions and regional chapters. (See Chapter 20, Marketing on the Web, for tips on how to do low-key marketing by participating in e-mail discussion lists and forums.)

Consider paying for a listing in the *Librarian's Yellow Pages* (www.LibrariansYellowPages.com); this directory is distributed free of charge to librarians, so you can assume that your client base has copies. You might also contact your local libraries—public and university—many of which maintain referral lists of independent info pros for requests that go beyond the scope of the library's mission. Provided that the librarians make it clear to their patrons that you are an information professional who charges for your services, this can be a useful secondary source of business. If you develop a good relationship with a local library, consider reciprocating by donating reference books, joining their Friends of the Library organization, or offering to do an occasional free seminar on Web research or another topic of interest.

Print Advertising

You may have noticed that, in a chapter devoted to print marketing, I haven't mentioned plain old advertising—taking out ads in newspapers, magazines, or other publications that your clients read. That's because print advertising is an expensive proposition, and you often don't see results for months. For advertising to be successful, you need to have a well-designed ad—which means paying a marketing pro to help you with the layout and wording—that appears in every issue of a periodical for at least six months. Remember the guideline about having to "touch" prospects at least five times before they'll call you? Well, when you run an advertisement, you have no assurance that your prospects will even notice the ads in any given issue; that's why consistent placement is important.

If you are considering running an ad, talk to a few of your existing clients and find out what kind of advertisement would make them pick up the phone and call you. What publications do they consider most reliable? Which ones do they read thoroughly? Look through a few recent issues and see what other types of companies advertise there.

One place for advertising that can pay off is in specialized directories. In addition to a regular listing in a directory—either paid or by virtue of membership in an association—you can often purchase quarter- to full-page display ads. The advantages of these ads are that you can be reasonably sure that your prospects will see your ad (assuming that you've selected an appropriate directory), you set yourself apart from your competition, and it's a one-time expense that pays off all year long. As with other ads, use a marketing pro to help you design one that will be effective and compelling.

Top Tips for Print Marketing

- Collect business cards from everyone you contact.
- Build your prospect list through qualified leads. Think quality over quantity.
- Consider direct mail only for clearly identifiable products rather than for information services generally.
- Send something to your prospects every month or so; a newsletter or postcard will do.
- Pay for listings in directories where you think your prospects will look for services like yours.

Chapter 22

Marketing by Writing and Speaking

Most new independent info pros don't have the advantage of being already well-known in their industry. One of the most effective ways of gaining credibility is to be seen as an authority, and that can come from writing articles or books your clients read, or by speaking at conferences they attend. An added benefit is that you can use these opportunities to remind people of what you know and what you do—although, of course, you can't turn either an article or a talk into a blatant sales pitch. However, you can mention your Web site and your newsletter, if you have one, in every speech and every piece of writing you undertake. Make it easy for your audience to find that Web site or subscribe to that newsletter by providing your e-mail address and your URL.

Marketing through speaking and writing can be tremendously effective, but it is a long-term process. It takes time to land a speaking gig or get an article written and published. Speaking and writing skills may not come naturally to you. Writing my first article was very difficult, and I was a nervous wreck during my first few speaking engagements, but I soldiered on under the assumption that (1) it would get easier in time and (2) I simply had to do this. It *did* get easier over time, and both writing and speaking have become good marketing tools. So, even if the thought of public speaking makes you cringe, read on.

Author, Author!

You can get a lot of mileage out of writing an article. If you write for an industry publication that your prospective clients read, you're immediately seen as an expert.

You can use that article as validation when you are trying to line up speaking engagements (more about this later in the chapter). If you purchase reprints of your articles—sometimes the publication will give you 10 or 20 copies if you ask—you can send them to your key prospects along with a marketing letter. Voila: instant credibility.

Try writing for your local business weekly; the audience is more limited and not as focused as for industry publications, but it's great practice and a good way for a wide variety of people to see your name. As with industry publications, you can include a reprint of the article with your marketing material for additional impact. And you can write for publications that your referral sources read. That includes *Connections*, the quarterly newsletter of the Association of Independent Information Professionals (www.aiip.org) and perhaps the publications of the Special Libraries Association and its divisions.

In fact, if you're really ambitious, you might consider offering to write a regular column for a publication whose readers you value. Of course, this presumes that you enjoy writing and that you'll come up with something to say in every issue. Before you pitch the idea to an editor, outline five or six columns and see whether you have enough ideas to sustain it.

The question that is undoubtedly at the front of your mind right now is, "How much will I get paid?" The minimum for professional writers is currently around $1 a word, but mention this to an independent info pro who writes regularly and she will probably collapse in helpless laughter. If you contribute an article to a local business weekly, don't expect to be paid at all. That goes for AIIP's *Connections*, too. If you write for an industry publication, the going rate is generally somewhere between $200 and $500 for an article of several thousand words. You probably won't be paid, either, until the article is actually published. No, you're not going to get rich from your writing, at least not directly—but as a loyal member of the National Writers Union (www.nwu.org), I always encourage writers to negotiate the best rate they can for their work. The real payoff comes in the reputation you build and in the other ways you manage to leverage your writing. Be sure to tell your clients about any articles you've written. Arrange with the publisher to have the final version of the article posted on their Web site, where you can link to it, or get permission to post it on yours. Mention it in your newsletter and, where appropriate, in the e-mail groups and discussion lists you participate in.

Writing a Query Letter

How do you figure out what publication to write for? To identify the important publications in your clients' industry, go to your local library and look through the *Encyclopedia of Business Information Sources* (Gale Group, published annually). In fact, consider purchasing this invaluable research tool. It's a great resource for identifying the key associations, directories, periodicals, Web sites, and databases for industries from Abrasives to Zinc. Then look at *Writer's Market* (Writer's Digest Books, published annually), the bible for freelance writers. This directory lists contact information for thousands of publications, and tells you what they pay, and whether they publish articles by freelancers as well as their own staff writers. Most public libraries have a copy, or you can buy it for $29.99 in print or through a Web subscription at www.WritersMarket.com.

Look up each publication you've identified through the *Encyclopedia of Business Information Sources*, make sure they publish articles by freelancers, and note any particular submission guidelines. You should also check the publication's own Web site for a link to "author's guidelines" or "submission guidelines." These tell you what type of material the publisher is looking for, the format in which to submit articles, the style and tone expected, and so on. Look through recent articles on the publication site, if they're posted there, or the indexes of recent issues, to see what types of stories the publication generally carries.

Now it's time to think about what to write. I can't give you ideas; you know what you know, and you know (or can figure out) what your clients would find interesting to read. Focus on topics that are timely, useful, and that tie together your expertise and the concerns of your client base. Once you have an idea of what you'd like to write about, send a query letter to the submissions editor to find out if they're interested in your article. You needn't write the article in advance, but you should be able to describe your idea in a paragraph or two. Explain why you think this article would be appropriate for the publication, why it's timely and interesting, and why you are the person to write it. If you have written other articles, you can include two or three of them with your letter. These previously published articles are called "clips;" they are often used to demonstrate to an editor that an unknown writer is, in fact, competent and has indeed been published before. Ask publishers for original copies (called tearsheets) of your article when it's published, so you can distribute them with your query letters.

Do send this material in hard copy, not through e-mail. Many editors won't open unsolicited e-mail attachments, and your query will have more impact on real paper. Enclose a self-addressed, stamped envelope for the editor's response; editors receive query letters all the time, so you want to make it easy to reply. It's all right to send query letters to several publications about the same general topic. If you're fortunate enough to have your proposal accepted by two editors, make sure that you can write two distinct articles, taking a different perspective or emphasis in each one. It is verboten to submit the *same* article to two publishers.

Always get a publication agreement in writing. Spell out the topic of the article, the length, the deadline for delivery, who owns copyright of the article and details of payment. Some publishers will insist on seeing the article before agreeing on a price, particularly if you're a new writer. Ask for the right to publish the article on your own Web site after a suitable embargo period, such as three months.

Writing Well

What about actually putting words to paper ... er, to computer screen? First, look through some back issues of the publication you're writing for, to get a sense of the style and tone of published articles. Make your article inviting by starting out with an attention-getting or intriguing first paragraph that catches the readers' attention and makes them want to read more. Ask the editor for a style sheet or author guidelines. Some editors like lots of sidebars and checklists; others want a list of referenced URLs; some have specific rules for subheadings, and so on. Pack your article full of useful information, so that people will want to keep it around for future reference. Remember, every time they look at it, your expertise is reinforced.

I remember a discussion among AIIP members in which one person maintained that it wasn't smart to give away your trade secrets in an article. On the contrary, I've always operated from the belief that whatever I put down on paper just serves to highlight my background and years of experience. Our "trade secrets" consist of our skills, experience, intuition, and contacts, and you can't give those away.

As for the more mundane aspects of writing a professional article:

- Write in simple, straightforward language, not "academese." Forget the extensive footnotes and pedantic prose.

- Keep your article focused and on point. Most readers don't have a long attention span or a lot of spare time to read articles, so don't inflate the length of your article beyond what you think the subject requires.

- Use descriptive subheadings to break up the text.

- Include a mention of your client newsletter, Web site, or other marketing tools in your author biography at the end of the article, along with your contact information and a brief description of your services and expertise.

- Stay within the word count agreed upon with the editor.

- Have a couple of colleagues give you their honest assessment of the article before you submit it, and make any necessary changes to ensure that it's as polished as possible.

- Meet the agreed-upon deadline. Remember, the editor may be holding space in an issue for your article. If you can't deliver the article on time, you've just made an editor's life a whole lot harder. Missing a deadline is one of the most unprofessional things you can do—when writing an article as well as in your own info pro business.

Once the article has been published, contact the editor and ask how many copies she or the publisher can send you. Find out whether the article will appear on the publication's Web site and link to it from your own site. If it's not destined for publication there, ask how long the content will be embargoed before you can post it on your own Web site. And get more mileage out of the article by mentioning it in your marketing material and your client newsletter, as well as in any talks that you give on the same or a related topic.

From 3,000 Words to 100,000

If you find that you really enjoy writing, and you have a hankering to produce something more tangible, it's time to think about writing a book. This exercise isn't for everyone. It's a huge investment in time for which you may never be fully compensated, and it requires discipline and focus. You must have something you really want to say, the ability to say it in depth, in an organized and engrossing way, and the drive to see the project through to completion, within the deadline agreed upon with your publisher. Writing a book is not for the faint-hearted.

That said, having written a book that relates in some way to your business or your clients' business is a great way to increase your visibility and establish yourself as an expert. It's immensely rewarding, and if you promote the book throughout your marketing efforts, you will see the benefits of all that work.

Writer's Market, mentioned earlier, can help you identify publishers in the industry you are covering. Your publisher will want a detailed proposal, including an outline and a description of each chapter. Unless you're already a published book author, your proposal will be taken more seriously if you submit one chapter in full. There is no reason to write more than that—you want to make sure you'll have a publisher before you invest all that time—but providing a publisher with a sample chapter shows that you are capable of stringing together enough words to fill eight or ten pages, at least.

Writing book proposals is an art. It's partly a matter of knowing your audience—the publisher as well as the eventual readership—and partly a matter of the kind of book you intend to write. The proposals for my *Super Searcher* books, which are collections of interviews with expert researchers, included a general idea of what I would cover but not the names of the experts to be interviewed, or a sample chapter, since I hadn't interviewed anyone yet. But the publisher was Information Today, Inc., for whom I'd already done other writing, so I was a known quantity. When I wrote a proposal for a book on how to find investment information, I submitted two completed chapters, copies of other books I had written, and a much more detailed outline, because it was for a publisher who didn't know me.

A number of guides to writing book proposals are available. Here are a few that I have found helpful:

- How to Write a Trade Book Proposal: www.adlerbooks.com/howto.html#TradeBkProp
- Developing Winning Book Proposals: www.studiob.com/res/propkit.asp
- Proposal Guide: www.waterside.com/proposalguide.html

Reva Basch, the editor of this book (and the author of four books herself), wrote a series of articles for AIIP's *Connections* on how to get a book published. If you're an AIIP member, you can download the articles from the members-only page of the AIIP Web site. Look for "Cover to Cover: What Aspiring Book Authors Need to Know," appearing in the Spring, Summer, and Fall 2001 issues.

Speaking Your Piece

Writing—either articles or an entire book—is one way to establish your credibility within your client market. Another technique that works for many independent info pros is public speaking. A room full of people staring at you may not be your idea of a fun time, but it does get easier with practice. Every time you give a talk, you have the undivided attention of everyone within earshot. You can offer a door prize as a way to collect attendees' business cards for marketing purposes. (See Chapter 21, Print Marketing, for a discussion of what to offer and what to do with those business cards once you have them.) And you can mention your talk in all of your marketing material, as another way to get added visibility from your presentation.

Starting Local

Unless you're already well-known in your field, you probably won't get invitations to speak, with expenses paid, at conferences around the world. That's okay; you can start local and work out from there. To begin with, identify the events and association meetings that your prospective clients are likely to attend. If they're marketing executives, look at the local chapter of the American Marketing Association. If you're targeting competitive intelligence managers, there's the Society of Competitive Intelligence Professionals. Find the appropriate organization's Web site and identify the person responsible for planning the local meetings. Write, e-mail or call the meeting planner and offer to speak (for no charge, of course) on a topic that you think would interest the group and that highlights your expertise. Offer to send the planner copies of any articles you've written. You'll probably find that you'll be welcomed with open arms. It's difficult to pull together local events, and an offer to speak, for free, is usually the best thing a meeting planner can hear.

Prepare, Prepare, Prepare

Once you've landed a speaking gig, do your homework—make sure you develop a talk that addresses the interests and concerns of the audience. The traditional formula for speakers—tell them what you're going to tell them, then tell them, and finally tell them what you've told them—still works. Build your talk with an introduction in which you set the stage and tell the audience what they'll be learning; followed by the body of the talk, in which you cover each of the topics you promised at the beginning; and concluding with a wrap-up that summarizes what you talked about and, if appropriate, ends on a thought-provoking or inspirational note.

Some speakers feel most confident if they write their speech ahead of time. If you take this approach, assume that between 10 and 15 pages of single-spaced text translates into a one-hour talk. Others work best with just an outline or PowerPoint presentation to speak from. If you're that type of speaker, figure on roughly three minutes of speaking for each PowerPoint slide.

Whichever mode works best for you, you'll give a better presentation if you practice your talk ahead of time. Stand in front of a mirror, set a timer to the number of minutes you've been allotted, and start talking. Allow 10 or 15 minutes for questions, and make sure that your talk fills but doesn't exceed the agreed-on time. Whether it's a half-hour talk or an all-day workshop, it's disrespectful to have too much or too little content for the time allotted. If you try to cover more material than you have time for, your audience will leave feeling confused, frustrated, and unsatisfied. If you have too little material to fill the time, you'll give the impression that you don't have much to say. Either way, you won't look good.

Be brutally honest with yourself as you practice your presentation. If you find yourself trying to cram too much information into the time you have, cut back. Yes, there's always more to say on a topic as fascinating as the one you've chosen to cover, but rushing through your slides because you've run out of time looks unprofessional and doesn't add to your or your audience's comfort. And don't be tempted to exceed your allotted time. You will accomplish nothing except alienating your audience and ensuring that the organization won't invite you again.

Finding a Test Audience

Joe Flower, an experienced writer, speaker, and consultant (www.Imagine WhatIf.com), has some great advice for anyone considering public speaking. Because so much of successful speaking is practice, he recommends finding volunteer speaking opportunities where you can improve your skills before making your big presentation at that major conference. As he said to me once: "Where do you find volunteer audiences? Local organizations such as women's clubs or the Rotary. The human resources or education specialists of companies in industries that might be affected by your talk. Offer them a free lunchtime talk that is relevant to their people. I once called up every stock brokerage in town, and gave a bunch of lunchtime talks about dealing with an aging population, for example. You need real audiences; there is no substitute."

Going Global

Once you've gotten a few talks under your belt, it's time to expand your horizons. Instead of just speaking to local chapters of national associations, get in touch with the annual conference planner or program committee and propose a talk that you think would be of interest to the membership as a whole. It might be an expanded version of your presentation to the local group, or something else that a broader audience would find appealing. Keep in mind that conference planners often work six to eighteen months out, so you may be making a pitch for a talk quite a ways in the future. The opportunity is worth waiting for, though; your credibility among your clients will grow significantly once you're known as a speaker at the national or international meeting of their professional or trade association.

When you reach this point, you may be in a position to ask for money. Depending on the organization, they may pay an honorarium to speakers. Even if they don't pay speakers directly, it's reasonable to ask for reimbursement of some or all of your travel expenses, and to expect them to waive any conference registration fees. After all, you're providing the content that their attendees are paying for, right? If you want to expand your speaking into a more regular part of your business, see Chapter 35, Other Services You Can Offer.

Learning to Speak

What if you're just not comfortable as a public speaker? Look for nonthreatening opportunities to speak in front of a group of people, even if they're not prospective clients. That might be a talk at the AIIP annual conference or at the local Chamber of Commerce. Think about taking on a role that requires occasional public presentations at your place of worship, or with an organization where you volunteer. Toastmasters International (www.toastmasters.org) is perhaps the best-known organization for honing your public-speaking skills. More than anything else, learning to speak publicly just takes a decision on your part to put yourself out there. The first few times you speak in public are difficult, but it really does get easier the more you do it. You may even end up enjoying the limelight, who knows?

PowerPoint Tips

The greatest tool I've discovered for public speaking is PowerPoint (www.microsoft.com/office/powerpoint). Even if you haven't used PowerPoint, you've

Public Speaking Pep Talk

The first time I stood up in front of a roomful of people and started talking, I was a nervous wreck. I had trouble maintaining my train of thought, I worried about keeping the audience's attention, I even worried that I couldn't see over the podium! But I survived, and I've found that, with practice, public speaking has become something I look forward to doing. Over the years, I've developed a few mantras that help me calm down when my stomach starts to clench up.

- The audience wants you to do well; they're silently cheering you on. As long as you make it through your talk and don't run screaming off the stage, you'll do fine.
- Most people can't imagine getting up in front of a room and speaking. They respect you for having the guts to do this. Your audience knows how brave you are, because they know how scared they'd be in the same position.
- What is the worst thing that could happen? Your clothes aren't going to fall off your body, so at least you know you won't wind up stark naked in front of a roomful of people. If you lose your place in your talk, you can stop, take a deep breath, smile, and start over at whatever point you find yourself. At worst, people may think you made a rather abrupt transition from one thought to the next.
- Perception is reality. Fake it 'til you make it. If you project an air of self-assurance and sound like you're having fun, your audience will pay attention to what you're saying and will enjoy your talk. They don't need to know that your stomach is in knots.
- Never tell the audience that you're nervous or that you don't have much to say. They don't need to know the former, and the latter isn't true, or you wouldn't be standing at the podium.
- Find a few friendly faces in the crowd and speak to those people directly. Make eye contact, smile, and imagine that you're just practicing your speech in front of a few friends.

probably seen it in action; no speech, sales presentation, or executive summary seems complete without PowerPoint slides. And there's something to be said for the PowerPoint approach. People absorb information better if they can both hear and see it, so slides that show your key points as you go along make it easier for your audience to follow you. You can turn your slides into handouts (with one, two, three, or six slides on a page) for your attendees to take with them; handouts reinforce your talk, give your audience something to write notes on, and—if you put your contact information on the last slide—ensure that they know how to get in touch with you later. In fact, I also insert a slide mentioning my free client newsletter and encouraging people to e-mail me for a subscription or to leave their business card so I can sign them up. In Chapter 21, Print Marketing, I also talk about sending postcards to the attendees after the meeting, reminding them of the highlights of your talk and supplying your contact information for future use.

Developing an effective PowerPoint presentation isn't difficult, if you keep in mind the need to keep it simple. Don't pack too much information on a single slide—no more than three or four lines per slide. Avoid animation, flashy text features, or anything else that distracts the audience from the *content* of your talk. Do you want them to remember what you said or how cool the effect was when the screen faded from one slide to the next?

As I've watched other PowerPoint presentations and gotten audience comments on my own, I've come up with a few more PowerPoint tips for independent info pros.

- Use a simple background—you can't tell ahead of time what it will look like on a projection screen, so the cleaner the better.

- Watch your colors. High contrast between text and background makes the text easier to read.

- Avoid animated text and transitions (when the text "flies" onto the screen from a corner or appears a letter at a time).

- Include your URL on the bottom of every slide. If the conference organizer won't pay for the cost of handouts, offer to e-mail copies of your PowerPoint presentation to people who give you their business cards. (This is a way of building your prospect list, by collecting business cards and sending them some marketing material, along with the slides they've requested, after the conference.)

- Consider posting your presentation on your Web site, and giving the direct URL to the audience in advance. It's less work than e-mailing it individually, but the disadvantage is that you don't have a chance to collect business cards or send out your marketing package.
- Keep the text of your slides simple and terse. Use a simple font such as Arial or Tahoma.
- Include screen shots or graphics if necessary, but remember that they may be difficult to read.
- If you're speaking from your slides rather than from a prepared script, use the number of slides in your presentation to gauge the length of your talk. Expect to spend about three minutes per slide.
- Put your name, URL, and e-mail address on the first and last slide, so people can write down your contact information before your talk or at the end.
- Spell-check and proofread your presentation when you first create it and after every change.

Lessons Learned as a Writer and Speaker

- ✦ You gain instant credibility once you're a published author.
- ✦ Write for publications your clients are likely to read.
- ✦ Write clearly, in straightforward language. Short articles are more likely to be read than longer ones.
- ✦ Get used to public speaking; practice, practice, practice.
- ✦ Plan on lining up speaking engagements for annual conferences at least 6 to12 months in advance.
- ✦ Use PowerPoint skillfully to emphasize key points, and to put your contact information in front of your audience.

Chapter 23

Starting the Word of Mouth

As I have said repeatedly in this book, you'll get most of your clients from referrals. A client will mention you to a colleague; a librarian will refer patrons when he gets requests he can't handle; a fellow independent info pro will send a client to you if the research goes beyond your colleague's expertise. As Sue Rugge, a pioneer in the info pro business, so memorably said, "It's all word of mouth, but you have to be the first mouth." This chapter looks at ways to get that word of mouth going.

Promoting "Brand You"

Many new entrepreneurs find it difficult to market themselves. We were taught as children not to brag or be overly boastful. When you're running your own company, though, you *are* the product. If you find it difficult to promote you, you, you, then focus on your company name. You're marketing Pat Smith Infotronics, not just Pat Smith.

In any event, keep in mind that everything you do has an impact on the reputation of your company and you as a professional. In a sense, you're always "on"—at least whenever you're in a business or professional setting. When you contribute to an electronic discussion group, watch your language and tone of voice. When you're at a professional meeting, dress appropriately; I usually try to dress a bit more conservatively than the average, just to ensure that I'm taken seriously.

"What Does Your Company Do?"

When someone asks you what you do, what will you say? You'll want to have a concise, memorable response prepared and ready to go. Give this some careful thought, keeping in mind that everyone you talk to is a potential client or referral source. Paul and Sarah Edwards, the authors of a number of books about home-based businesses, describe a useful formula for developing your 10-second introduction. The template they use is:

"You know how [describe typical clients' information problem]? Well, I [solve problem] by [doing this]."

For example, "You know how frustrating it is when you spend an hour looking for market research on the Web and never do find what you're really looking for? Well, my company helps you solve business problems by finding information that does not even appear on the Web." Or, "You know how hard it is to find 'soft' information about your industry or your competitors? Well, as a telephone researcher, I can gather the insights of the industry leaders for my clients, and since my clients' names are never associated with the research, I can put my finger on information they couldn't have obtained themselves."

I like this formula because it forces me to focus on the benefits I provide to my clients, rather than simply describing what I do, and it keeps the entire description to 10 or 15 seconds. As you work on your personalized version of the answer to "so, what do you do?", focus on the following:

- Avoid industry jargon or buzzwords such as "solutions." Word of mouth travels a lot farther if people outside your field understand and can describe to others what you do.

- Keep it short. They're asking you for a description of your business, not your life story.

- Make yourself recession-proof. What are your clients' critical information needs—things they view as essential, not just nice to have?

- Focus on benefits that provide clear added value. Offer services that your clients can't or won't do for themselves and that enhance their bottom line.

- Make sure you can deliver your introduction with enthusiasm. If you're excited about your business, others will be as well.

The Art of Schmoozing

Whether you're promoting your services at an exhibit booth, attending a local professional association meeting, or just chatting with someone at a conference, learn about the other person before you start describing your own business. Ask problem-seeking questions—"What do you use the Internet for at your job?" "What frustrates you most about your work?" "What do you do when you can't find the information you need?" Display a genuine interest in the other person's work and profession. Doubtless, you'll learn something interesting about her line of work. You'll also find out specifically how you can help her, and can fine-tune your introduction to address her particular information problems.

Many people are shy by nature and find it hard to make conversation with strangers. I had one of those "ah-ha" moments when I realized that most other people are equally concerned, and are delighted when they find someone willing to listen to what they have to say. I repeat the following reminders to myself before I walk into a room full of strangers.

- Pay attention. Focus on the person you're talking with, and listen to what he's saying.

- Be enthusiastic. Use your face and body to show emotion and to indicate that you're interested in the conversation. Show that you're passionate about what you do and that you love working for your clients. (And if that isn't the case, think about refocusing your business on a client base and type of work that you do love.)

- Perception is reality. Act self-confident, even if you don't feel self-confident, and eventually you'll start feeling as confident as you act.

"How Did You Hear About Me?"

Whenever a potential client contacts you to ask for an estimate or to learn more about your business, ask how she heard about you. That's invaluable market research; it tells you how your word-of-mouth marketing is going, and who's talking. I keep track in my client database of how each client found out about me, and once a year I look through it to see where most of my new clients have come from. Was it from my Web site? Are several of my existing clients frequent sources of referrals? Did people hear me speak at a conference? Did they read a book or an article I wrote, which prompted them to call me? Use this information to maximize your marketing efforts by focusing on the word-of-mouth tools that work best for you. (See Chapter 17, Strategic Planning, for more about conducting an annual review of where you are and where you're going.)

Susan Detwiler, a longtime independent info pro, took a systematic approach to this word-of-mouth analysis. As she described it, "A few years ago, I did a genealogy of my business—that is, I looked at each job I had done that year and thought through how I had gotten that particular client. Client A was a colleague of Client B, whom I had met at a Medical Surgical Market Research Group meeting. Client C was a member of the MSMRG. Client D was a referral from someone in the Association of Independent Information Professionals. Client E was a referral from someone who exhibited at AIIP. And so on. I realized that most of my well-paying work came from my *active* participation in two organizations—MSMRG and AIIP." Susan learned that it took more than just being a member of an association; she was active, visible, and known for a specific type of research service. She hasn't done much work directly for AIIP members as a subcontractor, but she has found that AIIP members are a good source of referrals.

Working the Associations

Susan Detwiler discovered that being active in selected associations can connect you to crucial sources of client referrals. The key is to look at an association's membership list before joining, and determine whether its members represent businesses or other organizations that are likely to use your services. If access to the membership directory is restricted to existing members, use your research skills to get a sense of who the members are. Look through the association's Web site and note the affiliations of elected officers and committee chairs. Review its annual conference program and see what kinds of speakers are invited. You might call the headquarters office and ask for a rough breakdown of the types of organizations its members come from.

Once you've identified one or two professional associations that seem to be likely sources of leads, join and become an active volunteer. Membership itself is worth very little beyond a listing in the association's membership directory. Your prospective clients will get to know you by seeing you in action. Identify a volunteer opportunity that involves contact with members—writing for the newsletter or organizing local programs, for example. At one point, I volunteered to handle the logistics for local meetings of the Special Libraries Association. RSVPs came to me, which meant that every time members mailed their checks and registration forms, they were reminded of Bates Information Services. And I was the one at the door handing out name badges and collecting tickets. It wasn't a sexy job, but it gave me the opportunity to meet most of the members of the local chapter, and they all knew my name and the name of my company. It was definitely a good investment in name recognition and brand awareness when I was just starting my business.

Maximizing Your Exhibiting Dollar

I mention attending professional conferences in Chapter 16, Professional Development. The focus in that chapter is on keeping yourself up to date on current resources and issues. However, conferences offer another marketing angle to consider—turning into one of those perky sales reps who stand at the front of their exhibit booths all day and try to talk to you about their company's services. Actually, it's not that bad an experience, and it can be a great way to build name recognition, credibility, and your prospect list.

Renting exhibit hall space is a big investment—in time, expense, and energy. The direct cost for the smallest typical exhibit space can run several thousand dollars and up, depending on the size of the conference. You'll need some kind of display—you're a fascinating person, but just you standing in an empty booth space isn't a very effective marketing approach. With some creativity, you can furnish your booth fairly modestly, but expect to spend at least $400 to $500, once you factor in the rental of a table and draping, a professionally done sign, and a plant or flowers to brighten the booth space.

The more challenging aspect of exhibiting is, of course, the fact that you have to be there, in the booth, during the entire time the exhibit hall is open. Trust me, no one stops to pick up marketing literature at an empty booth. It's tiring to be upbeat and positive when you've been on your feet for hours and given the same spiel to 50 or 100 people. On the other hand, the fact that you *have* a booth puts you in a league with the serious vendors, as far as your clients are concerned. Years after I invested in a booth at a couple of national conferences, people still remember that I'd exhibited. And I can trace a number of referrals back to people I met, and added to my mailing list, when I exhibited at those conferences. If the cost of a booth at a national conference is daunting, consider exhibiting at a local or regional event, as long as the attendees are client material.

Although every exhibit and every conference crowd is different, the following tips will help you maximize your investment in that exhibit hall space.

- Have plenty of brochures and business cards. Of course, you will collect visitors' cards as well, but people expect to be able to take something with them.

- Resist the urge to hand out pens, toys, or other giveaways unless you have something you know people will use daily. A pad of sticky notes with your logo, tag line ("Research for the advertising industry"), and contact information might be effective.

- Offer a daily drawing for something information-related, such as a book on Internet research. Don't offer wine, candy, or some other unrelated prize; your goal is to collect business cards from people who are interested in your services, so give away an item that will attract prospects, not just anybody who wants to win a bottle of wine.

- Be prepared to talk about the benefits you offer rather than simply describing your services. Hone a 10-second description of how what you do will change your prospective client's life. (Okay, maybe you won't change their lives, but you want prospects to think, "Good heavens, how have I managed to get along without your services?" Or, "This is terrific! I had no idea there were people who did this!")

- Don't try to demonstrate online research at your booth. You'll get bogged down while sitting at the PC, and you'll miss the opportunity to talk to people while your attention is focused on your search. Note, too, that connectivity costs in many exhibit halls are very high. Instead, consider preparing one-page examples of the type of research you do, with testimonials from satisfied clients. (The exception is if you are exhibiting at a very small conference, if the charge for a phone line is reasonable, and if you expect to have plenty of time to talk with each prospect.)

- Mentally prepare yourself to be exhausted by the end of the day. You'll be standing for long periods, looking friendly, enthusiastic, and upbeat for every single person who comes by. It can get tiring after a while but, if you psych yourself up ahead of time, you can pace yourself so that you don't burn out by 3 p.m.

- Be sure that your booth looks professional. It can be simple, but make sure your signs are professionally done and that your material is displayed well. Bring display stands so that your brochures and other handouts are easy to see.

- Avoid eating or drinking in the booth, police your area to get rid of clutter that others might have deposited there on their travels through the exhibit hall, and don't sit down when there are prospects around.

- Ask for a business card from anyone you talk with who sounds like a prospect, and make a note on the back of the card to remind you of the conversation. Send personalized follow-up letters when you return to the office.

- At the end of the conference, go through the business cards you've collected from your prize drawings and save those from organizations you think could become clients. Send every person a letter thanking them for participating in the drawing, enclosing your business card and a copy of your newsletter, or telling them how to subscribe to it electronically.

Asking for Referrals

It may seem odd, but we often forget to ask our clients and contacts to recommend others who might use our services. People appreciate the chance to spread the word about someone they enjoy working with, but they often need a reminder. I include one in my newsletter and marketing postcards: "Spread the word! Do you know anyone who might want to hear about Bates Information Services? Send me their e-mail or postal address, and I'll send them a one-time mailing to let them know about my research services." Note that I assure my clients that I'm not going to put their colleague or friend on a junk-mail list, nor will I call them with a sales pitch. When I do send out that mailing, I include the name of the client who referred me, which gives me instant credibility by saying, in essence, "This isn't a random sales pitch ... Your colleague Robin recommended that I contact you."

Some independent info pros offer an incentive for a client referral—a discount on the next job for that client, for example, or a token gift. I'm not convinced that such gestures are necessary or that they even make a difference. Use your judgment, based on your knowledge of your client base.

Another source of referrals may be the reference staff at your local public library. Although I usually recommend marketing outside your local area (see Chapter 11, Managing Your Clients), public librarians can be great word-of-mouth marketers. First, get to know the reference staff, and particularly the business reference librarians if your local library has a separate desk for business reference. You may not be a business researcher per se; you're simply targeting the librarians who deal with patrons whose information needs are more likely to be commercial in nature, and who are therefore more likely than the average library user to be willing and able to pay you for in-depth research services.

Find out if the librarians outsource or refer out questions that go beyond the level of service they normally provide. Some libraries have policies that prohibit the staff from recommending any outside information professionals; other libraries maintain lists of local independent info pros that they hand out to patrons on request. Consider offering to give a free workshop on your specialized area of research to the reference staff; it's a nice way to give something back to a valuable local resource, and it doesn't hurt to be seen as a supporter of the library. I have occasionally worked with public libraries to present a half-day workshop on business research that they open to the public. I make sure to highlight all the services and resources available at the library, and of course I mention my free newsletter at the end of the workshop. Everybody wins; the library is able to offer a valuable service to its patrons, the patrons are exposed to some of the more advanced services the library provides, and I can market myself to a group of information-hungry prospects.

Leads and Networking Clubs

While asking for informal referrals from clients is a great way to generate word of mouth, you might also consider joining a formal organization designed to fast-forward the referral process. These groups, called leads clubs or networking groups, offer members a structured way to exchange qualified business leads. Local groups often attract people from a wide variety of businesses—stock brokers, printers, interior decorators, cleaning services, and even independent info pros. Groups usually meet once a week, and each member has an opportunity to describe his or her business and exchange leads with other members. Expect to pay a yearly membership fee as well as local group dues.

Some independent info pros find these groups good referral sources; others value them for moral support and as resources for local business services such as accounting or graphic design. Networking groups also provide a comfortable setting for you to practice your 15-second introduction. Since the other members of the group are trying to provide you with qualified prospects, they need to grasp what you do. At each meeting, you can hone the description of your business so that it's memorable and understandable.

Look at networking groups as a part of your long-term marketing effort. You have to attend meetings with a spirit of generosity and a willingness to share your thoughts and suggestions with others, rather than just expecting to generate business leads. You get out of a networking group what you put into it.

Some of the larger networking groups are:

- Ali Lassen's Leads Club (www.leadsclub.com)
- Business Network International (www.bni.com)
- eWomenNetwork (www.ewomennetwork.com)
- LeTip (www.letip.com)

You may also find independent networking groups in your area; check with your local Chamber of Commerce for listings or pointers.

Viral Marketing

When marketing pros speak approvingly of viral marketing, they're usually talking about techniques that encourage people to spread a company's marketing message to others. If one person tells three others about your company, and each of them tells three others, your message is passed along to 243 people within five "tellings." One of the classic examples of viral marketing on the Web is Hotmail.com. They offer free e-mail, with the condition that a brief plug for Hotmail is appended to the end of every e-mail message you send. Every subscriber's friends see the ad, some of them sign up, all of their friends see the ad, some of them sign up, and so on.

Granted, you probably aren't in a position to give away a product or service for free. In fact, the last thing an independent info pro wants to do is to encourage the perception that all the information anyone might need is available for free on the Web. But you can think of ways to encourage people to pass along your name voluntarily. For example, every issue of my e-mail newsletter encourages clients to forward it, in its entirety, to colleagues, and includes a link to the subscription page on my Web site.

Another option is to add a "Recommend This Page" link to your Web site. Create a page of annotated links to Web resources, a newsletter, or other content that would be of use to your client base. Have your Web designer build a script so that, when people click the "Recommend This Page" button, they're prompted for the e-mail address of a colleague and given a space to add their own comments. Obviously, you include a clear promise that you will not harvest those e-mail addresses for marketing purposes. The script then generates an e-mail to the colleague, directing them to your page.

Whatever technique you use to generate buzz and to stimulate viral marketing, be sure that your efforts actually promote your business and expertise. Developing a great Web resource is a wonderful way to share your expertise and contribute to the collective wisdom on the Web, but if the resource doesn't also include a description of your services and a prominent link back to your company's Web page, it's altruism that can easily turn into a time sink. Maintaining a resource site that doesn't also function as a marketing tool for your business means that you're spending your valuable time on something that doesn't generate business. Make sure that whatever you develop highlights your unique abilities and expertise.

Top Tips for Starting Positive Word of Mouth

- Develop a memorable and descriptive 10- or 15-second introduction.
- Focus on benefits, not features; answer the question "What's in it for me?"
- Keep track of how new clients hear about you.
- Become active in any professional associations you join.
- Consider exhibiting at conferences – big investment but potentially big return.
- Remind your clients to refer colleagues to you.
- Leads clubs can be a good source of referrals and suppliers.

Chapter 24

Public Relations

Public relations, also called media relations, involves efforts to get third-party news coverage of you and your business. You aren't talking directly to prospective clients, as you are with most of your marketing efforts. Rather, you're addressing people who will deliver your message to their audience. Public relations can be an effective component of your total marketing strategy, but it won't, by itself, bring you many clients. What a successful public relations campaign can do is greatly increase your credibility; nothing enhances your authority like being quoted in a publication your clients read or, better yet, having an article written about you.

Of course, generating publicity about your business means doing something newsworthy. It also means being comfortable talking with reporters, writers, and TV and radio interviewers. Like everything else, public relations takes practice. I remember an early interview I did with a reporter from a local business journal. I spoke too casually, and one quote that made it in the article was my comment that "my clients are clueless about finding information, and they're delighted that I can help them get what they need to make important decisions." I was mortified that I'd called my clients "clueless," but I had only myself to blame. Reporters are entitled to use anything you say; you can't go off the record after the fact and try to take back something you said. It was a great learning experience, and since then I've trained myself to pause before answering any question and think about what I want my on-the-record response to be.

To learn more about the fine points of public relations, check out the Web site All About Public Relations (AboutPublicRelations.net), a well-done collection of articles, reference sources, and guidelines for the do-it-yourselfer. The book *Guerrilla Marketing for the Home-Based Business* by Jay Levinson and Seth Godin (Houghton Mifflin, 1995), although not specifically written for info pros, also contains useful tips.

Doing Something Newsworthy

Some reporters and broadcast producers may locate you through articles you've written, referrals from the Association of Independent Information Professionals (www.aiip.org), or even by doing a Web search. But they're more likely to call if you take the initiative and contact the media first with a story idea or newsworthy item. How do you find a newsworthy angle if you've just started your business? Think about what a reporter might find interesting.

- Send out a brief survey to your clients or prospects, asking them to estimate how much time they spend on the Web looking for information and their favorite search starting points. Guesstimate the average salary of your contacts, multiply that by the amount of time it would take them to find the information, subtract what it would cost if they paid you to find it, and the result of this admittedly unscientific survey is how much money they would have saved by calling an independent info pro. You might also mention the fact that a professional researcher can find richer, deeper information in X percent less time than the average non-info pro. Summarize the results, along with a list of the respondents' favorite search sites and a pointer to AIIP's referral service.

- Identify the 20 or 30 publications most frequently read by your client base—advertising executives, chemists, healthcare administrators, or whoever your target market happens to be. Do some research to identify how many of those publications are available in full text, with both current and archived material, for free on the Web. Odds are that less than 50 percent of the publications you've selected will meet these criteria. Pointing out two or three of the most outstanding gaps as examples, write this up in terms of "it ain't all on the Web for free, at least if you're looking for professional information."

- If you provide telephone research, develop a list of, say, the five best ways to get past executives' gatekeepers and the five conversation-stoppers that you should never use during a telephone interview. Package this list and present it as a tool to find the hidden information that never makes it into print—anywhere.

- Develop a specialized information product that you can offer at a flat fee—a weekly summary and analysis of industry news delivered electronically, for example—and pitch this as a value-added service that eliminates the glut of information that can overwhelm even the most savvy business professional. Why rely on a clipping service when you can tap into the expertise of an independent info pro?

- If you are speaking at a professional conference, ask the conference organizer for help in contacting the local press and reporters in the industry. They may share their media contact list, for example, or set up a "meet the speakers" reception for the press.

Amelia Kassel, owner of MarketingBase, developed a specialized information product and sent a press release to about a hundred regional business journals, from the Albany, New York, *Business Review* to the Honolulu *Pacific Business News*. Several publications picked up the story and she was able to track some new clients back to that publicity. As she commented later, though, "Keeping something like this going on a consistent basis is tough to do as a one-person business. I tried another press release about some new services, sending it out just to business journals in my state, and I got no bites." The lesson she learned is that what works best is sending out a press release as widely as possible and featuring a tangible and easy-to-describe product.

Writing a Press Release

Once you have something newsworthy to publicize, the next step is preparing a press release to send out to the relevant reporters and broadcast producers (see the section "Getting Noticed" for more about selecting the appropriate media). Most press releases use a standard format; this is not the time to show your creativity by doing something wild and crazy. Make it easy for the recipient to skim the release and figure out what you're up to and what's interesting about it.

Press releases usually follow the following conventions:

- Use your company letterhead, or type your company name, address, phone number, e-mail address, and URL, if you have one, at the top.

- In all caps, center the phrase PRESS RELEASE.

- Indicate that the information can be released immediately (FOR IMMEDIATE RELEASE).
- List your contact information—your name, phone number, and e-mail address.
- Write a headline that emphasizes what's newsworthy; make sure your company name is part of the headline.
- Indicate your city and state, and the date of the press release.
- In the first paragraph, tell who, what, when, where, and why. Summarize the important points. Readers should be able to tell immediately why they should care about your story.
- In the next paragraph(s), provide additional information. Include a quote from you as the principal or president of the company; this adds interest and makes the reporter's work easier.
- In the last paragraph, summarize what your company does, give a brief company history if you've been in business for a while, and list your contact information.
- Double-space the body of the text, with at least one-inch margins. This makes it easier for the reporter to skim the release and make notes in the margins.
- Indicate the end of the press release with '# # #' or the word END, centered on the page.

If possible, keep your press release to a single page, and never exceed two pages. Write clearly and in plain language, avoiding buzzwords, industry jargon, and acronyms. Although you know what you mean by "reinventing interactive paradigms," a reporter may not. Avoid adjectives and hyperbole; you're delivering news, not a sales pitch. Use the active rather than passive voice ("The company provides business research" rather than "Business research is provided by the company"). Proofread—not just spell-check—your release before you send it out, and double-check that you've included today's date. See the sidebar "Sample Press Release" for an example of what a short press release looks like. The "Press" section of most corporate Web sites will show you many more examples.

Sample Press Release

BATES INFORMATION SERVICES

PRESS RELEASE
FOR IMMEDIATE RELEASE
Contact: Mary Ellen Bates, 202.332.2360
mbates@BatesInfo.com

BATES INFORMATION SERVICES WEB SITE NAMED
"HOT SITE OF THE DAY" BY USA TODAY

Washington, DC (May 2, 2002)—Bates Information Services' Web site, offering a free Tip of the Month for Internet researchers, was named the Hot Site of the Day by USA Today. The Tip of the Month, available at www.BatesInfo.com/tip.html or through a free e-mail subscription, provides practical advice on how to find information on the Web and the value-added online services.

Mary Ellen Bates, principal of Bates Information Services and the editor of the Tip of the Month, has more than 20 years' experience as an online researcher. "I'm delighted that USA Today selected our Tip of the Month as today's Hot Site," says Bates. "I enjoy the opportunity to share some of the lessons I've learned over the years as an electronic librarian, and to help people search the Web more efficiently."

Mary Ellen Bates is the author of six books about the information industry, including the upcoming Building and Running a Successful Research Business: A Guide for the Independent Information Professional (Information Today, Inc., 2003). Bates Information Services, established in 1991, provides business research to business professionals and consulting services to the online industry. For more information about Bates Information Services, visit the Web site at www.BatesInfo.com or phone +1 202.332.2360.

# # #

Getting Noticed

You can address your press release to "Editor" in care of a particular publication, but that won't get you very far. Editors receive unsolicited press releases by the ream, every day. Take time to identify individuals to contact directly. Look through the print or online issues of publications you'd like to be mentioned in. Identify the columnists or staff writers who cover your area. Enclose a personal note with the press release, mentioning something they've written that you read recently, and telling them what your company is doing that you think the writer would find interesting. Showing that you've actually read the writer's work makes a big difference in whether your press release gets used or tossed.

Use some creativity in developing a media list of editors, reporters, and columnists with whom you want to stay in touch. You may want to send a release to the weekly business journals in major cities; if so, see BizJournals.com for links to about 40 business weeklies. Your local public library has media source directories you can consult for leads to publications in your industry. These directories include:

- *Bacon's Publicity Checker* (www.bacons.com)
- *Gale Directory of Publications and Broadcast Media* (www.galegroup.com)
- *All-in-One Directory* (www.gebbieinc.com)
- *MediaFinder* (www.mediafinder.com)

You'll certainly want to find out what publications your clients read (hint: ask them!), and to include in your contact list any publications produced by your industry's trade or professional association. Think about online publications as well as print; what e-journals or Web-based periodicals, if any, cover your market?

What about marketing to TV and radio and other nonprint media? My experience has been that this kind of exposure doesn't translate into business, perhaps because people are accustomed to having TVs and radios on almost as background noise. I've been interviewed several times on TV and by at least 20 radio stations over the course of my business, and I can't point to a single serious prospect I've gotten from any of those exposures. On the other hand, mentions in print media, and articles and books that I've written, have brought me a number of clients and prospects. I suspect that when people sit down to read, they're paying more attention, and they can clip the article and file it for later reference.

"According to Client X"

It's always nice to mention success stories or interesting projects you've worked on. Reporters like examples, and they're a great way to show your range of services. However, always ask permission from your clients—before the interview—to describe a project of theirs or to mention their name. Some clients are delighted to be quoted, but some organizations prohibit their employees from endorsing outside vendors. If your client is agreeable, be sure to give the reporter their contact information. I have a client who is a communications consultant and speech writer. She was happy to talk to a reporter about how she uses my services, and she got some free publicity from the article as well. In fact, she called to tell me that she'd put her name into a search engine and found that, despite not having a Web site of her own, she does have a presence on the Web—in the online version of the article in which she was quoted.

Also, encourage your clients to tell journalists about your services. Ask your clients—yes, ask 'em—whether they know anyone who writes for publications that they and their colleagues read. I am always amazed and gratified at my clients' responses when I try this. Because so many of them are consultants and independent professionals, too, they understand the need to publicize one another. I refer reporters to my clients for quotes whenever I can, and they return the favor. Cultivating your good-karma network can be a splendid public relations technique.

It's great to imagine yourself on the cover of *Time* or *Newsweek*, but save that fantasy for when you're already famous. For now, it's more realistic—and you have a much higher chance of success—if you focus on publications and writers that speak directly to your audience. If you provide information services to design professionals in the automotive industry, instead of pitching your story to the editor of the

Wall Street Journal, contact the journalist who covers the automotive industry for the *Journal*. Also, identify the leading publications that your clients read and get in touch with the journalists who cover automotive design.

Although it's tempting to send press releases by e-mail rather than in hard copy, resist. Journalists and editors get even more PR in e-mail than they do in print, and they tend to treat it the same way—straight into the trash. You're even easier to ignore in e-mail than you are on paper. An e-mail press release looks indistinctive if you include it in the body of a message; if it uses special formatting, it may not display correctly depending on how the recipient's mail program is set up—and many people find formatted e-mail annoying and a waste of time and bandwidth. And a press release sent as an attachment is, almost without exception, deleted unread. Even discounting the annoyance factor, your stationery has more impact; you can include clippings of other press coverage you've received and a copy of your brochure and business card, and—unlike unsolicited e-mail—it doesn't look or feel like spam.

Becoming a Certified Expert

In addition to sending out press releases and staying in touch with the editors, writers, and producers you're cultivating, you can take steps to become recognized as an expert in your field. In fact, you can get a listing in the *Yearbook of Experts, Authorities, & Spokespersons* (www.expertclick.com). This directory is targeted to the media, and is used by television, radio, and print journalists when they need to interview an expert on a particular topic. Yes, as crass as it sounds, you can buy your way into expert-hood—assuming you do have expertise in a given subject area and can learn how to give good sound bites. It isn't cheap, but if you compose a compelling listing you'll probably get calls from journalists and radio and TV producers looking for a pithy quote. Of course, it's your responsibility to turn what can be a very general quote or a brief mention into something your clients will hear about. Reference your interview in your client newsletter, on your Web site, and on the e-mail discussion lists you participate in. Be sure to add each reporter or producer who calls to your media contact list for future press releases.

Building a Press Kit

A press release, accompanied by a personal letter, is a good way to let an editor, reporter, or TV or radio producer know about a specific news item. But you'll also want a press kit that you can send to media contacts when you want to give them additional information about you and your business. A press kit is similar to your marketing kit, which is described in Chapter 19, Your Business Image—a presentation folder with everything they need to know about you—but what you put in a press kit will differ from the contents of a marketing kit.

Your press kit should include:

- Your business card
- A professionally done black and white photograph. Don't rely on family or friends to take a nice picture of you in your backyard. Pay a professional photographer.
- A biographical profile. It should be no more than one page, highlighting your professional accomplishments, your educational background, and any awards you've won or professional recognition you've received. This isn't a résumé and it shouldn't look like one; rather, it's a single page of publicity giving the highlights of your professional career.
- A one-page description of your business and the services or products you provide
- Copies of articles you've written, articles written about or featuring you, and speeches you've given
- Recent press releases
- A page of pithy quotes and testimonials from clients willing to provide them. Even an "anonymized" quote is worth using: "Around The World Information Services helped me win a half-million dollar account. Their market research and analysis were tremendous; I don't know what I'd do without them." —Marketing Director, *Fortune* 500 pharmaceutical company

Be sure to include a pitch letter—a one-page letter that introduces you and invites the recipient to review the contents. The letter should concisely and clearly explain why that person's audience—magazine readers, television audience, radio listeners, and so on—would be interested in your story. The pitch must be customized for each contact. Suggest a few different angles for coverage or for an interview, such as "did you know that 90 percent of the information on the Web can never be found in a search engine? Let me explain why" or "some of the most useful information on your company's competitors is right out there for anyone to find ... but no one thinks to look at these sources." After you've sent your media kit to your contacts, complete with personalized pitch letters, follow up with phone calls to make sure they've received the material and to see if they have any questions. When you call, be cognizant that media people are often on deadline, and be considerate of their time. Be prepared to give your pitch in less than two minutes, or to call back at a more convenient time. But stay in regular touch with your contacts. Send them press releases, any new articles you've written, copies of your newsletter, and so on. Even if they can't use your story now, they'll keep you in mind for later projects.

If you attend a professional conference, bring copies of your press kit; industry publishers often exhibit at conferences. Wait until the publisher rep isn't busy talking with potential subscribers—their first priority—and ask which editor would be most interested in your press releases and other material. Ask if any of the editors are attending the meeting; if so, try to arrange to meet with them to learn about their interests and the interests of their colleagues. Give them your press kit directly instead of just leaving one at the booth where it'll probably get lost or discarded. If the editors you really want to meet with aren't in attendance, send them press kits afterward, with a note saying how much you enjoyed talking with their colleague(s) at the show.

Giving Good Sound Bites

If your marketing efforts pay off, you'll eventually be asked to appear as a guest on a radio or television program. This can be a fun experience, and an excellent opportunity to establish your credibility. Although some people worry that they'll be asked a difficult question or made to look bad, that almost never happens. The host wants the audience to learn something and to be entertained; unless you go in looking for an argument, you'll find that the interviewer just wants to give you an opportunity to tell people about what you do and know.

The key to a successful interview is to prepare ahead of time, and to relax. The following tips will help you stay calm and self-confident while you're on the air.

- Know the program. Is it informal and chatty, or businesslike and to the point? Will the audience be familiar with the type of services you offer, or do you need to explain them in layperson's terms? Is it a call-in show, a lengthy interview and conversation with the host, or a three-minute slot in a news program?

- Provide the interviewer or the show's producer with a list of questions ahead of time. Make them interesting and thought-provoking and, of course, have interesting, concise, focused answers ready. The interviewer may not use any of them, but it doesn't hurt to offer some pertinent questions that may help focus the interview better.

- Provide the producer with a brief written background on you and your company.

- Even if the show is being taped for later broadcast, it may not be edited, so don't assume you'll have a chance to redo an answer. Speak thoughtfully. It's all right to pause for a second to collect your thoughts before you answer a question.

- Speak clearly and at a normal pace. Don't use industry jargon or acronyms without first explaining what they mean. Keep such usage to a minimum.

- Answer each question as concisely as you can, without giving monosyllabic answers. Think and speak in sentences, not paragraphs, to hold the audience's interest. Two or three sentences, or about 20 seconds, is enough for most questions. Focus on the most important points rather than on details.

- Relax. You've been invited because you and your work will appeal to the program's audience. Tell the audience what they would find most interesting. Use concrete language and anecdotes where appropriate to illustrate your point.

- Don't argue with the interviewer or with a listener, if it's a call-in show. If you do get a sticky question or one that you'd rather not answer, emphasize what's important and positive. Stay "on message"; don't get bogged down or sidetracked.

- Remember that anything you mention to the interviewer or production staff before you go on the air is fair game. Don't say anything off-air that you wouldn't want repeated to the audience.

- After the interview, send a thank-you note to the interviewer and the program producer. Offer yourself as a source for information in the future, and suggest any additional program ideas you might have.

Note that many of these suggestions apply to telephone interviews with print reporters as well as to radio and TV appearances. Reporters are looking for a few good quotes, so keep your answers short and focused. Save the detailed explanations for follow-up questions, if there are any. And, as I mentioned at the beginning of this chapter, be very, very careful about what you say, because the default assumption is that every utterance is fair game.

Public Relations Checklist

- ✦ Create something newsworthy—a survey, a report, a list of tips, or a unique information service—and write a short press release featuring the news.
- ✦ Develop a media contact list—editors, writers, and producers whom you want to cover your news.
- ✦ Send press releases and newsletters to your contact list regularly.
- ✦ Ask your clients for press referrals, and for permission to quote them.
- ✦ Prepare a media kit to introduce you to editors and producers.
- ✦ Plan ahead for interviews, and follow up afterward.

Section Four

Researching

Chapter 25

The Reference Interview

Librarians call it a "reference interview." Consultants call it a "client information needs assessment." Researchers call it a "client interview." They all refer to the conversation you have with a client in which he tells you what he needs, you negotiate the scope, deadline, format, and budget for the project, you thank him for his business, and you get to work. It seems like such a simple process, but if a project goes bad, you can usually trace it back to a reference interview that was poorly done.

The reference interview is the one time when you're guaranteed to have your client's full attention. He's calling you, he needs information and he knows it, and he wants you to do the work. This is the best chance you'll have to negotiate with your client, and probably the only point at which he's willing to take the time to explain the details of the work he wants you to do. If you don't nail down all the particulars now, you'll find it a lot harder to call back and explain that, well, you didn't really understand what he was talking about, and can we just have another little conversation to straighten out a few things?

This is also your best opportunity to make a subtle sales pitch. You can send out all the marketing material you want, but the stage at which the client will really listen to you is when he is calling *you* to perform a job for him. You can point out the added-value services you provide, in-depth research that he didn't know you could do, or an approach to the project that he hadn't thought of.

Steps in a Reference Interview

You wouldn't think that a simple conversation would require a series of steps, would you? Believe it or not, I teach a half-day workshop for librarians on the art of the reference interview. It's amazing how much is involved when you look at the dynamics of the negotiation that takes place.

Step One: First Contact

Your client contacts you and tells you what she wants done. If this initial contact is via e-mail, try to set up a time to have a live conversation. While an e-mailed request may look straightforward, you'd be surprised how often the request has morphed into something else by the time the conversation is over. In my experience, most e-mailed requests wind up developing into entirely different projects. Even—especially!—if an e-mailed request sounds simple, do what you can to talk to your client on the phone before you begin. If that's not feasible, prepare yourself for a series of e-mail messages to clarify and define the request.

Step Two: Explore the Question

Assume that what you're hearing from your client is probably *not* what you are going to wind up researching. No, your client isn't a fool; it's just that she doesn't know, most likely, what sources you'll be using, or how much information is available, or what kinds of research you're actually able to do. Here's the key: Your client is asking a question that she thinks you can answer. She is not necessarily articulating her underlying information need. Your job at this point is to ask open-ended questions to help your client explore the topic and explain what exactly she's looking for. See the sidebar "Getting at the Underlying Question" for some sample questions.

This is the point at which you listen and let the client talk. Focus on what she's saying and try not to jump to conclusions about the approaches you'll take to the research, the sources you'll use, or the information you'll find. Make sure that you're not distracted by other projects, another phone call (that's why voice mail was invented), or whatever's on your computer screen right now. Be here now; turn all your attention to your conversation with the client. Whatever else you're working on can wait; this is not the time for multitasking.

What if you have no idea what your client is talking about? Yes, it does happen, and it's difficult to conduct an effective reference interview if you don't know the first thing about the subject. You have a few options at this point. If you have absolutely no knowledge of the subject matter (I know nothing about medical research, for example), you might want to halt the conversation and refer the client to a colleague who specializes in that type of research. Alternatively, if the subject falls outside your area of expertise but you want to retain "ownership" of the project, you may choose

Getting at the Underlying Question

How do you get a client to explain what she really wants, without sounding like you're prying? Try some of these open-ended questions—and remember, this is the time to let your client talk.

- What do you mean by ____________?
- What do you already know about ____________?
- What do you expect me to find?
- Are there any sources you have already checked, or that you would recommend?
- Are there any other terms used to describe ____________?
- I'm not familiar with ____________. Can you explain it to me?
- If you were writing an article about this, what would the headline be?
- If I can't find exactly ____________, what would be second best?

to subcontract all or part of the work. If that's the case, the reference interview process will be somewhat different, because you may want to let your client know that you are bringing in "an associate" (or however you want to characterize your subcontractor). You may want to arrange a conference call, in which your subcontractor and your client can discuss the project. Then the subcontractor can get back to you with an estimate and you can work up your own estimate to give to the client. (See Chapter 14, Subcontracting, or I'll Scratch Your Back if You Scratch Mine, for more information.) On the other hand, perhaps the project just involves a topic you don't know much—or anything—about, but you're fairly confident that you can come up to speed quickly and do a competent job. In that case, you can tell your client that you need to do some preliminary research in order to develop an estimate. Spend a little time, no more than 15 or 20 minutes, getting familiar with the subject area. This assumes that your general research skills are fairly well developed; you don't want to flail about helplessly wondering where to begin. (If you do find yourself flailing, it's an indication to do what I suggested earlier in this paragraph—subcontract the project or refer it out to a more experienced colleague.) Remember, you can build some learning time into the project budget; this initial research is simply to get familiar with the terminology and to ascertain whether it's an area that you can get up to speed on later. Then you call the client back and resume the reference interview.

Step Three: Negotiate Everything

Now that you and your client have explored what she's really looking for, it's time to negotiate. Does this project call for specialized research techniques such as telephone interviews or public records research? Does your client want an executive summary along with the research? Would she like relevant information extracted into a spreadsheet or a PowerPoint presentation? Would she like you to present the results in person or on a conference call with her colleagues? Does she need the results in hard copy or would she prefer the material in electronic format? What about the deadline? Does she really need it in two days? Would she be willing to wait a week in order to get more in-depth research?

This is also the point at which you manage your client's expectations. You explain that, although you will use what you believe are the most appropriate resources available to you, you can't promise ahead of time what you'll find. The client is paying for your time and expertise, *not* for information per se. That means that, even if you don't find what she is looking for, she will still pay you for your research. Listen closely to your client at this juncture. Is she balking at "paying for nothing?" Is she asking you for a guarantee of what you'll find? Is she telling you that she just *knows* that you'll find lots of information? If so, this is when you'll have to spell out the rules of engagement—you can't make any assurances of what you'll find, you are not like a trial lawyer who only charges if he wins the case for you.

If your gut tells you that your client has unreasonable expectations, and if you don't seem able to change those expectations with a reasonable explanation of what you can and cannot do, it's time to walk away from the job; it has Disaster written all over it. This is not a failure on your part or your client's. It's usually a matter of different personalities or communication styles that just don't mesh. Presumably, someone else will be able to approach this client in a way that she hears and can acknowledge the inherent uncertainty of research. My usual tack in such cases is to say, "You know, I just don't think I'd be the right person for this job. Let me recommend a couple of colleagues who have more expertise in this area," or, "Let me give you the number to AIIP's referral service, which will give you names of other researchers who might be able to help you."

Step Four: Stop and Estimate

Note that we still haven't talked about budget. The first three steps in our reference interview have established what research the client needs and when she needs it. Now you have to figure out what it'll cost. Until you've been estimating projects for a year or more, don't try to come up with an estimate while you're conducting the reference interview. Nine times out of ten, you'll significantly underestimate the time involved. Instead, review what you understand the project to entail and tell the client that you'll work up an estimate and fax or e-mail it back to her shortly. Be sure to describe the work in your own words; if the client originally asked for "background information on the shipping industry," you might reword and refine her request, as a result of the clarifying questions you've asked her, as "a review of the overnight package delivery industry, such as Federal Express and UPS." Rephrasing the request ensures that you catch any hidden assumptions—yours or the client's—about what's involved in the project.

So you hang up the phone. You sit back and start noting down everything you think the job will require. For example, if you're estimating the overnight package industry project, your list might include:

- Review the major players' company Web sites to see how they describe their services.
- Download and extract information from companies' U.S. Securities & Exchange Commission filings.
- Obtain industry surveys from government agencies and trade associations.
- Search one of the professional online services for articles from industry publications.
- Obtain market research reports on the industry.
- Conduct telephone interviews with major customers such as L.L. Bean, Amazon.com, and Dell Computers to find out what concerns they have.

Would you have thought of all these possible research aspects while you were on the phone with the client?

Next, spell out what value-added services you will provide, such as an analysis of the results of your research or an executive summary of trends in the industry. See Chapter

13, Setting Rates and Fees, for more discussion of how to price a project, and a worksheet for estimating costs. Now, write a summary of what you'll do, what you expect your deliverables to be, when you will finish the project, and your not-to-exceed budget. Include some verbiage to the effect that you can't promise that you will find the exact data that the client is hoping to find, but you will make your best effort, and you will consult with the client during the course of the project if you encounter unanticipated roadblocks or find that very little information is available. You also need to include a disclaimer; see Chapter 15, Ethics and Legalities, for a discussion of disclaimers.

Step Five: Get Buy-In

Finally, you're at the step where you submit the budget to your client. Follow up with a phone call to discuss any last-minute questions and to nail down the project officially. Listen for any hesitancy about the budget. Does your client accept your proposal? Do you get the sense that she really expects you to deliver something more, or that she hopes it will *really* cost much less than your not-to-exceed budget? If you do, speak up now, as this is the last time you can easily clarify these expectations before getting underway. Also listen for any clue that your client had expected a much higher budget. If so, that's an indication that either you're pricing your services too low or you miscalculated the extent of the work involved. You can't correct your too-low pricing, but you must make sure that you haven't seriously underestimated the amount of effort required. Talk through the work you plan on doing and the format and scope of the deliverable, and check to see that you and your client are in agreement before you proceed.

Make sure your client knows that you'll call or e-mail if you have any questions as you go along or if you aren't finding as much information as you had anticipated. Ask if her accounting department will require any special information in order to pay the invoice, such as a purchase order or authorization number. The time to deal with this is before you begin working; if there's going to be a delay because of paperwork that must be completed, you have a much better chance of getting your client to expedite the process now, when she's eager for the work to be done, rather than after she has the results in hand and you're waiting for your invoice to be paid.

Unless you have an established track record with the client, you should get something in writing confirming the description of the project and the agreed-upon budget. Some independent info pros send a formal contract; others simply ask that the client okay the e-mail message describing the job; their response is confirmation. The larger the project, the more formal the proposal. Ask your lawyer to draft a sample contract that you can use for projects that require a formal agreement. I tend to avoid anything that looks like a contract for smaller projects; I've found that they just scare clients and they often delay the project while the client gets her legal department to go over them. On the other hand, if I am going to be working on a 40- or 50-hour project, I definitely want the client to take it seriously. In fact, I'll probably require prepayment of a portion of the not-to-exceed budget, so a formal contract is called for.

Am I Giving Away My Secrets?

Some clients require more hand-holding than others when it comes to a reference interview and an estimate. If they need a detailed description of the kind of research you plan to do, just build the extra time required to prepare that description into the budget for the project. They may become more confident after you've done a few projects for them, or they may just be the type of person who needs to feel in control. In any event, their need for hand-holding is not a reflection on your abilities, so look at it as a good exercise in thinking through a project and chalk up the experience to the wonderful diversity of humanity that you get to work with as an independent info pro.

Some independent info pros are reluctant to spell out the particulars of how they plan to approach a research project, fearing that they will be disclosing their trade secrets or giving the client a roadmap with which he can do the project himself. I think this is a misplaced fear. What we offer our clients isn't a secret stash of resources but rather the ability to search for information efficiently, follow clues to find information in unexpected places, and present the information in a way that makes it easy for the client to use. Telling our clients what resources we'll begin with hardly gives them the tools and expertise to do the work themselves, just as a doctor explaining what procedure she's going to use on me certainly doesn't give me the ability to do it myself, thank goodness.

Sources of Ambiguity

If all goes well, you will walk through the five steps of the reference interview, nail down the job and be on your way. If, however, there seems to be some miscommunication, you may have stumbled into one of the following pitfalls. You can't necessarily avoid these sources of ambiguity, but being aware of them will help you address any misunderstandings during the initial interview, instead of at the end of the project.

- The client's familiarity with the subject. If the client doesn't know much about the topic, he may provide what he thinks are helpful tips or buzzwords, which turn out to be dead ends. One way to catch this is to ask your client if he would like you to find some basic background information on the subject. (Note that this avoids the head-on question "Do you know what you're talking about?" but elicits the same information.)

- The client's assumptions about what information is available. It's human nature; we tend to ask the questions that we think people can answer. Your client may be asking for only the information he thinks you'll be able to locate, instead of describing the deeper question he really needs answered.

- The client's personality. No, you can't do anything about that, but you can recognize when your personalities clash, or your communication styles don't mesh. If that happens, see if you can bring in a subcontractor or just refer the job to a colleague.

- Misspellings or faulty memory. Librarians joke about the client who comes in asking for "that article from the *Times* a couple of weeks ago about fly fishing." Any experienced librarian will tell you that at least one and quite possibly two of those items is wrong—the article was from six months ago, it was in the *Journal*, or even *Angler*, or it was about deep sea fishing. Treat any statement along the lines of "I read about it last week" with similar skepticism. Likewise, double-check the spelling of any company or personal names.

- Dealing with intermediaries. One of the most difficult situations arises when a client's secretary or assistant calls you to relay a request for research. You can't negotiate directly with the client, you can't clarify or expand on the request, you can't offer additional services, and you can't discuss the budget. If you have worked with the assistant before, you may be able to simply ask to speak to the client directly. If not, see if you can e-mail a list of questions that the assistant can pass along to your client. If you hit resistance, the only alternative—short of declining the job altogether—is to document what you understand the project to be, spell out in detail the kind of information you will be providing, and make sure that the client signs off on the budget directly. Be careful; this is the kind of situation in which misunderstandings are much more likely to happen, and they're usually not detected until after the project is completed. Again, listen to your gut. If you just don't feel comfortable doing a project that you can't negotiate directly, offer to refer the client to a colleague. Turning down a project is almost always a better alternative than ignoring your instinct and winding up with a disappointed client who won't pay your invoice.

Top Tips for Negotiation

- Pay attention; don't try to multitask during a reference interview.
- Assume that there is a deeper question behind the initial question.
- Ask questions that elicit useful answers; ask open-ended questions.
- Avoid premature diagnosis; don't jump to conclusions regarding
- what the project entails.
- Paraphrase and reword the project to your client.
- Examine and be willing to negotiate all aspects of the request—information needed, deadline, budget, delivery method.
- Look for ways to up-sell—to tell your client about additional analysis or more in-depth research you can do on top of what he specifically asked for.
- Watch for possible areas of miscommunication and try to resolve them at the outset.

Chapter 26

Thinking Like a Researcher

I suspect that every researcher has a unique mental map he consults when preparing to tackle a research project. Your mental map will be built from your experiences in finding information over time—whether you learned to use the library as a child, how well the readily available Web sources cover your area of expertise, your familiarity with relatively obscure information sources such as government documents, your comfort level with regard to calling and interviewing industry experts, and so on. (For thoughtful discussions of researchers' mental maps, see Marylaine Block's article "Mapping the Information Landscape," *Searcher*, April 2002, available at www.infotoday.com/searcher/apr02/block.htm, and Barbara Quint's seminal pieces, "Inside a Searcher's Mind," *Online*, April and June, 1991.) I can't construct your research map for you, but I can show you some of the ways that info pros approach the research process.

Ready, Fire, Aim

The sequence for target practice or for research, of course, should be prepare, aim, and fire. However, researchers are often guilty of getting the order wrong and launching into a search before they've figured out what they should be looking for—the ready, fire, aim approach.

Assuming that you have already completed your initial interview with the client (see Chapter 25, The Reference Interview), the first thing you'll want to do is sit back and think. It's tempting to hop on the Net, throw in some key terms, and see what pops up, but your initial research will be more productive if you have done some preparation first. Remember, you may not incur any out-of-pocket expenses in searching the Web, but your client is paying for your time, and you have to manage it wisely.

What Form of Information Are You Looking For?

What do you really need to find? Does your client want white papers, policy statements, or position papers? Articles from magazines or trade journals? Conference papers? Chapters from authoritative books on the subject? Statistical material? Multimedia such as an audio clip, animation, video file, or image? Information from online discussion forums or newsgroup postings? Does your client want straight textual material, an Excel spreadsheet, Web pages, or some other format? Is the information you're looking for too current for a standard Web search engine to retrieve? Is it too old to appear online at all?

Looking at the question of form from a slightly different angle, does your client need:

- The full text of articles, or will summaries do?
- Very current material, or information from 10 years ago?
- Introductory material, or more advanced treatments that assume the reader's familiarity with the subject?
- A good overview, or an exhaustive search of everything written on the subject?

After you have answered these questions, jot down a checklist of what you are *really* looking for, and keep it close at hand as you begin your research. I'm always surprised when I realize how easy it is to get distracted as I become engrossed in my research. It's tempting to follow tangential leads. Peripheral vision is a useful skill and will often enable you to discover new and valuable sources, but you can wind up far afield if you lose focus and try to follow every lead.

Will You Know It When You See It?

Do you have a clear understanding of what your client needs? For example, I worked on a project to identify the impact of imported Chinese tungsten products on the U.S. market, specifically the use of Chinese tungsten in strengthening sharp edges in products such as snowplow and saw blades. Before I began, I had to decide whether I wanted *anything* that mentioned Chinese tungsten, or only material that looked at U.S. manufacturers as well. I knew I'd have to look at import and export statistics to see the trends in Chinese tungsten trade, and I had to determine the current strength of the market for U.S. tungsten. I had to identify experts to interview, which meant figuring out who would know about this specific issue; I couldn't just talk with an authority on the mining and processing of tungsten in general.

If you've done a thorough reference interview with your client, you will have reworded the goals of the project in your own words, to ensure that you understand exactly what the client expects. Justice Potter Stewart of the Supreme Court famously said that he couldn't describe obscenity but "I know it when I see it." That might work for Supreme Court justices, but it's not a good approach for independent info pros. If you don't know ahead of time what would answer the question and you're just hoping that you'll know it when you see it, you might easily miss a spot-on reference.

How Much Do You Know About the Subject?

Is this topic one you're already familiar with or must you do preliminary research in order to educate yourself? Be sure to factor into the total cost of the project the time required to bring yourself up to speed. Yes, it's all right to bill the client for that groundwork. My rule, though, is to not spend more than 30 minutes to an hour on self-education. If it takes me longer than that to get familiar with the topic, it's probably far enough outside my area of expertise that I should subcontract or refer the project to someone else. For instance, the entire area of chemistry happens to be foreign territory to me. I don't know what any of the terminology and symbols signify. I don't understand what happens when you combine certain elements. I have no sense of which components might be significant in a search, and which are common building blocks that I could safely ignore. I would be totally at sea if I accepted a search in this area. However, a topic like the Chinese tungsten market felt "safe" to me, even though I'd never researched anything quite like it before. I knew I could grasp what tungsten was and was used for; I knew from experience that certain questions and issues are common to searches of this general type. And I'd done similar research on other types of saw blades, so I had a list of resources that could get me started.

What's at Stake?

How you approach a research project will be determined in part by what the information will be used for. Does the client just want to come up to speed on a new technology or product? Does he simply want an overview of the trends in an industry? Does a client need to know what the market is like because he's considering going into a new line of business? Is the client making a strategic business decision and counting on the results of your research to help her reach a conclusion?

While clients may be reluctant to disclose the exact nature of the project they are working on, a skillful reference interview should give you at least a general sense of whether they expect you to deliver essentially a get-smart package or the informational equivalent of everything but the kitchen sink.

Seeing Horizons and Setting Limits

We info pros are a strange breed. We think about information in ways that most people don't. We know how much information is available *beyond* the Web—in fee-based online services, government documents hidden in the recesses of a courthouse, print material in libraries, even telephone interviews with experts who could never put all their knowledge into print. We see how far the information horizon stretches, and part of our role when we discuss a project with clients is to expand their understanding of the wide range of resources available.

I find that one of the greatest challenges in providing research services is figuring out how to narrow down my approach to the best, most relevant, most cost-effective sources for any given job. Do I start with one of the professional-grade online services? Should I look for a trade association's Web site? Would it be best to search market research companies' catalogs for an appropriate consulting report? Should I pick up the phone and call an expert? The approach you take first will be determined at least in part by the deliverable your client wants. If she's expecting articles from the trade press, you'll start with a fee-based online service. If she wants analysis, you might focus on market research reports or interviews with the leading players in the field.

In fact, one of the biggest challenges for a longtime researcher is to get out of your rut and try new approaches. It's easy to get accustomed to using the same databases, Web sites, or printed reference works over and over again for a particular type of research. But your clients hire you because you are an expert in finding the best information sources today. Just as your computer automatically clears its memory cache on a regular basis, consider purging your "assumptions cache" every six months or so. Seek out new information sources instead of, or in addition to, your usual sources. It's a useful exercise, and it helps keep you refreshed and current on the newest and latest resources. See Chapter 16, Professional Development, for more thoughts on staying on top of information resources and trends.

Whatever strategy you use, assume that you will be able to find *something*, even if the research topic is as focused as the market for replacement shower heads, as one of my projects was. If you come up with nothing on your first attempt, try broadening your search by adding synonyms and other alternative terms, eliminating date or language restrictions, and so on. For my research on shower heads, for example, I expanded the research to plumbing fixtures generally, and looked for statistics on trends in bathroom repair. We independent info pros sometimes forget that our clients need answers, not just data, and the information that fills their needs may not look at first glance like an exact match. We often have very high expectations of what will be relevant—"If this article isn't specifically about the market for replacement shower heads, forget it." Actually, the client is often just as happy with related information that points to the answer. Statistics on home renovation and repair and articles discussing general trends in consumer purchases of plumbing fixtures were sufficient for my client, who understood that it wasn't likely that anyone had studied the replacement shower head market specifically.

The flip side of expanding our vision of the information horizon is needing to know when to call it quits. I've always believed that what makes a good researcher is the presence of the "finder gene"—that urge to dig deeper, to try one more approach, to look through one more source to find the very best answer. It's a valuable trait but, like many skills, can be taken to an extreme. Once we're on the chase, it's hard to stop.

It's time to say "when" if:

- You run out of time. You have to have the answer by 3 P.M. and it's now 2:59.
- You start seeing references to the same sources over and over again; you feel like you're walking in circles. (Do you remember the story of Winnie the Pooh and Piglet tracking a Woozle around the tree, and eventually realizing that they were only tracking their own footprints?)
- You've found enough information to satisfy the client, and doing an exhaustive search isn't appropriate for the project or the budget.

Working for Free

You're in the middle of an interesting research project. You're enjoying the process of learning everything you can about the ice cream parlor industry, and you're finding leads for all kinds of great sources. During searches like this, it's hard to rein yourself in when you hit the end of your budget. "But there's so much more useful information out there!" you tell yourself. "My client is paying me to find the best information available, so I have to keep going. I just won't charge for these extra two hours."

BZZZT! Wrong answer. Giving free time to a client devalues your expertise and sets up the expectation that they'll get loads of research at a low cost. We have to stop when the client has decided it's time to stop; when you negotiated the not-to-exceed budget, your client was indicating how much value he assigned to this job. If he is only willing to pay for an overview of a topic, that's what he gets. Any additional time that you put into this project comes straight out of your bottom line. Even if you couldn't bill that time to other projects, you could have spent it on marketing, continuing education, investigating new computers for your next upgrade, or other productivity-enhancing tasks.

Of course, there are times when you might be justified in throwing in a free hour of work, particularly if you feel that you haven't been working up to capacity. Were you distracted and not focused on the client's job? Were you off on a tangent that you should have recognized as irrelevant? If so—and this shouldn't happen often—then absorb the time and resolve to avoid the problem in the future.

- You ask colleagues for suggestions, and they don't suggest anything you haven't already seen.
- You're doing research in a field or geographic region that simply doesn't offer many information sources, and you've tapped those out.
- You sense that the 80:20 rule has kicked in. You're pretty sure that you've found 80 percent of the information available, but the time, effort, and

expense required to find that last 20 percent would match or exceed what you've already spent.

Sometimes you just have to sit back and decide whether you've found an answer that works, even if it isn't an exact match with what the client asked for. Fortunately, charging for your time makes this task a bit easier. If the client is only willing to pay for an hour or two of your labor, then you know that he isn't looking for a comprehensive report on the subject. We can see how far the information horizon extends, but often our client does not want us to go all the way to the horizon.

Mapping Out a Large Project

Some research jobs are so straightforward that your search strategy is determined for you. "I need a bibliography of what so-and-so wrote about organic farming in the 1970s." "I need an Excel spreadsheet with five years of financial statements for these 10 companies." "Tell me the latest trends in retinal scanning for security systems." Other projects are more involved, and require research in a number of different types of information sources. For those more complex jobs, expect to spend time outlining your research strategy, thinking about all that is involved, and what kinds of resources you'll use. If you can, negotiate some interim deliverables; it's useful to get feedback from the client during the project, to make sure that your expectations match hers. It's a lot easier to adjust your approach mid-way through the process than after you've invested 20 or 30 hours of work. A mid-course check-in can also buy you additional time; your client, assured that you're making progress, is often less anxious to get the final report as quickly as possible.

When I map out a complex project, my timeline includes the following elements:

- Outlining all aspects of the research, listing what I need to find, what format it should be in, and what sources I think might be most appropriate.
- Calculating how much time to budget for analysis, synthesis, and review of the material after I have done all the research I can.
- Educating myself on the subject; checking for industry buzzwords and acronyms.

- Running a preliminary search using whatever research tool is most appropriate (professional online service, Web, phone, or library research).
- Reviewing what I have so far, identifying problematic areas, deciding which aspects I've covered sufficiently.
- Continuing research for the aspects of the project that I haven't nailed down.
- Evaluating my progress.
- Continuing research and evaluation until I have all angles covered or have exhausted the time I budgeted for research.
- Reviewing my results, writing my report and overview, adding whatever analysis my client has requested.
- Setting it aside for at least a few hours or overnight, reviewing one last time before sending to the client.

Note that one of the first things I do is calculate how many hours I can spend doing the actual research. If my client has agreed to a budget that includes 25 hours of my time, that *doesn't* mean that I'll be spending 25 hours doing research. I'll probably spend an hour or two preparing for the research, bringing myself up to speed on terminology, organizing my thoughts, reviewing the power tools available in the professional online services, and so on. I'll also set aside four or five hours at the end of the project to pull all the material together, put it into a format that is easy for my client to use, write an analysis and executive summary of my results, and outline any additional research that could be done if the client needs more information.

Tutorials on Research Techniques

There are a number of Web-based tutorials on how to embark on a research project. Most of them cover Web research as well as the use of some other, more traditional tools such as library resources and the fee-based online services. Many of these tutorials were prepared by university librarians, either in conjunction with a basic course in library reference or in an effort to teach students that there's more useful information out there than can be found through Web search engines. As a result, the focus of such tutorials is fairly basic; a longtime independent info pro probably won't learn anything new. If, on the other hand, you're coming to this profession without years of experience as a researcher and you want an overview of what's involved, you'll find these tutorials valuable.

California Polytechnic State University has an excellent Web tutorial on "information competence" at www.lib.calpoly.edu/infocomp/modules. It covers how to decide what approach to take, what types of material will answer the question, how to evaluate information sources, and how to organize and synthesize the information.

The Gale Group, an online information provider, and ALISE, the Association of Library and Information Science Educators, have jointly developed a Bibliographic Instruction Support Program, available at www.galegroup.com/customer_service/alise. This program was written from a reference librarian's point of view, but the insights are useful to independent info pros as well.

William Badke, a librarian at Trinity Western University, has written an electronic textbook, *Research Strategies: Finding Your Way Through the Information Fog*. The book is available at no charge on the Web at www.acts.twu.ca/LBR/textbook.htm.

Your local public or university library may also offer useful information on research basics—online tutorials, hands-on workshops, and other training material.

A Researcher's Checklist

- ✦ Do I have a clear understanding of what I'm looking for?
- ✦ Do I know what type and form of information my client wants, and ✦ why she wants it?
- ✦ Am I looking beyond my "usual suspects" to see what other information sources might be appropriate?
- ✦ Have I mapped my research strategy in advance, and allowed for time to evaluate and organize the information?
- ✦ Do I know when to stop, and am I willing to quit even though I ✦ know I could do more?

Chapter 27

Approaching Online Research

This chapter will give you an overview of what online research entails; the following chapters cover in more detail the various types of online information resources. Information Today, Inc., the publisher of this book, also publishes a series of books that focus on specific types of online research. I have written two of these "Super Searcher" books—*Super Searchers Cover the World: The Online Secrets of International Business Researchers* (2001), and *Super Searchers Do Business: The Online Secrets of Top Business Researchers* (1999). Other books in this series include *Super Searchers on Health & Medicine, Law of the Super Searchers* (on legal research), and even *Super Searchers Make It On Their Own: Top Independent Information Professionals Share Their Secrets for Starting and Running a Research Business.* Information on the entire series, including links to the resources described in each book, is available at www.infotoday.com/supersearchers.

For the purposes of this chapter, I've divided the online world into four broad categories:

- The open Web—that portion of the Web that you can access with standard search engines
- The invisible or hidden Web—sites that are accessible but hidden from most search engines
- The gated Web—content on Web sites that require registration and/or payment, such as Britannica.com or eLibrary.com

- The professional online services—the high-end aggregators of information from many sources, such as Dialog or LexisNexis

I cover the open Web and the invisible or hidden Web in more detail in Chapter 28, Web Research 101. I discuss the gated Web in Chapter 30, Specialized Online Services, and the professional online services in Chapter 29, Professional Online Services.

It's All on the Web for Free, Right?

You already know that not all the useful information in the world is available via the Web, just a mouse-click away—but sometimes it feels like the rest of the world is still laboring under that illusion. Every time another content-rich Web site starts charging for its services, I'm tempted to smile. I know that it will remind at least one more Web surfer, somewhere in the universe, that, no, it's not all on the Web for free.

Let's look at some of the places where information exists that a Web search engine won't find. Search engines miss a lot of the information that's on the Web. They may not know about a newly added or recently changed Web site. They may not dig deep enough into a site to find every page. They may not be able to read the textual or numeric data on a site if the information isn't in HTML or plain text; word-processed files, graphics, spreadsheets, databases, and multimedia files generally fall into this category. Some experts estimate that as much as 90 percent of the content of the Web is invisible to search engines. For a thorough guide to the Web's hidden information resources, see *The Invisible Web: Uncovering Information Sources Search Engines Can't Find*, by Chris Sherman and Gary Price (Information Today, Inc., 2001).

In addition to material that's on the Web but just not accessible to search engines, a surprising amount of content isn't on the Web because its publishers choose not to put it there. Factiva published a white paper, "Free, Fee-Based and Value-Added Information Services" (www.factiva.com/collateral/files/whitepaper_feevsfree_032002.pdf) that looks at the availability of information on the Web, based in part on a study that I conducted for them. I found that two-thirds of a random selection of 800 publications either had no Web site or provided no current articles on the site. And when I looked for archives of back issues, I found that more than 80 percent provided no archive on their site. The bottom line is that, if you want to conduct an in-depth search of trade or professional publications, you can't rely on finding the information you need on the Web.

Other limitations of conducting research on the Web include the impermanence of material—you have no assurance that what you find today will be there tomorrow—and the lack of sophisticated search and retrieval tools. Even the advanced search features of search engines resemble blunt tools rather than surgical instruments.

What's Missing?

As much as we would like to think that an electronic archive exists somewhere of everything that's been published, it isn't so. As the Factiva white paper I cited confirmed, publishers aren't putting their content on the Web in any complete or consistent manner. And we can't count on the professional online services to maintain a comprehensive archive of articles either. Even those databases that claim to provide complete, full-text coverage of a publication have gaps. Some very short articles are often omitted. Errors happen when articles are loaded into a database, and records get dropped. Syndicated features are routinely eliminated from the publications in which they appear. Advertising supplements, even if they include articles, are not preserved. Letters are transposed during data entry, so, for example, an article by Walter Mossberg won't be found if his name was input as Walter Mosbserg.

And then there are the Tasini gaps. *Tasini v. New York Times* was a case heard by the U.S. Supreme Court in which the justices ruled that database producers had to negotiate specifically for the rights to include articles written by freelancers. The fact that the articles had already appeared in print didn't automatically give the publishers the right to license those articles for resale by a third party, the electronic database producer or aggregator. The result of this decision was that some online information providers deleted all material by freelance writers rather than attempt to secure the rights from the individual authors. So, databases that at one point did attempt to include every article from a publication may now have gaps.

To further confuse the matter, many aggregators explicitly choose not to include every article from a publication. If the focus of a particular database is the insurance industry, for example, the producer may add selected articles from a wide variety of sources, while omitting anything that isn't focused on the insurance industry. And the articles themselves may not be complete. The records in most databases are straight text, which means that graphics, photos, charts, and graphs are usually not included, even on the Web. (One exception to this is the TableBase file, available on Dialog and DataStar, which extracts tabular material from business-related articles.)

Other factors that affect whether you'll find a specific article include embargos and lag time in updating online files, policies of the aggregators regarding which edition of a wire service or newspaper to include, and the policy of the database or Web site regarding the retention of older records.

Free vs. Fee

Given the wide range of information sources on the Web and in the fee-based online services, and given the fact that there isn't a tremendous amount of overlap between what's available on the Web and in the fee-based services, how do you decide where to start an online search? Longtime online searchers tend to default to the professional online services, valuing the power search tools, depth and breadth of information, search efficiency, and consistency among databases that they find there. Researchers who learned how to search the Web before they'd heard about Dialog or Factiva usually start with a Web search engine, knowing that they can skim a wide range of information sources and that the only cost will be their time. Understanding the pros and cons of both approaches, I developed a mental checklist to help me decide where to go first for any given research project.

- Who cares about this information? Would anyone be likely to collect it and give it away for free? If so, I'll start with the open Web.
- Do I need high-value search tools such as consistently applied subject indexing or the ability to construct a complex search statement? If so, I'll start with the professional online services.
- Am I looking for information in a form other than plain text, such as an audio or video clip, a spreadsheet, or a picture? If so, I'll start with the invisible Web.
- Do I need all the output in a single consistent format? If so, I'll start with the professional online services.

- Do I need very current material? If so, I'll start with news sources on the open Web.
- Do I need material from more than a year or two ago, or material that I can be sure of retrieving again later? If so, I'll start with the professional online services.
- Do I need articles from professional or trade publications? If so, I'll start with the professional online services.
- Is this a quick search just to see what information is available on a subject? If so, I'll start with the open and the invisible Web.
- Is this project in support of a high-stakes decision? Is it crucial that I find a wide range of material? If so, I'll start with the open Web, then go to the professional online services, then look for invisible Web material.

Boolean Basics

If you've ever used one of the professional online services or clicked the Advanced Search link on a Web search engine, you've probably been exposed to Boolean logic, which uses AND, OR, and NOT to define the relationship between your search terms. And if you made it past elementary school, you were probably exposed to Venn diagrams like the one in Figure 27.1, in which the left circle represents articles about running and the right circle represents articles about Boston. Articles that talk about both running AND Boston (*A* AND *B*) are represented by the center area of the figure, labeled C, where the two circles intersect. Articles that talk about running or about Boston or about both topics (*A* OR *B*) are represented by all the areas of the figure, that is, the two circles as well as their intersection, labeled *A*, *B*, and *C*. Articles that talk about running but do not mention Boston (*A* NOT *B*) are represented by the part of the left circle labeled A (it looks like a circle with a bite out of it).

The professional online services all use the syntax AND, OR, and NOT. Web search engines often support Boolean logic as part of their "advanced search" options. However, there is very little consistency in how search engines handle multiple words in a default or basic search. If you typed `running Boston` into a search

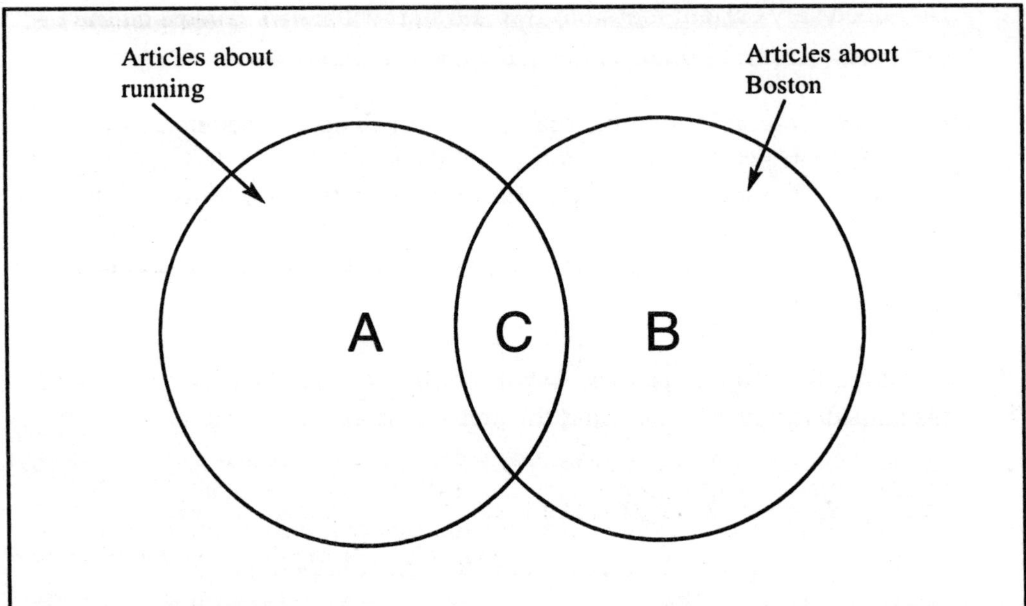

Figure 27.1 Venn Diagram

engine, it might be interpreted as `running AND Boston`; it might be read as `running OR Boston`; it might even be processed as the exact phrase "`running Boston`." To complicate matters, some search engines let you indicate words or phrases that must appear in each retrieved Web page, either by putting a "+" at the beginning of each required word, or by using a pull-down menu that indicates "This word must appear." In this case, the search `+running +Boston` would be interpreted as `running AND Boston`, and the search `running Boston` would be interpreted as `running OR Boston`. If you aren't sure how a search engine or online service is going to interpret your search, read the help files or search tips page before you get started.

Adjacency, Truncation, and Other Power Tools

The basic Boolean operators are pretty straightforward, as long as you keep those overlapping circles in Figure 27.1 in mind. But most online services and Web search engines offer additional search tools to help you refine your query. Some of the more common power tools include:

- Phrase searching, interpreted as look for these words in this exact order, with no intervening words. Most Web search engines require that you enclose a phrase in quotation marks. Example: `"tour de france"`

- Proximity searching, interpreted as look for these words within X words of each other, and in this order. This feature is more commonly available in the professional online services. Example: `asteroid near10 dinosaurs`
  Some also let you indicate that you want the two words within the same sentence or paragraph. Example: `asteroid same dinosaurs`

- Truncation, interpreted as look for any word that begins with these letters. This is used to search for variations of a word. Example: `vaccin*` (to search for vaccine, vaccines, vaccination, and so on)

- Field searching, interpreted as look for this word only in this part of the document. This is an effective way to narrow a search by looking for the key concepts in the title or first paragraph of an article, for instance. Search example: `title(exxon)`

- Date searching, interpreted as look for any records before/on/after this date. This is useful for finding articles published within a certain time frame; however, limiting by date is not reliable when searching the Web. Search example: `date from 12/01/02 to 3/01/03`

- Nested logic, interpreted as look for this word AND any of these words. This is useful when you want to use synonyms or other alternative terms in a complex Boolean search. Search example: `electric near2 (car or vehicle or automobile)`

Top Tips for Online Research

- Use Boolean logic when appropriate. It gives you more control over how the search engine processes your request, and the more control the better.
- RTFM. Yes, that's geek-speak for Read the Fabulous Manual. Click on the Help or Search Tips links, use the Advanced Search options, and read the printed documentation that comes with your subscription to an online service. Every online service has its own quirks and power tools; you're wasting your time and money if you don't take advantage of all the resources available.
- Practice pearl culturing. Just as a pearl begins with a small grain of sand, start with a narrow search to identify a few key articles on a topic. See what keywords are assigned to those articles, which acronyms are mentioned frequently, and what synonyms exist for the term or concept you're looking for. Then expand your search based on the new terminology you've learned.
- Use tools for limiting your search. Restrict your search by publication year, if you're looking for current material only; by source, if you want material from a specific publication or type of publication; by article length, if you only want in-depth coverage of a topic.
- Use search terms to define the type of material as well as the subject, particularly when searching the Web. If you are looking for statistical material, for example, include words like table, chart, or graph in your search.
- Use synonyms and alternative phrasings. A search for road rage might also call for "aggressive driving," "defensive drivers," and "traffic calming."
- Remember to account for variant versions of English. As George Bernard Shaw said, "England and America are two countries separated by the same language." Retirement in the U.S. is superannuation in Australia. Aluminum in the U.S. is aluminium in the U.K.
- Watch for gaps in coverage. Not everything that you want to find is online—either because the source is incomplete or because the information simply isn't available in an online format.

Chapter 28

Web Research 101

Almost all independent info pros use the Web as a research source, even if the primary focus of their businesses is something other than online research. Telephone researchers use the Web to look up contact names in companies, associations, and government agencies. Document delivery companies use it to confirm the title of a conference proceeding or obscure periodical. Library researchers consult Web-based public access catalogs before they head out the door, to make sure that the books they need are actually at the library.

Aspiring independent info pros often ask me whether it's possible to successfully run a business based exclusively on searching for information on the Web. Unfortunately, that's not a viable business model. As much as we would like to think that everything we need to know is on the Web, much of the most useful information is hidden within proprietary databases such as those offered by Dialog and LexisNexis (see Chapter 29, Professional Online Services, for more information on these resources). Limiting your research to what you can find on the Web does your clients a disservice; you are ignoring most of the high-value information sources and search tools that help you work most efficiently.

Whether they're correct or not, most people assume that they are expert Web searchers. Outsell, Inc., a consulting firm for the information industry, conducted a survey of self-described experienced online searchers. According to the Outsell report, 86 percent said that they didn't know what information is available, and 66 percent admitted that they didn't know how to evaluate information sources—yet 88 percent still consider themselves to be "skilled" searchers. (Source: Outsell e-brief, January 25, 2001.) That suggests to me that it's going to be difficult to convince anyone who already uses the Web to find information—even if they're just looking for news headlines or consumer health tips—to pay somebody else $75 or $100 an hour for Web research. Yes, you probably are a better searcher, you've identified some great resources, and you have the persistence of a bulldog. It's still a hard sell when the dominant perception is that anyone can find anything on the Web.

That said, I never cease to be amazed at the kinds of information and the types of research that are only possible on the Web. It's an invaluable tool, and a critical component of my searching toolkit. Clients do value our ability to find information more efficiently than they can, to evaluate Web information sources, and to select the most authoritative sources. We understand the limitations of the various Web search engines, and we know how to find sources that lie hidden in areas of the Web that search engines can't get at. As you read this chapter, think not so much about how you might build a business on Web-based research alone, as about how you can integrate the Web into the full range of information services you provide to your clients.

How Search Engines Work

Most people begin their research on the Web by typing a few words into a search engine such as Google (www.google.com) or AltaVista (www.altavista.com). It's a simple way to find hundreds—or hundreds of thousands—of Web pages, at least some of which might be useful. You'll get better search results if you understand how search engines are built, and their strengths and weaknesses. Note that this is a simplified description of how search engines work. For a more detailed explanation, see *The Extreme Searcher's Guide to Web Search Engines*, 2nd edition, by Randolph Hock, Information Today, Inc., 2001.

Contrary to appearances, search engines do not conduct a live, real-time search of the Web when you type your keywords in the search box. Instead, they search already-compiled indexes of the Web sites they have reviewed in the past. And where do those indexes come from? Starting with a core database of Web sites, a search engine reviews each Web page it already knows of to make sure it can "read" it (that is, that the content is in plain text or in a format that it can understand). It indexes all the useful words on the page, omitting common and relatively meaningless words such as *and*, *if*, and *the*, and then looks for any outgoing links to other Web sites. It goes to each of those linked-to sites, repeats the process of indexing all the useful words on those sites, looks for outgoing links, and so on. You can picture the automated program crawling through a site, and from site to site, and in fact these search engine indexing programs are called crawlers or spiders. Needless to say, crawling the Web is a time- and resource-intensive process; there is an inevitable delay between when a page is added or changed and when a search engine gets around to looking at it. There are also many pages that search engines can't or won't read at all. See the later section, "The Invisible Web," for more about what search engines *cannot* find.

When you type your search terms into a search engine, the retrieval software analyzes your input and figures out, based on its own internal algorithms plus any special instructions you might have supplied, how to process your search. The software determines whether all the words you've specified—or most of the words, or any one of the words—must appear on a Web page in order for that page to be retrieved. It figures out which combinations of words, if any, it should interpret as phrases. It evaluates the words to determine which ones are uncommon and, therefore, probably more important to your search. The retrieval program then checks the search engine's index and finds the entries for Web sites that match your search criteria.

The final step is a relevance-ranking process in which the search engine sorts the sites—often tens or hundreds of thousands—so that the ones most likely to be useful appear at the top of its list of results. How the search engine does this calculation is a deep, dark secret; search engines live and die by their ability to present users with the most relevant material at the top, and none will disclose exactly how their relevance algorithms work. In general, the calculation is based on some combination of factors, including the number of occurrences of your search words on the site, where and how prominently the words appear on the site, how close to each other they appear, the relative rarity of the words in normal usage, the "popularity" of the site as calculated by the number of times users have clicked on it or other sites have linked to it, and numerous other considerations.

Because of all these variables—the frequency with which they "crawl" sites to build and update their index, the method they use to interpret and process your search, and their proprietary relevance ranking algorithm—no two search engines have quite the same view of the Web. Try it for yourself: Type the same search into three search engines, and see how much (or how little) overlap you find among the top 20 or 30 sites in each one's search results list.

Getting the Most from Search Engines

Studies of search engine usage report that the average search only includes two or three words. That means that most people don't use synonyms or alternate phrasing or concepts, or take advantage of any of the search engine's advanced search techniques—limiting a search by type of site, language, format, or date; searching for two words near each other; looking for a word in the title of the page; and so on. The best way to keep up to date on these features is to get in the habit of periodically clicking the "advanced search" link or the "help" link in any search engines you use regularly.

Many search engines provide power-search features like these:

- Phrase or proximity searching (X near Y)
- Truncation (any word starting with the letters ABCDE)
- Field searching (the word X in the title, for example)
- Date search (find sites updated within the last X months)
- Language (limit this search to sites in a particular language)
- Adult filter (eliminate any porn sites from the search results)

Several excellent reviews of search engine features are available on the Web. These help you decide which search engine to use, based on the advanced features they offer. Two such reviews that are consistently reliable and current are

- Search Engine Showdown (www.searchengineshowdown.com/features)
- Search Engine Watch (www.searchenginewatch.com/facts/ataglance.html)

I also use these two resources to keep track of which search engines are the most comprehensive and most frequently updated (this seems to change every few months). I've also gotten in the habit of asking colleagues and clients about their favorite search engine. They may tell you about one that you haven't tried, and you may be on to a valuable new resource.

Web Directories and Guides

Search engines are built to find and index as many Web sites as possible. Sometimes, though, you don't want *every* site that mentions a particular word, but just the best, most authoritative sites. That's where human-built directories and Web guides come into play. The best-known Web directory is probably Yahoo! (www.yahoo.com), which two Stanford University students started way back in 1994 to keep track of Web sites that interested them. Web directories are distinguished from search engines by the following characteristics:

- Web sites are selected for inclusion by humans
- Sites are organized by category and subcategory (Science->Environment->Hazardous Wastes), so they can be browsed
- Emphasis is on selecting the best sites rather than the most sites

In addition to Yahoo!, well-organized, authoritative Web directories include the Librarians' Index to the Internet (www.lii.org) and the Open Directory Project (dmoz.org).

Web guides or portals are similar to directories; they consist of sites selected by an expert and are intentionally not comprehensive. However, Web guides usually focus on a particular topic or type of information and are often more useful if you want to dig deeper into the Web than you can with a general-purpose Web directory.

You can find Web guides on virtually any topic—government information, the plastics industry, professional associations, online newspapers, or everything you wanted to know about German Shepherds. A Web guide is usually built by someone with a passion or a professional interest in a specific subject, or by a librarian with an interest in building the best finding tool for a specific type of information. These guides are often excellent sources for independent info pros, as they provide a shortcut to the most useful and reliable resources on a topic.

Unfortunately, a single comprehensive directory of Web guides doesn't exist, so how do you find these resources? You can start with a general Web directory, click down to the topic you're researching, and then search within that category for the word "directory" (Yahoo! even has a subcategory for Web Directories). As you read articles about the subject you're researching, watch for mentions of online portals, meta-sites, and guides.

Here are some Web guides that independent info pros rely on:

- About.com (www.about.com) covers a variety of general-interest topics
- Business.com (www.business.com)
- Fast Facts (www.freepint.com/gary/handbook.htm) features links to almanacs, fact books, and other quick reference sources
- FedStats (www.fedstats.gov) helps unearth statistical information from the U.S. government
- FindLaw (www.findlaw.com) aids in legal research

The Invisible Web

Earlier in this chapter, I described in general terms how search engines look for new Web sites. However, much of the most valuable information on the Web is *never* indexed by search engines, so it is "invisible" to anyone who is using only a search engine for research. A number of reasons account for why search engines overlook or choose not to include information from particular Web pages:

- The page is not written in plain HTML text (some search engines can "read" word-processed files, spreadsheets, or PDF files, but no search engine can read text that might be embedded or expressed in a graphical or multimedia format).
- No other page has linked to the page, so the search engine hasn't learned about it.
- The Web page requires users to register before they can view its content.
- The information is contained in a database and can only be extracted via a separate search query at the Web site itself.
- The Web page has changed since the search engine last visited it.

- The content on the page changes frequently, so the search engine has elected not to index it.
- The information resides on a Web bulletin board or discussion forum which search engines don't "read."
- The Web site was down when the search engine attempted to index it.
- The page is many layers deep within a Web site, and the search engine doesn't look below a certain number of subdirectories.
- The Web page includes a metatag indicating that search engines are not to index it.

Obviously, many barriers exist to finding information on the invisible Web with a simple search engine search. Then how do you get to this often-useful information? First, look for resources listed in Web directories and guides like the ones I described earlier in this chapter. Note, especially, pointers to databases and to PDF files and other file formats not usually readable by search engines.

Remember, too, that even if some content is hidden from search engines, related pages may be visible. Say, for example, I want to find an interview I heard on National Public Radio concerning bioengineered foods. The Web page containing that interview (www.npr.org/ramfiles/me/20011128.me.07.ram) won't be accessible via a search engine, because search engines can't interpret audio files. But if I enter the words *bioengineered, NPR,* and *listen*—assuming that somewhere on the Web site I'll find a phrase like "click here to listen to this interview"—I get the page that describes the program and, indeed, has a link to the audio file. If you're looking for a page that you don't think a search engine will pick up, think of search words that imply invisible content. *Listen* suggests a link to an audio file; *search* suggests access to a database with a "click here to search" link; *video* or *view* suggests a video clip you can watch.

And, finally, remember that much of the invisible Web that's of particular interest to independent info pros consists of published material—articles on publications' Web sites, databases of market research reports, and so on. Develop your own collection of key Web resources for the type of research you do, focusing on the sources that search engines won't pick up. You can maintain links to these sites in your Web browser's bookmarks or favorites file, on a private (unlinked-to) page on your own

Web site, or just in your head. Wherever you keep it, this customized list of Web resources can be a valuable tool in your research.

For a much more in-depth discussion of how the invisible Web works and how to find information hidden beyond search engines, I recommend *The Invisible Web: Uncovering Information Sources Search Engines Can't Find*, by Chris Sherman and Gary Price (Information Today, Inc., 2001). The authors also maintain a Web site (www.invisible-web.net) with links to all the resources described in their book.

Discussion Forums and Lists

Although most research projects involve looking for written material or interviewing experts, sometimes we need to tap into the pulse of a particular group of people—electrical engineers, digital photography buffs, or international researchers, perhaps. The first stop may be e-mail discussion lists, newsgroups, and Web-based discussion groups. See the sidebar, "Mining Yahoo! Groups for Gold," for an example of how valuable such contacts can be. Locating these sources can be difficult; as a rule, they're part of the invisible Web described in the previous section. Fortunately, some directories exist that can help, and creative thinking will also guide you to the resources you're looking for.

In my experience, the most targeted discussions and best collections of experts can be found in e-mail lists. Although there is no comprehensive catalog of e-mail discussion lists, Web sites that host public e-mail lists usually provide searchable directories. Several of the most popular sites include

- Yahoo! (groups.yahoo.com)
- Topica (www.topica.com)
- Tile.net (www.tile.net)

Online forums hosted by particular Web sites are also good sources for identifying experts. Unfortunately, as I said, such discussions are difficult to identify and search engines often don't pick them up. Your best bet may be to identify a Web directory or guide that covers the industry or topic you want to research, and then look at likely sources to see if they host a forum. You can also search within a relevant subject category for the word *discussion* or *forum*.

For example, when I was doing the research on public safety radio systems that I describe in the sidebar, "Mining Yahoo! Groups for Gold," I wanted to find discussions specifically on "800 MHz interference." My first approach was to use a search engine and search for the phrase *800 MHz* and the words *interference* and *discussion.* (In Google.com, that would be written as *"800 MHz" interference discussion.*) Among the results were links to the StrongSignals.net Message Board, the archives of the Telecom Digest discussion list, and, ultimately, the groups.yahoo.com site for the 800Interference discussion group.

Mining Yahoo! Groups for Gold

I had a client who was interested in issues related to public safety radio systems in the 800-MHz range. One of the specific issues was interference problems encountered by police and other public safety officials using radio systems in this frequency range. I came across a mention of a public e-mail discussion group pertaining to this subject hosted by Yahoo! Groups. I went to groups.yahoo.com, located the group, and joined it, since it was open to anyone interested in the issue. Once I subscribed, I had access to the files that members of the group had uploaded to a separate library within Yahoo!. I found a treasure trove of information there—results of a questionnaire on 800-MHz interference sent to public safety agencies around the U.S., a best-practices guide on how to avoid interference between public safety radio systems and commercial wireless communications systems, and several PowerPoint presentations on the 800-MHz issue given at industry conferences.

Since this was a public discussion group—anyone could join—I told my client how he could subscribe to the discussion group and where to find the library files. He was delighted at what he found, and I was amazed at the quality of the information, none of which I could have retrieved using a search engine.

Finally, don't overlook Usenet newsgroups. These discussion groups predate the Web, and they tend to contain a high proportion of spam—off-topic messages promoting anything from porn to bogus investment opportunities. However, Usenet archives can turn up useful pointers, as well as background information on (and sometimes intemperate remarks made by) individuals you might be researching. Google now maintains the Usenet archive; you can search Usenet from 1981 to the present at groups.google.com. You can browse the directory of newsgroups or—sometimes a more efficient option—search the entire archive for postings on a particular topic.

As with other resources that are not indexed directly by search engines, you can also find pointers to discussion groups by typing in a keyword or two and the terms *list, listserv, forum,* or *discussion.*

Evaluating the Reliability of Web Sites

One of the most difficult parts of any research project is evaluating the sources of the information we've retrieved. Is this person really an expert? Is this article as impartial as it appears to be? Does this organization have a hidden agenda in its apparently objective white papers? When independent info pros send material to our clients, we are implying—whether we intend to or not—that we think that the information is reliable. It's our responsibility to make sure that we have evaluated the trustworthiness of any information that we pass along to our clients.

One check I use is whether it passes the straight-face test. Does it sound right? Is this the only source with this point of view, or is it corroborated by other sources? Can I find similar information in print sources? Is the writing clear, or riddled with spelling or grammar mistakes? Does it rely for effect on inflammatory language or impassioned arguments, or does it sound even-handed? And be aware of the JDLR (Just Doesn't Look Right) factor; if something looks off, it's probably not a reliable site.

Look to see if the Web site identifies who is behind the site. Is the "Consumers for Better Home Protection" that's advocating aluminum siding a real consumer organization, or is the site actually maintained by an aluminum siding trade association? If you question the legitimacy of an organization, call them and ask to speak with some members. Ask them who funds their organization.

I also look at the Web site's top level domain. That's the last part of a URL before any slashes or other punctuation, and is usually .com, .gov, .edu, .net, or a two-letter code indicating the country that hosts the site. If it's a government site, I assume that the information is relatively unbiased, except for whatever political bent you care to assign to government information sources. If it's an educational organization, I investigate further. If it's maintained by a university library, it's probably pretty reliable. If it's a student's Web page, all bets are off. If it's a .com site, particularly if I don't recognize the entity behind it, I'll look for an "about us" page or for additional information on the company or individual in question.

Be careful of "spoof" sites. Someone intent on defrauding or misleading investors can set up a page that looks similar to a trusted Web news source such as CNN or Bloomberg and that appears to feature late-breaking news about a company. The giveaway is that the URL will *not* be www.cnn.com or www.bloomberg.com but instead something like 123.33.123/CNN/index.html or www.BL00MBERG.com (replacing the letter O with the number 0). Another way a site can be spoofed is by using a URL that visitors might assume points to one organization but instead is owned by an opponent. See, for example, www.GATT.org, which many people would assume is a site maintained by the World Trade Organization that has to do with the General Agreement on Tariffs and Trade. Instead, it's owned by a group that opposes the WTO and GATT. Compare www.gatt.org and www.wto.org to see how similar they are in layout. When in doubt, look up the ownership of the domain through a WHOIS service search such as www.allwhois.com.

Look at how frequently the site has been updated, and don't rely on the notice at the bottom of the page that says "This site was updated on ...". Less-than-scrupulous Web site designers can embed a program that automatically generates today's date in that notation, suggesting that the site is updated much more frequently than it really is. Instead, look at the information itself. How current is it? Do they list "upcoming" events that have come and gone months before? Is the latest press release dated this month or a year ago?

You might also compare the current version of the site to prior versions. Alexa Internet maintains a selective archive, called The Wayback Machine (web.archive.org), of what many Web sites looked like on specific dates going back to 1996. It's not comprehensive to begin with, and Web sites can request that their entries be removed from the archive, but it does offer a way to see if a site has been around for more than six months. Type the Web site's URL in The Wayback Machine's search box and see what that site looked like two or three years ago, or if it was even in existence.

A fun example of a Web site that appears to be authoritative, but isn't, is the Dihydrogen Monoxide Research Division at www.dhmo.org. This site informs readers that "you should be concerned about DHMO! Although the U.S. Government and the Centers for Disease Control (CDC) do not classify Dihydrogen Monoxide as a toxic or carcinogenic substance (as it does with better known chemicals such as hydrochloric acid and saccharine), DHMO is a constituent of many known toxic substances, diseases and disease-causing agents, environmental hazards and can even be lethal to humans in quantities as small as a thimbleful." Sounds awful, doesn't it? Despite the page's numerous supporting documents and links to legitimate environmental groups, it's a farce. If, like me, you didn't know this before, dihydrogen monoxide is another term for water.

Searching Efficiently

Using the Web for research can result in information that will amaze your client; it can also be an enormous waste of your time. As you think through your research strategy (see Chapters 26 and 27 for tips), keep in mind that the true cost of research includes both your out-of-pocket expenses and your time. If you can find the material on a professional online service for $10 and in a quarter of the time that it would take you to find and download it from the Web, you offer your clients more for their money by using the value-added research services.

Keep your research goals in mind as you search the Web. It's easy to get distracted by sites that are only tangentially related to your topic. Set a limit for how much time you will spend on Web research. When you reach the end of the allotted time, stop and evaluate what you have and what more you're likely to find if you continue. The 80:20 rule applies to the Web just as it does to any other research; you'll find 80 percent of the useful information during the first 20 percent (or so) of your time, and you can easily take four times as long to find the remaining 20 percent. Given the breadth and variety of the information available on the Web, it's usually not cost-effective to attempt to find that last 20 percent. Your client's budget will guide you, of course. If the client is only willing to pay for two hours of research and $100 in online costs, your time, and the number and variety of sources you can consult, are limited. As I mentioned at the beginning of this chapter, in some situations you and your client might be better served by using the professional online services. Although you incur charges when you use these services, you can often find the information you need much more quickly, thus providing more complete information at a lower total cost to your client.

To help stay on track, keep a list of the Web sites you've looked at. (I just copy each URL from the browser location bar as I go to a site, and paste it in a word-processing document. I keep the list sorted alphabetically with Word's Sort command, so I can easily tell if I've been to the same place twice.) You may want to include the list of the sites in the material you deliver to your client; it's not only a valuable research resource, it's also a great marketing tool. It demonstrates that finding information on the Web is not as simple as plugging a couple of words into a search engine or pressing the secret "Find It" key that some people assume all info pros have on their keyboards.

Top Tips for Internet Research

- Use "type of document" searches to narrow your search: include the word listen to identify audio files, forecast to find industry projections, search to identify databases.
- Always use several search engines when conducting a comprehensive search. There is surprisingly little overlap among search engine coverage.
- Get to know the power search features of the search engines you use frequently. Know how to use field searches, truncation, phrase searching, and so on.
- Remember that much of the most valuable information on the Web is not included in search engines. Tap into your invisible Web resources as well.
- Watch for mentions of new resources, white papers, and other hard-to-find material in the articles and discussion groups you read.
- Carefully evaluate the authenticity and reliability of Web sites before passing information along to your clients.
- Searching the Web can be a time sink. Set a limit on the time you will spend researching on the Web and re-evaluate when you hit the limit.

Chapter 29

Professional Online Services

Long before the Web, other vast electronic warehouses of valuable information were available to anyone with a subscription and the patience to learn the arcane command language involved. I remember taking a class in online research when I was working on my Masters in Library Science back in 1980. We learned how to log on to Dialog (see later in this section for a description of each of the major online services); once we'd signed on, the system responded simply: ?. Not very user-friendly, I'd say. And it got worse; a search request would look something like this: *s raychem/ti and (fib??optic? or fib??()optic? ?)*

A lot has changed since those heady days when we librarians-in-training were delighted with the novelty of electronic access to material that previously could only be found in printed indexes. Some things haven't changed, though. The value-added online services still charge for access, and they still require somewhat arcane search syntax, at least compared to the simplicity of a Web search engine. They also still offer an array of information you can't find anywhere else—not on the Web and often not even in printed sources.

This chapter isn't a substitute for the training offered by the professional online services themselves and for the real-world experience of using them on a regular basis. In fact, I wrote an entire book about the various online search services (now out of print and out of date, alas), and even then I felt that I could have said a lot more about each vendor. Use this chapter as a tool to help determine which online services you should focus on. Then expect to spend at least six months learning how to make the best use of them and honing your search skills. Plan to spend several hundred dollars a month in the process of becoming proficient; this is probably not an expense you can bill back to clients, at least not in its entirety.

"This Costs How Much?!?"

Let's talk about the cost first, because that's what first-time users of any professional online service notice right away. Obviously, the price of online searches will vary, depending on the source you're using and whether you are downloading a single article or 50 market research reports. To give you a rough idea of the charges you'll incur, expect to pay $10 or $20 for a few articles on a topic, $150 or $200 for a company profile, and $15 or $20 per page for market research or investment analysts' reports.

Each vendor has its own set of pricing plans, some of them more attractive than others to the independent info pro. In general, we info pros look for subscriptions that don't impose a monthly minimum fee but charge us only for actual use. Most online services offer so-called transaction pricing, based on some combination of the amount of time you're online, the number of records you view on the screen or download, the number of searches you run, and the complexity of those searches. Needless to say, most independent info pros gravitate to the plans that are the most straightforward and predictable. Factiva.com, for example, does not charge for the time you spend online or the number of searches you run; you pay $2.95 for each article you download, period. You can't get much simpler than that.

Cheaper by the Dozen?

When I signed up with a local health club, I was given two options—I could pay $10 for each visit, or I could pay $75 a month for unlimited use. I knew I'd be going at least two or three times a week (or at least that was my intention), so I figured that I'd be better off with the flat monthly fee. However, the economics of saving money by buying unlimited access to a service don't apply to online services, at least for the average independent info pro. As I mentioned earlier, most of the professional online services offer some form of transaction-based pricing—at full retail price, of course—as well as a discounted rate if you commit to spending a certain amount every month. Most of these flat fee arrangements allow you to download as much as you want, with the proviso that if your usage winds up being much higher than expected, the fee will be adjusted up. It sounds tempting; you can do $2,000 worth of searches, bill your clients full price, and only pay your flat $1,000 for the month. That's a cool $1,000 profit, isn't it? Well, it is for *that* month, but what about the months when you can only bill out $500 to your clients and you're still stuck with that $1,000 invoice? Ouch!

On the other hand, some gated Web sites charge relatively modest fixed fees for a year's unlimited access. Hoovers.com, the business information site, offers members of the Association of Independent Information Professionals (www.aiip.org) full access to its value-added material for less than $200 a year. STAT-USA.gov, a database of international market research produced by the U.S. Department of Commerce, costs $175 a year for unlimited use.

My general rule is that anything that requires a minimum payment of $100 or more a month is a gamble, at least until I have used the online service for a year on a transaction-priced basis and the records show that I will consistently incur at least that much billable usage every month. Otherwise, I opt for the undiscounted rate on a pay-as-you-go contract. Sure, I miss out on the windfall those months when I use the service more than usual, but I also avoid having to pay a high fixed cost that I can't bill out during months when my workload is lower.

That said, sometimes a flat-fee contract makes sense. Alex Kramer, owner of Kramer Research, was offered unlimited access to one of the major online services for $400 a month. She took that offer in a heartbeat, knowing that (1) her usage was at least half that amount already, (2) she could promote her online research business more aggressively to build up usage, and (3) the monthly fee was low enough for her to absorb as overhead during those months when she didn't do many online searches. Alex has been in business for more than 10 years and can anticipate her usage and her cash flow needs pretty well, so this was a smart decision. If you're just starting out, though, I would caution you against signing a flat fee contract until you have a better handle on your average usage. A new independent info pro simply doesn't need another fixed expense that must be paid every month.

The Big Three (Plus a Few)

There are three major online services in the U.S. market—Dialog, Factiva.com, and LexisNexis. All three are available throughout most of the world, either directly or through third-party marketers, and additional professional online services exist that are particularly competitive in other regions. This section will give you a brief introduction to the big three, along with some of the other major players in the value-added online arena. Members of the Association of Independent Information

Professionals (www.aiip.org) are eligible for discounts and the waiving of monthly fees or minimums on many of these online services.

Dialog

www.dialogweb.com

Description: Dialog has rightly been called the supermarket of online services; the breadth, depth, and scope of its databases are arguably the best in the business, particularly for independent info pros. In one online service, you have access to the full text of articles from a wide range of sources, including newspapers, business, and marketing literature, as well as patent and trademark data; industry and company directories from around the world; chemical structure databases; summaries of articles from obscure medical, science, and technology publications; even a database of tables and charts extracted from articles. Just about the only type of information Dialog lacks is legal material such as case law and statutes.

Pricing: Dialog offers two transaction pricing options, one based on how long you spend connected to the system plus per-record charges for every item you display, download, or print; the other based on the amount of system resources required to process each command you enter, plus per-record charges. Both plans also involve a $168/year Dialog Services fee and a $14/hour telecommunications fee; the annual fee is waived for AIIP members.

Ease of use: Dialog offers you a choice of three user interfaces—Classic Dialog, accessed via the telnet protocol; DialogClassic Web, the same minimalist look and feel as Classic Dialog but accessed via the Web; and DialogWeb, the most user-friendly of the three. Although DialogWeb is the easiest to navigate, all three versions require a familiarity with the Dialog search syntax, which hasn't changed in 25 years and is more arcane than most. You have an astounding array of power search tools and information sources at your disposal, but this is a system that cannot be mastered quickly. DialogWeb has a Guided Search option with forms that help you select files and build a simple search without having to use the Dialog search syntax—but you lose access to much of the system's functionality. You can download an extensive user manual, *Successful Searching on Dialog*, at support.dialog.com/searchaids/success.

Factiva.com

global.factiva.com

Description: Factiva is a joint venture of Reuters and Dow Jones, two high-powered business information providers. As you would expect from its parentage,

Factiva.com is strongest in business-related information sources. It offers an impressive array of publications, and it's particularly strong in non-U.S. sources. Factiva also offers what it calls Intelligent Indexing across all its content. That means that, regardless of the origin of the information, you can look for articles on a specific topic or about a particular company, using standardized terms. Factiva is weak in coverage beyond the business press and consumer news sources; you won't find specialized directories, medical news, or intellectual property resources here.

Pricing: Factiva has by far the simplest transaction-based pricing plan. You pay $69 a year for the "password fee" (waived for AIIP members) and $2.95 for each article you download. Some financial and market analysis reports are more expensive, but all carry a set price and there are no additional fees associated with your search.

Ease of use: This is a relatively easy-to-use online service. It doesn't have some of the specialized search tools that are available on Dialog (see the discussion later on Power Tools), but the search syntax is fairly intuitive. The fact that you incur no charges for searching means that you have more freedom to noodle around, try different search strategies, and fine-tune your search until you're happy with the results, all free of charge.

LexisNexis

www.lexisnexis.com

Description: Along with Dialog, LexisNexis is one of the oldest of the professional online services. It began as a resource for lawyers, offering the full text of court decisions, and branched out to include the full text of laws and regulations, public records, and related material. What began as Lexis eventually came to include Nexis—an extensive collection of full-text and abstracted articles from a wide range of sources. Because its original user base consisted of people who weren't trained info pros, its search syntax and tools are more intuitive than those of some other online systems. You can subscribe to Lexis.com, Nexis.com, or both.

Pricing: Of the big three, LexisNexis has the murkiest transaction pricing plans. You can choose among several options, including a per-search charge or a connect-time charge, plus output costs. It's difficult to ascertain the cost of a search ahead of time, as detailed pricing is not readily available.

Ease of use: LexisNexis manages to combine power search features with a reasonably intuitive interface. Info pros who aren't familiar with the service can use the Quick Search option, and more experienced info pros can tap into the more advanced alternatives. The fill-in-the-forms interface helps you build searches in areas you're not familiar with.

The Best of the Rest

DataStar (www.datastarweb.com) is owned by the Dialog Corporation, which also markets the Dialog service. DataStar's strengths are in its coverage of European sources—published articles, company directories, and financial information. Its Web interface is simple to use, and an advanced user option is also available. Costs include a $340 per year DataStar Services Fee plus a minimum usage fee—which is, in effect, a nonrefundable deposit account—of $560/year (both fees are waived for AIIP members). Search charges are based on how long you are connected to each database, plus a fee for each item you display, download, or print.

"Visitor" Access

You'll probably do most of your online research on the one or two systems you know well and subscribe to. But sometimes you need access to an online service you don't normally search but that offers a resource or search feature you require. That's when you might consider using the credit card option, or what I call visitor access to the vendor. All three of the major online services offer some kind of visitor access; LexisNexis, in addition to a pay-per-article option, lets you buy unlimited access to selected collections of sources for a day or a week. That's got to be the best option of any of the visitor access packages, particularly if you think you'll need to run a number of searches in a particular file.

Visitor access is most appropriate for projects in which you have a limited need for the online service in question. Visitor access isn't appropriate if your search is complex or you need to access many different sources because it's probably a system on which you're not an expert searcher. In such cases, subcontract that portion of the research to another independent info pro who is an experienced user of the service. Keep in mind, too, that some visitor access packages include just a limited range of databases and search options, as well as a higher per-item cost when compared to regular subscription access.

Questel*Orbit (www.questel.orbit.com) focuses on intellectual property (patents and trademarks) and sci-tech information, particularly European in origin. It is not a simple system to learn and, given that much of its content is in complex, highly structured databases, not for the faint of heart. If you intend to specialize in intellectual property research, this is a must-have online service; otherwise, you can access most of the databases you'll need through other, simpler online systems. Prices include an annual service fee of $125 and transaction charges based on connect time plus output fees. In addition, subscribers are subject to a 6-month minimum billing of $270 (waived for AIIP members).

Westlaw (www.westlaw.com) is LexisNexis' main competitor in the legal research arena. In addition to offering the full text of case law and legislative and administrative material, Westlaw provides business information directly from Factiva.com and through a link to Dialog. Its user interface is reasonably easy to use, and most of its power search tools are accessible with pull-down menus. Pricing is negotiated separately for each subscriber, with flat-fee subscriptions the norm.

Power Tools

Not only do the value-added online services provide access to material that you can't find elsewhere, they also offer tools for fine-tuning your search and analyzing your search results. Each professional online service has a different suite of power tools; the following is a list of what to look for when you're evaluating which services to subscribe to.

- Truncation: Search for all words that begin with a specified word stem. You should be able to indicate single character truncation (calendar*), multiple character truncation (humid***), unlimited truncation (librar+) and internal truncation (wom#n)

- Nested logic: Construct a complex search with a combination of Boolean ANDs and ORs ([alumina or [aluminium or aluminum] adj oxide] and tape).

- AtleastX: Require that a search term appear at least X times within the document (atleast5 nicotine).

- Field searches: Limit the search to specific portions of the document, such as title, author, lead paragraph, or source (headline[color or colour]).

- Boolean and natural language searches: Select either Boolean logic (AND, OR, NOT) or a "fuzzy" search algorithm that looks for close as well as exact matches (global warming polar Europe would retrieve articles that contain most or all of these words).

- Date and relevance ranking: Sort the results of a search either by date with the most current items first, or by relevance with the items calculated to be the best matches first.

Dialog also has a number of unique specialized tools, including RANK (which analyzes the number of times an author's name, patent assignee, journal title, or subject term appears in the search results) and MAP (which takes the results of one search, extracts key terms, and then runs a new search using those extracted key terms).

Make a habit of reading the help files and advanced search screen tips when you search a professional online service. Remember, you're paying good money to use this system, and you might as well get maximum search power out of it.

Controlling Searches with Controlled Vocabulary

Many database records in the professional online services consist of more than the summary or full text of articles; they also include subject words and other indexing terms that have been added to improve the relevance and completeness of search results. For example, an article on the health benefits of walking as a form of exercise may have appended the indexing phrase "walking—health aspects." Other articles on this same topic will also be indexed "walking—health aspects." Database producers, and in some cases the online services themselves, have built detailed controlled vocabularies—that is, indexes of words and phrases used consistently to describe particular topics and concepts. These indexing terms can make your search much more focused and efficient. They allow you to fine-tune what might otherwise be an overly broad query, by searching for the controlled vocabulary terms in addition to whatever other words you think might appear in the article itself. So, for example, a search using the subject phrase "walking—health aspects" may give you more focused results than a search for the words "walking" and "health" anywhere in the text of articles. Many specialized nonbibliographic databases also use controlled vocabularies; patent databases index each patent record by a complex classification scheme, company financial records are indexed by industry code, and so on. Each database or database family, and each online service that uses one, has its own controlled vocabulary. Check the database and system documentation for controlled vocabulary or thesaurus terms that may help you improve your search results. See support.dialog.com/searchaids/dialog/f009_industry_terms.shtml and www.delphion.com/derwent/docs/cpi_manual_codes.pdf for examples of database thesauri.

Depending on the type of material it contains, a database may offer several types of indexing. Many assign subject words that describe the focus of the article (Agricultural Machinery or Intranet Portals). Some include additional subject terms that describe the type or format of the article or the way the subject is treated (Interview or Industry Survey). Some use codes to identify companies discussed in the article; these are particularly useful for company names that are frequently misspelled (Siemens), that involve odd punctuation (E*Trade), or that are inconsistently identified (W.R. Grace / WR Grace / Grace).

There are also hierarchical classification systems that, while somewhat complex, can be tremendous tools for expanding or refining a search. Examples of hierarchical systems include:

- NAICS and SIC codes, used to describe types of businesses

  62: Health Care & Social Assistance

  621: Ambulatory Health Care

  6214: Outpatient Care Centers

- MeSH medical subject headings

  A07: Cardiovascular System

  A07.231: Blood Vessels

  A07.231.611: Retinal Vessels

These are often called "cascading" codes; you can select articles that have a very narrow focus (MeSH code A07.231.611.647 for Retinal Arteries) or you can select all articles that discuss the cardiovascular system (MeSH code A07), which will include all articles indexed with any MeSH code that starts with A07. If you frequently use a database that includes complex codes, buy the print thesaurus or set a bookmark on your browser to the online version.

Experienced searchers often use a search technique called pearl culturing to identify useful subject indexing terms (see Chapter 27 for more about pearl culturing). For example, I was looking for articles in a psychology database on the topic of road rage. A search for that exact phrase turned up 16 articles—not very many for such a popular topic, but I wasn't too surprised; "road rage" is a popular term, not a scientific one, and I assumed that the psych literature would use different terminology. So, instead of despairing when I retrieved so few references, I looked at the subject terms assigned to those 16 articles and found that most of them were indexed as Driving Behavior and either Aggressive Behavior or Anger. So I expanded my search to *road rage or (driving behavior and (aggressive behavior or anger))* and retrieved 76 articles, most of which appeared to be right on target.

Pearl culturing works best when you run a quick search that isn't comprehensive but that is likely to retrieve a high proportion of relevant records. (Sometimes I limit the search to the title, assuming that, even though I won't find many items, the ones I do find will be highly relevant.) Then, you review the subject terms or codes used in those records and expand your search using the appropriate indexing terms.

Personalizing Your Online Experience

Most of the professional online services let you set a number of the system defaults; one of the first things I do when I subscribe to a new service is figure out how much I can customize. I usually look for options such as:

- Simple or expert search
- Date range to be searched (usually limited to current and prior year)
- Sort results by relevance or date
- Databases or publication groups to search
- Whether and how the search terms are highlighted in the results
- How many records to display initially on the search results screen

On Dialog, the simplest way to change your defaults is to log onto DialogWeb, switch to Guided Search (assuming you don't wind up there by default) and click [Settings]. This is a simple, Web-based guide to most of the system's personalization features, including Command Search versus Guided Search, pricing method, the number and format of records displayed on the search results screen, whether you want your search results limited to English-language documents, and so on. There are more sophisticated options that you can only set by using Command mode searching and editing your Profile. For all the technical details, see *Successful Searching on Dialog*, the user manual I mentioned earlier, and skip to the section on the SET commands.

On Factiva.com, click [Preferences] to set a wide range of options, including default sources and date ranges to search, how you want search results displayed, whether you want to see the lead sentence and indexing terms for each article in your results list, and so on.

On LexisNexis, click [Customize] to change your default search screen (Quick Search or Power Search), the number and format of records to be displayed on the search results screen, and which Search Forms you'd like displayed along the margin of your search screen.

Tracking Your Costs

All three of the major online services let you assign a client name or number to each search session; this information will appear in the invoice, so you can track expenses for the online research component of any given project. Usually, this feature is called the "Subaccount" or "Client Billing" code. This is a useful tool because independent info pros generally bill out all of their research-related expenses.

Although you can wait to bill your clients until you receive your invoice and see how much you've spent online for each project, this often isn't the most attractive option. Many clients want to be billed as soon as the project is completed, and you probably prefer to bill them sooner rather than later, too. Dialog displays the total cost of a search when you log off, and both Factiva.com and LexisNexis let you check your invoice online, with a two- or three-day delay between when you run the search and when the cost appears online. I usually check the online invoice before I bill a client, to make sure that my estimate of the online costs correlates with what shows up on the vendor's side.

When in Doubt, Subcontract Out

As I noted at the beginning of this chapter, the professional online services are expensive and more complex than, say, a Web search engine. On the other hand, they offer powerful search features and deep resources of information not available on the Web. If you are already a skilled searcher on one or more of these online services, these tremendously powerful tools will greatly expand the scope of your research offerings. If, on the other hand, you aren't an experienced searcher, or you get a project that requires the use of a professional online service on which you aren't proficient, consider subcontracting that aspect of the research to a fellow independent info pro who *is* an expert. See Chapter 14, Subcontracting, or I'll Scratch Your Back if You Scratch Mine, for all you need to know about farming out research to a colleague. Given the high cost of a poorly done online search—in terms of both direct costs and information not found—subcontracting is often the best option for both you and your client.

Tips for Using the Professional Online Services

- Learn the power search tools of the online services and use the
- Advanced or Command Search option.
- Avoid flat-fee contracts; transaction-based contracts help control cash flow.
- Stay up-to-date on pricing plans and changes in vendor rates.
- Consider "visitor" access for infrequently used online services.
- Use controlled vocabulary searches when appropriate.
- Take advantage of system customization options.
- Subcontract online research if you aren't an expert.

Chapter 30

Specialized Online Services

So far in this section, we've looked at finding information on the Web and on the value-added professional online services. This chapter reviews some of the more specialized fee-based online services. It is by no means exhaustive; thousands of databases focus on narrow market niches, from an online directory of American hospitals (www.ahd.com) to everything you'd want to know about textile machinery (www.davisongoldbook.com).

Keep in mind that the professional online services also provide access to many highly specialized databases. Of the big three, Dialog is particularly strong in this area, offering files such as Ceramics Abstracts, Meteorological and Geoastrophysical Abstracts, and Oceanic Abstracts. As the word "abstracts" suggests, many of these niche databases are not full text; they consist of a bibliographic citation, or a citation and summary of the article, plus indexing, but they're still a great way to find references to obscure and very specialized publications.

Broad but Low-Powered Services

Several online services that I'll discuss here provide access to a wide range of published articles for a modest fee. They often cover the same sources you'll find in the professional online services. So why use the higher-priced services? For starters, your search options are usually quite limited in these alternative online services; they're typically designed for the Web surfer who's willing to pay a few dollars for a quick search to turn up an article or two, rather than for the professional online researcher who needs to do an exhaustive search on a subject. Your output options are generally more restricted on these low-cost services, too. And the charge will go on your credit card right away, as opposed to a monthly invoice, which means that you'll almost certainly pay the bill for the search long before your client pays you.

Since most of these low-end services don't charge for searching—you incur a fee only when you request the full text of an article—they are often useful for scoping out the range of a topic. I'll sometimes type in a few key terms and see how much material I retrieve. I'll scan the article titles and summaries if available, to get a sense of how I might need to broaden or narrow my search. Then I'll run the search on one of the professional online services, where I can take advantage of its power search tools to focus on the most relevant material.

I also use the low-end services when I just need a single article and know exactly what I want. This kind of simple document delivery search doesn't require any finesse; all I want is the full text, and any online service that includes that publication will do.

eLibrary

eLibrary (www.elibrary.com) was first built as a tool to help students with homework. It provides access to magazine and newspaper articles, reference sources such as encyclopedias and almanacs, broadcast transcripts, and images. It still retains some of the feel of a student-oriented resource; it rates the "reading level" of all its articles, for example. However, eLibrary is a useful tool for the rest of us as well, at least for simple searches and article look-ups. Searches are free; unlimited access to full-text content is $14.95 a month or $79.95 a year. It supports both Boolean and "natural language" searches (a looser search that looks for good but not necessarily exact matches), lets you limit your search by date range or publication, and allows you to search for a specific author. You can sort your results by relevance, date, publication, or—yes—reading level.

FindArticles.com

This site isn't just inexpensive—it's free (www.findarticles.com). It includes articles from Gale Group, one of the major online database producers, dating back to the mid-1990s. Because the content is provided by a single aggregator, you won't find quite the range of sources you see on other online services, but articles from the 300 publications it does cover are available at no charge. The search function is pretty rudimentary; you can search within a single title or a group of publications, and you can search for a word or phrase within the article. Unfortunately, you can't limit the search by date, which makes it difficult to find current material.

FT.com

The *Financial Times* of London provides the full text of its paper at www.ft.com. What's unusual, though, is that it also sells access to a broad collection of articles from other publications. All this was free of charge when it was first rolled out but, beginning in 2002, FT started charging a fee for access to its power search tools and for the full text of non-FT publications. The free search interface at search.ft.com is pretty limited; you can search for words or phrases in the full text or the headline, and limit the search by broad date ranges (today, last 7 days, last 28 days, 3 months, etc.). And the only articles you can view for free are recent articles from the *Financial Times*. For $225 a year, you have access to a number of more sophisticated search features, including the ability to select the publications to search, to search using indexed subject terms and company names, and to limit by geographic region. You also get unlimited access to full text or abstracted articles from 500 global news sources going back five years.

Low-Fee Specialized Services

There's more to online information than full-text articles; a number of specialized services provide access to other forms of value-added content. Most of these services offer flat-fee pricing; an annual subscription gets you unlimited access. As I discussed in Chapter 29, independent info pros are generally better off avoiding online services that charge a fixed fee. However, the following services are fairly modestly priced, and probably worth it if you expect to use them at least once a month.

EDGAR Filings

Edgar? Who's Edgar? The U.S. Securities & Exchange Commission requires that all publicly traded companies file their financial and stock-related reports electronically through EDGAR, the Electronic Data Gathering, Analysis, and Retrieval system. You can search and retrieve EDGAR files at no charge through the SEC's Web site (edgar.sec.gov). Although the SEC's search interface gets better all the time, in some instances you'll want more powerful search tools than are available at that site. Several commercial sites sell access to the same EDGAR files, but with sophisticated search, monitoring, and display options, including downloads in spreadsheet format and the ability to search by executives' names. Two major players in providing value-added EDGAR filings are EDGAR Online and 10kWizard. EDGAR Online (www.edgar-online.com) charges $14.95 a month, plus a per-document fee if you download more than a certain number of records a month. 10kWizard (www.10kwizard.com) charges $25 a month or $150 a year for similar services.

Hoover's Online

Hoover's (www.hoovers.com) offers company profiles for major public and private companies in the U.S. and selected European countries. Basic company information, including a description of the firm's lines of business, financial information, and major competitors, is available at no charge. More in-depth information, including a company history, extensive list of executives, comparisons to industry averages, and so on, is available to subscribers. It's a nice resource if you do any kind of business-related research; if nothing else, it's a great place to start your research. Business subscriptions range in price from $399 to $4,995 a year, depending on whether you just want access to Hoover's value-added information on large companies or whether you also want to be able to download sales contact lists from 175,000 companies and search a database of all U.S. companies with five or more employees. Members of the Association of Independent Information Professionals (www.aiip.org) are eligible for a significant discount.

Stat-USA

The U.S. Department of Commerce is charged with encouraging trade, both within the U.S. and internationally. To that end, it has created a rich collection of international trade information, called Stat-USA (www.stat-usa.gov). Most of the research-related material is in Stat-USA's National Trade Data Bank, which includes Industry Sector Analysis Reports, Best Market Reports, and International Marketing Insight Reports. These reports can be 20 or 30 pages long and are written by trade experts within the country in question. The reports tend to be quite specific—the telecommunications industry in Chile, the civil aviation industry in Austria, or the best markets for pollution control equipment worldwide. Unlike most government information sources, the National Trade Data Bank is not free; there is a fee to download reports, but it's a relatively modest $175 a year. You can also purchase individual reports for $25 each.

Market Research Services

Some market research and consulting firms sell a selection of their reports through the professional online services. Other online services specialize in providing access to market research. What complicates matters for researchers is that each of these services offers a slightly different collection of reports, search tools, and pricing policies. Some let you purchase selected pages from a particular report—usually $10 to $30 a page—while others require you to buy the entire, often several-thousand-dollar, report.

Profound

Profound, owned by the same company that owns Dialog and DataStar (two professional online services discussed in Chapter 29), offers a rich collection of market research reports from around the world (www.profound.com). You can search by market research firm, location, industry, company name, and free text. Most of the reports are available in both plain text and PDF format; virtually all can be purchased by the page, section, or chapter. One of the drawbacks of Profound is its pricing; most subscribers are required to pay a hefty deposit as well as per-document fees. AIIP members are exempt from the Premium subscription fee; they just pay the per-record charges—yet another reason to belong to AIIP.

Market Research Aggregators

Several Web-based services pull together reports from a number of market research firms. As much as they would like to differentiate themselves from each other, not much difference really exists. All offer fairly simple search options, all let you browse by industry or broad category, and none charge for searching, only for the reports or pages you display or download. Note that publishers occasionally put restrictions on how their reports can be sold, so some reports can only be purchased in full. Three of the main players in this arena are:

- ECNext (www.ecnext.com/commercial)
- MarketResearch.com (www.marketresearch.com)
- MindBranch (www.mindbranch.com)

Public Records Databases

Several specialized databases provide public records data—that is, information about individuals that comes from government sources. These services include ChoicePoint Online (www.choicepointonline.com/cdb), AutotrackXP (www.autotrackxp.com), and KnowX (www.knowx.com). They offer access to legally available personal information such as current and prior addresses, assets, real estate transactions, judgments or liens against the person, professional certification, driver's licenses, and so on. PACER (pacer.psc.uscourts.gov) provides access to information on all cases in U.S. federal district, circuit, and bankruptcy courts. It's not a single aggregated index but rather a collection of databases maintained by the individual court systems.

The challenge in using any of these public records systems is that none is complete and exhaustive. An inexperienced researcher may check for lawsuits against an individual, turn up no records, and incorrectly report to the client that the individual is clear—having missed a suit filed in one of the states not covered by a particular online system. See Chapter 32, Public Records Research, for more discussion about what's involved in finding information through public records.

It's not just court records or information on individuals that's tricky to research. Take the Agencywide Documents Access and Management System (ADAMS), an online service providing access to public documents at the U.S. Nuclear Regulatory Commission (www.nrc.gov). Not only do you have to download proprietary software in order to search ADAMS, but even its own documentation admits that finding records is difficult:

> Folders shown in ADAMS contain pointers to **some** of the documents and other objects that are stored and managed in the libraries. A single document may be found in more than one folder because of its subject matter (just as a copy of a paper document can be filed in more than one file folder). In the case of an electronic ADAMS document, each folder merely has an electronic link or pointer to the same document. A title viewed, printed, or copied from one file will be the same as if viewed, printed, etc., from another folder. WARNING: ** NOT ALL DOCUMENTS IN ADAMS COLLECTIONS ARE IN FOLDERS. If, by browsing through the folders in the Document Manager, you do not find the document for which you are looking, you can search to find documents in the library.

Confused yet? There are 30 pages of instruction on how to search ADAMS, because each collection of documents must be searched in a different way. ADAMS is not for the faint of heart.

Checklist for Using Specialized Online Services

- Can I track down the article I need more cost-effectively using a low-end online service than using the Web or a professional online service?
- Is the information in this specialized online service also available in a specialized file on a professional online service? Which is more cost-effective to use?
- Is this a research project that I'd like to "test-drive," just to see what
- I find, on an online service that doesn't charge for searches?
- Will I be searching a specialized online service as well as the professional online services for this project? If so, how can I best break out my research to make the best use of both types of online resources?

Chapter 31

Telephone Research

Info pros tend to think of all the information resources available online—on the Web, in the professional online services, and in the specialized, niche databases—but we sometimes forget that the best information may not exist as recorded text at all. If you need information on what motivates people to purchase hole saws, or the best industries for a sheltered workshop to market to, or a list of the minority-owned businesses that bid on a specific project, you're not going to have much luck online. These were all real-life research projects, and the answers were all found by interviewing real, live experts.

Telephone research isn't for everyone. It takes persistence, creativity, patience, and great interviewing skills—a set of talents that many independent info pros don't possess. When I talk about phone research, I'm not thinking about simple market surveys in which the interviewer is given a list of phone numbers to call and a script of questions to ask. That type of research isn't value-added, and companies generally pay low wages to the people who conduct such interviews. Rather, telephone research as I discuss it in this chapter involves getting up to speed on an issue, identifying the key players, conducting in-depth interviews, analyzing the results, and writing up your results and conclusions.

If, after reading this chapter, you think that you'd like to specialize in telephone research or add it to the mix of services you offer, I recommend *Super Searchers Go to the Source*, by Risa Sacks (Information Today, Inc., 2002). This is a great collection of interviews with 12 experts in primary research, including a number of phone researchers, in which you can learn about the challenges and joys of this kind of information business. Even if you don't focus on telephone research exclusively, it's a useful skill to add to your information arsenal. Phone research can often help you provide a more complete information package, filling in the missing pieces you can't get online.

What's Involved in Phone Research?

The idea behind phone research is that you often have to figure out more than just the facts. After you're read the articles, reviewed the market research reports, and gone through the annual reports, you need to dig deeper and figure out causes, motivations, and underlying factors. Why is this industry in such turmoil? What is the executive of this company most likely to do in the face of this new situation? How did this company get where it is today; what was its strategy? In addition to digging up soft information like this, phone research is great for updating published statistics and covering just-breaking developments.

There are several types of telephone research. One project I was involved in had to do with how a typical toddler spends his day. How much time does he spend watching TV, eating, playing by himself, playing with others, napping, and so on? In addition to a good deal of online research, we had to identify parents who could describe how their toddlers spent their day. This kind of specific, anecdotal information-gathering lends itself well to telephone research. Another type of phone research involves digging up information so specialized that very little has been written about it—for example, the market opportunities for a specific type of carbide-tipped blade. And sometimes telephone interviews are used to follow up on a quote you've found in an article, to discover what else the quoted expert has to say on the topic.

Doing telephone research usually involves working as a subcontractor a fair amount of the time. A significant portion of your work may come from other independent info pros and from librarians, because not many people can do phone research well, and most are willing to subcontract to an expert. You'll need to cultivate clients who understand and value telephone researchers; these include market research companies, competitive intelligence departments within organizations, and public relations firms.

Characteristics of a Good Phone Researcher

Every independent info pro has a telephone, but not every info pro can be a successful telephone researcher. Here's a list of the characteristics shared by the best telephone researchers:

- Take a real interest in people. You have to be compulsive about asking "why" and you have to really want to learn the answer.

- Have the tenacity of a bulldog. It's often a challenge to get past gatekeepers and voice mail and actually talk to the person you're trying to reach. You have to persevere and think creatively about how to get through. That might mean calling early in the morning or during lunch time.

- Avoid getting discouraged. You have to be able to hear "no" and keep on going, always assuming that you'll eventually find someone who will tell you what you need to know. All telephone researchers have days when they just don't want to talk to anyone, or they feel they did a horrible job on their last interview. Some phone calls are hard to make, and some interviews go badly, for whatever reason. You just have to pick yourself up and move on.

- Keep your schedule flexible. You have to call people when it's convenient for them to talk. If your target is five time zones away, you may have to set your alarm for 5 a.m., or be willing to call at 10 p.m.

- Be insatiably curious. To do phone research well, you must be able to get completely immersed in an obscure topic. You have to enjoy the process itself, the thrill of the hunt, the search for the one person in the world, perhaps, who knows everything you need to learn about this topic.

- Be polite and courteous. You're asking a favor when you call to interview someone, and they don't have to talk to you. Treat everyone you speak to with respect, whether it's a CEO, the receptionist, or the temp who's taking calls while someone is out sick. Try to make a personal connection with everyone you talk to. The person who answers the phone can either hang up or put you in touch with the ideal contact; a lot depends on how you treat that person.

- Listen carefully. Part of successful telephone interviewing lies in the ability to wait for people to say something interesting or useful. If you're patient, you will often get referrals to other sources that are vital to your research but hard to find—obscure Web sites, discussion lists, books, reports, other people you should talk to, and so on.

- Develop your online research skills as well as expertise in phone research. Almost every phone project involves a good deal of preliminary research—identifying candidates to interview, getting up to speed on an unfamiliar industry or topic, drilling down through company Web sites to see who is responsible for the product you're interested in, and finding out what a prospective interviewee has written already. You'll either have to do this research yourself or subcontract it to an expert online searcher before you can begin the telephone phase of the project.

- Hone your writing ability. Not only must you be a good listener, you also have to write reasonably well. The report that you provide to your client will be more than just a transcript of your interviews; it should include a summary of what you learned, an analysis of the key points and issues revealed in the interviews, leads on other areas of research, and so on.

For more in-depth discussion of each of these characteristics—straight from some of the best telephone researchers in the industry—see *Super Searchers Go to the Source,* which I described earlier in this chapter.

The Challenges of Telephone Research

Assuming you have the personality and skill set, phone work is one of the easier segments of the independent info profession to break into. You don't need training and years of experience searching the professional online services. You don't need a private investigator's license or nearby access to a world-class library. And because it's a type of research that many people find difficult or less attractive because it's not online, you may find less competition than in some other areas. Of course, the usefulness of telephone research is less well recognized than that of online and Web research, so your marketing efforts may take longer to pay off. Clients often think about bringing in an expert online searcher, but few people realize how much information never gets published at all.

Telephone research poses some unique challenges. For starters, you only have one chance with any individual contact; if you fumble an interview, you can't go back and try it again later. That means that you need to be prepared and energized for every phone call. In addition, telephone research can only be conducted, as a rule, during the normal business hours of the person you're calling. As a result, you're limited in the amount of work you can take on at one time. Unlike online researchers, who can always squeeze in one more project over the weekend if need be, telephone researchers must work when their subjects work. And telephone work during holiday seasons and peak vacation periods, such as July and August for those of us in the northern hemisphere, is very difficult. Your contacts are less likely to be in the office and less likely to be focused on work. (On the other hand, you may be able to get past gatekeepers more easily during these times, because they go on vacation too.)

Telephone research is by its nature time-consuming. Even a couple of 10-minute interviews can easily take two or three hours, once you factor in time to prepare for the interviews, identify the people to interview, schedule the interviews, and write up your results. You have to reconcile yourself to losing some jobs when clients need phone work done, but have limited budgets and don't realize how much is involved in doing this kind of research.

Successful Telephone Interviews

Telephone research differs from other types of research in that so much depends on human interactions. If you're having a bad day, or you catch your interview subject on a bad day, that's it. Online services don't care one way or the other how you're feeling. The computer responds just the same whether you're polite or rude. Since phone research is such a high-touch business, your success depends on your skill in getting each interview right the first time. Here are some suggestions from expert telephone researchers, many of whom were interviewed in *Super Searchers Go to the Source*, on how to succeed in this line of work.

- Know how to estimate. Figure that the total project will take four to five times longer than you expect to spend on the actual interviews. So a one-hour interview could take five hours altogether, including the time to identify the right person to talk to, make several calls before you get that person on the phone, conduct the interview, and write up the results. Allow extra time for developing your discussion guide or list of questions, and for a summary and final analysis of the results. Often, the write-up and analysis will take up 50 percent of the total time in a project. And remember, when planning your work flow and negotiating a deadline with your client, this process will stretch out over several days. Even if you're only doing five interviews, it's very unlikely that you'll get all five people on the same day—and you may have to make easily 20 or 30 calls to identify the right five people.

- Do your homework. Before you make any calls, educate yourself about the subject matter. Learn the buzzwords and acronyms used by people in the industry. You don't want to spend someone's valuable time asking questions that you could easily find answers to yourself; you want to use the interview to gather information that can't be found elsewhere. If you're planning to call a published expert, learn beforehand what that person has said or written on the topic.

- Think sideways. Rather than focusing specifically on where to find the information, think about who could answer your question. Who cares about this topic and might be willing to talk to you? Good sources for experts, or referrals to experts, include trade or professional associations, government agencies, directories, industry publications, educational institutions, nonprofit organizations, and even the exhibit and speaker rosters for trade shows and conferences. And think about people you know in your nonwork life who might be helpful. I've called family members for projects, as well as people I've known for years through online discussion forums (but have never met face to face), and even someone with whom I'd trained for a marathon.

- Have something to trade. See what you can offer your interviewees in exchange for their thoughts and comments. Will your client allow you to send an "anonymized" version of the summary report to a cooperative contact? Can you offer a summary, over the phone, of what you've learned from other interviews?

- Start with your least important or low-stakes interviewee, and work your way up. If you're going to ask a dumb question or flail around, you want to do that during a less-crucial interview. For that matter, it's often helpful to identify someone with a general knowledge of the topic to talk to first. Try to save your most important interview for later in the process, when you're knowledgeable about the subject, you know what issues are particularly difficult or important, and you are comfortable in your approach.

- Always ask for referrals. An experienced telephone researcher once said "Never, ever leave somebody without asking for a referral. And when you call the next person, say that you were recommended by the previous person. People respond so well to recommended calls." Always ask "who else could help me with this? Whom would you suggest I talk with? Do you know anyone else who is an expert on this topic? Where else would you suggest I look?"

- Prompt for more. It's useful to ask at the end of the interview, "Is there anything important that I didn't ask?" or "Is there anything else that you'd like to tell me?"

- Try to verify independently whatever someone tells you. Watch for bias in your interviews, particularly if you hear something from one interviewee that contradicts what all your other interviewees have said. Unlike published information, which an editor ensures passes the straight-face test, what you get in a phone interview hasn't been vetted by a neutral party. If you hear something that just doesn't sound right, be sure to question it, or at least flag it in your report to the client.

- Ask one question at a time. Multiple or complex questions confuse and frustrate interviewees and make it harder to concentrate on the key information you're trying to find. Make sure that your questions aren't "leading," so that you don't bias the responses you get.

- Stay focused. Before you make any phone calls, write up a paragraph spelling out what you're looking for, and keep that in front of you during your interviews. On the other hand, be willing to go where the interview leads, within reason. Sometimes the best information is what you didn't think to ask, or expect to find. That's the serendipity of telephone research.

- Enlist the help of whoever answers the phone. Despite your best efforts to find an appropriate contact beforehand, sometimes you have to call an organization and blindly ask for suggestions on the person to talk to. Use questions like "who in your organization lives and breathes this topic?" Sometimes it helps to throw yourself at the mercy of the receptionist or secretary with a question like "I need your help; can you tell me who I can talk to about this?"

- Know when to stop. Telephone research often involves soft questions that don't have definite answers, so it's hard to know when to quit. When most of your questions have been answered, or you keep hearing the same information over again, that's an indication that you're ready to wrap it up. If you keep hitting dead ends, or people tell you over and over that no one knows the answer to your question, rethink your strategy. Be willing to try an entirely different approach, or to scale back your expectations of what you'll be able to find. Keep a careful eye on your time and budget throughout the project. You have to be skilled at estimating costs and keeping track of your time as you proceed. Be sure to communicate with your client on an ongoing basis if what you're finding takes you in new directions or if something comes up that affects the time frame or budget. In one project I worked on, for example, we discovered midway through that many of the experts were at an industry conference in Beijing for the next ten days.

Telephone Research Ethics

If you provide telephone research, you will eventually get a call from a potential client who, when told that the information he wants is most likely too confidential to be disclosed, will respond, "Well, just lie and tell them you're a student writing a paper." You'll have to figure out a tactful way to tell the prospect that you simply can't do that.

Both the Association of Independent Information Professionals (www.aiip.org) and the Society of Competitive Intelligence Professionals (www.scip.org) address this issue. AIIP's Code of Ethical Business Practice states that members "uphold the profession's reputation for honesty, competence, and confidentiality." SCIP's Code of Ethics requires that members "accurately disclose all relevant information, including one's identity and organization, prior to all interviews." Of course, this does not mean that you are required to disclose the identity of your client; in fact, clients often use independent info pros because we do provide anonymity. When you call a contact, you will generally introduce yourself and tell them the name of your company and that you are conducting research. If they ask for the name of your client, you can respond that your client hasn't authorized you to disclose that information. Surprisingly, many people are satisfied with this answer and, even though they don't know whom the information will go to, will agree to talk to you. Some clients, though, have no objection to your disclosing their names. Be sure to clarify the level of required confidentiality at the start of each project. If there's any doubt, err on the side of maintaining confidentiality.

The bottom line is to listen to your gut. Don't accept projects that you aren't comfortable with, or that you consider unethical. If you're not happy doing the work, you probably won't be able to provide professional-quality research, anyway. If necessary, see if you can negotiate with your client to refocus the project on information that is available through legitimate sources. As Andrew Pollard said in *Super Searchers Go to the Source*, "Most information that's of value can be gathered from ordinary open sources and by open means."

Checklist for Telephone Researchers

- Be prepared. Conduct background research so you know the basics about the topic before you call.
- Put yourself in the right frame of mind. If you're truly interested in everyone you interview, you'll be able to learn much more from them.
- Stay focused and determined. Just because the last person refused to talk to you doesn't mean that you're stuck. Pick up the phone and make the next call.
- Remain unfailingly polite. As a telephone researcher, you are relying on people's generosity; no one owes you an interview.
- Keep within the bounds of the law and your personal ethics. Don't accept a job that you don't feel comfortable doing.

Chapter 32

Public Records Research

Public records research is a specialized field best suited for independent info pros who are detail-oriented, who enjoy doing on-site research at courthouses and government agencies, and who have good people skills. Unlike online research, there's no massive aggregated collection of sources or databases you can consult; public records work involves going directly to where the records are kept and just digging around. Public records research is more art than science; you learn how to be a good searcher through experience. No one has written a definitive how-to manual on public records research because the techniques used for one source are entirely different from those used for another. One courthouse may have its own internally built database to index court cases; another may have a purely manual filing and indexing system. One government agency might feed all its records into a fee-based online service, and another might require that all requests go through a clerk.

Before I go into more detail about public records research, I'll note that I am not a lawyer and I cannot tell you about the regulations that apply to public records research in your state or country. As an example of why this matters, in some states you are not permitted to disclose information about criminal cases if the person was not eventually convicted. Be sure to talk with a lawyer who is familiar with public records work before you start.

If, after reading this chapter, you decide that you'd like to learn more about providing public records research, you can read more about it in *Naked in Cyberspace: How to Find Personal Information Online*, 2nd edition, by Carole Lane (Information Today, Inc., 2002) and *The Sourcebook to Public Record Information*, 3rd edition (BRB Publications, 2001). You can also read interviews with several leading public records researchers in *Super Searchers Go to the Source: The Interviewing and*

Hands-On Information Strategies of Top Primary Researchers—Online, on the Phone, and in Person, by Risa Sacks (Information Today, Inc., 2001).

What Does a Public Records Researcher Do?

Public records research involves getting documents from official sources. Those sources include:

- Courts—for information on court cases, tax liens, divorce filings, and other legal matters
- Government agencies—for documents that companies must file with regulatory agencies, reports and studies prepared by agencies, and documents generated by the agency that are available through the Freedom of Information Act or similar public-access requests
- Government records—for real estate deeds and property assessments; aircraft, car, and boat registrations; birth and death records; marriage licenses; and driver's license and occupational license information
- Government archives—for both published and unpublished material from government agencies

Some of this information is available online, through government Web sites or specialized online vendors. But much of it exists only in printed form, and/or must be searched on-site at the courthouse or government agency office. Public records research is definitely hands-on research.

You might be surprised by the questions that can be answered using public records. Some of the more common types of research projects include:

- Pre-employment screening—checking to see if a job applicant has a criminal record that she's not disclosing, whether any civil litigation or restraining orders have been filed against her, if she has made workers' compensation claims or filed for bankruptcy, whether she has the proper occupational licenses, and that she really did graduate from the institution she claims.

- Asset searching—finding out what a person owns—real estate and other major assets such as cars, boats, aircraft—as well as company ownership or significant stock holdings, so that a divorced spouse or the victor in a court case can collect money owed.

- Environmental research—tracking down which companies conducted operations at a particular site. When toxic waste sites must be cleaned up, there is a search for all the "potentially responsible parties" or PRPs. That means digging through archives and government records to discover all the companies that occupied the site—sometimes going back 100 years or more—in order to see which ones might be held responsible for the toxic waste.

- Executive due diligence—verifying whether an executive is who he claims to be. This involves discovering whether a potential director or executive has been involved in any litigation; whether he has a criminal record; whether he is living within his means; the value of any property he owns; and what he has said in interviews, articles, and even Internet chat rooms.

- Corporate due diligence—looking into a company that may be acquired or that a venture capitalist wants to fund, to determine the company's assets, whether it has been sued, if there are any outstanding tax liens against it, and whether it is in good standing with the state or regional agencies that regulate corporations and industries.

- Competitive intelligence—finding out about a corporate competitor. For example, to research how a particular manufacturing plant is configured, you might get an evacuation plan from the local fire department, or filings with the government agency that regulates environmental safety and health. This may also involve tracking down former employees—through searches of resumes, chat rooms, or online discussion forums—and interviewing them about their experience with the company.

- Labor union campaigns—discovering financial information about a company and its management in order to determine executive compensation plans, company profitability, political campaign donations the company has made, who is accountable for corporate decisions, and so on.

- Opposition research—investigating a political candidate, tracking down contributors to his campaign, learning his positions on issues over the years, confirming that the biographical information provided by the campaign is accurate, finding out his community activities, and so forth.

Is a Public Records Researcher a PI?

There are important distinctions between a public records researcher and a private investigator. Many public records researchers also have PI licenses, and some PIs also do public records research. To further complicate the matter, not all jurisdictions define a private investigator the same way. For example, Virginia considers public records research to be PI work; you can search public records databases, but you can't tell your client about the results of your research without a PI license. Before you set yourself up as a public records researcher, check with your state or local licensing board to find out what's permitted.

The process for getting a private investigator's license also varies from one jurisdiction to another. You may have to take a test or show that you have a certain number of years of experience working for a licensed PI, or that you have attended continuing education courses. In some areas, you have to be bonded. Unfortunately, reciprocity among jurisdictions is the exception rather than the rule, so you must check with every state or province in which you plan to conduct research to see what regulations apply.

Learning How to Research Public Records

As I mentioned earlier in this chapter, there aren't any comprehensive user manuals or step-by-step guides to conducting public records research. That's because every government agency and courthouse has its own system for organizing its records and making them available. Unlike online researching or telephone interview skills, what works in one region doesn't necessarily work in another. You can learn the general concepts involved in public records research, but after that it's a matter of discovering how each agency or court operates, how its information is organized, and how its online system, if any, works. Learning the craft of public records research also means knowing what the actual documents look like and contain. If you simply rely on online information sources, you only know about documents in the abstract. Digging around in the files themselves is the only way you'll learn what you can expect, what to look for, and where the pitfalls lie in public records research.

Curiously, even the vocabulary is different from one jurisdiction to another. In most courts, you consult with the clerk of the court. But in Pennsylvania, this position is called Prothonotary. If you're looking for information on real estate, you might have to ask the clerk for grantor/grantee files, mortgager/mortgagee information, real property files, or land records, depending on where you are. Likewise, information on court cases might be listed on a docket sheet, a file folder, or the table of contents to a case file. Asking for a case file index in a court that uses the term docket sheets may get you nothing but a blank look from the person behind the desk.

Although more and more indexes of public records are being made available electronically, either through the originating government entity or a fee-based online service, an online public records search is by no means complete. It's a great way to develop leads—which must be verified by a hard copy of the original record—but you still have to go to the source for additional information and to search through files that weren't included in the online source. And many jurisdictions load current records onto their databases but not information from five or ten years ago, which in many cases can be just as useful as the more recent information.

More than in most types of research, it is critical to identify the gaps in coverage of the public records you are searching, especially when using online sources. Part of this comes with experience; you use the sources at a particular courthouse often enough and you'll remember that their indexes only go back two years, for example. You also have to be persistent and verify every assumption you make. Ask the clerk how far back the information goes; ask whether there are other records stored elsewhere; ask if there are other ways a record might be filed. This is another reason why public records research is primarily conducted on-site rather than over the phone or online; you have to verify the results and comprehensiveness of every search, and that's very difficult to do if you aren't there in person.

It might appear that public records research is one type of independent info pro business that you can learn on the job. It is true that, unlike telephone research in which you only have one chance to conduct a successful interview, you can go back to the same public records source several times if you don't find what you're looking for at first. And unlike the professional online services, public records searching doesn't require extensive training in Boolean logic, cascaded thesauri, and arcane search commands. However, you may incur significant out-of-pocket expenses such as photocopying charges and per-search fees for online public records databases, not to mention the wear and tear of driving 20 or 30 miles to an out-of-town courthouse—multiple times, if necessary—to complete your work.

Challenges of Public Records Research

Public records research is one of the more challenging areas of specialization for independent info pros. It's not an exact science; you do the best you can and make sure that your clients don't have unrealistic expectations about how comprehensive a public records search can be. There is a potential for mistakes all along the way, and you have to watch for and recognize gaps in coverage and errors in the indexes and databases. A clerk might tell you that records aren't available when they are; information may be missing from a database; letters in a name might have been transposed by a data entry clerk. You try to think of all the possible ways you might locate what you're looking for, but the points of entry are limited. You're at the mercy of the way the index was set up for use, and the quality control imposed on the data by the court or government agency.

Public records research also involves a high level of client expectation management. You must help your clients understand that some things just can't be done—you can't get current personal bank account information, you can't unseal a court file that's been sealed by a judge's order, and you can't get a clerk to go to an off-site records storage facility to dig up a file for you just because your client needs it today. Clients who believe that "it's all available for free on the Web" have to be educated about the realities of finding public records, the vast majority of which are *not* on the Web at all.

As a public records researcher, much of your work involves dealing with gatekeepers—the civil servants who staff the desks and whom you must ask for help in locating documents, or for copies. They all have rules to follow and, like you, they have good days and bad days. You'll be dealing with them repeatedly, so you must be courteous and professional. But you also have a client who wanted results today—

and the clerk tells you that it'll take three days to copy the file. If you maintain a good rapport, they'll usually do what they can for you.

You have to watch carefully for name variations as well as outright errors. Jane Smith-Klein might be listed as Smith-Klein, Jane; Smith, Jane; Klein, Jane Smith; or Smithklein, Jane. Joe St. James could be indexed under St. James or Saint James or simply James. In most public records systems, each of these alternative names has to be searched separately. Some public records researchers charge by the total number of names searched rather than by the hour. If you're searching a printed index, or in a small town where there just aren't that many places to look, the by-name approach can be reasonably cost-effective. But that kind of pricing also encourages both the client and the researcher to skimp on the number of alternative names that might be checked. And that may leave your results incomplete and compromise your research efforts.

Sometimes, the information you want can only be released after you've made a request under the Freedom of Information Act or a local public records access law. That means that it could take months to get the information ... or to be turned down. These types of projects require a lot of persistence; you might be able to get the information if you ask again, or reword the request, or appeal the decision. And during the entire process, your client may be tapping her fingers on her desk, wondering why it is taking you so long to find one simple document.

Public records researchers have to be very detail-oriented, because it's all about following leads, making sure you don't miss anything. It can be tedious. You also have to be efficient, because the public offices are only open certain hours, and your client is paying you to travel there. You need to get as much done as you can during a single trip.

Making your added value visible to your clients is at least as important in public records research as in other types of information services. You need to distinguish yourself from court records retrievers or court runners, relatively low-paid workers—essentially clerical support—who go to courthouses, copy docket sheets, and deliver them to a professional to review and decide which individual files to order. Lynn Peterson, owner of PFC Information Services, makes the distinction this way: "I rarely go to the courthouse myself, but rely on a network of runners to go out to the various courthouses. I direct them, I tell them what I need, or I may make them go out several times—obtaining the docket sheet on the first trip, so that I can determine which documents I want copies of for my review. There is a world of difference between a court runner who goes out and grabs copies or checks the case index, and a public records researcher. It's similar to the distinction between a low-level clerk who shelves books at the library and a research librarian."

It's important to write a report detailing the research you did, all the name variations you tried, the techniques you used, and what you found and didn't find. Documenting your efforts is even more important than with other types of research. Not only must you distinguish your services from those of a court runner but, because what you deliver might contain very little actual material in relation to what you are charging, your client has to know what you did and didn't do on his behalf.

Your search strategies may not be obvious by looking at the deliverable, particularly because in public records work you deliver only exact matches. In regular online research, you're often looking for information on a subject or industry. That means that, even if you don't find anything exactly on point, you can include information that's close to what your client wants. For example, if you're researching the market for ice cream parlors, you're bound to find relevant data. On the other hand, if your client needs information specifically on Joe's Scoop Shop in Missoula, Montana—who owns it, whether there are any outstanding liens, what other companies Joe owns—you can't send her information on related companies; you either find information on Joe's or you don't.

Ethical and Legal Issues

Public records researching involves some unique ethical and legal concerns. For starters, as I mentioned at the beginning of this chapter, check with your local government to find out what aspects of public records research, if any, might be regulated or restricted to licensed private investigators.

One area of research that has been getting attention from law enforcement is what is called "pretext calling"—using deception to get information on an individual's bank account balance, stock portfolio, or other personal data. This type of information, unless disclosed in a divorce settlement or other legal filing, is considered off-limits; any independent info pro who promises to provide such information is waving a red flag in front of law enforcement.

Beyond the legal restrictions, there are types of research that some independent info pros simply don't want to tackle. The research itself is not illegal—public records are "pure" information, in the sense that they are available to anyone who looks for them. But some public records researchers choose not to do certain kinds of research, such as domestic cases (divorces, child custody, tracking down an old boyfriend), identifying birth parents for an adopted child, finding out the identify of that so-and-so who cut in front of you on the road last week, getting information on celebrities and other people in the news, and so on. Decide which types of research fall beyond your own comfort level, and be prepared to refer those jobs to other experienced public records researchers.

You have to be careful to protect the confidentiality of both your client and the subject of your research; simply knowing that someone is researching an individual may tip off the opposing side in a court case to your client's legal strategy. Don't ask a clerk how to search for "Marion Barry"; ask, generically, how to conduct a search on an individual's name.

Although all independent info pros should carry general liability insurance, public records researchers usually carry errors and omissions insurance as well. E&O insurance protects you from lawsuits in which a client claims that you failed to find information that you should have turned up. As Alex Kramer, owner of Kramer Research, noted, "Public records are not an exact science. If something is written wrong, if something's misfiled, forget it. There are just too many variables out there. You do the best you can. That's all you can guarantee to your clients."

You may also want to use a more formal disclaimer notice, as discussed in Chapter 15, Ethics and Legalities. For example, Lynn Peterson includes the following caveat with all her research: "The information provided was compiled from public records and from third parties with authorization, when required. PFC Information Services has exercised its best efforts to provide accurate information, but does not guarantee the accuracy of the data reported. PFC hereby expressly disclaims any and all liability for consequential, incidental, or punitive damages resulting from errors, partial data, or inaccuracies in the data provided." Be sure to consult with your lawyer about an appropriate disclaimer to include with your research results.

Getting Started as a Public Records Researcher

Like other independent info pros, public records researchers get most of their business through networking and word of mouth. Much of your business will be local, but some jobs will be subcontracts from other info pros or from private investigation firms. A number of networks of public records researchers and private investigators exist that you can market to and that you can use when *your* clients need out-of-town research. They include:

- Public Record Retriever Network, an online directory of public records researchers maintained by BRB Publications, Inc. (www.brbpub.com/PRRN).
- National Association of Legal Investigators (www.nalionline.org)
- National Association of Investigative Specialists (www.pimall.com/nais/nais.j.html)
- State associations or registries of licensed investigators, who may also provide public records research (You'll have to drill down from the state's main Web site to find a registry; some states don't make this information available online, but will at least give you contact information for the regulatory board. You can also use a search engine and include the words investigator, association, and the state you're interested in.)

Don't forget the Association of Independent Information Professionals (www.aiip.org), which includes not only public records researchers but a wide variety of other info pros.

In order to build a public records research business, you have to recognize and create your own market opportunities. Figure out what unique local resources you have access to and who would need this type of information. For example, Tom Culbert, a Washington, DC, area researcher with a background in the aviation industry, has built his business around access to the National Archives and the archives of the various branches of the U.S. military located in and around Washington.

What if you live in a small town? Public records work doesn't necessarily have to be done in a big city. Law firms, the major market for public records searches, often require local research. If you specialize in title searches, you can market to real estate companies. In fact, you can often market informally as you're out in the field doing research. If you notice a lawyer or paralegal struggling to figure out how to look up a case file, or frustrated at not being able to find anything on an individual, offer to help. It's a powerful marketing moment—you're face-to-face with a prospective client, and demonstrating your proficiency at something that person realizes is difficult to do. Although I usually counsel against spending much time on one-to-one marketing, it makes sense to seize the opportunity when it presents itself; personal interaction can be very powerful in this type of setting.

Public Records Databases

As I've said earlier in this chapter, no online public records database is complete or comprehensive. There is a lot of overlap, but there are gaps as well, so you usually have to search more than one database for any given project.

Several specialized databases provide information from U.S. government sources, including:

- CDB Infotek (www.choicepointonline.com/cdb)
- AutotrackXP (www.autotrackxp.com)
- KnowX (www.knowx.com)
- CourtLink (www.courtlink.com)

These online services offer access to legally available information such as individuals' current and prior addresses, assets, real estate transactions, judgments or liens, professional and driver's licenses, and so on. Some public records information is also available through professional online services such as LexisNexis (www.lexis nexis.com), Westlaw (www.westlaw.com), and Factiva (global.factiva.com). In addition, PACER (pacer.psc.uscourts.gov) is the U.S. federal court system's collection of databases covering cases in district, circuit, and bankruptcy courts. It provides PDF documents for those courts that are part of the Case Management/Electronic Case Files system. This includes many bankruptcy courts and a handful of U.S. district courts, with more coming online all the time. Keep in mind that not all federal courts make their case information available on PACER and that the system does not include state or municipal court dockets. Also, as I mentioned in Chapter 30, PACER is not a single aggregated index but rather a collection of systems maintained by each court system. That means that you'll have to search multiple systems if you're doing a comprehensive search, and you'll have to budget the time to learn how to use each court's online system.

Many local jurisdictions maintain their own online indexes to public records. No comprehensive list of Web sites where you can search these indexes exists, but the following sites provide links to a number of government Web sites where you can check to see if such indexes are available for a particular jurisdiction. (Note that most focus on U.S. jurisdictions.)

- Search Systems (www.searchsystems.net)
- BRB Publications (www.brbpub.com/pubrecsites.asp)
- Access Central (www.access-central.com)
- Search Enginez (searchenginez.com/public_records.html)

Many of the records in the local jurisdiction indexes include only cursory information on each case: the parties, the date the case was filed, the case number, maybe the attorneys of record, and perhaps a one- or two-word description of the type of case—divorce, say, or contracts. You still have to obtain the actual documents from the case file to find out what's really involved. Most jurisdictions won't take telephone requests, so you'll generally have to go in person to request the file you want, review it, and photocopy whatever material your client needs. Many files are kept off-site in storage facilities, which often means requesting the file one day and returning another day to review the material once it's been retrieved from storage and sent to the public research room.

To complicate matters, if you're researching an individual with a common name, you may have trouble determining whether the cases you've turned up involve your Henry Smith or another Henry Smith. Often, nothing in the court documents uniquely identifies the participants—they don't include Social Security numbers, addresses, or other identification—so you'll have to do additional research to figure out whether each case you identify actually involves your target.

As part of a public records job, you'll often want to search newspapers and other periodicals as well, to find any mentions of your target. That phase of the project might turn up issues in local jurisdictions you may not have thought of. See Chapter 29, Professional Online Services, and Chapter 30, Specialized Online Services, for descriptions of some additional online sources that public records researchers either search themselves or subcontract to other independent info pros who specialize in searching these services.

Lessons for Public Records Researchers

- There is no single aggregated index to public records resources.
- No online resource for public records is comprehensive or complete.
- Be sure you know the laws in your jurisdiction regarding access to and use of public records.
- Successful public records researchers are detail-oriented, persistent, and resourceful. If one approach doesn't work, they know how to pivot and try another strategy.
- Most public records work entails going on site to conduct research.

Chapter 33

Library and Other Manual Research

Although most aspiring independent info pros assume that they'll do research in their home office all day, some have successfully built a business around manual research—going directly to libraries, archives, and other information sources to gather information and conduct research. The secret to success in manual research is to find an industry or subject specialization, or to provide a service that most clients can't do on their own. Some independent info pros provide document delivery services (more about this later in the chapter); some track down photographs from archives; some create bibliographies of sources not available online.

Although it's possible to provide manual research in a small town, it's a lot easier if you live in or near a large city with access to public, academic, and government libraries. Think creatively about the unique resources in your area. Do you live in or near your state capital? Can you use resources in the state legislature? Does your city have a good historical society? Are you near a presidential library? Is there a well-known museum in town that has a library associated with it?

Manual research tends to be a low-margin business; it's often labor-intensive, and it doesn't use the "sexy" tools of online research or other esoteric sources. Be sure your deliverables showcase your value. (See Chapter 34, Deliverables, for more discussion of surfacing your value.) You need to be very client-oriented; you're providing a service that might appear clerical at times, so make sure your clients know that you're offering customized, personalized service that they couldn't get anywhere else.

Using Specialized Local Collections

I recently browsed through the membership directory of the Association of Independent Information Professionals (www.aiip.org), looking at the listings for "unique collections" among the members' entries. Entries ranged from the Public Relations Society of America library to the Canadian Tax Foundation, the Italian Patent and Trademark Office, the Harvard Business School library, the Georgia state archives, and the World Bank. That's a wide variety of sources, and I'll bet that each of the info pros who lists access to a special collection targets a client base that values access to the material in that collection.

Before you launch your business, spend some time becoming familiar with any special collections in your region. You can start by asking librarians at local universities and government agencies, or checking their Web sites for mention. Libraries all over the world maintain their own guides to special collections; many of these are available online. If there's a museum or historical society in your town, find out if they maintain a library that's open to researchers. You might want to make an appointment with a research librarian at your local public library and find out what local special collections the library has identified.

How would you take advantage of these unique collections once you've identified them? One independent info pro was providing research support for a movie on pre-war Poland. The client needed to know what the interiors of buildings were like during that period, how people dressed, what the streets looked like, and so on. The info pro wound up going through books and image files in the Library of Congress, looking for pictures of interiors of Polish homes, drawings and portraits of people in ordinary dress, and photographs of street scenes for her client.

Say you live near the Beinecke Library at Yale, which has a remarkable collection of early books and manuscripts going back to the days of Greek and Roman papyri. Could a historical research organization use your services? Might a public relations firm want you to find material dating back to when a client company was founded in the 1800s? Who else could use a researcher with access to a collection of household documents from the 14th century to the 18th century that details the daily life and social history of merchants, farmers, and wealthy families?

Document Delivery Services

Document delivery, fondly known as doc del, involves going to libraries or other sources and getting copies—and occasionally originals—of articles, papers, conference proceedings, patents, laws, or other documents as requested by clients. These clients are often librarians or other info pros who are trying to track down something that doesn't exist online, that isn't available in-house or from other local libraries, or for which they don't have a complete citation that might enable them to find it more easily themselves. Even though publishers are increasingly making their content available, either on their own Web sites or through the professional online services, a great deal of material still simply doesn't exist in electronic format. Doc del companies often work from an e-mailed list of citations from an online search, or a faxed photocopy of a bibliography or footnotes, with the troublesome items circled.

As a doc del service provider, you would first check to see if any of those citations are incomplete or clearly incorrect. What is the actual name of the publication that's cited as ADV CATAL? (Answer: *Advances in Catalysis.*) Is the date in the citation correct? Was that newsletter about the Internet really published back in 1989, or did someone transpose the last two digits of the year? Doc del providers often search a professional online service at this point, to try to find an accurate and complete citation. Even if the item itself isn't available in full text online, at least you'll be able to confirm the article title, author, source, and date.

Next, you would look through the list to see if any of the citations can, in fact, be found online (sometimes the client just doesn't have access to the database with the complete text of the material). A helpful resource at this step is *Fulltext Sources Online*, published twice a year by Information Today, Inc. (www.infotoday.com/FSO), which—as the name implies—is a directory of online sources, including publisher Web sites, for the full text of publications.

The next step is to determine whether any local libraries subscribe to the publication and have the issue you need. Most large libraries maintain a searchable version of their catalog on their Web site, so you can confirm that the library at least subscribes to *Advances in Catalysis*—although you won't know from looking at the Web site whether the issue you need is on the shelf, misfiled, lost or stolen, out at the bindery, or stored off-site in a warehouse. At this point, you would either go to the library yourself or send a runner—someone whose job is to go to the appropriate library and photocopy articles, book chapters, or whatever the clients need. Some doc del companies have their own runners who go from library to library as needed;

others rely on outside runners who specialize in one or two libraries and do photocopying for a number of document delivery services.

At this point, things sometimes get tricky. What if your client didn't supply a page number for the article, and none of the articles in the cited issue seems to be the right one? What if the publication changed names and the library only lists it under its new name? Sometimes you simply have to go back to the client and ask for clarification or additional information. Often you wind up consulting with the library staff to track down a publication that has changed names or is otherwise difficult to locate.

Another challenge of the doc del process is that a fair number of requests, typically, are for documents that were never published in a traditional journal or book. You'll get a citation such as "Trends in the Machine Tool Industry, presented by Peter West at 1997 International Machine Tool Show" and you'll find that the International Machine Tool Show doesn't publish its conference papers. You may have to try to track down Peter West, find out if he still has a copy of his paper and, if so, whether he will send you one.

At this point, you may have to check with your client, to get approval for any additional costs and to extend the deadline for delivery of the material. Some doc del clients are only willing to pay for orders that can be filled locally and reasonably quickly. If you can't get it right away, they would rather just cancel the order. In fact, often they are not willing to pay anything for an unfilled order, even if it took you several hours to try to track down the source. The challenge here is to demonstrate to clients that, although doc del may look to them like a simple, cut-and-dried transaction, it often involves a good deal of research to identify a source and obtain a copy of an article based on an obscure or ambiguous citation. You may also want to explain all that is involved in providing comprehensive doc del work, including citation verification, copyright clearance, arranging for someone to go on-site to photocopy, and so on. Regular contact with the client, and a good understanding of their expectations, is essential. Sometimes, despite your best efforts, you just can't deliver. The chapter the client requested is from a book that is out of print and not in any library you can find. The citation is to an article from an obscure Latvian magazine that ceased publication five years ago. The government report is classified, so no one will give you a copy. Or the citation is so mangled that you can't find a document that might match what the client wants.

Document delivery is a difficult industry to break into, although it can be a good niche if you are close to several large libraries and you have a knack for tracking down elusive material. Doc del companies don't have large profit margins; you make money on volume, so you have to find plenty of clients who need your services on a regular basis. That means intensive marketing, particularly when you first start out. It's a labor-intensive business, too; you can spend a lot of your time either going from library to library yourself or coordinating your runners. As Frank Warren, principal of Instant Information Systems, said, "Operating a successful doc del firm for the long-term is less about locating documents and more about locating repeat clients willing to pay for the service. Being able to find the document is necessary but not sufficient for long-term success."

And you have to be persistent, despite the difficulties I've mentioned, in tracking down the obscure, the incomplete, and the questionable. If you have to tell a client repeatedly that the material couldn't be found, the client will simply stop calling you. On the other hand, you could spend 80 percent of your time finding the last, most problematic 10 percent of the items your client has requested, and it's hard to make money that way.

I mentioned that profit margins are low in the doc del business. Pricing is difficult to get right. Some companies work on a per-document basis, charging a set amount per item plus photocopying and copyright fees (more about the latter in the next section). This method works well if the requests are easy to fill, but if you spend an hour tracking down an obscure cite and only make $10 on that item, you're barely earning minimum wage. On the other hand, if you charge by the hour to ensure that you are compensated for the time you spend, your clients may object, as they won't know ahead of time how much their order will cost.

If you want to find out more about document delivery work, see DocDel.net (www.docdel.net), which contains a collection of articles about the industry, a directory of doc del providers, links to useful doc del Web resources, and instructions on how to subscribe to the DocDel e-mail discussion list. DocDel.net was developed and is maintained by Frank Warren of Instant Information Systems.

Copyright Issues

As I mentioned in Chapter 15, Ethics and Legalities, copyright is a murky area, and interpretation of the law changes all the time. It's still unclear exactly what activities constitute "fair use" of copyrighted material, what we are allowed to pass along to clients, and what our clients can do with that material. AIIP has published a white paper by Stephanie Ardito, *Copyright & Information Professionals: Complying with the Law*, that addresses some of these issues (www.aiip.org/order.html).

Independent info pros who provide photocopies of material for clients are responsible for addressing copyright issues. (Content from the professional online services, on the other hand, include a copyright fee in the per-document cost, so no additional copyright fee is required unless multiple copies are to be made.) This means that each time you photocopy anything from a copyrighted publication, you have to determine the copyright royalty amount and to whom you must pay it. You pass this charge along to the client in addition to your own fee. Many publications charge a few dollars per article, but some highly specialized sources charge more. Remember *Advances in Catalysis*, which I mentioned earlier in the chapter? The royalty fee per article is $35. Sometimes the copyright fee will be the most expensive portion of the total doc del charge. And, just to add a few more gray hairs to the head of any info pro in the doc del business, some publishers ban any copying of their publications. In such situations, your only option may be to try to purchase a copy of the entire book or issue in which the article appeared.

Some doc del companies elect not to pay the copyright fee and simply provide the article to the client with a reminder that copyright compliance is the client's responsibility. This is not a particularly prudent path to take; publishers are becoming much more aggressive about copyright compliance and have been known to test doc del companies with "secret shopper" orders to see whether the company is not only charging for but submitting copyright payments to the publisher for each item provided. As a result, some doc del firms have been sued by publishers or forced to pay out-of-court settlements for copyright infringements. When it's you against a multinational publishing company, you can imagine who's going to blink first.

The administrative burden of figuring out the copyright fee and contacting the publisher for each document delivered is often more than an independent info pro can handle. One alternative is to use the Copyright Clearance Center (www.copyright.com), a for-profit company that handles the payment of copyright fees. Its Transactional Reporting Service lets you log the publication name, date, and number of pages you're copying; it calculates the royalty fee and bills you weekly, and pays the publisher the required amount. Although not all publishers have registered with the CCC, a high proportion do participate, and it's a convenient way to ensure that you've paid the appropriate fees.

You can read more about U.S. copyright law at the Library of Congress' U.S. Copyright Office Web site (lcweb.loc.gov/copyright). DocDel.net also has a collection of links to copyright-related sites at www.docdel.net/Copyright_Sites.html.

Online Tools for Manual Researchers

Before you head out to your local library with a handful of document orders, you have to make sure that the library actually has what you need. Almost all large libraries make their catalogs available on the Web, so you can check to see if the conference proceeding or book is in the library's collection, or if they subscribe to the magazine you need. Of course, as I pointed out earlier, this still won't tell you if the item is on the shelf, but at least you know your odds are good. An excellent directory of library online public access catalogs, or OPACs, is LibDex (www.libdex.com). You can browse by geographic region or search by library name.

But what if your local library doesn't have what you're looking for? First, you'll have to find a library that *does* list the item in its catalog. Fortunately, several services offer shared or union catalogs, which are the combined online catalogs of hundreds or thousands of libraries. They're primarily designed to help librarians catalog their own material; a cataloging librarian can look to see if someone else has already cataloged a particular book so that she doesn't have to figure out the Dewey Decimal or Library of Congress classification number and subject headings herself. (Speaking as a former solo librarian with no particular skill in cataloging, I can tell you that these services are a godsend.) But union catalogs also allow subscribers to see which participating libraries have cataloged a particular book or periodical. If they've cataloged it, presumably they own, or owned, a copy. Once you've figured out what library has the item you need, you can identify a document delivery company in the same area—using the AIIP directory or the list of doc del firms at www.docdel.net—and subcontract the job to that company.

Some of these online cataloging systems are only available to bona fide libraries—the ones with actual books to catalog. Fortunately, most public libraries do subscribe to one of these systems and will run individual searches for you to see what libraries own a publication you're looking for. If you keep your requests to a modest volume and ask politely, you may be able to rely on this cost-free method of determining where to get a specific title. One of the largest shared catalogs, the Online Computer Library Center or OCLC, offers independent info pros prepaid access to its WorldCat database. This may be a useful tool if you expect to be doing a lot of this kind of searching. You have to purchase a minimum block of 500 "searches" and, at around $1 per search, it's not a trivial investment. These search units can also be used elsewhere in OCLC's FirstSearch collection of bibliographic databases, although individual records from these article databases cost an additional five search units, making it a more expensive option than some of the professional online services. If you want to subscribe to OCLC's WorldCat database, contact the regional network of libraries in your area; all subscriptions, training, and customer support are provided by local library consortia rather than directly by OCLC. The list of regional networks is at www.oclc.org/contacts/regional.

Most document delivery firms also use the catalogs of some of the large, authoritative libraries when they simply need to confirm or clarify an ambiguous bibliographic citation. If you aren't sure about the exact title of a book, want to verify the spelling of an author's name, or need to see a list of all the books a particular author has written, your resources include the Web-based catalogs of the Library of Congress (catalog.loc.gov) and the British Library (blpc.bl.uk).

Top Tips for Library Researchers

- Look for unique collections in your region. For marketing purposes, think creatively about who would be interested in this information.
- Document delivery work is a low-margin business; focus on building volume by finding regular, repeat clients and providing great customer service.
- Persistence and creativity are key skills for a manual researcher.
- Even manual researchers often need to use online sources to help locate information.
- Copyright is a big issue for manual researchers. Become familiar with the law, and be prepared to be overly cautious in handling payments and otherwise complying with it.

Chapter 34

Deliverables

We often spend so much time focusing on determining our clients' needs, managing our clients' expectations, and doing the research itself that we forget what might be the most important part of any project—the information we send to the client. We know how much work went into that final package but, unless we make it obvious, our client may not appreciate everything that was involved. You probably don't want to give your client a blow-by-blow description; indeed, your client almost certainly doesn't expect or need to hear all the gruesome details. But you do have to make sure that, when you present your invoice, he'll pay it knowing how much value he received. When you provide analysis, synthesis, and a summary of the key elements of your research, you are providing tremendous added value. Be sure to surface that value so your client sees what you've contributed.

No Added Value = No Perceived Value

Every independent info pro knows that it's the content that matters, not the packaging, right? Well, yes and no. We're experts at finding information because we look past the hype and focus on whether the source is authoritative, accurate, and up-to-date. Our clients come to us because they know we're good at finding information efficiently; that's a given. What sets us apart from the competition—and by that I mean other info pros, our clients' internal information sources, and do-it-yourself searching—is that we add tangible value *after* the research, and we package the material in a way that makes it accessible and user-friendly.

As every project draws to a conclusion, look at the information you have gathered and think about how you can make it more digestible, more easily absorbed, by someone who is looking at it for the first time. That's harder than it sounds; you have been immersed in this project and, in a sense, swimming in the data. You're probably perfectly clear on what all this material is and why you've selected it. But try to step back and think about what it looks like to your client—someone who no doubt understands the concepts covered in the documents you're sending, but who does not see the context until you make that clear. Your client hasn't spent the last three days doing the research, digging around in various resources, and sorting through an array of documents, Web sites, spreadsheets, and other information, and your job is to put the retrieved information in context.

Basic Data Massage

There are various levels of post-processing, from simply cleaning up and reformatting the output of an online search, to sophisticated analysis and distillation of the information. If you are planning to send a set of electronic documents (articles, reports, patents, Web sites, and so on), I assume that you will at least insert page breaks at the end of each document and delete any extraneous material such as indexing terms. If you include plain text material in a tabular format, make sure that it's in a nonproportional font such as `Courier`, which will retain the proper spacing.

Some online services deliver their output with no embedded manual line breaks—that is, the text flows from one line to the next and will adjust automatically if you change the font or margins. Other online services insert a line break at the end of each line. If you change the font, especially to a proportional font such as Times Roman, the formatting suddenly looks different. For example, the following text looks fine as displayed by the online service:

```
Researchers   have   been   experimenting   with   substances   that
stimulate  blood  vessel  growth  for  nearly  a  decade,  but  a
landmark study published this week is the first demonstration
such substances can make patients better.
```

But when you download it into a word-processing program and change to a better-looking proportional font, it looks like this, due to those embedded carriage returns:

Researchers have been experimenting with substances that
stimulate blood vessel growth for nearly a decade, but a
landmark study published this week is the first demonstration
such substances can make patients better.

If your output routinely includes such unwanted manual line breaks, you can purchase shareware that removes them. One such product is SmartWrap (www.selznick.com/products/smartwrap), which lets you copy the text of an article to a clipboard, remove all line breaks except those at the end of paragraphs, and then paste the text back into your document. You can also write a macro for your word processor that removes all line breaks other than those at the end of paragraphs. See the sidebar "Macro for Removing Manual Line Breaks" for an example.

Macro for Removing Manual Line Breaks

This macro for Microsoft Word removes manual line breaks at the end of each line of text, but preserves line breaks at the end of paragraphs. It assumes that each paragraph is separated by two line breaks. If, instead, paragraphs are separated by a single line break and a set number of spaces, change this macro accordingly.

- Find <manual line break><manual line break> [If paragraphs are separated by a line break and four spaces, change this to Find <manual line break><space><space><space><space>]
- Replace with ~~ [this is a symbol that is unlikely to appear in a document]
- Find <manual line break>
- Replace with <space>
- Find ~
- Replace with <manual line break>

(If you have any problems recording or using macros, consult the Word Help file on macros.)

Packaging Your Results

Now that you've massaged the information so that it's cosmetically more attractive to your client, what else can you do to enhance the value of your deliverable? For starters, you can generate a table of contents that helps guide your client through the material you're delivering. See the sidebar "Generating Tables of Contents" for an example of how to do this in Microsoft Word. Other simple ways to enhance the usability of your work include:

- Highlighting, underlining, or bolding the key sentences or paragraphs in each item, so that your client can easily locate the most useful information
- Summarizing the results in your cover letter, telling the client what you found and extracting the key points from your research results
- Providing a list of the resources you used, including Web site URLs, names of databases or files searched on the professional online services, contact information for the individuals you interviewed, and so on

I also always add a footer at the bottom of every page consisting of my company name, address, phone number, and e-mail address. This ensures that, even if the package of material is taken apart and distributed within my client's organization or beyond, readers will know who provided the information.

Be aware of how your clients are accustomed to looking at information. Chances are they don't do research themselves on a regular basis, but they are probably comfortable reading newspapers or wire stories on the Web, checking sports scores online, and so on. The more you make your work product look similar to what your clients see elsewhere, the more user-friendly and accessible your work becomes. For example, look at Figure 34.1—the beginning of an article from the *New York Times*' Web site—and Figure 34.2—the same article, downloaded from Dialog. Which one is easier to read? Which one will look more familiar to a client?

By the way, did you notice the difference in the two titles? The *New York Times* Web site titled the article "F.T.C. Urged to Take a Hard Line on Advertising of Snuff," while the Dialog version of the same article is titled "F.T.C. Is Urged to Take a Hard Line on Snuff." The lesson here is that, even if a client gives you an exact title, saying "I know I saw it a few weeks ago," search broadly enough to catch the article even if the title isn't quite the same. And keep the output format in mind when you're deciding which source to search. For most clients, the unadorned Dialog format may be

The New York Times
ON THE WEB

June 5, 2002

F.T.C. Urged to Take a Hard Line on Advertising of Snuff

By GREG WINTER

Antismoking advocates in Congress opened an offensive against snuff makers yesterday, urging the Federal Trade Commission to derail the industry's attempts to promote chewing tobacco as a safer alternative to cigarettes and contending that its largest company, UST Inc., unfairly focuses on children with its advertising.

In a letter to Donald S. Clark, the secretary of the F.T.C., two Democratic opponents of big tobacco — Representative Henry A. Waxman of California and Senator Richard J. Durbin of Illinois — said the agency would be "acting outside of its authority" if it allowed companies to say that snuff poses fewer health risks than smoking.

Figure 34.1 An article from www.nytimes.com

2/3,TX/3
04232341 **NYT Sequence Number:** 379948020605 **(USE FORMAT 7 FOR FULLTEXT)**
F.T.C. Is Urged to Take a Hard Line on Snuff
GREG WINTER
New York Times , Late Edition - Final ED , Col 04 , p 7
Wednesday June 5 2002
Document Type: Newspaper **Language:** English
Record Type: Fulltext **Section Heading:** SECTC
Word Count: 480

Text:

Antismoking advocates in Congress opened an offensive against snuff makers yesterday, urging the Federal Trade Commission to derail the industry's attempts to promote chewing tobacco as a safer alternative to cigarettes and contending that its largest company, UST Inc., unfairly focuses on children with its advertising.

In a letter to Donald S. Clark, the secretary of the F.T.C., two Democratic opponents of big tobacco -- Representative Henry A. Waxman of California and Senator Richard J. Durbin of Illinois -- said the agency would be "acting outside of its authority" if it allowed companies to say that snuff poses fewer health risks than smoking.

Figure 34.2 An article from DialogWeb

just fine, but for the CEO, you might want to make the extra effort of providing a more user-friendly and familiar-looking version.

In addition to formatting your material, find out if your client has any specific needs and preferences. Does she like to see bullet points of the key issues? Does she work extensively with charts, graphs, and spreadsheets? If so, would she like you to extract data from your results and create graphics that illustrate the information you found? Even something as simple as knowing whether your client prefers color or black and white can make a difference. And make sure your word processing software and delivery defaults are compatible with your clients'. Some clients' organizations upgrade their software regularly, but some, especially smaller businesses, do not. Also, be sensitive to the fact that formatting features that work beautifully for you and most of your clients may be more of a hindrance than a help for clients with a different computer setup. One of my clients, for example, can't handle footers at the bottom of pages—something in the interaction between his word processing software and his printer means that pages with footers get garbled. I'm not going to attempt to troubleshoot his set-up, but I can make a note to remind myself to send him more lightly formatted documents.

Generating Tables of Contents

You can generate a table of contents in Microsoft Word by marking each title and then indicating where you want the table of contents to be generated. Here are the steps in Microsoft Word 2000:

- Highlight the title of the first item
- Pull down the Format menu and select Style
- Select Heading1
- Repeat for all items
- Insert a Section Break before your first item (Pull down the Insert menu, select Break, then Section Break: Next Page)
- Restart the page numbering for the content at page 1 (Move the cursor to the first page below the section break, pull down the Insert

menu, select Page Numbers, click Format, click Page Numbering:

- Start At, and make sure it starts at 1)
- Before the section break, insert your table of contents (Pull down the Insert menu, select Index and Tables, then Table of Contents)

And here are the equivalent steps in Word 2002:

- Highlight the title of the first item
- Pull down the Format menu and select Styles and Formatting
- Select Heading 1
- Repeat for all items, then close Styles and Formatting window when complete (NOTE: the Styles/Formatting window remains on the right side of the screen until you close it with the x)
- Insert a Section Break before your first item in the document (Pull down the Insert menu, select Break, then Section Break Types: Next page)
- Restart the page numbering at page 1 (Move the cursor to the first page below the section break, pull down the Insert menu, select Page Numbers, click Format, click Page Numbering: Start At, and make sure it starts at 1)
- Before the section break, insert your table of contents (Pull down the Insert menu, select Reference, then Index and Tables, then Table of Contents)

Moving Beyond Research Results

In addition to simply providing your research results, pleasantly formatted as they are, consider developing added-value reports that your client might find useful. I was taken aback the first time a client asked for a PowerPoint presentation of the results of my work. How could I reduce all the information I found to five slides, I thought? Then I realized that he was accustomed to seeing information delivered that way, and that presenting my results in the same familiar format was the most efficient way to let him see the key points before he dug deeper into the material. Your job is not only to find the most useful information you can, but also to make that information as easy to use as possible. If your client is developing a PowerPoint slide show and needs information to insert into the presentation, provide the results in that format. If your client is accustomed to receiving reports from his staff in the form of one-page bulleted memos, use that format too.

Another feature that you may want to make part of your cover letter or summary report is what I call an "information topography" report. We info pros sometimes forget that we learn a lot in the process of doing research that isn't obvious in the results we send. For example, here are some snippets of information I gleaned during a recent online research project:

- Contrary to the client's expectations, the topic was not being discussed in consumer publications.
- There seems to be a lot of interest in this topic in Europe, based on the number of articles I found from European sources.
- An industry only tangentially related to my client's is tracking this topic closely. This may indicate possible synergies that my client had not previously thought of.

What I told my client in this case was, essentially, information *about* information—what I found as I was doing my research that would not have been surfaced simply by delivering the research results. As we conduct research, we see the lay of the information landscape; we see where deep pockets of information reside and where little information exists. We get a sense of what kinds of publications, groups, and industries care about the topic we're researching. All of this can be tremendously useful to our clients, but we have to spell it out in order for our client to see the information topography that we have mapped out.

Less Is More

It's difficult for new info pros to figure out what *not* to include in the final report to a client. You've found all this great information—pages and pages and pages of it—and since you'll be charging the client for the cost of obtaining it all, shouldn't you include every single page? The answer is no—unless you have previously discussed the issue with your client and he has said that he really, truly does want everything you can find. In most situations, your client is using you because he *doesn't* want everything—he wants the key information, the best of what's out there.

Clients will often pay more for five pages of information than they will for 105 pages. I'll never forget a project I did for a client who wanted to know what people were saying about a specific aspect of color inkjet printers. She authorized a budget that included 30 hours of my time, and I gathered information from all over—articles from consumer publications, photography and digital printing magazines, and newspapers; postings from Web discussion forums on digital cameras and printing; newsgroup and e-mail discussion list messages; and market research studies. She told me that she wanted just a three-page summary of my results, but I couldn't believe that, for such a big budget, she'd settle for so little material. So I sent her a 10-page report on what I found, along with all the material I had gathered. She called and said she was happy with the report, but was still waiting for my three-page summary. Sure enough, once I managed to distill all I'd found down to three pages, she was completely happy with the results. What she was paying me for was not just my ability to gather the information, but to make sense out of it and provide some analysis of what I'd found.

When I first started my business, I did a good deal of subcontracted research work for Linda Cooper, an information consultant in Pennsylvania. In addition to doing the research, she had me explain in a sentence or two why I was including each article in the package. So, for example, I'd write something like, "Article 1 includes a useful chart on the company's market share in the women's apparel industry, and a discussion (which I highlighted) on its strategic plans. Article 2 is an interview with the leading women's apparel designer, discussing trends in the industry." If I'd decided to eliminate any article from the package I sent her, she asked to have it enclosed at the end, as supplemental material. What surprised me as I did this was how many articles I moved to the "supplemental" category. Once I had to articulate why I was including an article, I often realized that it wasn't really that useful, or it covered a tangential topic, or it duplicated what another article provided. After a while, Linda stopped asking for the article annotations, since I had learned how to weed out the extraneous material. But, more than 10 years later, I still conduct the Linda Cooper Exercise in my head each time I prepare a package of material for a client.

Output Options from the Professional Online Services

Most of the major professional online services provide formatting tools and display options that help you deliver better-looking search results. The following is a brief overview of what's available on the major online services. Note that, in addition to the options listed below, all of these services let you send the search results to any e-mail address. You will probably not want to send the results directly to your client, because you'll usually need to sort through the results, eliminate items that are repetitive or less relevant, and put your own "brand" on the results as I discuss elsewhere in this chapter. If, however, you're short on time and simply need to send one or two documents to a client, e-mail delivery can be a useful option.

Dialog

Dialog (www.dialogweb.com) includes a number of output options to customize the format of material you've downloaded. One of its more powerful features is the Report function, which creates tabular output of selected information in the records you've retrieved. This is particularly useful for creating lists of companies and their revenue, government contracts awarded and the amount of each contract, patent assignees and patent numbers, and so on. For more detailed information, see support.dialog.com/searchaids/success/report.shtml

Dialog also lets you indicate the specific document fields you want to display and the order in which to display them. You can create and save output formats consisting of certain fields (called User Defined Formats), and you can design customized output formats on the fly, as you issue the display, type, or print command. If you've retrieved a list of patents assigned to a certain company, for instance, you may not want to repeat the company name in every item; UDF allows you to display just the patent number, patent title, and date, for example. For more information about user defined output, see support.dialog.com/searchaids/success/set_un.shtml

The default display order for Dialog search results is reverse chronological, that is, with the most recently added material first. "Most recently-added" usually means most recently published, but if the database has just added a backfile of articles from a new source or picked up older material from an existing publication, you may get some older references as well. You can easily override the default by sorting the results of your search by title or publication date; by author or journal title (in bibliographic databases); by company name, city, state, or ZIP code (in directory databases); or even by sales (in company profile databases). The

Successful Searching on Dialog manual includes detailed information on using the Sort command.

DataStar

DataStar (www.datastarweb.com) is owned by the same company as the Dialog service described above, and offers many of the same output customization features. You can build your own customized output formats, and you can sort the results by a wide variety of fields such as title, author, source, date, length, and so on. DataStar also offers what it calls WebChart software, a free tool you can download that enables you to import the results of a search into a chart format. From there, you can massage and reformat the data and export it to HTML, Excel, or Word. See the description of WebChart at www.dialog.com/sources/subject/webcharts.shtml. You can also get output from DataStarWeb in PDF format, with a nice-looking table of contents and the search statement on a separate page.

You can download the *DataStar Search Guide*, which includes a section on customizing output, at support.dialog.com/searchaids/datastar/pdf/dssearchguide.pdf.

Factiva

Factiva.com has a drop-down box that lets you select the fields you want displayed and save the customized format. You can sort the search results by date or by calculated relevance. You can format the output in RTF as well as in plain text and a more polished-looking format.

LexisNexis

LexisNexis' (www.lexisnexis.com) output formats include citation, keyword-in-context, and full format. There is also a "custom" tab, through which you can select the specific fields you want displayed. The results are displayed in plain text; you can download documents in either HTML or RTF.

Branding and "Sealing" Your Results

Earlier in this chapter I suggested some ways to highlight the added value you bring to the research process by packaging your results in a manner that your clients will find easy and convenient to use. But it's also important to think about the medium in which you deliver your results, and about making that package look as professional as possible.

The last time I reordered my company letterhead, I was struck by the fact that it had been a couple of years since the last order. I'm just not sending out as many projects in hard copy as I used to, and much of my marketing has migrated to digital format as well. As tempting as it is to shift entirely to electronic delivery, there are times when hard copy tells a better story. A well-designed, nicely bound paper report on company letterhead will be passed around your client's office, and is often perceived as more valuable, somehow, than an electronic version of the same report. Print also gives you complete control over how the output looks; if you e-mail a Word file to a client, you are at his mercy when it comes to printing and binding the results. Your logo may be printed in black and white instead of color; his printer may spit out blank pages or mangle a nonstandard font; he may just paper-clip the report together when it's printed out, and so on. Also, if you are including printouts of Web pages in your report, it's often easier to deliver the results in hard copy rather than try to incorporate the pages into a word-processed document.

If I'm concerned about maintaining the appearance and format of a report, I will often convert it to a PDF file before sending it to the client. This ensures that, when my client prints the report or looks at it on the screen, it will appear the same as when I sent it. Some word processing software packages come with a feature that lets you convert a file to PDF. If you buy the Adobe Acrobat software (www.adobe.com/store), you also have the ability to "lock" a PDF report so that the recipient cannot change it.

Of course, it's faster to zap a file to a client via e-mail, and it avoids the expense of an overnight delivery service. An electronic file is easier for a client to forward to her boss or colleagues. And if you use your word processor's table of contents feature described earlier in this chapter, your client can jump directly from the table of contents to any item in the report. Of course, you should use whatever delivery format is most convenient for your client. Some corporate cultures run on electronic communications and expect their vendors to do the same. Other clients prefer receiving the material in hard copy, so they can mark up the results, tear out a page for later use, or read the results while they're on the road.

If your client tells you that he wants to distribute copies of your report to others, or to store the material in an internal database or on his intranet site, you will need to discuss copyright concerns. Dialog and DataStar offer an Electronic Redistribution and Archiving Service (support.dialog.com/searchaids/era) that streamlines the licensing of additional use of material from their systems. For content from other online services, your best bet is to contact the customer service office and ask how to proceed. Factors that affect the ease and cost of buying redistribution rights include the number of copies to be made, whether or not the information will be housed in an internal database, and the source of the documents. Note that Dialog, DataStar, and Factiva.com specifically grant permission for subscribers to "occasionally and on an infrequent basis" distribute copies of material within an organization. Whether that applies to material provided by an independent info pro is not clear; if in doubt, put your client's general counsel in touch with the online vendor.

Archiving Search Results

What do you do with the results of your research after you have sent your report to the client? You will probably want to archive a copy of your search, although some professional online services impose restrictions on how long you can maintain such a file on your PC. I usually keep search results for three to six months, as permitted by my service agreements with the various online vendors. The only reason to keep a copy, really, is in case a client loses the report you sent and you need to send a replacement. After a month or so, the odds are pretty low that the client will come back asking for a replacement copy—although it does occasionally happen, sometimes many months later. One way to deal with copyright restrictions in a situation like this is to keep a record of your search strategies and the databases searched, so you can at least recreate them if a client asks for the results again. You can offer to charge just the database costs plus a smaller labor fee than if you had to totally restrategize the search. You can point out to the client that the redone search will also retrieve more current information along with their original results.

Of course, you will never send the results of a search to another client, especially if it includes material from any of the fee-based online services; when you download content from an online service, you are only buying it for a single client.

Another reason to save a copy of your search results is in case a client or someone else questions your search strategy. Although I only save the report itself for a few months, I retain a printout of all my search strategies as well as any Web pages I relied on, a list of the databases searched, the cover letter, and all other correspondence with the client regarding the extent and limitations of the research. Web pages can be changed at any time, so you may want to use software that lets you save the original page—as opposed to just the URL—including all formatting, frames, links, and graphics. One of the more powerful applications for preserving Web pages is SurfSaver (www.surfsaver.com), available free from askSam Systems, which also markets database management systems.

Top Tips for Preparing Deliverables

- Format your report to look attractive and familiar to your client; plain text often appears too "dense."
- Highlight the key information in the text and/or include bullet points for important findings in your cover letter.
- Offer to provide analysis and synthesis of the information.
- Include an "information topography" report as part of your summary to the client.
- Less is more. Weed your search results ruthlessly; don't overwhelm your client with data.
- Use the output-customization tools available on the professional online services.
- Consider "sealing" your results in PDF to maintain their professional appearance.

Chapter 35

Other Services You Can Offer

The focus of this book has been on information businesses that provide some type of research service. However, many independent info pros also offer services that go beyond providing information. Some give workshops and seminars. Some write user manuals and training material for the online information services. Some provide consulting services to the information industry—to information providers that need help developing or improving their user interface, for example, and to libraries and information centers that require assistance in resolving a management problem or improving their service. And finally, some independent info pros offer outsourcing—that is, practical personnel services such as library-staffing-in-a-box, temporary help, or specialized staff for specific library jobs such as cataloging or intranet Web site maintenance.

All these services require a fair amount of marketing, particularly if you're offering them as a sideline to your main focus. However, if you present your various services in a way that highlights your background and experience, your clients will see the synergies that come from hiring someone with a broad range of skills. When editor Reva Basch was an active online searcher, her business card, brochure, and Web site all said "research, writing, and consulting to the online industry." When I am invited to teach workshops on advanced Web research techniques, I often hear the comment, "It's great to find someone who doesn't just teach this kind of research but actually does it for a living." As long as the various services that you provide tie together somehow, you'll benefit by reminding clients of *all* the information services you can provide. Just don't include a blurb for your sideline selling Tupperware; that's a fine business, but it doesn't relate to your skills as an information professional.

Training, Workshops, and Seminars

Chapter 22, Marketing by Writing and Speaking, talks about using conference presentations to market your business. But more in-depth speaking opportunities can be a source of revenue as well. Some independent info pros offer customized or one-on-one training in areas such as searching the Web, effective telephone research, or advanced search techniques on the professional online services—essentially, teaching clients about what the info pro does every day. These personalized training sessions require a good deal of preparation, because the focus is the needs, interests, and skills of the one or two clients you're teaching. On the other hand, you can charge a premium for the customization, and it's rewarding to see your student's eyes light up as he finally realizes how to do something he didn't think possible.

Other training possibilities include half- or full-day workshops or seminars on specific types of research or information skills. The advantage of developing a workshop or seminar is that, unlike the personalized training, creating the course content and handouts is a one-time investment; after that you need only do minor updating each time you give the workshop. You might arrange to teach such workshops in conjunction with professional conferences or trade shows, usually on the days just before or after the main program. You can also organize and market your own workshop, but the amount of marketing required is generally beyond the scope of an independent info pro unless you intend to do this kind of work full time. Promoting a workshop usually requires a very large mailing list of people potentially willing to pay several hundred dollars for training. It also requires administrative backup to handle registrations and credit card payments, and access to an appropriate training facility and the required audiovisual equipment. Renting a room, a digital projector, and an Internet connection alone can run $1,000, and that doesn't include the cost of your handouts or the coffee and snacks that workshop attendees expect. Until you know that you'll be able to attract enough people to pay your overhead and make a profit, it is usually wiser to focus on offering workshops or seminars through the professional associations you belong to or other professional conferences or trade shows.

If you are considering doing a substantial amount of professional speaking, consider joining the National Speakers Association (www.nsaspeaker.org). Membership is limited to people who, within the preceding 12 months, have given at least 20 paid presentations or made at least $25,000 in speaking fees. However, NSA also has local chapters, many of which offer "apprentice" membership for anyone interested in professional speaking. They usually have monthly meetings that focus on topics such as how to improve your delivery or presence, how to involve an audience, how to keep up with technology, and so forth.

Technical Writing

I also discuss writing articles and books in Chapter 22, Marketing by Writing and Speaking. Technical writing is another form of authorship that, even though it often requires that you labor in anonymity, can pay reasonably well. Whenever you read a software user's manual, online service training documentation, or a Web site's Frequently Asked Questions file, you're looking at technical writing. Tech writing jobs are not the sexiest of projects, but it can be enormously satisfying to know that you have translated the arcane notations of a computer programmer or systems designer into a clear, user-friendly description of, for example, all the nifty ways a searcher can get the most out of a particular online system.

The requirements for a good technical writer include your ability to:

- Learn a new software program or online service quickly
- Write clearly and concisely
- Put yourself in the users' place and imagine how they will most likely use the system, what problems they will encounter, and what questions they will have
- Work well with a variety of staff members within the client organization, including marketing, programming, and systems people

Pricing a technical writing project is particularly tricky. You don't know ahead of time how long the project will take or how many times system features and functionality will change before you finish the job. Most technical writers will advise you to bid a job at a straight hourly rate rather than by the project. Give a rough estimate of how long you expect it to take, with the proviso that you and the client can renegotiate once a certain percentage of the work has been completed. A clearly written contract, with well-defined deliverables and deadlines, is essential. Otherwise, "project creep" sets in and you find that you are suddenly responsible for twice as much work as originally anticipated.

If the field of technical writing interests you enough to pursue it as a sideline, consider joining the Society for Technical Communication (www.stc.org). STC has local chapter meetings where you can meet fellow technical writers, special interest groups that focus on specialized concerns of members (indexing, consulting and independent contracting, usability, and so on), several membership publications, and an annual conference. With more than 20,000 members, STC is the leading organization for the tech writing profession.

I also recommend you join the online conferencing service The WELL (www.well.com), which features lively discussion forums for technical communications (Tech) and for freelance writers (Byline), populated by both newcomers and people who've been doing this kind of work for years. The subscription to The WELL is $10 a month and is, in my experience, one of the best bargains around.

Outsourced Library Services

Although most independent info pros focus on research services, a subset within the profession offers more direct library-related services. These are info pros who take over some or all of the functions of the libraries themselves. Their clients tend to be corporations, nonprofits, government agencies, or other types of organizations, rather than public or academic libraries.

Some libraries outsource functions beyond their core competencies so that they don't have to find or develop internal expertise. Specific tasks that are often outsourced include:

- Handling requests for photocopies or original documents, and providing interlibrary loan services
- Cataloging
- Managing the library's network and PCs
- Developing and maintaining intranet Web sites

- Filing pages in loose-leaf reference manuals (primarily in law firm libraries)
- Managing subscriptions, checking in periodical issues, and routing periodicals
- Shelving books and other clerical tasks

Most of these jobs require information-professional skills but are relatively generic. So, unlike a library's reference and research services, for example, they can be outsourced fairly easily.

Some libraries outsource in order to address specific problems—a backlog of uncataloged books, a sudden upsurge in research requests, conversion from a card catalog to an online catalog, moving the library, or covering the workload of a librarian out on extended leave. Some of this kind of work borders on consulting, particularly if you are brought in not only to manage a library automation project but to make recommendations regarding which system to select. And some libraries outsource some or most of their research work on an as-needed or ongoing basis.

Most libraries manage to serve remote branch locations by putting information on an intranet and offering telephone and e-mail reference services. But some libraries need to maintain a physical presence in branch offices that aren't adequately served by the main library. Rather than hire and supervise a remote staff, some library managers simply contract with a library outsourcing company to handle the management of the remote library. Similarly, some libraries in multinational companies (as well as companies with round-the-clock employees) need to provide reference and research services 24 hours a day, seven days a week. Rather than struggle to find staff willing to work the graveyard shift, they may opt to outsource that coverage to someone who *is* willing to work such hours. Alternatively, some libraries have arrangements with outsourcers in other parts of the world; they simply hand off the phone calls to the outsourcer when the library's workday ends and the outsourcer's day is just beginning.

Sometimes libraries are outsourced entirely; the existing library employees are reassigned or fired, and all the library functions are handed over to an outsourcing firm. The contractor is responsible for hiring and managing staff, who usually work on the client's premises and, as far as most employees can tell, are just like any other employees. This type of situation can be difficult and involves a delicate balance.

Specialized libraries often rely on the support and cooperation of other local libraries for borrowing and lending materials, sharing resources, brainstorming, and so on. However, librarians in other organizations may harbor quite a bit of ill will toward the staff of an outsourced library, who are perceived as having taken over the "real" library and prompted the decision to fire the staff. Obviously, this perception isn't based on reality, because the decision to outsource a library is almost always made before any consideration of who or what entity will be hired to provide the services that employees still need. But the feelings are still there, and as a result, it can be difficult to hire and retain staff for an outsourced library.

In most outsourcing situations, the independent info pro has to find a way to provide the same level of service as an in-house info pro, while costing the client less and still making a profit. For short-term outsourced projects, the cost savings are obvious; it's almost always cheaper to pay a contractor for the duration rather than bring a new employee on board. And for jobs that involve specialized expertise such as cataloging or network management, the client may be willing to pay a premium to avoid having to build the expertise in-house. Outsourcing a branch library or the entire library function is the most difficult situation of all. The contractor wants to hire and retain good employees, but is under pressure to keep costs down.

Needless to say, neither the American Library Association nor the Special Libraries Association offer wholehearted endorsements of outsourcing library services, but if you know what librarians see as its advantages and disadvantages, you will be better equipped to handle objections and to address the issues that come up. The following resources will tell you what some of the library associations have to say about outsourcing:

- American Library Association: Outsourcing in Libraries (www.ala.org/alaorg/oif/outsourcing.html) Also, try the "Search The Website" link with the word outsourcing

- Special Libraries Association: Exploring Outsourcing: Case Studies of Corporate Libraries (www.sla.org/pubs/books/out.html). SLA members also have access to a bibliography of outsourcing materials (www.sla.org/content/memberonly/electrinfo/contract.cfm)

Consulting Services

Consulting—to information vendors, to libraries, or to groups or companies that need help organizing, managing or using information—is a service that a number of independent info pros provide, either as a sideline or as the major focus of their business. Helpful books that address issues consultants frequently face include *The Consultant's Calling: Bringing Who You Are to What You Do* by Geoffrey M. Bellman (Jossey-Bass, 2001) and *Getting Started in Consulting* by Alan Weiss (Jossey-Bass, 2000).

Running a consulting practice has much in common with running a research business, but presents its own set of challenges as well. Projects are usually much larger in terms of scope, budget, and duration. You're selling your expertise and your opinions, as opposed to information created by others. That's difficult for some info pros, who are more comfortable searching for information rather than providing their own opinions and conclusions.

Types of consulting that info pros provide include:

- Library consulting—conducting information audits, providing guidance in selecting a new library automation system, developing a marketing program for the library, providing strategic planning, and so on
- Enterprise information consulting—working with a group or organization that needs to create and develop a library or information center or otherwise organize and manage their information
- Information industry consulting—providing advice regarding the usability, functionality, and content of an existing or proposed online system or product; advising on training and marketing issues

Consulting can be a way to keep you fresh; you have a chance to go into an organization, ask lots of questions, see how things are done, and come up with recommendations on how things could be done better. Consulting can also be immensely frustrating. Often, you are dealing with many personalities, not all of whom see eye-to-eye on the problem at hand and how to resolve it, and you may feel pressured to come to a conclusion that your client wants but that you don't feel is the best solution for the organization.

The skills required to succeed as a consultant include the same ones needed by any independent info pro—the ability to run a small business, manage cash flow, market yourself and your company, manage your time, and so on. The unique demands of consulting also need a special set of skills. These include the ability to

- "Read" a situation and sort out the personalities, agendas, and concerns of all the players
- Even-handedly assess the needs and priorities of the organization
- Build relationships of trust with the key players
- Evaluate alternatives, thinking beyond the options your clients perceive

You also need good writing skills, because your deliverable usually consists of a report and set of recommendations. If you can't clearly articulate the problem, the alternative solutions, and your recommendation, your clients aren't going to be happy with your work. And although it may seem obvious, you do have to have some experience as an information expert before you can provide consulting services; this isn't an entry-level job. In order to successfully market yourself as a consultant, you need contacts and references, or a solid reputation in the information community. You may not be able to provide consulting services when you first start your information business, but later on it can be a great way to take advantage of all the contacts and experience you've built up. My first few consulting jobs all came from existing clients who said something like, "I know you specialize in doing online research for us, but we really need some help in using our in-house online resources. Can you help?" It's gratifying to be able to sell not only your expertise in finding information but also your knowledge and broad perspective on the information industry.

Checklist of Other Information Services Independent Info Pros Can Offer

- Personalized, one-on-one training
- Packaged workshops and seminars
- Writing user manuals, documentation, and FAQ files for online information providers
- One-time or permanent outsourced staffing for libraries
- Consulting to libraries
- Needs analysis and information management consulting to organizations
- Consulting on product design and content, and other issues, to information providers

Appendices

Appendix A. The Association of Independent Information Professionals

The Association of Independent Information Professionals (www.aiip.org) was established in 1987 by 26 info pros, who met at the invitation of Dr. Marilyn Levine, a professor of Library and Information Science at the University of Wisconsin and the owner of Information Express. The composition of AIIP has changed over the years, as has the information industry itself and the expectations of our clients.

Today, AIIP has more than 600 members throughout the world, about 80 percent of whom are based in the U.S. There are four classes of membership:

- Full members—those who own a business that provides information services
- Associate members—those who are interested in the profession but don't own an information business
- Student members—those who are interested in the profession and are currently enrolled in an accredited college or university (student members pay a discounted membership fee)

- Supporting members—individuals or organizations that support the objectives of AIIP (and are willing to show their support by paying a significantly higher membership fee)

I joined AIIP before I started my information business, and it was one of the best investments I made. I was able to read and participate in AIIP's lively members-only electronic discussion forum, which gave me a good sense of the daily concerns of independent info pros. I also saved up money and airline frequent flier miles in order to attend the annual AIIP conference—again, before I launched my business. The conference was an extraordinary experience. Everyone there was serious about their business, and it seemed that all the conversations revolved around research, information, or being an entrepreneur. It also appeared that everyone knew everyone else, and, in fact, they did; the electronic discussion forum kept people in touch during the year. I remember taking detailed notes during the conference sessions, and being astonished at how willing people were to share their experiences. One session was titled something like "My Biggest Marketing Mistakes." It consisted of a panel of four independent info pros telling all their colleagues what did and didn't work.

Obviously, one of the key benefits of AIIP membership is the ability to tap into the expertise of a network of longtime independent info pros, both in person at the annual conference and electronically on the private e-mail discussion list. You'll meet people with a wide range of backgrounds and experiences, you'll find people you can subcontract work to and who will subcontract work to you, and you'll develop a network of friends you can bounce ideas off who understand what it's like to run an information business.

The more tangible benefits of AIIP membership include:

- Significant discounts from a number of information vendors, including waiver of monthly minimums or annual fees (some vendor benefits are limited to Full members)

- Access to the members-only e-mail discussion list, AIIP-L

- Participation in the Referral program, through which potential clients who call AIIP headquarters are given the names of three qualified AIIP members (this benefit is limited to Full members)

- A listing in the AIIP directory, along with a description of your services and background
- Access to the free volunteer mentoring program, which connects new members with more experienced independent info pros
- Listing in the speakers' bureau (limited to Full members)
- A New Member Guidebook—extracted discussions from AIIP-L on a variety of business topics such as marketing, research skills, niche markets, disclaimers, and subcontracting
- A sample subcontracting form and sample nondisclosure agreement
- Subscription to a quarterly newsletter with practical articles on various aspects of the independent info pro business

You can download the membership application form from the AIIP Web site.

The AIIP Membership Directory is available on the Web site, as is material describing the independent info profession, a link to the AIIP referral program, and an online store where you can purchase AIIP white papers and tapes of conference sessions.

Given the importance of maintaining the trust of clients, vendors, colleagues, and the public, AIIP has a code of ethics that all members are required to sign when they join the association. Once in a while, there is a flurry of news coverage when an unscrupulous company tries to market access to information obtained illegally, and this makes a strong code of ethics even more crucial for our profession. We independent info pros must ensure that we not only comply with this code but that we avoid even the appearance of impropriety. Here is the current version of AIIP's Code of Ethical Business Practice:

An Independent Information Professional is an entrepreneur who has demonstrated continuing expertise in the art of finding and organizing information. Each provides information services on a contractual basis to more than one client and serves as an objective intermediary between the client and the information world.

An Information Professional bears the following responsibilities:

- Uphold the profession's reputation for honesty, competence, and confidentiality.

- Give clients the most current and accurate information possible within the budget and time frames provided by the clients.
- Help clients understand the sources of information used and the degree of reliability which can be expected from those sources.
- Accept only those projects which are legal and are not detrimental to our profession.
- Respect client confidentiality.
- Recognize intellectual property rights. Respect licensing agreements and other contracts. Explain to clients what their obligations might be with regard to intellectual property rights and licensing agreements.
- Maintain a professional relationship with libraries and comply with all their rules of access.
- Assume responsibility for employees' compliance with this code.

Copyright, Association of Independent Information Professionals (www.aiip.org/aboutaiip/aiipethics.html)

(Initially approved by the membership May 5, 1989, last amended on April 20, 2002)

Appendix B. Staying Up-to-Date

As a one- or two-person business, you'll find that one of the biggest challenges is keeping up with the information industry, with new technology, and with trends in the marketplace. The following publications, e-journals, and Web sites can help.

Print Publications

The CyberSkeptic's Guide to Internet Research. Information Today, Inc., 10x/year. $104 (www.cyberskeptic.com)

Newsletter written for the experienced Internet researcher. Each issue includes a review of a Web site, comparisons of similar Web products, discussions of search techniques and tools, and brief industry announcements.

The Information Advisor. Find/SVP, monthly. $165 (www.informationadvisor.com)

Newsletter that focuses on reviews and evaluations of online information sources, with an emphasis on business resources. (Note that I am the contributing editor of *The Information Advisor*.)

ONLINE. Information Today, Inc., 6x/year. $110 (www.infotoday.com/online)

Magazine targeted to information professionals, covering electronic information products, the Internet, and search techniques. (Note that I am a columnist for *ONLINE*.)

Searcher. Information Today, Inc., 10x/year. $75.95 (www.infotoday.com/searcher)

Magazine targeted to professional online researchers. Includes in-depth articles on search techniques, industry trends, and evaluations of online resources.

Electronic Publications

Ex Libris. (marylaine.com/exlibris)

A weekly e-mail newsletter written by former librarian, now independent info pro, Marylaine Block. She describes it as "an e-zine for librarians and other information junkies."

Free Pint. (www.freepint.com)

Web-based portal for information professionals. This site includes an electronic bulletin board (called the Bar) and a lengthy electronic newsletter that comes out biweekly.

Neat New Stuff I Found on the Web This Week. (marylaine.com/neatnew.html)

Also produced by Marylaine Block, this newsletter (and Web site) has an annotated list of the interesting and useful sites she has come across.

Netsurfer Digest. $20/year (www.netsurf.com/nsd)

Weekly e-mail newsletter with an eclectic collection of new Web resources, Internet-related news, book reviews, and miscellany.

ResearchBuzz. (www.researchbuzz.com)

Weekly e-mail newsletter covering online research and news.

Search Engine Report. (www.searchenginewatch.com/sereport/index.html)
Monthly e-mail newsletter on trends in the search engine industry.

SearchDay. (www.searchenginewatch.com/searchday/searchday.html)
Daily e-mail newsletter focusing on Web search news, reviews, search tips, and search engine news from across the Web.

Web Sites
Search Engine Watch. (www.searchenginewatch.com)
A wide variety of information on how to use search engines and to optimize a Web site for search engine indexing.

Search Engine Showdown. (www.searchengineshowdown.com)
Ongoing detailed comparisons of the major search engines, evaluating relative size, features, timeliness, and so on, as well as news about search engines.

The Resource Shelf. (www.resourceshelf.com)
Daily Weblog of information sources, online articles, tools, and resources, compiled by Gary Price.

Appendix C. Independent Info Pro Tools and Resources

The following are the books, associations, Web sites, government agencies, and other organizations that are useful for independent info pros.

Books
The Consultant's Calling: Bringing Who You Are to What You Do by Geoffrey M. Bellman. Jossey-Bass, 2001. $19.95
Although at times a bit touchy-feely, a very useful book on how consultants can best work with clients. Some of his advice applies to any independent info pro business.

Copyright & Information Professionals: Complying With the Law by Stephanie Ardito. Association of Independent Information Professionals, 1998. $25 (www.aiip. org)
Written by an expert in the field of copyright, this white paper looks at copyright issues from the perspective of an independent info pro.

DataStar Search Guide. Dialog, 2001. No cost (support.dialog.com/searchaids/datastar/pdf/dssearchguide.pdf)

User manual for DataStar subscribers. Available in PDF format only.

Encyclopedia of Business Information Sources Published annually. Gale Group. $370.

Excellent directory of the key resources—books, reports, publications, Web sites, associations, and so on—for industries from Abrasives to Zinc.

The Extreme Searcher's Guide to Web Search Engines 2nd edition, by Randolph Hock. Information Today, Inc., 2001. $24.95 (www.extremesearcher.com)

Detailed coverage of eight search engines and directories, along with chapters on other search tools and techniques.

Fulltext Sources Online. Published twice yearly. Information Today, Inc. $129.50 per issue (www.infotoday.com/FSO)

Directory of publications available online in full text. Includes publishers' own Web sites as well as the major professional online services.

How to Avoid Liability: The Information Professional's Guide to Negligence and Warranty Risks by T.R. Halvorson. Association of Independent Information Professionals, 1998. $25 (www.aiip.org)

White paper explaining how independent info pros can get themselves in trouble by promising too much or by relying too heavily on disclaimers.

The Invisible Web: Uncovering Information Sources Search Engines Can't See by Chris Sherman and Gary Price. Information Today, Inc., 2001. $29.95 (www.invisible-web.net)

In-depth coverage of what the invisible Web is and how to find information that search engines can't locate. Also includes 18 chapters of the best invisible Web resources in specific subject areas. Links to all the Web resources are also available at www.invisible-web.net.

Naked in Cyberspace: How to Find Personal Information Online 2nd edition, by Carole A. Lane. Information Today, Inc., 2002. $29.95 (www.technosearch.com/naked)

Coverage of the online tools—both on the Web and in fee-based online services—for finding public records and other information on individuals.

The Sourcebook to Public Record Information 4th edition. BRB Publications, 2002. $76.95 (www.brbpub.com/books)

Directory of public records sources in federal, state, and local government agencies and courts. Particularly useful if you need to find sources outside your own local jurisdiction.

Successful Searching on Dialog Dialog, 1998. No charge (support.dialog.com/searchaids/success)

In-depth user manual for Dialog subscribers. Available as a PDF file (for printing) and in HTML (for browsing).

Super Searchers Go to the Source: The Interviewing and Hands-On Information Strategies of Top Primary Researchers – Online, on the Phone, and in Person by Risa Sacks. Information Today, Inc., 2001. $24.95 (www.infotoday.com/supersearchers)

Interviews with 12 info pros who specialize in conducing primary research, including telephone researchers, public records researchers, and journalists.

Super Searchers Make It On Their Own: Top Independent Information Professionals Share Their Secrets for Starting and Running a Research Business by Suzanne Sabroski. Information Today, Inc., 2002. $24.95 (www.infotoday.com/supersearchers)

Interviews with 11 independent info pros (including the author of this book) on how they started and successfully run their businesses.

<u>Organizations and Government Agencies</u>

The Chartered Institute of Library and Information Professionals: www.cilip.org.uk

U.K.-based association of librarians and other information professionals. Includes corporate librarians, independent info pros, and public librarians.

Service Corps of Retired Executives: www.score.org

Organization associated with the U.S. Small Business Administration, consisting of volunteer executives who offer free e-mail and in-person counseling to small business owners.

Society of Competitive Intelligence Professionals: www.scip.org
An international association of competitive intelligence practitioners. Members are primarily people involved in corporate competitive intelligence, but include a number of CI consultants and independent info pros as well.

Special Libraries Association: www.sla.org
An international association of librarians in specialized libraries—primarily those in corporations, associations, and government agencies—as distinct from public and school libraries.

U.S. Small Business Administration: www.sba.gov
Offers many useful resources on planning a business, marketing, managing cash flow, and related general business issues.

Fee-Based Online Information Services

DataStar: www.datastarweb.com
Professional online service with a stronger European focus than some of its competitors, particularly in the area of company directories.

Dialog: www.dialogweb.com
One of the major professional online services. Wide variety of databases. In addition to several subscription plans, Dialog offers Open Access, which lets nonsubscribers use the service and pay by credit card.

Factiva: global.factiva.com
Another one of the major professional online services. Its focus is business and financial information; good global coverage of news sources. Best transactional pricing plan of the major online services.

LexisNexis: www.lexisnexis.com
Another one of the major professional online services. Wide variety of databases, covering business, news, and legal sources. Also allows you to search current news items on the Web. Pricing is not as favorable for independent info pros as that of other major online services.

Questel*Orbit: www.questel.orbit.com
Specialized professional online service, focusing on patent and trademark information and science and technology databases.

Westlaw: www.westlaw.com
Full text of legal case law and legislative and administrative material. Business information is provided directly from Factiva.com and through a link to Dialog.

Appendix D. People Quoted in This Book

Here is contact information for the independent info pros and consultants that I quote directly in this book. I am grateful to all of them for their assistance and contributions. Note that each person's listing includes his or her preferred methods of contact.

Reva Basch
Aubergine Information Services
P.O. Box 116
The Sea Ranch, CA 95497
reva@well.com
www.well.com/~reva

Linda Cooper
Information Consultant
Quakertown, PA
lindacooper@erols.com

Thomas Culbert
Aviation Information Research Corp.
73 Fendall Ave.
Alexandria, VA 22304
703.823.1264
tcairc@avinforsch.com

Susan Detwiler
Founder, The Detwiler Group
www.detwiler.com

Jan Goudreau
Principal, Information Crossroads LLC

6028 Snow Crystal
Columbia, MD 21044
www.infoxroads.com

T.R. Halvorson
President, Synoptic Text Information Services, Inc.
HC56 Box 6038
Sidney, MT 59270
406.433.4180
trh@midrivers.com
www.lexnotes.com

Amelia Kassel
President, MarketingBase
707.829.9421 or 800.544.5924
amelia@marketingbase.com
www.marketingbase.com

Laurie Kauffman
Owner, Net Worth Consulting
1316 Kenyon Street NW
Washington, DC 20010
202.462.6549
lkauffman@compuserve.com

Alex Kramer
Owner, Kramer Research
Washington, DC

John Levis
John E. Levis Associates, Inc.
32945 Indiana St.
Livonia, MI 48150-3766
734.422.8029
John@jelevisassoc.com
www.jelevisassoc.com

Lynn Peterson
President, PFC Information Services Inc.
Oakland, CA
www.pfcinformation.com

Risa Sacks
Owner, Risa Sacks Information Services
risa@rsacksinfo.com
508.799.8810

Suzanne Sabroski
Principal, Sabroski & Associates
2416 London Road, Suite 884
Duluth, MN 55812
suzanne@sabroski.com
www.sabroski.com

Jan Tudor
President, JT Research LLC
P.O. Box 8705
Portland OR 97207
503.827.7241
jt@jtresearch.com
www.jtresearch.com

Frank Warren
Principal, Instant Information Systems
13345 Copper Ridge Rd.
Germantown, MD 20874
301.540.4864
IIS@docdel.com
www.docdel.com

About the Author

Mary Ellen Bates is the owner of Bates Information Services, now in its second decade of operation. She provides business research to business professionals and backup research services to corporate librarians. She also conducts workshops and seminars for information professionals. Prior to starting her own business in 1991, she worked in corporate and law libraries for 15 years. She received her Masters in Library and Information Science from the University of California, Berkeley and has been an online researcher since the late 1970s.

She is the author of five other books: *Super Searchers Cover the World* (Information Today, Inc., 2001), *Mining For Gold on the Internet* (McGraw-Hill, 2000), *Researching Online For Dummies*, 2nd edition, co-authored with Reva Basch (Hungry Minds, 2000), *Super Searchers Do Business* (Information Today, Inc., 1999), and *The Online Deskbook* (Information Today, Inc., 1996). She writes for *EContent, ONLINE,* and *Searcher*, and is the contributing editor of *The Information Advisor*. She is a frequent international speaker, and has given presentations at information industry conferences around the world. The first two-time president of the Association of Independent Information Professionals, she is also active in the Special Libraries Association and the Society of Competitive Intelligence Professionals.

Mary Ellen received AIIP's first annual Sue Rugge Memorial Award, created to recognize an AIIP member who, through mentoring, has significantly helped others establish their businesses. She also received the 2002 Professional Award from the Special Libraries Association, and was named member of the year by the Communications Division and the Washington, DC, Chapter of SLA.

In her spare time, Mary Ellen is a back-of-the-pack marathon runner. She lives in Washington, DC, with her companion and two dogs. She can be contacted at mbates@BatesInfo.com or www.BatesInfo.com.

Photo by David Torres

About the Editor

Reva Basch, executive editor of the Super Searcher book series, has written four books of her own: *Researching Online For Dummies* (Hungry Minds, 2nd edition with Mary Ellen Bates), *Secrets of the Super Net Searchers* (Information Today, Inc., 1996), *Secrets of the Super Searchers* (Information Today, Inc., 1993), and *Electronic Information Delivery: Evaluating Quality and Value* (Gower, 1995). She has edited and contributed chapters, introductions, and interviews to several books about the Internet and online information retrieval. She was the subject of a profile in *WIRED* magazine, which called her "the ultimate intelligent agent."

Prior to starting her own business in 1986, Reva was Vice President and Director of Research at Information on Demand, a pioneering independent research company. She has designed front-end search software for major online services, written and consulted on technical, marketing, and training issues for both online services and database producers, and published extensively in information industry journals. She has keynoted at international conferences in Australia, Scandinavia, Europe, and the United Kingdom, as well as North America.

Reva is a Past-President (1991–1992) of the Association of Independent Information Professionals. She has a degree in English Literature, *summa cum laude*, from the University of Pennsylvania, and a Masters degree in Library Science from the University of California in Berkeley. She began her career as a corporate librarian, ran her own independent research business for 10 years, and has been online since the mid-1970s. She lives on the remote northern California coast with her husband, cats, and satellite access to the Internet.

Index

A

B

C

D

E

F

G

H

I

N

O

P

Q

R

X

Y

Z